The Ethics of War and Peace

THE ETHIKON SERIES

Series Editor:
Terry Nardin

The Ethikon Series publishes comparative studies on ethical issues of current importance. By bringing scholars representing a diversity of moral perspectives into genuine dialogue with one another, the series aims to broaden the scope of ethical debate and to identify commonalities and differences between alternative views.

THE ETHIKON INSTITUTE

The Ethikon Institute is an organization concerned with the social implications of ethical pluralism. Its programs in intersocietal relations, civil society, bio-environmental ethics, and family life are designed to explore a diversity of moral outlooks, secular and religious, and to identify commonalities and differences between them. The Institute pursues these objectives by organizing focused dialogue between authorities on influential ethical perspectives. By encouraging a systematic exchange of ideas, it aims to advance the prospects for agreement and to facilitate the accommodation of irreducible differences. The Ethikon Institute takes no position on the issues that divide its participants. It serves not as an arbiter but as a forum for the cooperative exploration of diverse and sometimes opposing views.

The Ethics of War and Peace

RELIGIOUS AND SECULAR PERSPECTIVES

Edited by Terry Nardin

PRINCETON UNIVERSITY PRESS

PRINCETON, NEW JERSEY

Published by Princeton University Press, 41 William Street,
Princeton, New Jersey 08540
In the United Kingdom: Princeton University Press,
Chichester, West Sussex

Library of Congress Cataloging-in-Publication Data

The ethics of war and peace : religious and secular perspectives /
edited by Terry Nardin.
p. cm.
"Conference on 'The Ethics of War and Peace' held in January 1993
at the Notre Dame of Jerusalem Center"—Pref.
Includes bibliographical references and index.
ISBN 0-691-03713-2 (alk. paper)
1. War—Religious aspects—Comparative studies—Congresses.
2. War—Moral and ethical aspects—Congresses. 3. Peace—Religious
aspects—Comparative studies—Congresses. 4. Peace—Moral and
ethical aspects—Congresses. I. Nardin, Terry, 1942–.
BL65.W2E74 1996 172′.42—dc20 95-691 CIP

This book has been composed in Janson

Princeton University Press books are printed
on acid-free paper and meet the guidelines
for permanence and durability of the Committee
on Production Guidelines for Book Longevity
of the Council on Library Resources

Printed in the United States of America by
Princeton Academic Press

10 9 8 7 6 5 4 3 2 1

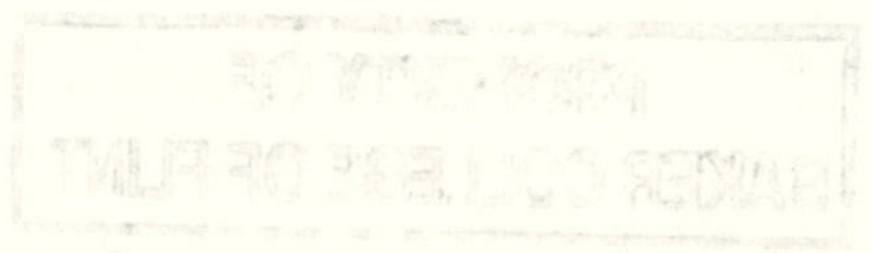

Contents

Preface vii

Contributors ix

INTRODUCTION — *Terry Nardin* 3

PART ONE: *The Classic Debate: Natural Law and Political Realism*

CHAPTER 1
The Ethics of War and Peace in the Catholic Natural Law Tradition — *John Finnis* 15

CHAPTER 2
Just War Thinking in Catholic Natural Law — *Joseph Boyle* 40

CHAPTER 3
Realism and the Ethics of War and Peace — *David R. Mapel* 54

CHAPTER 4
Realism, Morality, and War — *Jeff McMahan* 78

PART TWO: *Expanding the Dialogue: Judaism and Islam*

CHAPTER 5
War and Peace in the Jewish Tradition — *Michael Walzer* 95

CHAPTER 6
Prohibited Wars in the Jewish Tradition — *Aviezer Ravitzky* 115

CHAPTER 7
War and Peace in Islam — *Bassam Tibi* 128

CHAPTER 8
Interpreting the Islamic Ethics of War and Peace — *Sohail H. Hashmi* 146

PART THREE: *Critical Perspectives: Christian Pacifism and Feminism*

CHAPTER 9
Christian Nonviolence: An Interpretation — *Theodore J. Koontz* 169

Chapter 10
Conflicting Interpretations of Christian Pacifism —
Michael G. Cartwright 197

Chapter 11
Is There a Feminist Tradition on War and Peace? —
Jean Bethke Elshtain 214

Chapter 12
Toward a Feminist Ethic of War and Peace — *Sarah Tobias* 228

Part Four: *Comparative Overview*

Chapter 13
The Comparative Ethics of War and Peace — *Terry Nardin* 245

Chapter 14
Divine Justice, Evil, and Tradition: Comparative Reflections —
Richard B. Miller 265

Index 283

Preface

THIS BOOK originated at a conference on the ethics of war and peace held in January 1993 at the Notre Dame of Jerusalem Center. The event was organized by the Ethikon Institute in cooperation with the University of Wisconsin-Milwaukee/Marquette University Center for International Studies and was made possible by a grant from The Pew Charitable Trusts.

The Ethikon Institute is engaged in an ongoing program of dialogues and publications designed to increase our knowledge of the diversity of ethical perspectives that may be brought to bear on major issues of public life. As in other Ethikon projects, the contributors to this book were asked to address a common set of questions. All have revised their chapters to take account of the discussion in Jerusalem and to insure that each chapter contributes to the comparative and dialogic exploration of ethical ideas. The book is thus a product of the Institute's continually evolving efforts to facilitate a useful exchange of ideas between authorities on different ethical traditions and between the communities shaped by those traditions. We hope the chapters that follow will help readers to acquire a better understanding of viewpoints that may be unfamiliar to them and a better sense of the assumptions and limitations of their own points of view.

By dialogue we mean a conversational and comparative inquiry into different views about a common topic—not a debate that can be won or lost, but an exchange of information. In an Ethikon dialogue, the emphasis is on discovery, not persuasion. Dialogue presupposes difference and need not seek to overcome it. But it also presupposes information about the different views, and this means listening to those who can articulate those views.

To generate the information needed for comparison, two chapters have been commissioned on each perspective. The first is a presentation of how the perspective deals with the topic of war/peace ethics, as this topic is defined by the questions that all the contributors were asked to consider. The "presenter" is a reporter, not necessarily an adherent or advocate, though he or she must have enough sympathy with the described perspective to explain its distinctive character. Given the comparative aims of this study, it is not the job of the presenter to refute critics, or to "advance the debate" on a given aspect of the topic, but simply to state, carefully and dispassionately, how the topic-related questions are handled within the tradition on which he or she is reporting. The second chapter on each perspective has been prepared by a "reactor" who also knows the perspective well and whose task is to present an alternative interpretation of controverted issues. Finally, the presentations and reactions are reviewed in two comparative overviews that seek to identify commonalities and differences, substantive and methodological, among the presented views.

This book is the first in a series of Ethikon Institute studies published by Princeton University Press. Each study will bring together scholars representing a diversity of ethical perspectives, secular and religious, to discuss an important issue of public life. The volumes will be structured to identify significant points of agreement and disagreement among the presented views. The approach taken in individual volumes in the series will depend on the topics discussed and the current state of reflection on those topics, but all will be carefully designed comparative studies rather than collections of loosely related articles.

Like any collaborative project, this one could not have been completed without the cooperation and support of many persons in addition to the authors represented here. Among them were other participants in the Jerusalem conference, many of whose ideas and arguments have found their way into this book: Shukri Abed, Ruben Apresyan, Shlomo Avineri, Chris Brown, Naomi Chazan, Henry Clark, Marie Egan, Sharif Kanaana, Bruce Nichols, Khalil Shikaki, Peter Steinfels, Mark Tessler, Philippe Van Parijs, Margaret-Rose Welch, and Noam Zohar. Though he was unfortunately unable at the last minute to travel to Jerusalem, Stanley Hauerwas shared his understanding of Christian pacifism with us. We are especially grateful to Michael Cartwright, Sohail Hashmi, and Sarah Tobias, who, though they did not attend the Jerusalem conference, agreed to write chapters for this book. The project owes most, however, to Ethikon's founder and president, Philip Valera, who developed the model of comparative analysis and focused dialogue on which this series is based.

Special thanks are due to Msgr. Dr. Richard Mathes, chargé of the Holy See and director of the Notre Dame of Jerusalem Center, for the excellence of his hospitality. Dan McIntyre, formerly of The Pew Charitable Trusts, provided much excellent advice. Lea Ann King, who chairs the Ethikon board of directors, lent valuable assistance in the organization of the conference. We benefited from the criticism of several anonymous readers, and we are especially grateful to Ann Himmelberger Wald, our editor at Princeton University Press, for her confidence in the project. We also thank Jane Nardin for providing substantive and editorial guidance.

All royalties from the sale of this book go to the Ethikon Institute to support its programs on intersocietal relations, civil society, bio-environmental ethics, and family life.

Contributors

JOSEPH BOYLE is professor of philosophy and principal of St. Michael's College at the University of Toronto, and past president of the American Catholic Philosophical Association. He writes on applied ethics and moral theory, and is coauthor with John Finnis and Germain Grisez of *Nuclear Deterrence, Morality and Realism.*

MICHAEL G. CARTWRIGHT is assistant professor of religious studies at Allegheny College. He is the author of articles on biblical hermeneutics and the use of scripture in Christian ethics.

JEAN BETHKE ELSHTAIN is professor of social and political ethics at the University of Chicago. Her books include *Public Man, Private Woman: Women in Social and Political Thought*, *Women and War*, *Democracy on Trial*, and an edited collection, *Just War Theory*, as well as articles in scholarly journals and journals of civic opinion.

JOHN FINNIS is professor of law and legal philosophy at the University of Oxford, and a fellow of University College, Oxford. He is a fellow of the British Academy, has been a member of the Holy See's International Theological Commission, and is a member of the commission's Council for Justice and Peace. His books include *Natural Law and Natural Rights*, *Nuclear Deterrence, Morality and Realism* (with Joseph Boyle and Germain Grisez), and *Moral Absolutes: Tradition, Revision, and Truth.*

SOHAIL H. HASHMI is assistant professor of international relations at Mount Holyoke College. His research and teaching interests include comparative international ethics, specifically just war theory, and Middle Eastern and South Asian history and politics. He is currently writing a book analyzing the contemporary Islamic discourse on ethics and international relations.

THEODORE J. KOONTZ is professor of ethics and peace studies at the Associated Mennonite Biblical Seminary in Elkhart, Indiana. He has served with the Mennonite Central Committee as executive secretary of the peace section and as a visiting professor at Silliman University in the Philippines. His publications include articles on Mennonite political thought and conscientious objection.

DAVID R. MAPEL is associate professor of political science at the University of Colorado at Boulder. He is the author of *Social Justice Reconsidered* and coeditor, with Terry Nardin, of *Traditions of International Ethics*. He writes and teaches in the fields of political theory and international relations.

Jeff McMahan is associate professor of philosophy at the University of Illinois at Urbana-Champaign, having previously been a research fellow in philosophy at St. John's College, Cambridge. His books include *British Nuclear Weapons: For and Against* and *The Ethics of War* (forthcoming).

Richard B. Miller is associate professor of religious studies at Indiana University. He is the author of *Interpretations of Conflict: Ethics, Pacifism, and the Just-War Tradition* and editor of *War in the Twentieth Century: Sources in Theological Ethics*. He has also written on medical ethics, sexual ethics, and feminism.

Terry Nardin is professor of political science at the University of Wisconsin-Milwaukee and vice president of the Ethikon Institute. He is the author of *Law, Morality, and the Relations of States* and coeditor, with David R. Mapel, of *Traditions of International Ethics*.

Aviezer Ravitzky is chairman of the department of Jewish thought at the Hebrew University of Jerusalem. He is a specialist in medieval Jewish philosophy and contemporary Jewish thought, as well as the relation between religion and politics in modern Israel. He has published on these topics in English and in Hebrew. His most recent book is *Messianism, Zionism, and Jewish Religious Radicalism*.

Bassam Tibi is professor of international relations at the Georg-August-University in Göttingen, where he also heads the Center for International Relations. His books include *Arab Nationalism: A Critical Inquiry*, *Islam and the Cultural Accommodation of Social Change*, *The Crisis of Modern Islam*, and *Conflict and War in the Middle East*.

Sarah Tobias is a Ph.D. candidate in political theory at Columbia University. She is currently writing a dissertation on feminist ethics.

Michael Walzer is a permanent member of the School of Social Science at the Institute for Advanced Study in Princeton, New Jersey. He is a coeditor of *Dissent* magazine and a contributing editor of *New Republic*, and is the author of *The Revolution of the Saints*, *Just and Unjust Wars*, *Spheres of Justice*, *Interpretation and Social Criticism*, and other books.

The Ethics of War and Peace

INTRODUCTION

Terry Nardin

THIS BOOK IS CONCERNED with the reasons for making war, for fighting with restraint, or for repudiating war as an instrument of policy, as these issues are understood within six distinct and important ethical perspectives. Its premise is that there is more than one way of looking at the ethics of war and peace, and that to understand the topic is, in part, to understand these alternative views. A few words about how we have approached our task may help the reader to understand the substantive chapters that follow this introduction.

Though moralists usually argue about the rights and wrongs of conduct from within a given set of ethical ideas, our aim has been to move beyond the usual boundaries of moral argument. The first-order discourse that goes on inside a moral tradition seeks primarily to elicit the implications for conduct of a particular system of values. In contrast, the dialogue in which we are engaged here constitutes a second-order discourse, designed to clarify how recurrent questions of war/peace ethics are handled in different ethical systems.

One important set of questions concerns conceptions of peace and war, as these are understood within each perspective. What types of peace and war can be distinguished? How are they related? What attitudes toward peace and war are reflected in these conceptions? Is there a presumption against war, and if so, on what is it based? To what extent is it morally proper to adopt nonviolent, pacifist, or abolitionist attitudes?

Another set of questions concerns reasons for waging war. What grounds for war, if any, are recognized within each perspective? What criteria distinguish justifiable from unjustifiable wars? Do intentions matter? How important is one's internal motive or the spirit in which one acts? Are acts of war rendered unjust if done for the wrong motives? And because wars can occur within as well as between communities, how should we think about the ethics of civil war? Which situations, if any, warrant armed resistance or conscientious objection?

Finally, there are questions concerning the conduct of war, once the fighting has begun. What constraints apply to military conduct? Are these merely prudential constraints, or do they have moral force? How can respect for moral principles be reconciled with a concern for consequences? Can one ever be excused from observing constraints on the conduct of war? In particular, can these constraints be overridden in emergencies that threaten to destroy a community? What does a commitment to peace require of those who must decide when and how to fight?

These are the questions that have guided our inquiry into the ethics of war and peace in the traditions of natural law and political realism, in Jewish and Islamic ethical discourse, and in the arguments of pacifist and feminist critics of these established ethical systems. Building on the answers we have found in each of these perspectives, we have sought through dialogue and comparative analysis to discover areas of divergence and convergence among them. Where do they differ? Can these differences be reconciled? What areas of agreement can we identify? What conclusions, if any, can we draw regarding the prospects for a common ethic of war and peace, despite persisting disagreement?

This comparative approach to the ethics of war and peace is not without precedent. Standing behind it are long traditions of scholarship concerned with the comparative study of religion, law, and morals. Comparative inquiry is relatively rare in the study of international ethics, but it is implicit in efforts to distinguish alternative ethical positions. The debate over the place of ethics in international affairs, for example, was for many years defined in terms of an opposition between "idealism" and "realism." This distinction, though often pronounced to be simplistic and outdated, has a way of reasserting itself—in fact, it does so in this book, where we take the debate between natural law and political realism as our point of departure—because it reflects the basic tension between deontological and consequentialist ethical concepts, a tension that is starkly evident in the ethics of war and peace. More recently, students of international ethics have emphasized another opposition, one that distinguishes between "cosmopolitan" and "communitarian" viewpoints.[1] This distinction, too, is at work in the present volume, for its dialogue takes place between those whose judgments are rooted in the commitments of a particular faith-centered community and those who ground their judgments on principles regarded as universal because they rest on tradition-independent ideas of reason and human nature. In my judgment, both dimensions—one defined by the clash between deontology and consequentialism, the other by the opposition between universalism and particularism—are required to make sense of differences both within and between the major ethical perspectives.

As an alternative to multiplying dichotomies, one might attempt to organize the richness of ethical worldviews in terms of three, five, or more categories. The effort to distinguish and compare different modes of thought provides the tripartite framework (realism, rationalism, and revolutionism) for Martin Wight's recently published lectures on international relations, and the comparative and dialogic approach he cultivated has been carried on by Michael Donelan.[2] Wight's goal was to articulate a typology that would systematically order the major alternatives. Others have proceeded in a more eclectic manner, identifying viewpoints that have achieved a certain historical identity or philosophical coherence without claiming that the resulting collection is either systematic or comprehensive.[3]

Often the viewpoints identified for investigation are those that make sense in relation to a particular issue. A comparative approach based on this more pragmatic criterion can be found in studies undertaken by the Ethikon Institute on global resource distribution, transnational migration, and political change in Europe.[4] Inquiry into actual, historical ethical traditions has also been important in several studies focusing specifically on the ethics of war and peace.[5] In a period in which scholarship in international relations, as in other fields, is increasingly influenced by hermeneutic, historicist, and multiculturalist concerns, we can expect to see more research on international ethics that proceeds by comparing diverse ethical perspectives, and that is attentive to what may emerge from dialogic encounters between these perspectives.

The comparative study of international ethics raises some difficult methodological issues. To discuss these issues fully would distract attention from the substantive concerns of this book, but a few words should be said about the character of the enterprise we are inviting you, the reader, to join. On what grounds have we selected the viewpoints represented here? Why these particular perspectives? Are they comparable entities? These questions are most easily answered by discussing some of the difficulties inherent in the comparative study of ethical ideas.

One difficulty comes from the sheer diversity of viewpoints to be understood. A possible objection to the comparative approach we take in this book is that our concept of an ethical viewpoint is ill defined and that those we have identified are not comparable entities. Several of these perspectives are explicitly based on religious premises, but others are not. Although some display impressive coherence, others are marked by wrenching disagreement. Some are historical traditions, others philosophical constructs. And even if the perspectives are in some sense comparable, the discussions of them that we have assembled here differ both in aim and in style. Finally, the reader who is satisfied on all these points may still conclude that we have not chosen the right perspectives to study.

Despite the hazards of the enterprise, there is much to be learned from the comparison of different viewpoints, even when they rest on different assumptions and are expressed in different idioms. Noncomparability may be a problem in statistical studies, where one is trying to isolate relations between certain variables while holding others constant, but it is irrelevant to the comparison of ideas or practices: the fact that two viewpoints may be different in significant ways is a conclusion, not an obstacle to understanding. Thus, it cannot be an objection to the comparative study of ethical viewpoints that some are religious and others secular. We have included both religious and secular perspectives in this study because ethical views are often linked with religious beliefs shared by a large number of people, and because these beliefs are a part of the ethical experience that moral and political philosophy must seek to comprehend. Nor is comparison barred by the fact that some viewpoints display substantial agreement on war and peace issues whereas others do not. The extent to which there is or is not agreement within a given viewpoint is something we want to discover and to understand.

A more radical objection to comparative ethics arises from the claim that we cannot understand viewpoints connected with ways of life different from our own. A version of this historicist argument has been made against those who criticize Christian pacifism from an external perspective. Moral precepts cannot be understood abstractly, apart from the experience of particular historical communities, the Christian pacifist argues, so it is futile to make context-independent distinctions between just and unjust wars. What matters is who is making the distinction and for what purposes.[6] But the argument sometimes goes beyond this quite plausible insistence on the hermeneutical importance of context to assert the more extreme conclusion that a communal worldview can be understood only from within the community whose view it is. Christian nonviolence, its adherents sometimes argue, is not an abstract ethical theory that can be usefully contrasted with other theories; it is a set of convictions and practices that defines a community of believers. To comprehend these convictions and practices one must take part in them, and to do that one must be a member of the community of nonviolent Christians. Its principles are not fully intelligible to those who do not embrace its beliefs and way of life.

The fallacy in this argument is that it equivocates between different meanings of "understanding." It does not follow from the fact that belief is required for the understanding available to an insider that it is required for *any* understanding. Belief is merely an aspect of understanding. The religious historicist is in effect making the circular claim that the understanding one can achieve by faith can be achieved only by faith. The argument undermines itself: if understanding is impossible without belief, any effort to communicate with those who are not believers is pointless. The historicist argument implies that there can be no significant dialogue or understanding between authentic Christians and those outside this community, or, more generally, between those who are members of different moral and intellectual communities.

It is true that observation from afar, which is so often accompanied by ignorance, incomprehension, and hostility, can be an obstacle to interpretation. But emotional and intellectual involvement can blind as well as illuminate. To understand something may in part be to understand it "from the inside," but understanding also means knowing what a thing is not, and this requires distance. Interpretation presumes the possibility of access by outsiders to the object of interpretation. This possibility is denied by the claim that only the believer can understand Christianity.

The alternative to historicist hermeneutics need not rest on the foundationalist premise that real understanding presupposes an objective standpoint. Such foundationalism is simplistic: you cannot have access to "facts" in the absence of interpretive devices.[7] Our premise in this volume is that to understand a system of moral ideas requires neither a standpoint located wholly within that system, nor a single, indisputable standpoint that lies outside it. We can criticize one system using the ideas of another. We are members of many overlapping ethical communities, and our participation in each gives us critical distance on the ideas of the others. Michael Walzer, who shares the view that significant conversation between people shaped by different communal experiences is possible, moves toward the historicist position when he argues that the most effective moral criticism is the "connected criticism" of those inside a community's moral system. Intercommunal criticism, Walzer fears, is apt to be abstract or rationalist, and for this reason is likely to lead to coercion rather than to dialogue and voluntary agreement.[8] In other words, authentic dialogue is more likely within communities than between them. But to the extent that communities overlap and appropriate one another's ideas, the force of this argument is diminished. And it is precisely because dialogue between those committed to different ideas is difficult that special effort is required to bring it about and to help it succeed.

It is inherent in dialogue not only that speakers will say different things but that they will speak in different idioms or voices. One of the challenges of dialogue is to listen to the manner in which others make their arguments and disclose their beliefs, assumptions, and commitments. Style and substance, one soon learns, are not easily disentangled. As the following chapters illustrate, the way a speaker argues his or her case is related to the history and conceptual content of the case argued.

John Finnis's chapter on natural law, for example, presents a carefully organized structure of precepts and distinctions that draws upon a heritage of centuries of debate within a largely Christian context. But it is not the only interpretation of this heritage, and it may be fairly said that the coherence that the position achieves in Finnis's hands is accomplished in part because his chapter articulates a single version of natural law, Catholic natural law, and indeed a particular version of this version, the so-called new natural law. David Mapel's presentation of realist ethics is equally analytical, but it constructs an argument that departs in many ways from the views of Machiavelli, Hobbes, Niebuhr, Morgenthau, and others who are often labeled "political realists." Because realists characteristically think of themselves as making a fresh start rather than as reinterpreting a tradition, it may be argued that Mapel's approach is entirely in keeping with the spirit of political realism. Realists, even more than natural lawyers, dismiss the authority of the past and assert an ethic as reasonable because it rests on premises that seem reasonable to them.

The other chapters also illustrate different ways of approaching the topic. Michael Walzer reports faithfully on a strand of Jewish thought little known to outsiders, though its principles differ markedly from those he has defended elsewhere.[9] Bassam Tibi is more openly critical, examining Islam with the lens of a self-confessed internationalist. In doing so, he provides insight into an issue currently dividing the Islamic world. Jean Elshtain observes that the most striking feature of feminism regarding the ethics of war and peace is disagreement, and this disagreement is reflected in her own ambivalent stance as both an advocate and a critic of feminism. And Ted Koontz, who speaks as a Mennonite whose pacifist convictions are often treated as irrelevant by those who think it obvious that war is sometimes warranted, does so in an idiom, critical and passionate, that both reflects and protests this marginalization. The reactors, too, speak in a diversity of idioms.

Would it be better if these contributions were stylistically more uniform? Would that make the viewpoints presented more "comparable"? It seems unlikely. The chapters are not only representative accounts but also individual representations of the viewpoints they describe. They are the products of real voices in conversation, and what they say cannot be forced into the Procrustean bed of a common analytical scheme. The authors adopt different ways of dealing with the common questions we have asked them to discuss because the questions mean different things in different viewpoints. We need to take these different meanings seriously.

Because the patterns of ethical thought we have identified are in many ways significantly different entities, it sometimes seems best, in seeking to encompass them all in a single term, to speak of perspectives or viewpoints instead of traditions or systems. Feminism offers a recognizable approach to many issues, but nothing so unified and directive as a system of moral precepts. Political realism is a consistent viewpoint—an ethic of responsibility or of expediency, depending on how you judge it—but it is not a self-conscious tradition like rabbinic discourse or Catholic natural law, both of which display an impressive degree of coherence and continuity. Yet every viewpoint is to some extent an analytical construct resting on distinctions articulated through a process of abstraction rather than the mere description of particulars. And even description requires interpretive categories.

Ethical thinking, like other kinds of thinking, can be analyzed by a procedure of historical inquiry or philosophical abstraction into positions, discourses, schools, movements, paradigms, or modes of thought. Any identified viewpoint can be further dissected into increasingly particular arguments, strands, idioms, voices, etc., or combined with other viewpoints to generate a more inclusive framework of ideas. A tradition or perspective is an interpretive tool, a way of organizing experience. It is not a "thing," an ontologically given object of perception, a natural kind. The idea that there is a fixed and objective roster of ethical viewpoints waiting to be correctly identified is absurd.

This is not to say that our choice of viewpoints for study is beyond criticism. But it has a rationale. We begin with the classic confrontation between natural law and political realism because the terms of debate have been set, in Western political discourse at least, by these perspectives. As suggested earlier, they reflect the poles of ethical thought, natural law tending toward the universal and deontological, political realism toward the particular and consequentialist.[10] Against pacifism, both insist that there must be an ethic of war because wars may be forced upon us even though we wish to avoid them, and because ethical choices are unavoidable if we choose to fight. And in contrast to the messianic withdrawal of rabbinic Judaism and the messianic engagement of classical Islam, both natural law and political realism accept the existence of a plurality of states, recognizing that coexistence is inescapable and perhaps even desirable.

We might have captured the tension between political realism and natural law in other ways, perhaps by contrasting realism with what is sometimes called "the just war tradition," a label that embraces a diversity of views holding that war is subject to moral constraints. We might have chosen, as an alternative to Catholic natural law, some other strand of Christian ethics or the Kantian version of natural law that is today embodied in many nonreligious theories of morality and human rights.[11] We might have examined an even more inclusive family of natural law arguments, including those of Grotius, Hobbes, Pufendorf, and Vattel.[12] Or we might have focused on the tradition of positive international law, especially the law of armed conflicts. But these viewpoints are, with the exception of Kantian ethics, less clearly distinguished from political realism than is the Catholic tradition of natural law in the thoroughly anticonsequentialist version articulated by John Finnis and his colleagues.[13] The coherence of this interpretation, as well as its dependence on an ancient and fully developed literature, makes it an especially useful tool for exploring the tension between law-oriented (moral) and outcome-oriented (consequentialist) conceptions of war/peace ethics.

In Part Two of this book, we seek to expand the dialogue by bringing in the voices of Jewish and Islamic ethical thought. How does the classic debate look from the standpoint of perspectives somewhat removed from this debate, yet clearly related to it? The dialogue becomes more difficult here, for Jewish and Islamic perspectives on war and peace are shaped by ideas, methods, and sources peculiar to these traditions. It is, for the scholar coming from a concern with Christian, Western, or secular ideas and issues, also inherently risky—if one attempts it at all, one may be chided for lacking expertise, reproached for not doing more, or accused of orientalism. These are risks we choose to run, trusting that others will correct our mistakes.

The third part of this book adds two critical voices, those of feminism and Christian pacifism, that have for the most part been outside the mainstream Western debate on war and peace but whose moral significance is undeniable. Like Judaism and Islam, these perspectives have proven hard to incorporate into the debate between realism and natural law, for they, too, seem to challenge the assumptions of that debate. Our effort to come to terms with this challenge has been illuminating for all sides, and we hope it will prove illuminating for the reader.

It may be that we should have paid more attention to what Ted Koontz in his chapter calls the "abolitionist" perspective of Penn, Saint-Pierre, Kant, the founders of the League of Nations and the United Nations, and other advocates of global federation. The main concern of this tradition is not the ethics of war but the construction of a just international order in which law will substitute for war. For that reason, the tradition takes us away from our concern with how states and individuals should deal with war when it cannot be avoided. For better or worse, our focus in this book is on how the choice to fight or not to fight should be made, not on how a world might be created in which such choices are no longer required.[14]

The comparative overviews that make up the final section of this book compare and contrast the presented viewpoints in relation to the questions each author was asked to keep in mind while preparing his or her chapter. Many of these questions reflect the "just war" categories of the classic debate between political realism and natural law. As the chapters to follow illustrate, those committed to other viewpoints will often ask different questions. One of the things we want to discover is where these viewpoints challenge not only the familiar answers to the classic questions but the questions themselves. We also want to learn something about differences within each viewpoint—differences the exchanges between the presenters and reactors for each perspective are designed to illuminate. What emerges is a picture of continuing debate, both within and between the viewpoints represented here. Moral traditions are often seen as doctrinal relics, the hardened deposits of past debates. As the following chapters make clear, they are also a resource for future debates and moral choices—choices and debates that will, in turn, reshape our multivocal heritage.

Notes

1. Chris Brown, *International Relations Theory: New Normative Approaches* (New York: Columbia University Press, 1992).

2. Martin Wight, *International Theory: The Three Traditions* (Leicester: Leicester University Press, 1991), and Michael Donelan, *Elements of International Political Theory* (Oxford: Clarendon Press, 1990). Wight's three traditions are the Machiavellian (realism), the Grotian (rationalism), and the Kantian (revolutionism), whereas Donelan identifies five views: natural law, realism, fideism, rationalism, and historicism.

3. See Terry Nardin and David R. Mapel, eds., *Traditions of International Ethics* (Cambridge: Cambridge University Press, 1992).

4. Symposium on the Ownership and Distribution of the World's Natural Resources, *Journal of Value Inquiry* 23 (1989), 169–258; Brian Barry and Robert E. Goodin, eds., *Free Movement: Ethical Issues in the Transnational Migration of People and of Money* (University Park, PA: Pennsylvania State University Press, 1992); Symposium on Capitalism, Socialism, or Mixed Economy, *Ethics* 102 (1992), 447–511; and Chris Brown, ed., *Political Restructuring in Europe: Ethical Perspectives* (London: Routledge, 1994).

5. Thomas L. Pangle, "The Moral Basis of National Security: Four Historical Perspectives," in Klaus Knorr, ed., *Historical Dimensions of National Security Problems* (Lawrence: University Press of Kansas, 1976), 307–72; Reiner Steinweg, ed., *Der Gerechte Krieg: Christentum, Islam, Marxismus* (Frankfurt-am-Main: Suhrkamp, 1980); James Turner Johnson, *The Quest for Peace: Three Moral Traditions in Western Cultural History* (Princeton: Princeton University Press, 1987); James Turner Johnson and John Kelsay, eds., *Cross, Crescent, and Sword: The Justification and Limitation of War in Western and Islamic Tradition* (New York: Greenwood Press, 1990); John Kelsay and James Turner Johnson, eds., *Just War and Jihad: Historical and Theoretical Perspectives on War and Peace in Western and Islamic Traditions* (New York: Greenwood Press, 1991).

6. Stanley Hauerwas, "Whose Justice? Which Peace?" in David E. DeCosse, ed., *But Was It Just?* (New York: Bantam Doubleday Dell, 1992), 84. The hermeneutical issues raised by Hauerwas in this article and other writings are discussed at length by Ted Koontz and Michael Cartwright in Chapters 9 and 10 below.

7. A point emphasized in the context of war/peace ethics by Richard B. Miller, *Interpretations of Conflict: Ethics, Pacifism, and the Just-War Tradition* (Chicago: University of Chicago Press, 1991), 241, and in Chapter 14 below.

8. Walzer, *Interpretation and Social Criticism* (Cambridge, MA: Harvard University Press, 1987). In the absence of a "thick" set of shared values, members of different communities must fall back on articulating prohibitions rather than positive duties, so this "thinner criticism" is about as much as one can hope for in international ethics. Walzer develops this line of thinking in *Thick and Thin: Moral Argument at Home and Abroad* (Notre Dame, IN: University of Notre Dame Press, 1994).

9. Michael Walzer, *Just and Unjust Wars: A Moral Argument with Historical Illustrations*, 2d ed. (New York: Basic Books, 1992).

10. It is worth noting that although individual realists are often particularist, concerned with the security of their own states, political realism as an abstract doctrine makes the universal claim that every state must be concerned with its own security.

11. Alan Donagan makes an effort to sketch the outlines of a "common morality" along Kantian lines in *The Theory of Morality* (Chicago: University of Chicago Press, 1977). See also Gene Outka and John P. Reeder, Jr., eds., *Prospects for a Common Morality* (Princeton: Princeton University Press, 1993).

12. On what is sometimes called the "Grotian tradition," see Hedley Bull, "The Grotian Conception of International Society," in Herbert Butterfield and Martin Wight, eds., *Diplomatic Investigations: Essays in the Theory of International Politics* (Cambridge, MA: Harvard University Press, 1968), 51–73; also Hedley Bull, Benedict Kingsbury, and Adam Roberts, eds., *Hugo Grotius and International Relations* (Oxford: Clarendon Press, 1990).

13. See John Finnis, *Natural Law and Natural Rights* (Oxford: Clarendon Press, 1980); *Fundamentals of Ethics* (Washington, DC: Georgetown University Press, 1983); *Moral Absolutes: Tradition, Revision, and Truth* (Washington, DC: Catholic University of America Press, 1991); and, with Joseph M. Boyle, Jr. and Germain Grisez, *Nuclear Deterrence, Morality and Realism* (Oxford: Clarendon Press, 1987). The "natural law" theories of Hobbes, Spinoza, and Rousseau contain many realist arguments, and have been understood as realist by some interpreters.

14. The place of law and institutions in the international order is the subject of another Ethikon project, the results of which appear in David R. Mapel and Terry Nardin, eds., *The Constitution of International Society: Diverse Ethical Perspectives* (forthcoming).

PART ONE

The Classic Debate: Natural Law and Political Realism

CHAPTER 1

The Ethics of War and Peace in the Catholic Natural Law Tradition

John Finnis

Peace and War

Law, and a legalistic morality and politics, can define peace and war by their mutual opposition. Any two communities are either at peace or at war with one another. If they are at war, each is seeking a relationship to the other ("victory over," "prevailing over") which that other seeks precisely to frustrate or overcome. If they are at peace, each pursues its own concerns in a state of indifference to, noninterference in, or collaboration with the concerns of the other.

But sound moral and political deliberation and reflection is not legalistic. Despite some tendencies towards legalism, the Catholic tradition of natural law theory very early articulated and has steadily maintained a richer and more subtle conception of peace and war. From the outset, the philosophers in the tradition have accepted that social theory (a theory of practice) should have a distinct method, appropriate to its uniquely complex subject matter. It should not seek to articulate univocal terms and concepts which, like the concepts a lawyer needs, extend in the same sense to every instance within a clearly bounded field. Rather, it should identify the central cases of the opportunities and realities with which it is concerned, and the focal meanings of the terms which pick out those opportunities and realities. What is central, primary, and focal, and what peripheral, secondary, and diluted, is a function of (that is, is settled by reference to) what is humanly important, which in turn is a function of what are the good reasons for choice and action. So there are central and secondary forms of community, of friendship, of constitution, of the rule of law, of citizenship—and of peace. The secondary forms are really instances. But a reflection which focuses on them will overlook much that is important both for conscientious deliberation (practice) and for a fully explanatory reflection (theory).

So: to describe or explain peace as the absence of war is to miss the important reasons why, as the tradition affirms, peace is the point of war. That affirmation is not to be taken in the diluted and ironical sense of the Tacitean *solitudinem faciunt pacem appellant*.[1] The tradition knows well enough that wars are sometimes, in fact, waged to annihilate, out of hatred or sheer delight in inflicting misery, destruction, and death, and that even such wars can be said to be "for the sake of peace," that is, for the inner peace of satiation of desire and the outward peace of an unchallenged mastery over one's domain.[2] But even the inner peace attainable by such means is partial, unstable, and unsatisfying, and the peace of an unfair and cruel mastery is deeply disordered and deficient. More adequately understood, peace is the "tranquillity of order," and "order is the arrangement of things equal and unequal in a pattern which assigns to each its proper position."[3]

But a definition of peace in terms of things resting tranquilly in their proper places still fails to articulate the peace which could be the point of war. It remains too passive. The account needs to be supplemented by, indeed recentered on, what Augustine had treated as primary in the two immediately preceding sentences: *concordia* and *societas*, concord and community. For concord is agreement and harmony in willing, that is, in deliberating, choosing, and acting, and community is fellowship and harmony in shared purposes and common or coordinated activities. Peace is not best captured with metaphors of rest. It is the fulfillment which is realized most fully in the active neighborliness of willing cooperation in purposes which are both good in themselves and harmonious with the good purposes and enterprises of others.

Peace, then, is diminished and undermined generically by every attitude, act, or omission damaging to a society's fair common good—specifically, by dispositions and choices which more or less directly damage a society's concord. Such dispositions and choices include a proud and selfish individualism, estranged from one's society's (or societies') concerns and common good;[4] contentiousness, obstinacy, or quarrelsomeness;[5] feuding with one's fellow citizens[6] and sedition against proper authority;[7] and, most radically, war.

To choose war is precisely to choose a relationship or interaction in which *we* seek by lethal physical force to block and shatter at least some of *their* undertakings and to seize or destroy at least some of the resources and means by which they could prosecute such undertakings or resist our use of force.[8] (Do not equate "lethal" with "intended to kill": see under "Attitudes toward War and Nonviolence" below.) In the paradigm case of war, the *we* and the *they* are both political communities, acting as such—what the tradition called "complete or self-sufficient (*perfectae*) communities." But there are only "material," not "formal" (essential, morally decisive), differences between that paradigm case ("war" strictly so called) and other cases:[9] the war of a political community against pirates; the revolt of part of a political community against their rulers, or the campaign of the rulers against some part of their community, or some other form of civil war; the armed struggle of a group or individual against gangsters, bandits, or pirates; the duel of one person against another. In each case, the relationship and interactions between *us* and *them* which we bring into being in choosing to go to war replace, for the war's duration, the neighborliness and cooperation which might otherwise have subsisted between us and them. But the tradition teaches that a choice of means which involves such a negation of peace (of concord, neighborliness, and collaboration) cannot be justified unless one's purpose (end) in choosing such means includes the restoration, and if possible the enhancement, of peace (concord, neighborliness, and collaboration) as constitutive of the *common* good of the imperfect community constituted by any two interacting human societies.[10]

This requirement of a pacific intention is, for the tradition, an inescapable implication of morality; it is entailed by the truly justifying point of any and every human choice and action. For peace, in its rich central sense and reality, is materially synonymous with the ideal condition of integral human fulfillment—the flourishing of all human persons and communities.[11] And openness to that ideal, and the consistency of all one's choices with such openness, is the first condition of moral reasonableness.[12]

In the classic sources of the tradition, that primary moral principle is articulated not as I have just stated it, but as the principle that one is to love one's neighbor as oneself, a principle proposed as fundamental not only to the Gospel law but also to the natural law, to practical reasonableness itself.[13] Accordingly, the tradition's classic treatments of war are found in the treatises on *caritas*, precisely on love of neighbor.[14] Justice removes obstacles to peace, and is intrinsic to it, but the direct source of peace is love of neighbor.[15] And war is to be for peace.[16]

For true peace, not a false or seeming peace. War might often be averted by surrender. But the peace thus won would often be a false peace, corrupted and diluted by injustices, slavery, and fear. Preserving, regaining, or attaining true peace can require war (though war will never of itself suffice to achieve that peace[17]).

Motive or Intention

An act, a deed, is essentially what the person who chooses to do it intends it to be. Intention looks always to the point, the end, rather than to means precisely as such; intention corresponds to the question, "Why are you doing this?" But any complex activity is a nested order of ends which are also means to further ends: I get up *to* walk to the cupboard *to* get herbs *to* make a potion *to* drink *to* purge myself *to* get slim *to* restore my health *to* prepare for battle *to*. . . .[18] So, though intention is of ends, it is also of all the actions which are means.

English lawyers try to mark the distinction between one's more immediate intentions and one's further intentions by reserving the word "motive" for the latter. The spirit in which one acts, the emotions which support one's choice and exertions, can be called one's motives, too, but become the moralist's direct concern only if and insofar as they make a difference to *what* is intended and chosen. If the proposal one shapes in deliberation and adopts by choice is partly molded by one's emotional motivations (more precisely, by one's intelligence in the service of those emotions), then those motivations are to be counted among one's intentions (and motives), help make one's act what it is, and fall directly under moral scrutiny.

A war is just if and only if it is right to choose to engage in it. A choice is right if and only if it satisfies all the requirements of practical reasonableness, that is, *all* relevant moral requirements. If one's purpose (motive, further intention) is good but one's chosen means is vicious, the whole choice and action is wrong. Conversely, if one's means is upright (say, giving alms to the poor) but one's motive—one's reason for choosing it—is corrupt (say, deceiving voters about one's character and purposes), the whole choice and action is wrong. The scholastics had an untranslatable maxim to make this simple point: *bonum ex integra causa, malum ex quocumque defectu*, an act will be morally good (right) if what goes into it is entirely good, but will be morally bad (wrong) if it is defective in *any* morally relevant respect (bad end, or bad means, or inappropriate circumstances). Treatises on just war are discussions of the conditions which must *all* be satisfied if the war is to be just.

The preceding three paragraphs enable us to see that, in the tradition, no clear or clearly relevant distinction can be drawn between "grounds for" war and "motive or intention" in going to war. The proper questions are always: What are good reasons for going to war? What reasons must not be allowed to shape the proposal(s) about which I deliberate, or motivate my adoption of a proposal?

In the first major treatise on war by a philosophical theologian (as opposed to a canonist), Alexander of Hales (c. 1240) identifies six preconditions for a just war. The person declaring war must have (1) the right *affectus* (state of mind) and (2) authority to do so; the persons engaging in war must (3) not be clerics, and must have (4) the right *intentio*; the persons warred upon must (5) deserve it (the war must have *meritum*); and there must be (6) *causa*, in that the war must be waged for the support of the good, the coercion of the bad, and peace for all.[19] Here the word *causa* is less generic than in the maxim *bonum ex integra causa*, but less specific than in Aquinas's discussion of just war, about thirty years later. Aquinas (c. 1270) cuts the preconditions down to three: authority, *causa iusta*, and *intentio recta*. Aquinas's *causa* is essentially what Alexander of Hales had called *meritum*. There is a just *causa*, says Aquinas, when those whom one attacks deserve (*mereantur*) the attack on account of their culpability; just wars are wars for righting wrongs, in particular a nation's wrong in neglecting to punish crimes committed by its people or to restore what has been unjustly taken away.[20]

Thus it is clear that, in Aquinas, the term *causa* is not equivalent to "a justifying ground." Rather, it points to something more like the English lawyer's "cause of action," a wrong cognizable by the law as giving basis for a complaint, a wrong meriting legal redress. As Francisco Suarez notes, 350 years later, a discussion of such *iustae causae* for war is primarily a discussion of the justifying grounds for war *other than* self-defense:[21] to act in self-defense really needs no *causa*. (Throughout I shall follow Article 51 of the UN Charter in using the term "self-defense" to include all cases of justifiable defense, *légitime défense*.) So there is an important difference between a present-day inquiry into the justifying grounds for war and a medieval inquiry into *iusta causa*. Aquinas had more reason to distinguish (as he firmly does[22]) between *causa* (in his sense) and *intentio* than we now have to distinguish between "ground" and "motive or intention."

Is there nonetheless some room, in considering the rightness of initiating or participating in a war or act of war, for an inquiry into the spirit or sentiment in which a people, an official, or a citizen acts? Perhaps there is. We might draw a distinction between "grounds" and "spirit" by recalling that war is paradigmatically a social and *public* act. Now, just as an individual's act or deed is essentially what the person who chooses to do it intends it to be, so the acts of a society are essentially what they are defined to be in the public policy which members of the society are invited or required to participate in carrying out. That defining policy, which organizes the *actions* of individual participants in a war (thus constituting their acts a social act),[23] and does so by more or less explicit reference to war aims and strategy, can often be distinguished both from any accompanying propaganda and from the emotions and dispositions of the leaders who shaped and adopted it. Thus individual citizens can, in principle, assess the public policy, the announced reasons for going to war, the announced war aims, and the adopted strategy (so far as they know it) and assess the justice of the war (taking into account the facts about the enemy's deeds, operations, and plans so far as they can discover them). Such an assessment can set aside the moral deficiencies of the society's leaders, except insofar as those deficiencies—manifest bellicosity, vengefulness, chauvinism, and the like—should be taken into account in judging the truth of the leaders' claims about facts and about the absence of suitable alternatives to war.

Notice that this does not carry us very far. Individual citizens have (in varying measure) some duty to consider the justice of the war, even if there is a weighty presumption in favor of accepting the public policy; in carrying out that duty, they must not allow themselves to be swayed by exciting but evil motivations: "the craving to hurt people, the cruel thirst for revenge, a bellicose and unappeasable spirit, ferocity in hitting back, lust for mastery, and anything else of this sort."[24] The same goes for the leaders: the shaping and adoption of their choice to go to war, of their war aims, and of their strategy will be wrongful if *affected* by any such seductive emotions.

Yet that malign influence might (and perhaps not infrequently does) remain undetectable by those who are called upon to participate in the war. To these citizens, the grounds for war, and the war aims and strategy which provide the grounds for particular operations, may reasonably seem morally acceptable. Indeed, those grounds may sometimes *be* morally acceptable even when the leaders of the society would in fact not have acted on them but for their own immoralities of disposition ("spirit") and motivation ("intention").

Grounds for War

It is primarily by harnessing reason to devise rationalizations that emotions create temptations to injustice (and to other immoralities). Rationalizations are plausible grounds which make proposals for choice and action attractive to reason and will but which, in truth (as indeed the deliberating or reflecting agent could discern), fail to satisfy all the requirements of practical reasonableness. As we have seen, the first such requirement is openness to integral human fulfillment, articulated in the tradition as love of neighbor as oneself. (The tradition—even, tentatively, in its purely philosophical articulations[25]—adds, "Out of love of God, source of the very being and life of self and neighbor alike.") All other moral principles are specifications, more and less general, of this primary moral principle. One of the most immediate specifications is the Golden Rule of fairness, in each of its forms, positive and negative: do to/for others as you would have them do to/for you; do not do to others what you would not be willing to have them do to you. This in turn is specified in the presumptive obligations to keep promises, to respect the domain and goods of others, to compensate for wrongful harm, and so forth. And these obligations in turn rule out a good many alleged grounds for war.

Sifting the types of reason put forward to justify or explain a decision to fight, the tradition became clear that only two could justify such a decision: self-defense, and the rectification (punitive or compensatory/restitutionary) of a wrong done.

Aquinas runs the two grounds together in a single, foundational proposition: "Just as rulers rightly use the sword in lawful *defense* against those who disturb the peace within the realm, when they *punish* criminals . . . so too they rightly use the sword of war to *protect* their polity from external enemies."[26] Later scholastics, such as Vitoria (c. 1535) and Suarez (c. 1610), while not repudiating Aquinas's resort to arguments which assimilate defense to punishment, do distinguish between defensive and offensive wars: war is self-defensive if waged to avert an injustice still about to take place; it is offensive if the injustice has already occurred and what is sought is redress.[27] And while they consider self-defense a ground so obviously just that it scarcely needs argument,[28] they consider offensive wars to be justified basically by the justice of retribution (*vindicatio*).[29] An offensive war is like the action of the police in tracking down and forcing the surrender of criminals within the jurisdiction, action assimilated (in this line of thought) with the action of the judge and the jailer or executioner.

As so often, Suarez's care brings nearer to the surface of the discussion an issue which seems to me to present the tradition with a notable difficulty. Private persons may forcibly defend themselves,[30] but "a punishment inflicted by one's own private authority is intrinsically evil," that is, it is wrong in all circumstances, even when one cannot get retributive or compensatory justice from a judge.[31] (For punishment is essentially the restoration of a fair balance between the offender and the law-abiding, a balance which the commission of an offense disturbs by enacting the offender's willingness to take the advantage of doing as one pleases when the law requires a common restraint; and persons who are not responsible for upholding the balance of fairness in distribution of advantages and disadvantages in a community *cannot* by "punitively" repressing wrongdoers accomplish that restoration of fairness which their act, by purporting to be punishment, pretends to accomplish.) It is because private punishment is always immoral that the tradition, following Cicero,[32] insisted on public authority as one of the essential preconditions for just war (meaning just offensive war). But in a world without any world government, are not states and their rulers in precisely the position of private persons? How can they punish if they are not world rulers, or even international rulers, and so lack the type of responsibility that grounds acts of punishment—responsibility for maintaining and restoring a balance of justice between wrongdoers and the law-abiding, or between wrongdoers and their victims? This difficulty is often raised in a slightly different form: how can a state or government rightly act as both judge and party? That is a fair question, which Suarez identifies and tries to answer,[33] but I think the form in which I have framed the difficulty is the more fundamental.

The issue is complicated, above all by the flexible extension of "defense" and "punishment" and their convergence or even overlap in a range of situations. Note first that a war, or a military operation, is not taken out of the class of *defensive* acts by the mere fact that it is initiated to forestall a reasonably anticipated and imminent unjust attack.[34] More importantly, defense is of rights and does not become inapplicable on the first success of a violation of them. If it is self-defense to resist forcibly the entry of squatters into my family house, is it not self-defense to eject them forcibly when I discover them on returning home in the evening? Defensive measures seem to extend to self-help reclamation of what one has just lost.[35] And why should the mere temporal immediacy, or delay, of one's measures make an essential difference? Again, Vitoria, without seeking to justify the Spanish appropriation or colonization of the Americas on this ground, upheld the right of the Spanish to make war on the Amerindians *in defense of* the many likely innocent Amerindian victims of Amerindian cannibalism, human sacrifice, and euthanasia of the senile.[36] "For the defense of our neighbors is the rightful concern of each of us, even for private persons and even if it involves shedding blood."[37]

Moreover, much of what the tradition says about the *punitive* function of war between polities relates not to the punishment's primary, retributive rationale but to punishment's function as a deterrent, general or special. "Without the fear of punishment to deter them from wrongdoing (*iniuria*), the enemy would simply grow more bold about invading a second time."[38] May not the same thought play a legitimate part in one's deliberation as a private person deciding whether or not to expel squatters from some part of one's domain? Note how Vitoria not only moves back and forth between defense and punishment, but also treats each as an aspect of the other:

> The license and authority to wage war may be conferred by necessity. If, for example, a city attacks another city in the same kingdom, . . . and the king fails, through negligence or timidity, to avenge [impose retribution for] the damage done (*vindicare iniurias illatas*), then the injured . . . city . . . may not only defend itself but may also carry the war into its attacker's territory and teach its enemy a lesson (*animadvertere in hostes*), even killing the wrongdoers. Otherwise the injured party would have no adequate self-defense; enemies would not abstain from harming others, if their victims were content only to defend themselves. By the same argument, even a private individual may attack his enemy if there is no other way open to him of defending himself from harm.[39]

Thus the conceptual boundaries between defense and punishment are somewhat blurred. Still, the distinction remains, and with it the question: why is punishment morally allowable in the state and its government, but not in the individual whose rights are not and perhaps cannot be vindicated by the state? Suarez gives the technical answer:

> Just as the sovereign prince may punish his own subjects when they offend others, so he may exact retribution [*se vindicare*] on another prince or *state which by reason of some offense becomes subject to him*; and this retribution cannot be sought at the hands of another judge, because the prince of whom we are speaking has no superior in temporal affairs.[40]

But the proposition I have italicized smuggles the conclusion into the premises. If this wronged state or government has no rightful human superior in secular matters, the same will be true of the offending state or government, and the proposition[41] that the offense puts the offending state (morally speaking) into a state of subjection is question-begging or a fiction.

A number of recent writers have surmised that the issue was obscured from the tradition's classical writers by the notion that all Christendom was one realm, so that the wars of a state or government within that quasi-universal realm could the more readily be supposed to be analogous to the use of police power to bring to justice wrongdoers within a realm.[42] But this hypothesis, though not altogether groundless, is scarcely satisfying; the emperor's sovereignty over Christendom was manifestly a fiction, and the existence of states outside the empire was all too well known. Moreover, the traditional position that punitive war is justified survived after the replacement of Christendom by states which everyone accepted were wholly independent sovereignties.

Without, I think, the benefit of much clear discussion among the tradition's representatives, recent witnesses to the tradition—notably Pius XII, John XXIII, and the Second Vatican Council—have spoken as if the only justifying ground for war were defense.[43] Several moralists who uphold the main lines of the Catholic natural law tradition argue that this is a legitimate development of the tradition, that it renders the tradition more consistent with its own principles.[44] Inasmuch as they rely on a supposed change in the nature of warfare by virtue of technological developments, their argument is unpersuasive. Many present-day wars are fought in traditional ways at more or less traditional levels of limited destructiveness. Moreover, although a world government can now be envisaged as in some sense a practical possibility (again by virtue of technological development), and although leaders and people ought to do what (if anything) they responsibly can to bring such a world government into being,[45] these considerations do not justify the conclusion that, in the meantime, states must behave precisely as if they already had a common superior, effectively responsible for maintaining the worldwide common good, on whom exclusively they must treat the police power (of bringing wrongdoers to justice) as having been devolved. If self-defense (*légitime défense*) is to be held to be the only just ground for war, it must be on the ground that the tradition (1) rightly judged that private individuals as such have no right to punish those who have wronged them, but (2) erred in supposing that independent states purporting to punish states which have wronged them are in an essentially different moral position from private persons purporting to punish people who have wronged them. Vitoria and Suarez uneasily ascribed the supposed moral difference between the positions of private persons and independent states to "the consent of the world" and the customary positive law (*ius gentium*), not to natural law.[46] The same consent and custom grounded slavery.[47] As the customary institution of slavery came to be discerned by the tradition itself as contrary rather than supplementary to natural law, so the tradition has come (or is coming) to discern the true moral character of the custom ascribing to states the authority to levy punitive war.

Other Distinguishing Criteria

Having a good ground is not the only prerequisite for justly going to war (and fighting it). *Bonum ex integra causa, malum ex quocumque defectu*; there are other conditions which must all be satisfied if one's warring is to be justifiable. All of these further conditions are, I think, implications of the Golden Rule (principle) of fairness, rather than of the principle that one must never choose to harm the innocent. The most important of these implications is that it is unfair not only to the enemy but also to one's own people (1) to initiate or continue a war which has no reasonable hope of success, or (2) to initiate a war which could be avoided by alternatives short of war, such as negotiation and nonviolent action.

The condition that the foreseeable side effects of going to war be not excessive ("disproportionate") was usually stated by the tradition in connection with the justification-conditions of punitive wars. A government's initiation of a war for the sake of retributively restoring an order disturbed by a wrong done to its own country could not be justified if the war were likely to expose that country unfairly to loss and risk of loss (for example, great risk of substantial loss, or significant risk of great loss). Indeed, it seems to be only such wars that the tradition explicitly declares to be subject to this condition.[48] But there can be little doubt that even the decision to put up a defense must be subject to the same sort of precondition. Modern restatements of the tradition which make defense the only just ground for war do treat *probability of success* and *proportionality* (of anticipated damage and costs to expected good results) as preconditions.[49]

That is not to say that a military unit faced with overwhelming odds must, in fairness, surrender. Everyone knows that one unit's willingness to fight to the last man can sometimes inflict such losses that the enemy's overall operation and strategy is weakened or delayed and so can be defeated—its victory over the unit destroyed was Pyrrhic. And everyone knows that an isolated unit, in the dust of conflict, can rarely discern with confidence how its resistance would affect the overall outcome of the war. Military discipline is therefore not unfair in imposing a strong presumption in favor of fighting on. But, when standing alone against the enemy, those in command of the whole nation or its armed forces as a whole must very seriously ask whether it is consistent with the Golden Rule to undertake a hopeless resistance which will impose immense losses on the combatants of both sides, on noncombatants of both nations (especially the nation attacked), and perhaps on the citizens of neutral states lying (say) in the path of the fallout.

The same sort of fairness-based considerations underlie the requirement that war be considered a *last resort* after the exhaustion of peaceful alternatives.[50] The losses accepted in a negotiated settlement, however unpalatable, must be compared with the losses that would be borne by all those likely to be destroyed or injured by the alternative option, war.

How are such comparisons and judgments of (dis)proportion to be made? Not by the simply aggregative methods taken for granted by utilitarian, consequentialist, or proportionalist ethics, which blandly but absurdly ignore the incommensurability of the goods and bads at stake in human options.[51] It is a matter, rather, of adhering to the *rational* requirement of impartiality by an intuitive awareness of one's own *feelings* as one imaginatively puts oneself in the place of those who will suffer from the effects of the alternative options (not forgetting the different status of the various classes of potential sufferers, some of whom would have willed and initiated the war and thus accepted the risk). As the US Catholic bishops indicate, to identify proportionality one must "tak[e] into account" both the expected advantages and the expected harms, but with the purpose (not of measuring incommensurables but rather) of "assess[ing] the justice of accepting the harms," an assessment in which "it is of utmost importance . . . to think about the poor and the helpless, for they are usually the ones who have the least to gain and the most to lose when war's violence touches their lives" (not forgetting, however, their fate in an unjust peace).[52] As we shall see when we consider unfairness ("disproportion") in the conduct of military operations, the deliberations and conduct of a party to the conflict will provide a referent against which to assess the requirements of impartiality as they bear on other conduct of that same party.

The Conduct of War

All the moral requirements which bear on the decision to go to war apply also to the willingness to carry on fighting and to the conduct of the war in particular military operations. Indeed, they apply also to the adoption of a deterrent strategy in the hope that war will thereby be averted.[53] The distinction between *ius ad bellum* and *ius in bello* is scarcely part of the Catholic natural law tradition. Nor is it a helpful distinction. True, it teaches that the rightness of a decision to fight does not entail the rightness of everything done in fighting; but that is more fundamentally taught by the more general principle, applicable to all decisions and actions, *bonum ex integra causa, malum ex quocumque defectu*: *every* choice must satisfy all moral requirements.

So it must be clear at the outset that, in the Catholic natural law tradition, there can be no question of different moral constraints pulling against one another. Each of the constraints is a necessary condition of justifiability, and compliance with one or some of them is never a sufficient condition. The combatants, like the leaders who opted for war, must have upright intentions: their motivations must be free from unfair bias and cruelty, they must intend to fight on some just ground, they must not be willing to impose unfair devastation. And, just as their leaders in deliberating about whether to go to war must not intend the death of innocents (noncombatants), either as an end (malice and revenge) or as a means (of breaking the enemy's will to fight, for example, or of bringing neutrals into the war), so, too, those who plan and carry out military operations are subject to precisely the same constraint, the same exceptionless requirement of respect for (innocent) human life. So too, indeed, are those who participate in the public policy and act of maintaining a strategy of deterrence involving threats which they hope will never (but could and, as far as the policy is concerned, would) be carried out.[54]

Curiously, Aquinas's little treatise *de bello* makes no reference to the exceptionless moral norm that innocents must not be deliberately killed. But there is no doubt that he held that norm to be applicable to war. For the norm itself is one which, a little later in the same part of the *Summa theologiae*, he clearly affirms and defends as exceptionless.[55] And, as we shall see in the next section, he explicitly affirms (with the whole tradition) that such norms remain requirements of reason and thus of morality whatever the circumstances. As if to make the point economically, his treatment *de bello* affirms the exceptionless applicability to war of another moral norm which many people violate in war, indeed violate perhaps even more freely and with even fewer qualms of conscience: the moral norm excluding all lying (as distinct from subterfuges which do not involve affirming as true what one knows to be untrue).[56] And the whole tradition after him peacefully accepts the absolute immunity of noncombatants from deliberate attack, that is, attack intended to harm them either as an end or as a means to some other end.[57]

Combatants are all those whose behavior is part of a society's use of force; if we are engaged in just defense, enemy combatants are those whose behavior contributes to their society's wrongful use of force. Anyone whose behavior during warfare could not be used to verify the proposition, "That society is at war with us," is clearly a noncombatant. But some of those people whose wartime behavior could be used to verify that proposition (little old ladies knitting khaki socks, for example) nevertheless contribute so little, and so merely symbolically, to the acts of war whose violation of just order is ground for war that they are reasonably considered noncombatants. The principle of discrimination—that one must not make noncombatants the object of attack as one makes combatants—requires one to respect the distinction between combatants and noncombatants, but does not presuppose that drawing the distinction is easy. There are in fact many borderline cases: farmers, workers in public utilities, members of fire brigades, and the like, who engage in certain performances specified by war and essential to it, yet very little different from their peacetime occupations and essential to the survival and well-being of all who are certainly noncombatants. Some theorists in the tradition have called them combatants, others in the tradition have called them noncombatants. But, on any view, the population of a political community includes many people who are certainly noncombatants; their behavior would in no way help to verify that the society is engaged in operations of war against another society. They include in particular those who cannot take care of themselves, together with those whose full-time occupation is caring for the helpless. The behavior of people of these sorts contributes nothing to a society's war effort, but actually diverts resources which might otherwise be used in that effort.

Noncombatants, then, are innocent; that is, they are not *nocentes*, not engaged in the operations which most of the tradition assimilated to capital crimes and which the newer conception proposed by (say) Grisez treats as activities warranting forcible resistance in self-defense. Noncombatants may not be directly harmed or killed; "directly" here means "as a means or as an end."[58] (Does it follow that combatants may be directly killed? See the last section below.) But, without intending any harm to noncombatants, one may choose to plan and carry out military operations which one knows will in fact cause noncombatants injury or death; and such a nonhomicidal choice can be justified provided that the choice is otherwise fair and well motivated (*malum ex quocumque defectu*). The proviso just mentioned is often expressed as "provided that the death-dealing or other harmful effects on noncombatants are not disproportionate." Here "proportionate" can have a rational meaning which it could not have if it referred simply to sheer magnitude; its rational meaning is *unfair*, imposed by a biased and partial, not an impartial, measure and judgment. The standard is the Golden Rule, and I have sketched in the preceding section the ways in which it gains content. The basic measure is: what people do, or are unwilling to do, to themselves and their friends. For example: In 1944, Allied air forces followed a policy of precision bombing when attacking German targets in France, and a policy of blind or other imprecise bombing when attacking German military targets in Germany.[59] Thus they showed themselves willing to impose on German noncombatants a level of incidental harm and death which they were not willing to impose on French civilians.

This was unfair; the collateral damage to German civilians was, therefore, disproportionate.

Are there prudential as well as moral constraints on the conduct of war once it has begun? Here I take "prudential" in its modern meaning: in my/our own interests. Doubtless sane leaders will regulate their decisions with an eye to the consequences for themselves and their community. But the tradition is quite clear that there is no coherent and nonarbitrary prudence apart from a morally regulated, indeed morally directive, prudence which respects *all* the requirements of reasonableness, including fairness and respect for the humanity of *all* persons in every community. So, in the final analysis, it is futile and misleading to investigate a prudence distinct from morality. Machiavellianism, for all its impressive rules of practice and its attractions to the emotions of self-preference and the aesthetics of technique, is a mere rationalization which cannot withstand rational critique. For it cannot justify its horizon, its presupposed demarcation of a range of persons or communities whose well-being it will then take as the measure of prudentially "right" action. The so-called paradoxes of nuclear deterrence are merely one exemplary sign of the unreasonableness of every prudence which falls short of the requirements of morality's first principle.

Morality in Extremity

The remarks in the preceding paragraph indicate the tradition's fundamental response to the question of morality in extremity. For "extremity" denotes the grave and imminent danger that *we* will be overwhelmed or destroyed (unless we take certain measures). The tradition does not suggest that the requirements of morally decent deliberation take no account of such a danger. On the contrary, all the requirements of the Golden Rule are liable to be profoundly affected by the presence and degree of such risks.

The so-called rules of war include many norms which are valid and binding because they have been *adopted* (posited) by custom or agreement or enactment by some body empowered by custom or agreement to make such enactments. This is true not only of modern international conventions, but also of much in the tradition's moral treatises on war, where such norms are described as *de iure gentium* (as distinct from *de iure naturali*).[60] Now, the moral force of positive law, including the *ius gentium* inasmuch as it is positive law, rests on the Golden Rule (taken together with the rational requirement that one be concerned for the well-being of others and thus of the communities to which one belongs). Having taken the benefits of others' compliance with the rules, I cannot fairly renege on one of those rules when it requires compliance from me. But the principle articulated in the preceding sentence, though reasonable and usually decisive, is not absolute. That is to say, it does not apply exceptionlessly. For if the situation now is such that, had it obtained when compliance with some rule by others was in issue, I would not have wanted and expected (demanded) those others to comply, it can be fair for me to withhold my compliance; I can fairly do as I truly would have been willing for others to do in a like case.

So, in principle, those rules of war which depend on custom, agreement, or enactment are liable to be set aside in extremity. On the other hand, the tradition holds that where a rule, though positive (de iure gentium, not de iure naturali), has been adopted precisely *for* and *with a view to* regulating conduct in situations of extremity, it cannot rightly be set aside. Thus, since the rules of fair trial for a capital crime are designed precisely for the extremity in which persons on trial for such crimes find themselves, those who are convicted on perjured testimony must patiently endure death,[61] and judges who know the truth but after every effort can find no legal way of proving it (or of excluding the false evidence) must follow the rules of evidence and sentence to death someone whom they know to be innocent.[62] So there may well be rules of war which, though positive, are not subject to dispensation in emergency, since they were adopted precisely for that type of extremity.

Moreover, not all "rules of war" are merely positive. Some are true implications of the basic requirements of practical reasonableness, which are morality's (natural law's) foundational principles. And some of those basic requirements entail exceptionless moral norms. What Kant identified as the requirement that one treat human persons always as ends in themselves and never as mere means is a bundling together of the requirement that one never meet injury with injury (even when one could do so fairly), which excludes all acts of mere revenge, and the requirement that one not do evil (such as intentionally to destroy, damage, or impede a basic human good) for the sake of good—each requirement being, in turn, an implication of the first moral principle of openness to integral human fulfillment (love of neighbor as oneself). One of the exceptionless moral norms entailed by the requirement that evil not be done for the sake of good is the norm which excludes intending to kill, and intentionally killing, any (innocent) human being.

But, at least in situations of extremity, would it not be the lesser evil to kill a few innocents (say hostage children) to prevent the extermination of thousands and the utter ruin of a decent community? The whole tradition, while very attentive to the need to prevent bad consequences and to the bearing of likely bad consequences on duties of fairness, denies the claim that reason can identify such a killing of the innocent as the lesser evil.[63] It accepts the Socratic, Platonic, and Catholic maxim that it is better (a lesser evil) to suffer wrong than to do wrong,[64] and rejects as an understandable but ultimately unreasonable temptation the thought[65] that it is better for one innocent man to be framed and put to death than for the whole people to perish. It accepts that self-defense is a situation of necessity,[66] but rejects as unreasonable and morally false[67] the Roman and Cromwellian maxim that necessity knows no law. Or rather, the maxim is given its proper, subordinate role: necessity (that is, great danger) can entitle one to make an exception to rules adopted for human convenience, or concerning human goods which are not basic; thus rules about fasting and sabbath observance, or about rights of property, can be overridden "by necessity," as fairness suggests and permits.[68] But the basic goods of the human person must be respected unconditionally.

One can find in the tradition occasional statements which clearly face up to the gravity of the matter:

> In such a situation, the law of God, which is also the rule of reason, makes exceptionally high demands. . . . The principles the Church proclaims are not for some ideal or theoretical world or for humanity in the abstract. They speak directly to the consciences of men and women in this world. They are principles that can on occasion demand heroic self-sacrifice of individuals and nations. For there are situations, for example in war, in which self-defense could not be effective without the commission of acts which must never be done, whatever the consequences. Innocent hostages, for example, must never be killed.[69]

But such statements are less frequent than one would think needful to prepare people to live up to the taxing responsibilities of suffering wrong rather than doing it in situations where everything is or seems to be at stake.

To be sure, the tradition's adherence to exceptionless moral norms is reinforced by faith in God's providence, redemption, and promise of eternal salvation. But it is not logically dependent upon that faith. Nor is it, ultimately, a legalism, in which exceptionless rules might be promoted for fear that allowing exceptions would have bad consequences (for example, by abusive extensions of the permission). It understands itself, rather, as an unconditional adherence to the truth about what reason requires. An understanding and defense of the tradition thus depends upon a critique of claims that reason does not warrant these (or any) exceptionless specific norms.[70]

Resistance to Political Authority

The tradition is not content with so cloudy, euphemistic, and characteristically modern a term as "resistance." The Resistance was trying to overthrow German rule in France, and in conscientious deliberations such a venture deserves to be known for what it is, and distinguished from disobedience, "civil" or otherwise.

The tradition's reflections on the forcible overthrow of governments proceed in the same dialectic of private right and public authority, of defense and punishment, as its reflections on war between nations. For such overthrow is truly a warlike venture. There are two main sorts of unjust government which might rightly be overthrown: (1) governments which seized power unjustly and by force and have not been legitimized by effluxion of time and absence of alternatives, and (2) governments which came to power lawfully but govern with manifest gross injustice (looting, murdering, framing, etc.).[71] If a government of either type pursues certain private citizens in an attempt to kill or mutilate them, they can rightly use force in the exercise of their rights of self-defense, and doing so is not necessarily made unacceptable by the fact that it will have the side effect of killing even the supreme ruler.[72] But no private citizen, as such, can rightly undertake to kill any or all of the rulers, as punishment (or revenge) for their wrongdoing, however wicked, any more than private citizens can rightly kill a well-known murderer on the score that they are administering capital punishment (or vengeance).[73]

Still, might not such a citizen claim to be defending the community against the future crimes of the government? In the case where the government had come to power justly or acquired a moral entitlement to govern, the answer given by the tradition was: yes, if the wrongs such a citizen seeks to prevent are violent, but not otherwise; for in any other case, the attempt amounts to levying offensive war, which is never within private authority, any more than a private citizen can rightly resort to personal violence to incapacitate a forger. In the case where the government came to power illegitimately and remains illegitimate, the tradition is willing to treat the government's acts of ruling, however peaceful in themselves, as amounting to a continuing act of violent injustice against the community (banditry). Accordingly, unless the community by some communal act makes it clear that it wishes no such deliverance, any private individual has the tacit and assumed public authority and constructive consent needed to seek an illegitimate government's violent overthrow, not as an act of punishment but as defense of self, country, and every innocent member of the community.[74] Such an act must, of course, satisfy all the other relevant requirements of proper motivation, exhaustion of alternatives, prospect of success, and fairness in accepting the foreseeable bad side effects.[75]

The risk that any attempt to overthrow a government by force will have very bad side effects is often great. The tradition, for the most part, inculcates caution and emphasizes the general desirability of preferring nonviolent or "passive" forms of resistance, always within the context of a wider teaching that government and positive law create moral obligations which, though by no means absolute or indefeasible or invariably strong, are significant and prevail over the contrary inclinations and desires of subjects in all cases save where the exercise of governmental power in question is certainly unjust. The tradition also recognizes other cases of justifiable disobedience, short of revolutionary violence intended to overthrow—that is, acts of war against—an unjust regime.

First, there is the important class of cases where administrative or legal requirements demand the performance of immoral acts (to surrender Jews to the Nazi authorities, for example). Violation of such requirements is both permissible and obligatory.

Second, government property may be specifically dedicated to wicked activities: concentration camps, slave ships, abortoria, human-embryo experimentation equipment, nuclear weaponry deployed for deterrence by a strategy involving city-swapping and final countervalue retaliation, etc. In circumstances where destroying the property and impeding the evil activities would be likely to save some persons from serious injustice, those actions would be justified.

Third, there is civil disobedience strictly so called. This involves essentially (1) overt violation of a law (2) to express one's protest against that law, or against something public closely connected with some application of that law, together with (3) ready submission to the law's sanctions (a submission not morally required in the other classes of justifiable disobedience). The violation must not involve doing anything otherwise immoral, and its manner and circumstances must make it clear to observers not only that it *symbolizes* opposition to some important and clearly identified matter of law or policy, but also that this opposition seeks justice, not advantage. Since civil disobedience must not involve doing anything otherwise immoral, its justification does not cover use of force against any person. Nor does it cover the destruction of property which is at all closely connected with the well-being of individual persons who would be damaged by its destruction, removal, or temporary or permanent inaccessibility. Above all, it shuns the maxim "Evil may be done that [greater] good may come of it"; indeed, that is the maxim which underpins most (though not all) attempted justifications of the laws or policies or proposals which are the objects of the civilly disobedient protest. So-called civil disobedience will be corrupted and corrupting if the campaigners subscribe to that maxim and so are willing to do real harm, not in self-defense but to advance their cause. The "harms" one does in justifiable civil disobedience must be actions which, in their full context (as set out in the definition just given), are of a type accepted by one's upright fellow citizens as essentially no more than vivid expressions of authentic moral-political concerns, and thus as not truly harms. The essential analogy here is with the blows given and received on the football field, or the touchings and jostlings in a rush-hour crowd; in their full context these are not harms, even though in other contexts they would constitute assaults.[76]

The most fundamental point and justification of civil disobedience is to *show* that the wickedness of the laws or policies in question takes them outside the ordinary web of politics and law, and undermines the very legitimacy of the state or government itself—a legitimacy founded on justice, not on calculations of advantage in which the lives of innocents might be directly sacrificed in the interests of others.

Attitudes toward War and Nonviolence

The tradition emerged and flourished in coexistence with a body of customary laws (ius gentium) which it in part reformed but in part accepted with a complacency which now seems disconcerting. But at no time was the tradition an apologia for war. Rather, its thrust has been, and ever more clearly is, to teach that wars are *certainly unjustified* unless a number of conditions are satisfied. It involves no belief that many wars are just, or that the conduct of any war is in fact free from wicked injustice. Even in teaching (as it used to do but now scarcely does) that offensive war could be justified to punish guilty rulers and their agents, the tradition required that war be the last resort, initiated only after communications, negotiations, and where practicable a ceding of rights for the sake of peace.

The tradition is still developing, on the basis of its own fundamentals. Those fundamentals entail, I think, that war can be justified only as defense. In the absence of a world government, no state or political community or ruler can rightly claim the authority to punish; the custom on which that authority was formerly rested[77] should now be regarded as immoral and ineffective. To purport to exercise such authority, in these circumstances, is to do no more than to reproduce the practice of feuding, writ large. And if there were a worldwide government, its rulers' justifiable powers against communities would be police powers: to take steps to bring offending individuals to justice, and to defend themselves and overcome resistance in the course of taking those steps, but not to administer punishment to whole communities, or to punish individuals otherwise than by impartial judicial trial and public sentence.

As it reaches this point in its development, one can discern that the tradition's fundamentals implicitly entail the rejection of a belief which is explicit not only in the tradition but also in both classic pacifism and "political realism"—the belief that war must involve *intending to kill.* The act-analysis involved in Aquinas's discussion of private self-defense entails, as Aquinas makes clear, that defensive acts foreseen to be likely or even certain to kill can nonetheless be done without any intent to kill. One's choice in choosing such an act of defense need only be to stop the attack, accepting as a side effect the attacker's death, unavoidably caused by the only available effective defensive measure. Such choices do not violate the exceptionless moral norm excluding every choice to destroy a basic human good. They will be justifiable choices only if they also involve no violation of any other requirement, especially the requirement of fairness: a deadly deed cannot be fairly chosen to fend off a harmless blow; those who are themselves acting unjustly cannot fairly resort to deadly force to resist someone reasonably trying to apprehend them.

And the structure of the action of political societies can be the same as that of individuals' acts of self-defense. Deadly deeds can be chosen, not with the precise object of killing those (other societies and their members) who are using force to back their challenge to just order, but simply to thwart that challenge. If the social act is limited to the use of only that force necessary to accomplish its appropriate purpose, the side effect of the death of those challenging the society's just order can rightly be accepted.[78] The distinction between innocents (combatants) and noninnocents (noncombatants) remains: lethal force may rightly be used against persons whose behavior is part of the enemy society's wrongful use of force (against combatants), but not against others. The innocent (noncombatants, those not participating in the use of force against just order) cannot rightly be made the objects of lethal force.

The tradition, even as substantially developed and refined by the exclusion of punitive justifications for war and of intent to kill in war, wholly excludes pacifism—that is, the claim that lethal force can never be rightly used. Pacifism is not to be found in the New Testament[79] (in which the Catholic understanding of natural law already emerges), read as an integrated whole. What does there emerge is the vocation of some individuals and groups to nonviolence (unconditional abstention from such use of force) in witness to the truths that peace, like all true goods, is a gift from above—of divine grace working in a privileged way by healing mercy and reconciliation—and that war, though its point is peace, can never be the efficient cause of peace.

Notes

1. Tacitus *Agricola* 30, imagining a speech by a British chieftain: "They [the Romans] make a wilderness and call it peace."

2. Cf. Augustine *De civitate Dei* 19.12.

3. Augustine *De civitate Dei* 19.13: "Pax omnium rerum, tranquillitas ordinis. Ordo est parium dispariumque rerum sua cuique loca tribuens dispositio."

4. Aquinas *Summa theologiae* II-II q. 37 aa. 1 & 2 (discordia in corde).

5. Aquinas *Summa theologiae* II-II q. 38 aa. 1 & 2 (contentio in ore).

6. Aquinas *Summa theologiae* II-II q. 41 aa. 1 & 2 (rixa).

7. Aquinas *Summa theologiae* II-II q. 42 aa. 1 & 2 (seditio).

8. The tradition is scarcely concerned with formulating a definition of war more satisfying than Cicero's *decertare per vim*, "contending by force" (*De officiis* 1.11.34).

9. On the many forms of war in a general sense, see Francisco Suarez *De bello* prol., in Gwladys L. Williams et al., trans., Suarez, *Selections from Three Works* (Oxford: Oxford University Press, 1944), 800.

10. "We wage war to gain peace. Be peaceful, therefore, even while you are at war, so that in overcoming those whom you are fighting you may bring them to the benefits of peace." Augustine *Epist. 189 ad Bonifacium* 6, cited in Aquinas *Summa theologiae* II-II q. 40 a. 1 ad 3. See also II-II q. 29 a. 2 ad 2.

11. "Perfect peace consists in the perfect enjoyment of the supreme good, . . . the rational creature's last end." *Summa theologiae* II-II q. 29 a. 2 ad 4.

12. See, for example, Germain Grisez, Joseph Boyle, and John Finnis, "Practical Principles, Moral Truth, and Ultimate Ends," *American Journal of Jurisprudence* 32 (1987), 99–151 at 125–31.

13. See Aquinas *Summa theologiae* I-II q. 100 a. 3 ad 1.

14. In Aquinas *Summa theologiae* II-II q. 41 (de bello), and embedded in qq. 34–43 (vices opposed to caritas); see prol. to q. 43. Suarez *De bello* disp. 13 in tract. 3 (*De caritate*) in his *De triplice virtute theologica* (1621).

15. Aquinas *Summa theologiae* II-II q. 29 a. 3 ad 3.

16. See note 10 above; also Plato *Laws* 1.628d–e; 7.803c–d; Aristotle *Nicomachean Ethics* 10.7.1177b5.

17. Leo XIII, Apostolic Letter *Nostis errorem*, in *Acta Leonis XIII*, vol. 9 (Rome, 1890), 48: "There should be sought for peace foundations both firmer and more in keeping with nature: because, while it is allowed consistently with nature to defend one's right by force and arms, *nature does not allow that force be an efficient cause of right*. For peace consists in the tranquillity of order, and so, like the concord of private persons, that of rulers is grounded above all in justice and charity" (my trans.; emphasis added).

18. The example, aside from the military purpose, is from Aristotle and Aquinas: Aquinas *In II Phys*. lect. 8 (no. 214); *In VII Meta*. lect. 6 (no. 1382); *In XI Meta*. lect. 8 (nos. 2269, 2284).

19. Alexander of Hales *Summa theologica* 3.466, carefully analyzed in Jonathan Barnes, "The Just War," in Norman Kretzmann, Anthony Kenny, and Jan Pinborg, eds., *The Cambridge History of Later Medieval Philosophy* (Cambridge: Cambridge University Press, 1982), 773–82.

20. Aquinas *Summa theologiae* II-II q. 40 a. 1c, quoting (in a slightly garbled form) Augustine *Quaestiones in Heptateuchum* 6.10; and see Barnes, "The Just War," 778.

21. Suarez *De bello* 4.1 (Williams, trans., p. 816).

22. "Even when a legitimate authority declares war, and there is *causa iusta*, it can be the case that the war is made immoral/illicit by wrongful *intentio*." Aquinas *Summa theologiae* II-II q. 40 a. 1c.

23. See John Finnis, Joseph Boyle, and Germain Grisez, *Nuclear Deterrence, Morality and Realism* (Oxford: Oxford University Press, 1987), 120–23, 131, 288, 343–44; John Finnis, "Persons and Their Associations," *Proceedings of the Aristotelian Society*, supp. vol. 63 (1989), 267–74.

24. "Nocendi cupiditas, ulciscendi crudelitas, impacatus et implacabilis animus, feritas rebellandi, libido dominandi, et si qua similia, haec sunt quae in bellis iure culpantur." Augustine *Contra Faustum* 22.74; Aquinas *Summa theologiae* II-II q. 40 a. 1c.

25. See, for example, Plato *Laws* 4.715e–716d; cf. Plato *Republic* 6.500c.

26. Aquinas *Summa theologiae* II-II q. 40 a. 1c: "Sicut licite defendunt eam [rempublicam] materiali gladio contra interiores quidem perturbatores, dum malefactores puniunt, secundum illud Apostoli, 'Non sine causa gladium portat: minister enim Dei est, vindex in iram ei qui male agit,' ita etiam gladio bellico ad eos pertinet rempublicam tueri ab exterioribus hostibus."

27. Suarez *De bello* 1.6 (Williams, trans., p. 804); cf. Vitoria *De iure belli* (1539) sec. 13; trans. in Vitoria, *Political Writings*, ed. A. Pagden and A. Lawrance (Cambridge: Cambridge University Press, 1991), 303.

28. Vitoria *De iure belli* sec. 1 (Pagden and Lawrance, eds., p. 297); Suarez *De bello* 1.4, 6 (Williams, trans., pp. 803, 804).

29. Vitoria *De iure belli* secs. 1, 44 (Pagden and Lawrance, eds., pp. 297, 319; but note that the editors often mistranslate *vindicatio* and its cognates as "revenge"; even "vengeance" is, in modern English, misleading as a translation of *vindicatio*); Suarez *De bello* 1.5 (Williams, trans., pp. 803–4).

30. Thus Vitoria *De iure belli* sec. 3 (Pagden and Lawrance, eds., p. 299): "Any person, even a private citizen, may declare and wage defensive war."

31. Suarez *De bello* 2.2 (Williams, trans., p. 807) and 4.7 (p. 820); cf. Vitoria *De iure belli* sec. 5 (Pagden and Lawrance, eds., p. 300). Behind them, Augustine *De civitate Dei* 1.17, 21. Contrast the non-Catholic tradition following Grotius *De iure belli ac pacis* (1625) 2.20.8.2, in Grotius, *The Law of War and Peace*, trans. Francis W. Kelsey (Oxford: Oxford University Press, 1925), p. 472, and thence Locke, *Two Treatises of Civil Government* (1689–90), 2.2.7.

32. Cicero *De officiis* 1.11.36–37.

33. Suarez *De bello* 4.6, 7 (Williams, trans., p. 819).

34. This is denied by some; for example, A. Ottaviani, *Compendium iuris publici ecclesiastici*, 4th ed. (Vatican Polyglot Press, 1954), 88.

35. Vitoria *De iure belli* sec. 3 (Pagden and Lawrance, eds., p. 299); contrast, however, sec. 5 (p. 300) and Vitoria *De bello: On St. Thomas Aquinas, Summa theologica, Secunda secundae, Question 40*, in James Brown Scott, ed., *Francisco de Vitoria and His Law of Nations* (Oxford: Oxford University Press, 1934), cxvi: "It is impermissible for a private person to avenge himself *or to reclaim his own property* save through the judge."

36. Vitoria "Lecture on the Evangelization of Unbelievers" (1534–35) para. 3, in *Political Writings*, 347; "On Dietary Laws, or Self-Restraint" (1538), in *Political Writings*, 225–26; *De Indis* (1539) para. 15, in *Political Writings*, 288–89.

37. Vitoria "Lecture on the Evangelization of Unbelievers" 347.

38. Vitoria *De iure belli* sec. 1 (Pagden and Lawrance, eds., p. 298); see also sec. 5 (p. 300).

39. Vitoria *De iure belli* sec. 9 (Pagden and Lawrance, eds., p. 302).

40. Suarez *De bello* 2.1 (Williams, trans., p. 806, emphasis added).

41. For example, Suarez *De bello* 2.3 (Williams, trans., p. 807).

42. Barnes, "The Just War," 776–77 and 775 n. 23; Anthony Regan, *Thou Shalt Not Kill* (Dublin: Mercier, 1979), 77–79; Finnis, Boyle, and Grisez, *Nuclear Deterrence, Morality and Realism*, 315 n. 3; Germain Grisez, *Living a Christian Life* (Quincy, IL: Franciscan Press, 1993), ch. 11.E.3.b.

43. Pius XII, Christmas Message (24 Dec. 1944), *Acta Apostolicae Sedis* 37 (1945),

18, teaches that there is a duty to ban "wars of aggression as legitimate solutions of international disputes and as a means toward realizing national aspirations." Pius XII, Christmas Message (24 Dec. 1948), *Acta Apostolicae Sedis* 41 (1949), 12–13, teaches: "Every war of aggression against those goods which the Divine plan for peace obliges men unconditionally to respect and guarantee, and accordingly to protect and defend, is a sin, a crime, and an outrage against the majesty of God, the Creator and Ordainer of the world." John XXIII, *Pacem in terris*, *Acta Apostolicae Sedis* 55 (1963), 291, teaches: "In this age which boasts of its atomic power, it no longer makes sense to maintain that war is a fit instrument with which to repair the violation of justice." Noting Pope John's point, Vatican II explains how "the horror and perversity of war are immensely magnified by the multiplication of scientific weapons," and draws the conclusion: "All these considerations compel us to undertake an evaluation of war with an entirely new attitude." *Gaudium et spes* (1965), para. 80, with note 2 (note 258 in the Abbott ed.). In para. 79, the Council states: "As long as the danger of war remains and there is no competent and sufficiently powerful authority at the international level, governments cannot be denied the right *to legitimate defense* once every means of peaceful settlement has been exhausted. Therefore, government authorities and others who share public responsibility have the duty to protect the welfare of the people entrusted to their care and to conduct such grave matters soberly. But it is one thing to undertake military action for the *just defense of the people*, and something else again to seek the subjugation of other nations" (emphasis added). None of these statements unambiguously repudiates the tradition's constant teaching that punitive and, in that sense, offensive war can be justified.

44. Grisez, *Living a Christian Life*, ch. 11.E.3.b; Augustine Regan, "The Worth of Human Life," *Studia Moralia* 6 (1968), 241–43; Ottaviani, *Compendium iuris*, 88.

45. John XXIII, *Pacem in terris*, paras. 43–46, in *Acta Apostolicae Sedis* 55 (1963), 291–94.

46. Vitoria *De iure belli* sec. 19 (Pagden and Lawrance, eds., p. 305) and sec. 46 (p. 320); but cf. sec. 5 (p. 300), seeking to derive the punitive authority of states from their self-sufficiency; Suarez *De legibus* (1612) 2.19.8 (Williams, trans., p. 348):

> The law of war—in so far as that law rests upon the power possessed by a given state . . . for the punishment, avenging (*vindicandam*), or reparation of an injury inflicted upon it by another state—would seem to pertain properly to the *ius gentium*. For it was not indispensable by virtue of natural reason alone that the power in question should exist within an injured state, since men could have established some other mode of inflicting punishment, or entrusted that power to some prince and quasi-arbitrator with coercive power. Nevertheless, since the mode in question, which is at present in practice, is easier and more in conformity with nature, it has been adopted by custom (*usu*) and is just to the extent that it may not rightfully be resisted. In the same class I place slavery.

47. Suarez *De legibus* 2.19.8 (Williams, trans., p. 348).

48. See, for example, Suarez *De bello* 3.8 (Williams, trans., p. 821).

49. Pius XII, Address to Military Doctors (19 Oct. 1953) *Acta Apostolicae Sedis* 45 (1953), 748–49; United States National Conference of Catholic Bishops, *The Chal-*

lenge of Peace, Pastoral Letter of 3 May 1983 (Washington DC: US Catholic Conference, 1983), paras. 98–99.

50. *The Challenge of Peace*, para. 96 (exhaustion of peaceful alternatives).

51. See Finnis, Boyle, and Grisez, *Nuclear Deterrence, Morality and Realism*, ch. 9.

52. *The Challenge of Peace*, para. 105.

53. Finnis, Boyle, and Grisez, *Nuclear Deterrence, Morality and Realism*, esp. ch. 4.

54. See Finnis, Boyle, and Grisez, *Nuclear Deterrence, Morality and Realism*, ch. 5, on the impossibility of bluff in a complex society.

55. Aquinas *Summa theologiae* II-II q. 64 a. 6.

56. Aquinas *Summa theologiae* II-II q. 40 a. 3; see also q. 110 a. 3. Likewise Suarez *De bello* 7.23 (Williams, trans., p. 852).

57. Vitoria *De iure belli* secs. 34–37 (Pagden and Lawrance, eds., pp. 314–17); Suarez *De bello* 7.6, 15 (Williams, trans., pp. 840, 845); *The Challenge of Peace* (n. 49 above), paras. 104–5.

58. Thus "direct" killing of the innocent is explained as killing either as an end or as a means by Pius XII (12 Nov. 1944, in *Discoursi e radiomessaggi* 6: 191–92); by Paul VI (*Humanae vitae* [1968], n. 14); and by the Congregation for the Doctrine of the Faith (*De abortu procurato*, 18 Nov. 1974, para. 7; *Donum vitae*, 22 Feb. 1987, n. 20). For similar explanations of "direct" in terms of "as an end or as a means," see Pius XII, *Acta Apostolicae Sedis* 43 (1951), 838 (killing) and 843–44 (sterilization), and *Acta Apostolicae Sedis* 49 (1957), 146 (euthanasia).

59. Finnis, Boyle, and Grisez, *Nuclear Deterrence, Morality and Realism*, 39–40, 264–65, 271–72. The attacks to which I am here referring are, of course, not the regular British obliteration or "area" bombing raids of 1942–45, directed at cities and their inhabitants as such, but attacks on railway yards or on the submarines congregated at Kiel, etc.

60. For example, Vitoria *De iure belli* sec. 19 (Pagden and Lawrance, eds., p. 305); Suarez *De bello* 7.7 (Williams, trans., pp. 820–41) and, very clearly and fundamentally, *De legibus* 2.19.8 (quoted above, n. 46).

61. Suarez *De bello* 9.5 (Williams, trans., p. 859).

62. Aquinas *Summa theologiae* II-II q. 64 a. 6 ad 3; q. 67 a. 2.

63. On the killing of innocent hostages, see Vitoria *De iure belli* sec. 43 (Pagden and Lawrance, eds., p. 319).

64. Plato *Gorgias* 508e–509d; Vatican II, *Gaudium et spes*, para. 27; see John Finnis, *Fundamentals of Ethics* (Oxford: Oxford University Press and Washington, DC: Georgetown University Press, 1983), 112–20; Finnis, *Moral Absolutes* (Washington, DC: Catholic University of America Press, 1991), 47–51.

65. Articulated for the tradition in John 1:50; 18:14.

66. Vitoria *De iure belli* secs. 1 (Pagden and Lawrance, eds., p. 298), 19 (p. 305); Suarez *De bello* 1.4 (Williams, trans., p. 803); 4.10 (p. 823).

67. See Finnis, *Moral Absolutes*, 51–55; Finnis, Boyle, and Grisez, *Nuclear Deterrence, Morality and Realism*, ch. 9.

68. Grotius, though not Catholic, states the tradition accurately enough: "'Necessity,' says Seneca, . . . 'the great resource of human weakness, breaks every law,' meaning, of course, every human law, or law constituted after the fashion of human

law." *De iure belli ac pacis* 2.2.6.4 (Kelsey, trans., pp. 193–94). In 1.4.7.1 (pp. 148–49), he exemplifies the latter category by pointing to the divine law of sabbath rest, subject to a tacit exception in cases of extreme necessity. See also 3.1.2.1 (p. 599). In Aquinas, the maxim *necessitas non subditur legi*, necessity is not subject to the law, is used just to make the point that, in an emergency so sudden that there is no time to consult authorized interpreters, it is permissible for the subjects to give to the law an interpretation that they think would have been approved by the lawmaker (assumed to be a morally upright lawmaker). "Keep the city gates shut," for example, can be regarded as subject to an interpretative exception "except to admit your own army in flight from the battlefield." *Summa theologiae* I-II q. 96 a. 6c & ad 1.

69. Archbishops of Great Britain, "Abortion and the Right to Live," 24 Jan. 1980, para. 24.

70. Such a critique is available in, for example, Finnis, *Moral Absolutes*.

71. Suarez *De iuramento fidelitatis regis Angliae* (1613) 4.1 (Williams, trans., p. 705).

72. Suarez *De iuramento fidelitatis* 4.5 (Williams, trans., p. 709). As always, the side effects of the ruler's death or overthrow remain to be assessed for the fairness or unfairness of incurring them.

73. Suarez *De iuramento fidelitatis* 4.4 (Williams, trans., p. 708).

74. Suarez, *De iuramento fidelitatis* 4.11–13 (Williams, trans., p. 714). Aquinas, in his youthful *Commentum in libros Sententiarum Petri Lombardi* II d. 44 q. 2 a. 2c, treats the killing of Julius Caesar as justifiable on this basis.

75. Aquinas *Commentum in libros Sententiarum Petri Lombardi* 4.7–9. "The Church's Magisterium admits [recourse to armed struggle] as a last resort to put an end to an obvious and prolonged tyranny which is gravely damaging the fundamental rights of individuals and the common good." Congregation for the Doctrine of the Faith, *Libertatis conscientiae*, Instruction on Christian Freedom and Liberation, 22 Mar. 1986, para. 79.

76. See further Finnis, Boyle, and Grisez, *Nuclear Deterrence, Morality and Realism*, 354–57.

77. Vitoria *De iure belli* sec. 19 (Pagden and Lawrance, eds., p. 305); see the quote from Suarez above, n. 46.

78. See further Finnis, Boyle, and Grisez, *Nuclear Deterrence, Morality and Realism*, 309–19.

79. See Grotius *De iure belli ac pacis* 1.2.6–8 (Kelsey, trans., pp. 61–81).

CHAPTER 2

Just War Thinking in Catholic Natural Law

Joseph Boyle

I AM IN SUBSTANTIAL AGREEMENT with the analysis in John Finnis's chapter. Indeed, it is as good a short statement of just war theory within the Catholic natural law tradition as I know of. Given this, I think the most useful contributions I can make are to underline certain points that seem to me to be important, to develop some of the distinctions Finnis makes, and to draw out some of the implications of his analysis. I will also say something more than Finnis does about conscientious objection and the duty of citizens to support their nation's war efforts.

Peace and War

Finnis portrays the natural law tradition as not having been greatly concerned with the definition of war; it appears satisfied with Cicero's unsatisfying "contending by force." Part of the reason is that, although there is a paradigm case of war—a relationship between polities in which one seeks by physical force to thwart some of the other's undertakings and to seize or destroy some of the other's resources—there are variations on the paradigm that raise the same or similar moral questions and are governed by the same principles and many of the same norms. So, the tradition proceeds on the assumption that the effort to develop a general definition is not of much help and may in fact mislead.

Furthermore, within the tradition there is a recognition that among the activities that are called "wars," either in ordinary language or according to any definition that is not purely stipulative, there are activities of differing moral character. The idea is that the moral significance of bellicose actions, like that of actions generally, emerges not from a definition of the ordinary usage of terms like war or violence, but from a determination of how actions, considered not as mere behavior but as voluntary undertakings in which people choose to do certain things for the sake of certain benefits, are related to the standard of right reason. By reference to this moral standard, two behaviorally similar or even identical actions, which can both correctly be called wars, can be essentially different from the moral point of view, if done for different purposes or under different circumstances.[1] So, from the perspective of natural law, justified and unjustified wars are not two species of the same genus; they are essentially different kinds of action.

According to Finnis, the relationship of wars to the good of peace is central to the distinction between just and unjust wars. This good is inevitably at stake when warfare is contemplated or undertaken. Other goods are also surely affected, but these are reasonably incorporated into this relational notion. For the norms of justice regulate the harms that may be inflicted on people, their holdings, and their institutions, and justice is a part of the wider social good of peace as understood within the tradition.

Now, the idea of peace that the tradition develops from Augustine is plainly the idea of a basic good, a reason for which action can be undertaken without any further benefit in view.[2] As social animals, human beings have reason to want to form a community with others, to cooperate with them, and to live in harmony with them. Unjustified wars are evil because of the harm they cause to this good and its component parts; even justifiable wars need special justification because of their at least apparent conflict with this good.

But why should this good, rather than some others, be the *point* of war, as Finnis holds the logic of the tradition to require?

To answer this, it is first necessary to underline Finnis's point that there is a kind of peace that is not the real thing, but only an appearance of peace that includes enough of the elements of true peace to provide a reason for acting, organized in such a way as to block the realization of genuine peace. Thus, the harmony one seeks when one undertakes to dominate or enslave others or to satisfy one's desire for vengeance is not peace; these actions may aim at a kind of order and at a form of tranquility, but they block the harmony of wills and the genuine community that peace includes. Perhaps morally unjustified wars inevitably aim at this inadequate kind of peace, but plainly that is not what Finnis is referring to when he claims that peace is the point of war.

His claim plainly is normative: morally justified warfare should aim at peace, should be for the sake of peace. And it is not the fact that peace is a basic human good, an ultimate reason for action, that underlies this claim. For peace has an especially intimate relationship with basic moral principles as understood within natural law. The practical reasonableness prescribed by natural law requires action compatible with a will open to an ideal human community in which all the goods of all people are realized in interpersonal harmony.[3] This is the ideal prescribed by the commandment to love one's neighbors as oneself. It is, among other things, a peaceful community of human beings. Since all upright choice and action must be ordered toward this ideal, all upright choices to engage in warfare must also be so ordered.

In short, within the natural law tradition, wars can be morally justified only if they are morally good actions, that is, justified by basic moral principles; and those principles can be usefully formulated in terms of peace. Both these points are important for situating the natural law approach to warfare in relation to other normative approaches.

First, the dependence of the moral evaluation of any war on moral first principles clarifies both the character and the purpose of natural law reasoning about warfare. This reasoning is an application of the basic principles of morality to the special conditions of warfare and to the particular circumstances of individual wars. Thus, according to the tradition, the precepts governing warfare are neither the result of a generalization from considered judgments about what is acceptable and unacceptable in warfare, nor the result of casuistical reasoning from certain paradigm cases of wars that are plainly wrong and of wars that are plainly justified. The considerable casuistry within the tradition's analyses of war is part of the effort to clarify the character of various bellicose actions to allow a precise application of moral principles to the case at hand.

There is a recognition within the tradition of the complexity of the process of applying moral principles and general moral norms to individual actions.[4] Although the structure of this reasoning is deductive, the clarification of the kind of action to be evaluated is achieved by informal conceptual analysis.[5] Moreover, this deductive and analytical procedure can result only in the evaluation of an action as described, that is, in the evaluation of an action insofar as it is an action of a certain kind. Since further redescription of the individual action being evaluated can in many cases turn up features that might cause a change in the action's moral evaluation, and since there is no rationally determined limit to the possibility for redescribing an action, there remains an aspect of moral evaluation not reducible to rational analysis.[6]

Nevertheless, the application of moral principles to individual actions is at the heart of moral analysis according to natural law. For the correct application of moral principles to individual actions is necessary for the determination that those actions are in accord with moral truth. And the determination of the truth of concrete moral judgments, including those about warfare, is the purpose of moral analysis on the natural law conception.

Thus, on the natural law conception, the judgment that a given war meets the standards for a just war is in fact the judgment that the choice to undertake the war is in accord with moral truth. This means that the communal choice of a nation to undertake a war that is just is a morally good choice, and that the choices of soldiers and other citizens to support that communal choice are to that extent morally good. These choices are not necessary compromises with evil, nor are they immoral choices constrained from even greater evil by conventional rules; rather, they are choices completely in accord with moral truth. The determination of the moral truth as applied to given wars is the purpose of normative analysis on the natural law conception, and no war that fails to meet the standards of moral truth can be justified by these standards.

Second, the formulation of moral principles in terms of peace is useful for situating the natural law tradition's approach to war in relation to pacifism, especially Christian pacifism. For this formulation makes clear that any war that is morally justified must be at a deep level compatible with and in the service of peace. This suggests that disagreements between pacifists and natural law theorists are not located at the level of fundamental moral principle, but emerge within the reasoning from principles to concrete moral evaluation.

This suggestion is underlined by the following implication of Finnis's analysis. The pacific character of the principles governing war, together with the *bonum ex integra causa* principle, which, as Finnis explains, requires that a morally good act be in every aspect in accord with reason,[7] implies that a justified war is one that involves no choice or intention incompatible with the reality of peace.

This looks paradoxical: taking up arms against others seems to involve choosing something contrary to peace with them, even if for the sake of future peace with them. No doubt, many, perhaps most, wars are fought with such intentions, and pacifists are correct in objecting that those wars are immoral—instances of doing evil so that good might come of it. But not all wars need involve such intentions: if peace does not exist or must be protected, and if one's bellicose actions are necessary to bring it about or to protect it, then those actions need involve no choice or intention contrary to peace. Moral principles do not appear to exclude war in these conditions.

Pacifists deny this conclusion. But the fact that pacifists and natural law theorists agree in rejecting, for reasons that appear similar, a considerable class of wars suggests that the disagreement here is not over moral principles, but over concerns whether the conditions ever obtain that allow war to be fought compatibly with moral principles. In particular, it would seem that pacifists reject the natural law conclusion because they believe that the dispositions of nations and of individual soldiers are such that when they fight, they must inevitably turn their hearts against peace, even when defending or protecting it. If warriors necessarily willed to harm their enemies when fighting them, then the pacifist claim to inevitability would be justified. But as Finnis indicates, the natural law tradition's view of justified killing in warfare can be understood as excluding the intent to kill,[8] and this can be generalized to apply to other harms inflicted on one's enemies.

If this analysis is correct, a pacifist claim that choosing to engage in warfare inevitably involves turning one's heart against peace cannot be grounded in the essential intentional structures of the choices and acts of belligerents. Thus, one crucial point of disagreement between pacifists and natural law theorists is the truth of the pacifist claim that warfare inevitably involves choices incompatible with the good of peace. The truth of this claim is not evident, but neither is its falsity.

Motive or Intention

Finnis plainly holds that intentions are intrinsic to actions as voluntary undertakings. He also assumes that voluntary undertakings are the subject of moral evaluation. The intention essential to a human action as voluntary is one's active interest in some benefit for the sake of which one chooses to do something. So what one intends, strictly speaking, is a benefit, what the reason for which one acts promises as a desirable outcome.[9] This non-behavioristic conception of human action often makes it difficult to determine from a third-person perspective what action a person, or a group of persons acting jointly, is performing. But these difficulties do not render impossible third-person identification of actions, and they surely do not preclude the possibility that individuals and groups, aware of their own practical reasoning and choices, can accurately identify their acts as voluntary undertakings. So, the conception of human action accepted by many within the natural law tradition is not incoherent.

Moreover, the tradition's judgment that actions so characterized are the subject of moral evaluation is not arbitrary, but is a function of a coherent, if controversial, understanding of the purpose of moral evaluation. As noted above, according to the natural law conception, the purpose of moral evaluation is to determine the truth of concrete moral judgments, and this purpose is realized when the morally relevant features of actions are correctly related to the principles of right reason. Why is it important that human actions be guided by moral truth, and so be determined to accord with right reason? The tradition's answer, more often left tacit than explicitly articulated, is that providing this kind of direction for human action is the only way human action as voluntary, as an exercise of the rationality and freedom in virtue of which humans are in God's image, can be rationally guided and genuinely fulfilling.[10]

In short, there are various conceptions of morality and its purposes, but the natural law conception is one according to which the point of morality is to allow one's practical reasoning and choices to be fully intelligent and good. Morality, on this conception, is not a constraining device to cause people to avoid the most socially destructive behavior of which they are capable or to get them to be as good as they can be without their own cooperation; rather, it serves to provide fully rational guidance for choices, for actions as voluntary undertakings.

It is perhaps worth noting that the doctrine of the double effect, an important component of the natural law casuistry of warfare, presupposes the tradition's conceptions of human action and of morality, but is neither equivalent to these conceptions nor implied by them. According to this doctrine, the difference between what a person intends and the side effects a person knowingly brings about in acting can have a decisive moral significance. For example, the just war requirement of noncombatant immunity is a prohibition of intentional attacks on noncombatants. The doctrine of double effect constrains the absolute prohibition to that of intentional attacks, and allows that, if certain other conditions are fulfilled, actions that predictably lead to the deaths of noncombatants may be undertaken.

Clearly, this doctrine is hardly intelligible without a conception of human action and morality like that held by the natural law tradition. Still, the attribution of decisive moral significance to the distinction between what is intended and what is knowingly brought about as a side effect is not a feature of these general ideas about action and morality. For it is clear that all the voluntary aspects of actions are governed by moral norms, not simply those included within one's intention. The significance of this distinction arises because there are absolute prohibitions, and those prohibitions cannot reasonably be extended to exclude bringing about harmful side effects.[11]

Given the natural law conception of human action and of the purpose of moral evaluation, it is not surprising that natural law statements of the conditions for just war include a requirement of right intention. But a puzzle emerges from standard statements of these conditions because of the addition of a condition requiring just cause. As Finnis notes, what one's reason for action promises and what one intends in acting are identical: why do Aquinas and the subsequent tradition treat right intention and just cause as two distinct conditions for the justifiability of a war? The assumption is that the just cause is the reason for action and that the benefit it promises is what one intends. Finnis's answer is that Aquinas had a technical, legal meaning for just cause according to which the just cause is not a justifying reason.[12] That seems plausible.

But I think there is a reason, compatible with the one Finnis proposes, for having two separate conditions here that would hold even if just cause were taken to be the justifying reason. Without the condition of right intention, the connection between one's action and the reason that justifies it remains contingent, and this allows for the possibility that just cause could be only a pretext or excuse for bellicose action aimed at some further goal beyond that which one's justifying reason supports, or at some completely independent goal that can be pursued using the justifying reason as a rationalization only. In other words, only to the extent that one acts for goals supported by the justifying reason, insofar as they are supported by it, and only for them, is one's bellicose action morally justified.

This does not mean that one cannot engage in war in anticipation of benefits that go beyond one's justified war aims. Those aims are goals that instantiate, often in a minimal way, the good of peace. Further goals that instantiate that good and that can be seen as possibilities if one's war aims are realized are thus justified if the war aims are. Thus, for example, the fact that in the Gulf War, the United States was motivated by the prospect of improved economic and political relations with some Gulf nations should its efforts to evict the Iraqis from Kuwait succeed does not seem to be the kind of further intention that violates the condition of right intention. That intention was for actions and benefits that became real prospects once the normal international relationships were restored by the successful achievement of the war aims. This kind of intention, which looks ahead to the future benefits of the peace created by achieving justified war aims, seems to me unavoidable and legitimate. The presence of such intentions has no tendency to suggest that the justifying reasons for war, and the specific goals they legitimize, are pretexts or rationalizations.

Acting with some intentions does, however, render one's justifying reason a mere pretext or rationalization. Suppose, for example, that the underlying motivation for the American involvement in the Gulf War were not the defense of Kuwait, but a desire to destroy Iraq's economic and industrial capacity to prevent future aggression, or to punish an erstwhile ally for insubordination. If one of these were the intention behind the war, then it would fail the condition of right intention, assuming (as I do) that intending these things is not justified. This would be so even though a just cause existed, and even if care were taken to carry out the war aims and to limit, for various reasons such as international opinion, military actions to those which carry out these aims. For in this scenario, the goals are pursued not as instantiating the justifying reason, but insofar as they instantiate the unjustified reasons. Indeed, when Elizabeth Anscombe in 1939 objected to the British decision to go to war with Germany, allegedly in behalf of Poland, her worry was not that there was no just cause available, but that it was not the reason for which Britain fought.[13]

Grounds for War

Finnis rejects the older tradition's belief that in addition to defensive grounds, the war of one nation against another can be justified on retributive grounds as a kind of punishment for wrongdoers. Representatives of the tradition in the last fifty years accept this judgment. But Finnis also rejects the reason commonly given, namely, that modern war is too destructive to be used except as a means of defense. His proposal is that the underlying rationale for retributive warfare is mistaken; the authority required to rightly punish other polities and those who act for them does not exist (although something similar to it would exist if there were a world government).

The rejection of retributive justice as a justifying ground for warfare seems to me to involve more than tinkering with the theoretical foundations of the natural law approach to war and peace. The idea is not that, although punishment is out as a justification, defense is a broader notion than we thought; with this approach, things would remain pretty much as they were at the practical level, except that the rationale of defense would now bear the justificatory weight that punishment used to bear. It is true that the notion of defense is broader than the older tradition assumed, but it is neither completely elastic nor coextensive with the notion of punishment.

One practically important respect in which the notions of defense and punishment differ is in the way they are related to past wrongs. A person cannot defend against a wrong already perpetrated, although he or she can defend against its continuing consequences. But a person can, and under the proper circumstances may, punish another for a wrong already perpetrated. Thus, if legitimate grounds for war are limited to defensive considerations, then just to the extent that standing grievances among polities are *past* wrongs, and not ongoing injustices, they are not legitimate grounds for war. There is no defending against them. (I am not suggesting that the casuistry needed to apply this distinction would be easy.)

Furthermore, and perhaps more importantly, defensive grounds limit the further goals one can adopt as a justified defensive war unfolds. The only deterrence one can legitimately seek is that which flows from successful defense, and the only punishment one can seek is that which is involved in successful defense. Thus, efforts to inflict punishment on the enemy beyond what defense justifies are immoral, as are efforts that go beyond what defense justifies to arrange the end of a war so as to put the enemy leaders on trial, or to destroy a polity or a regime. The desire to see war criminals punished is legitimate, and can be acted upon after the war, provided that an authority can be located that has the right to punish. But this desire cannot, if punishment is excluded as a legitimate ground for war, provide a justification for fighting, or for further fighting. I suspect that these limitations are widely ignored in modern warfare, as they were, for example, in the Second World War. They would be hard to maintain if punishment were a legitimate ground for war.

Resistance to Political Authority

In this section of his chapter, Finnis does not discuss the issue of conscientious objection. I will say something about this because it falls squarely in the middle of the natural law account of political authority and obedience. This account, at least according to some readings, has quite permissive implications concerning the responsibilities of individuals, especially soldiers, for their cooperation in war efforts, and in several ways seems to require a subordination of individual, conscientious judgment to the judgment of political leaders.

Alan Donagan has succinctly stated the norms that the natural law tradition regards as decisive in regulating the decisions of individuals in respect to their government's wars: "If it [a given war] is just, it is permissible to volunteer to serve in it, provided no other duty prevents it; and it is impermissible not to accept lawful conscription to serve. If it is unjust, it is impermissible to serve under any circumstances."[14]

These norms make sense only if the citizen is expected to make an independent moral evaluation of the justifiability of the war in which he or she cooperates. So natural law, along with the broader tradition Donagan calls "common morality," rejects the rationalization that Shakespeare puts in the mouth of one of Henry V's soldiers: "We know enough if we know that we are the King's men. Our obedience to the king wipes the crime of it out of us."[15]

The second of Donagan's three norms appears to exclude any interesting form of conscientious objection, that is, any refusal of lawful conscription based on any consideration other than the judgment that the war in question is immoral. Although the third of Donagan's norms states that this is a reason that requires one to refuse service, the second norm certainly suggests that there are no general grounds to which a citizen might appeal as a justification for refusing military service in his or her country's just war. This also has been the standard position of the Catholic tradition, at least up until about 1960.

The assumptions behind this view are worth noting: (1) that in a just war, political society may impose military service on its members; (2) that a citizen drafted for military service has a duty to obey and support the justified decisions of political authority; and (3) that this duty is very hard, if not impossible, to overturn. The first two of these assumptions are deeply embedded in the natural law conception of social life; but I doubt if the third can be justified, however deeply presumptions in favor of the prerogatives of political society may have permeated natural law thinking in the past. I do not see why this duty should be any less defeasible than any other structured and recognized social obligation.

Here are some reasons for being suspicious about this third assumption: the tradition includes an exception for a class of citizens—the clergy.[16] Their social role is such that they must not fight. So, this assumption cannot be accepted in its strongest version, namely, that the duty of citizens to fight in a just war when ordered is impossible to overturn. Moreover, one may also wonder whether reasons similar to those which exempt the clergy from the duty to fight do not also exempt others, either because of the special jobs they have or for other reasons having to do with special commitments they have undertaken. If the clergy is exempt, then why not also monks not in holy orders? If monks, then why not others like doctors or teachers or others whose work seems especially opposed to bloodshed? If these, then why not others who have adopted a particularly pacific or prophetic lifestyle? I doubt there is a good answer to questions like these. More generally, it is not clear why the duties people have as citizens should necessarily or generally trump the other duties they have within the other communities in which they live and work.

So, I think that the recent ecclesiastical statements that call for states to recognize a right of conscientious objection, a right that seems to go beyond protecting an individual who acts on the judgment that the war in question is immoral,[17] are a correct development of the tradition, and that this new teaching is justified by the tradition's growing wariness about excessive deference to the prerogatives of political society and perhaps of the clergy as well. If I am correct, this development does not imply an incipient willingness to accept the view that war is necessarily wrong, or that citizens do not have a real, though defeasible, obligation to fight in their country's just wars.[18] To recognize that a duty is defeasible is not to suggest that it might not exist.

Catholic teaching, then, does not endorse the position that pacifism—that is, the claim that war is always wrong—is a legitimate position. It does, however, appear to endorse the view that a conscientious refusal to fight in one's country's wars is easier to justify than earlier Catholic teaching or natural law theorizing have allowed.

So far, I have ignored the epistemic issues that complicate the efforts of citizens and potential soldiers to evaluate their nation's war. What should one do when one does not know that the war in which one is commanded to fight is unjust, but has doubts about the matter?

The standard answer seems to favor compliance with authority. Walzer quotes Vitoria: "A prince is not able . . . and ought not always to render reasons for the war to his subjects, and if the subjects cannot serve in the war except they are first satisfied of its justice, the state would fall into grave peril."[19] Walzer then goes on to look at the moral situation from the perspective of the draftee: under the circumstances he can hardly be blamed for going along with the authorities.

It is reasonable to refuse to blame those who out of fear of punishment, habits of law-abidingness and patriotism, or immaturity obey the commands of their political leaders. But considerations like these provide an excuse for those who comply, not a justification for the claim that even when in doubt about the justice of the war, they should comply.

Vitoria's brief argument addresses this question of justification, but inconclusively. He rightly notes that political leaders sometimes cannot and sometimes should not render reasons for waging a war to those they govern. But the inability of the leaders to explain the reasons for waging a war, even if this arises from their moral obligations as leaders, does not settle the responsibilities of potential soldiers in doubt about whether it is right to fight. Apparently to deal with this lacuna in his analysis, Vitoria adds that if subjects need to be satisfied of the justice of the war before they may serve, then the state will be in grave peril.[20]

Perhaps Vitoria means this to be a consequentialist argument: the peril of proceeding in this way provides a decisive reason for resolving doubts in favor of the decision of the political leaders. But this argument is problematic within a natural law context. First, it is not clear why, if consequentialist reasoning should be the tiebreaker in cases of doubt, it should not also be used more generally. But, plainly, consequentialist reasoning does not figure prominently in natural law analyses, and there is good reason to think it an alternative approach to moral thinking that is deeply alien to natural law.[21] Second, there is some reason to wonder whether a presumption for settling doubts in favor of the state will generally avoid the kinds of peril Vitoria is worried about, or whether avoiding such perils is generally a good thing. A docile citizenry may make it easier for a country's leaders to engage in warfare, but that has its own dangers; and facilitating warfare is frequently not a good thing, whether from the perspective of a morally defined conception of the common good or from a consequentialist conception of the overall benefit and harm brought upon those affected by the war.

It remains, therefore, that the presumption that doubts should be settled in favor of the judgment of political leaders must be justified, if it can be, either by something specific to the situation of choice when there is doubt about its moral character, or by something specific to the way political authority figures in such situations. In general, one's responsibility in situations of doubt is to try to resolve the doubt, but in no case to do what one has reason to think might be wrong; for to do this would be to be willing to do what is wrong.

Given these norms for resolving doubts, the role of authority in the process is limited. It is often reasonable for a person to accept the authority of experts concerning judgments within the area of their expertise, even if the person cannot judge for himself or herself about the matter. Thus, the authority of moral advisors, scholars, and others with relevant experience can be important, and sometimes decisive, in settling doubts.

But it is hard to see how authority in areas other than those in which truth is discovered and moral reasoning correctly carried out could be relevant to settling doubts. In particular, it is hard to see how a presumption in favor of the judgment of political authority would figure significantly in a procedure for settling doubts governed by these norms. For political authority is based on the need of a community to act in concert, and so those who have political authority do not have it because of any special expertise in determining the facts or in moral reasoning.

Still, political authority is real, and citizens have a real, though defeasible, obligation to obey the lawful commands of political leaders. This obligation is often relevant to the deliberations of a potential soldier in doubt about the justice of the war in which he is commanded to fight. His obligation to obey this command can be overridden only if a reason is present for thinking that obedience would be immoral. Mere feelings of distaste, worries, or a feeling that what is commanded might be wrong are not sufficient to override the duty to obey. They are not doubts that generate moral dilemmas. Similarly, a conviction that one's political leaders are untrustworthy, that they lie to the country, or that they act with bad will, is not a reason justifying a refusal to obey, unless it is based on evidence. Without evidence, such convictions may be no more than an expression of unwillingness to accept the moral legitimacy of political authority.

Consequently, the authority of political leaders can play a role in the deliberations of the potential soldier in doubt about the justice of the war in which he is commanded to fight. Besides providing part of the context for setting aside putative doubts that do not establish a reason for doubting that a war is just, the authority of political leaders sometimes provides a reason for taking their statements about the justice of the war at face value. When there is no evidence or specific ground for distrusting the statements of political leaders, cooperative citizens will accept them as true, and sometimes that is enough to settle the doubt.

However, if such considerations as these do not settle the doubt, that is, if, after considering fully the obligation to obey legitimate authority and the obligation to accept the authority's credible statements, there remains a reason to think that the war is unjust, then the potential soldier should refuse to participate. For in that situation, the authority of the political leaders would be used precisely to enjoin obedience to a command whose moral legitimacy is in question, and the potential soldier would be commanded to do what he had reason to think was seriously wrong. Since doing what one has reason to think is wrong is itself wrong, one cannot be obliged to obey commands to do such things. Indeed, one is obliged to disobey them.

In a word, the presumption in favor of obeying political authority in conditions of doubt about the justice of a war is a weaker one than Vitoria and many others in the tradition have allowed. The prince is obliged, at least in some circumstances, to "render reasons" to his subjects. As Donagan notes: "War is such a horrible evil that only a very clear and great cause can justify it; and when such a cause exists, it should not be difficult to show it."[22]

Moreover, whatever the prince's obligations, potential soldiers must satisfy themselves that there is no reason to believe that the war they are asked to fight is unjust. So, natural law implies, and natural law theorists should hold, that individual moral judgment, if not "individual volition,"[23] must be brought to bear on the decisions of citizens and potential soldiers about whether to participate in their country's war.

The restriction of individual moral judgment to what citizens can certainly *know* appears to make things easier for political leaders and for citizens. But the effect of this limitation has often been to render just war considerations a dead letter, at least as they figure in individual deliberation.[24] The laxism of this development is obvious, and has brought justified scorn on the just war theorists and religious leaders who defend it.

The central moral problem is that obedience has no tendency to excuse or justify individual action contrary to conscience. For obedience is a form of social cooperation in which one's choice to obey is intelligible only as a part of a social act in which the goals of the polity are pursued. Obedience is justified in this situation only when honest moral reflection reveals no reason to think that there is a crime, and obedience is not morally justified as long as one has a reason for thinking the war is criminal, or as long as one negligently fails to determine whether such a reason exists.

I am not suggesting that one cannot comply with the orders of those who have power over one's life without strictly obeying them, that is, without entering into a form of social cooperation in which one endorses and actively promotes the goals of the powerful party. What the natural law tradition calls "material cooperation" is possible in wartime; without endorsing their government's unjustified war, citizens can cooperate in various ways with the government, even if this cooperation furthers the war effort. This kind of cooperation can be morally justified, and often is for citizens whose support of a war they judge immoral is limited to paying tax and carrying on their lives in a law-abiding way.[25] But the decisions of citizens to fight or to actively support such a war, however reluctant, appear to be acts not of material cooperation but of formal cooperation and obedience.

Notes

1. St. Thomas Aquinas *Summa theologiae* I-II q. 1 a. 3 ad 3; see also q. 18.

2. See Germain Grisez, Joseph Boyle, and John Finnis, "Practical Principles, Moral Truth, and Ultimate Ends," *American Journal of Jurisprudence* 32 (1987), 103–8.

3. Grisez, Boyle, and Finnis, "Practical Principles," 128.

4. See Aquinas *Summa theologiae* I-II q. 100 a. 3.

5. See Alan Donagan, *The Theory of Morality* (Chicago: University of Chicago Press, 1977), 66–74.

6. See Germain Grisez, *The Way of the Lord Jesus*, vol. 1, *Christian Moral Principles* (Chicago: Franciscan Herald Press, 1983), 259–63.

7. Finnis, Chapter 1 above, under "Motive or Intention."

8. Finnis, Chapter 1 above, under "Attitudes toward War and Nonviolence."

9. See Grisez, Boyle, and Finnis, "Practical Principles," 104; Aquinas *Summa theologiae* I-II qq. 12–13.

10. See Aquinas *Summa theologiae* I-II prol.

11. See Joseph Boyle, "Who Is Entitled to Double Effect?" *Journal of Medicine and Philosophy* 16 (1991), 475–95.

12. Finnis, Chapter 1 above, under "Motive or Intention."

13. G.E.M. Anscombe, "The Justice of the Present War Examined," in her *Ethics, Religion and Politics: Collected Philosophical Papers, Volume III*, (Minneapolis: University of Minnesota Press, 1981), 74–75.

14. Donagan, *Theory of Morality*, 111.

15. Michael Walzer, *Just and Unjust Wars* (New York: Basic Books, 1977), 39.

16. Aquinas *Summa theologiae* II-II q. 40 a. 2.

17. Vatican Council II, *Gaudium et spes*, para. 79.

18. Cf. David Hollenbach, *Nuclear Ethics: A Christian Moral Argument* (New York: Paulist Press, 1983), 7–8.

19. Walzer, *Just and Unjust Wars*, 39.

20. Walzer, *Just and Unjust Wars*, 39.

21. See Donagan, *Theory of Morality*, 172–209.

22. Donagan, *Theory of Morality*, 111.

23. Walzer, *Just and Unjust Wars*, 39.

24. See Donagan, *Theory of Morality*, 15–17.

25. See John Finnis, Joseph Boyle, and Germain Grisez, *Nuclear Deterrence, Morality and Realism* (Oxford: Oxford University Press, 1987), 342–54.

CHAPTER 3

Realism and the Ethics of War and Peace

David R. Mapel

BECAUSE "REALISM" is a term with many meanings, it is best to begin this chapter by noting what will *not* be discussed here. Realism as it is understood in the current academic international relations literature of "neorealism" will not be discussed. This sort of realism is intended as a descriptive or empirical account of international relations, whereas the essays in this volume are primarily concerned with prescriptive views of international affairs. Nor will this chapter consider realism as the argument that morality should *never* govern state conduct. Some realist authors do make this argument, although it has seldom been put forward without some sort of qualification or equivocation. In fact, the self-appointed critics of realism are usually the ones who portray it as a completely unqualified rejection of morality in international affairs. Finally, this chapter will not try to summarize a disparate body of historical views that may fall under the heading of realism. That job has been ably performed many times before with respect to both classical realists like Thucydides, Machiavelli, and Hobbes, and modern realists like Morgenthau, Niebuhr, and Kennan.

Instead, realism appears here as a philosophical construct designed to respond to the concerns of pacifists, just war theorists, and other moralists of international affairs. Of course, this construct must bear at least a family resemblance to various historical views if it is to deserve the name of realism. Throughout this chapter, I note where similar views have been expressed by classical and modern realists (especially Robert W. Tucker, who perhaps comes closest to being a "realist" in my sense of the term). But my aim is not primarily historical in character. It is, rather, to elicit the logic of realism as a broadly ethical view of war and peace.

Understood in this way, the central claim of prescriptive realism is that morality should not *always* govern state conduct. Though historically realism has often been formulated in a more radical manner—for example, as the view that morality cannot govern state conduct or should never govern state conduct—it is this more moderate formulation of realism that poses the most serious challenge to other traditions of thought about the ethics of war and peace. Without pulling the teeth of realism, it forms the basis of a powerful challenge to more conventional ways of understanding the role of morality in international relations.

This challenge can be developed in three different ways. First, with respect to *ius ad bellum*, realism argues that strict observance of legal and moral prohibitions against aggression must sometimes compromise the state's security or survival. Second, with respect to *ius in bello*, realism argues that even wars fought for limited ends and with limited means must sometimes involve the deliberate killing of innocent people. Finally, some writers have insisted that both the ends and the means of war normally can and should be limited, but have argued that states are not bound to observe such limits in extreme situations. Although this last alternative is usually not thought of as fully realist in character, the idea of extremity as a justification or excuse has been of central importance in the realist tradition. For this reason, I will consider this last argument as a third way of expressing the central challenge of realism.

Unless the critic of realism can establish that morality is always of overriding importance, then any of these arguments, if true, is sufficient to establish the central claim of realism. For each argument identifies a different situation in which morality would appear to require a sacrifice of territorial integrity or political independence by the state. This is not to say that the state should never surrender some of its territory or independence for the sake of morality. Nor is it to deny that historically the requirements of morality have been understood in a variety of ways. It is to assert that unless the fundamental interests of the state are considered "just" by definition, the state will sometimes face situations in which those interests will conflict with morality.[1] Realists argue that in such situations, morality should not always prevail in the conduct of statecraft.

War and Peace

Historically, realists have often argued that international relations is a Hobbesian "state of nature" that is also a "state of war." If the three arguments above constitute the core of the realist approach to the ethics of war and peace, however, then prescriptive realism is not inherently committed to the view that international relations is a zero-sum game or war of all against all. The prescriptive claims of realism may remain plausible even in an international environment very different from the one we inhabit now. Let us make the "unrealistic" assumption that the normal condition of international relations is one of peaceful cooperation. Even in such a peaceable kingdom, it could remain the case, both in principle and upon rare occasion, that the state might require (and should use) force to defend itself, and that even a limited use of force would harm innocent people in unjust ways. Understood as a distinctive view of the role of morality in international relations, realism is logically compatible with a wide range of empirical assumptions about the character of international society. Many criticisms of realism as a descriptive view of international relations are therefore simply beside the point in the present context.

Nevertheless, it is true that the hard questions identified by prescriptive realism do not arise unless we assume that there are occasions when the state must use force to secure its own vital interests or survival. And historically, realists have often argued that international relations does resemble a Hobbesian state of war, understood not as a condition of actual force but as "a tract of time, wherein the will to contend by battle is sufficiently known."[2] But others have rejected this definition of war as broad enough to rationalize almost any kind of preemptive violence as defensive in character. Theorists in other ethical traditions have often focused on questions of definition because they wish to show that war is an inherently social activity and therefore both norm-governed and voluntary rather than necessary. Above all, these critics of realism wish to contest the sort of definition of war offered by Clausewitz: "War is an act of force . . . which must lead, in theory, to extremes."[3]

Clausewitz argued that the social conditions "which circumscribe and moderate [war] . . . are not part of war: they already exist."[4] Yet Clausewitz also argued that "if we keep in mind that war springs from some political purpose, it is natural that the prime cause of existence will remain the supreme consideration in conducting it."[5] In other words, Clausewitz appreciated that real, as opposed to theoretical or definitional, war involves choice. Realists have usually recognized both the social and the voluntary character of war. Yet they agree with Clausewitz that there is a dialectic of violence in war that tends to replace the aims of policy with the aims of total military victory. Realists thus acknowledge with Clausewitz that war "may be a matter of degree," but they are inclined to fear war precisely because it has a tendency to outrun initial policies and limitations.[6] The critical question for the realist is not therefore whether total war falls within the definition of war, but whether this kind of war represents the abandonment of policy. In many cases (most notably, nuclear war), some realists have argued that it does.

If we still want a definition of war, then perhaps we can say that for realists, war is "organized violence carried out by political units against each other," with organized interstate violence understood as one species of war.[7] According to this definition, what distinguishes war from other forms of violence is its official character, although questions remain about what makes it official and what degree or kind of violence is required to distinguish war from peace. The vagueness of this definition is unlikely to bother realists, however: they are comfortable with any definition broad enough to include undeclared wars, total wars, and some kinds of internal conflict and rebellion.

For similar reasons, realists have not been interested in defining peace. Realists are generally resistant to any equation of peace with justice, since this would suggest that there can be no peace in the absence of agreement about justice. They are more likely to define peace simply as the absence of organized violence. They insist that peace and justice sometimes can and do conflict, although they may grant that justice is sometimes a condition of lasting peace.[8] But only sometimes: claims of justice appear in many cases to be a condition of protracted violence, as current struggles over national self-determination illustrate.

War and Nonviolence

Though realists have occasionally celebrated war, they have usually deplored it on the prudential grounds that war always poses a risk to the state. Because they are skeptical about attempts to reconcile prudence and morality, they have often had a keen sense of the immorality of war as well. Not only are the causes and conduct of war often unjust, but character and even language deteriorate during war, as Thucydides noted in his frightening description of the civil war in Corcyra.[9] The same sorts of prudence and skepticism explain realist attitudes toward nonviolence, and particularly pacifism.[10] Both realists and pacifists are skeptical about many of the distinctions of just war theory. On this basis, some realists agree with pacifists that a consistent commitment to fundamental principles of common morality requires the rejection of war. But these realists think that the pacifist rejection of war is deeply imprudent: "For a man who wants to make a profession of good in all regards must come to ruin among so many who are not good."[11] Other realists think that the pacifist rejection of war is not only imprudent but immoral as well, since these realists think that the distinction that common morality draws between doing and allowing harm cannot be sustained. Pacifism should be morally condemned because in refusing to use force to prevent the ruin of some, it allows the ruin of all.

In response, it may be insisted that there is an important difference between doing and allowing. Much more broadly, it may be argued that it is realism, not pacifism, that is not only clearly immoral but imprudent as well. Nuclear weapons have finally revealed to everyone that the most serious threat to human values is the use of force in behalf of the state. Prudence dictates that we give up the state.[12]

Realists are inclined to doubt that the existence of nuclear weapons shows that the state can no longer secure the ends that human beings have traditionally desired, such as security, just change, and political independence. Instead, they are likely to argue that if we give up the state, we must also be prepared to give up those ends, like political freedom, that the state has traditionally defended. No prudent person can expect nonviolence to secure the traditional ends of the state against adversaries willing to use extreme measures. In other words, realists doubt arguments for nonviolence and against the state that appeal to our prudential self-interest.

They are equally dubious about appeals to our higher nature or to the possibility of moral transformation, and these doubts have usually reflected various theological or psychological assumptions about the sinfulness or natural egoism of human beings. But there seems to be no reason why realists must claim that such change is impossible. Instead, realism might simply argue that such change seems unlikely enough: with some rare exceptions, nonviolence is not a strategy for preserving political independence, and at present human beings appear to desire political independence as much as ever.

If human beings cannot be weaned from wanting what only the state can presently secure, then perhaps the state system can be replaced by a world authority with enough power to require world disarmament, to enforce world peace, to compel just change, and to preserve at least a large degree of political autonomy. Here realists are likely to worry about the tremendous dangers that must attend the tremendous power that such a world authority would require. Aside from standard worries about world tyranny, there is also a worry about chaos. Kenneth Waltz, for example, argues that if a central authority is strong enough to control secession, strong states will be tempted to struggle to control the reins of world government; if the center is weak, efforts to break free may be prevalent, leading to a world of civil war.[13] Of course, if the main sources of international conflict were to wither away, an effective world authority might not require such great power.[14] Realists who begin from pessimistic assumptions about human nature deny this possibility. But although such assumptions have historically been of great importance in the realist tradition, they do not seem to be a necessary part of realism. Again, realism understood as a prescriptive ethic of international relations is logically compatible with a wide variety of assumptions about the possibility and desirability of international transformation. It may be both a theoretical and a moral failing of realism that it has traditionally not paid much attention to questions about how states should act to transform international relations. On the other hand, questions about how states may act in nonideal circumstances would appear to be equally important. Indeed, we must be able to answer these questions before we can know what states may do in the process of moving toward a more peaceful world.

The Grounds for War

Realists think that war can in principle serve peace or justice by enforcing international law, by preserving a balance of power, or by promoting change. For this reason, realists do not subscribe to the view that war is no longer an effective means of achieving these ends. Yet although war may sometimes promote peace or just change, realists are much more concerned with war as a means of preserving the state, and are likely to feel some affinity for the view that the only justifiable wars are those fought in defense of the state or the political community. From a realist perspective, there are two objections to restricting the justification of war to self-defense. First, there is no very clear way of limiting the definition of aggression, and therefore the idea of self-defense, without sometimes undercutting the claim of states to preserve their territorial integrity and political sovereignty. Second, it may at times prove necessary to wage wars that clearly go beyond self-defense, however defined, in order to protect national security.

Realists are likely to agree that the most satisfactory definition of aggression includes the idea of imminent threat. This definition of aggression recognizes that the initiation of force can be defensive in character when it is a response to an immediate, grave, and manifest threat to state survival. Although some critics of the just war have objected that this definition of aggression permits states to initiate force whenever they believe that they face an imminent threat, this is not a criticism that realists are likely to make.[15] For although there are borderline cases, these criteria are clear enough to allow us at least sometimes to judge that beliefs about the existence of an imminent threat are unreasonable or insincere. From a realist perspective, the difficulty with this kind of definition is rather that the state's independence can also be compromised by measures that are nonforceful and less than imminent, such as economic destabilization or perhaps a prolonged state of mobilization that drains resources. In some situations, it may be indispensable for the state to act "aggressively" and therefore "unjustly" in order to avoid a nonforceful danger that will prove no less fatal than military conquest.

It has sometimes been argued that this notion of preemptive war as an indispensable means to state survival exaggerates the degree of strategic knowledge and foresight possessed by political actors.[16] The preemptive (actually, preventive) wars recommended by Machiavelli, for example, clearly rest on exaggerated claims to know how states will and must act. But though historically, realists often have made exaggerated predictive claims, only the most optimistic advocate of nonviolent national defense would assert that force has never been an indispensable means of defending the state against an immediate military threat. Realism insists that at least occasionally, preemptive war can also be an indispensable means of defending the state against grave but nonforceful threats.

In response to these difficulties, we might try to broaden the definition of aggression to include a wider range of threats. In doing so, we might find that we can sometimes agree about particular cases. Yet realists think there is little hope of general and lasting agreement on the interpretation and application of legal definitions of aggression, since in interpreting such definitions, states always have conflicting interests in stressing the importance of both world stability and national sovereignty.[17] Although the chances of agreement within the UN Security Council about the interpretation of aggression may have improved recently, realists doubt whether this development expresses anything except a temporary phase of American hegemony following the end of the Cold War. If the state does consistently try to conform to a definition of aggression that can be clearly interpreted and applied, the consequences may prove dire. In short, realism argues that it is impossible for the state to conform to clear rules of ius ad bellum without sometimes compromising its own security.

Historically, realists have also argued that sometimes not only preemptive but also preventive wars are necessary. In the case of preventive war, such claims of necessity may indeed attribute a kind of strategic clairvoyance to governments. Such claims of necessity may also reflect exaggerated fears about long-term political trends that will eventually leave a state isolated in a hostile world. Writers in the tradition generally agree with Hobbes, however, that it is natural for human beings to reason about dangers before they become immediate, and that such reasoning is often far from paranoid. As Michael Howard asks, was it paranoid for the British to worry about the revival of German power in the 1930s? Was it unreasonable in 1939 that "nearly all the British felt justified in going to war, not over any specific issue that could have been settled by negotiation, but *to maintain their power* while it was still possible"?[18] Since Germany had already violated international law in 1939, the Second World War was not, strictly speaking, a preventive war. But as Michael Howard suggests, the principal reason for the British decision to declare war was fear of German hegemony. Of course, the retrospective conclusion drawn by many that there should have been a preventive war in the 1930s has strongly influenced postwar conceptions of the legitimate use of force (the so-called Munich analogy), as illustrated by President Bush's rationale for his war against Iraq. Nevertheless, it may be argued that all wars that are motivated by fear of hegemony alone are unjust: there must be a more definite threat before war can be justified. Realists, however, are reluctant to condemn all such wars on the grounds that aggression itself is wrong, or that aggression anywhere is a threat to peace everywhere, or that aggression is a crime against international society. They are even more reluctant to move beyond the condemnation of aggression to the waging of war *against* aggression. For this tradition, enforcing international law cannot by itself constitute a sufficient reason for going to war.

Because realism refuses to justify war on legal, moral, or religious grounds, it is a doctrine that in some respects limits violence. Indeed, realists have argued that it is really moralism in foreign policy that most frequently leads to violence, not realism. But moralism is not morality: morality is not a set of simple rules but a complex structure that includes many distinctions and exceptions.[19] Yet some realists have argued that morality should occupy a subordinate role in foreign policy precisely because the complex character of moral reasoning tends to get lost in practice. In practice, the following fallacious line of reasoning is all too tempting: Because aggression is an evil, it is something states are morally responsible for choosing. If there is moral responsibility, then aggression is not merely an evil, but an unnecessary evil. Aggression must stem from the miscalculations of aggressors, not from powerful underlying social and political grievances. Such miscalculations must therefore be deterred and punished. The realist claims that historically, this way of viewing aggression has tempted statesmen to oversimplify: from this perspective, peace tends to become indivisible, war tends to become a stark conflict over justice, and the distinction between ius ad bellum and ius in bello tends to become blurred. Traditional statecraft, which has historically focused on discriminations of "power, interest and circumstance," is gradually replaced by the idea of collective security, which tends to disregard these considerations in favor of the rights of all states, great and small, against aggression wherever and however it may occur.[20] No doubt this crude reasoning is not inherent in a moral approach to foreign policy: moralists can indeed make sound prudential judgments, and the doctrine of collective security can be given a more sophisticated formulation. It may also be doubted whether historically there is such a stark opposition between traditional statecraft and the sort of Wilsonian idealism that is the usual target of realist criticisms. Yet realists have often argued that even if the idea of national security is itself quite vague, their approach to foreign policy is in practice less subject to abuse than its alternatives.[21]

Realism is in one sense more permissive about the grounds for war than many other traditions, since it sometimes sanctions wars of self-preservation as well as wars of self-defense. But realists claim that their principles are in another sense far less permissive than those of other views, since they do not sanction wars between the forces of good and evil. In criticism of realism, it may be said that realism is more willing to permit aggression and less willing to oppose it than other traditions. In reply, it may be said that realism is more tolerant of peaceful negotiation with the devil than other traditions, on the grounds that negotiation is usually less risky and less destructive than confrontation on the basis of principle.[22] As we shall see in the next section, realists generally refuse to demonize the unsavory foreign states with which governments must sometimes deal.

Resistance to Political Authority

In considering realist views of resistance to political authority, it will be helpful to distinguish between two versions of reason of state. "Patriotic" reason of state regards the state as being of fundamental value. Pericles' speeches, for example, express the view that Athens has "attained an independent existence such that her preservation means more than the happiness or misery of all her inhabitants."[23] In contrast, "liberal" reason of state regards the state as merely an instrument or condition for realizing more fundamental values, albeit an indispensable condition. Lincoln's speeches, for example, express this view of the Union as indispensable to the preservation of universal moral and political principles. In practice, this distinction between patriotic and liberal reasons of state sometimes may not make much difference, for in the actual conduct of foreign policy, an indispensable condition of fundamental value might just as well be regarded as itself a fundamental value. In theory, the distinction is important because it suggests that realism is compatible with a wide range of views about the basis of state authority and resistance to authority.[24]

The importance of the distinction between patriotic and liberal reasons of state can be illustrated by considering a standard criticism of realism. It is sometimes argued that because realism is committed to doing whatever is necessary to preserve the state, nothing in the logic of realism forbids the hunting down of internal enemies of the state. This logic is most clearly illustrated in Machiavelli, who recommends political murder as a tool of statecraft. In response, it should be said that a great deal depends on the kind of view in question. Liberal realists regard the state as being instrumental to other ends, and in many cases the principal end is political liberty. For this reason, liberal realists have sometimes insisted that conscription can only be justified given a compelling threat to the state; that free speech, conscientious objection, civil disobedience, and every other form of peaceful protest must be tolerated by the state up to the point of imminent constitutional crisis, rebellion, and civil war; that free elections, free speech, and many forms of protest must be permitted during the course of civil (and foreign) wars; and that during such crises political leaders may sometimes suspend certain rights but should resist taking on any new, unconstitutional powers.

Nevertheless, should all constitutional measures to preserve the state fail, even liberal realists are likely to argue that a state may temporarily use unconstitutional measures against its own citizens, as long as those measures ultimately serve to reestablish the liberal state.[25] This is simply the internal side of realism's more general approach to politics itself: if the state may sometimes make war against foreigners when its survival is threatened, and if war involves forcing innocent people to kill each other, then the state may sometimes take extreme measures toward its own citizens for the same reasons. There is some truth, then, in the criticism that realism finds itself on a slippery slope with respect to the way in which the state may treat its citizens. The realist rejoinder is that states do sometimes find themselves on such a slope, whether they like it or not. Liberal realists add that the slope is not as slippery as their critics suggest. There may be safe stops on the way down.

Realists take much the same position with regard to foreign repression. In principle, liberal realists will discriminate between foreign states that permit peaceful resistance to authority and those that do not. On liberal principles, only the former are entitled to resist revolution. Though liberal realists may condemn foreign repression, they do not regard such repression as remarkable, nor do they think that we should always respond to foreign repression by breaking off diplomatic recognition (much less by launching reform interventions). Realists recognize that a repressive or illiberal form of government can sometimes express the history, culture, and values of a community. In other words, the state can serve as an indispensable condition for a variety of political values. More importantly, realists usually view the state as an indispensable condition of order. Although revolution is sometimes the expression of a just desire for self-determination, realists think it has more often been an occasion for bloodletting on an enormous scale that has spilled across borders and become international. In short, with respect to internal resistance both inside and outside the state, the security perspective predominates. This perspective sometimes leads realists to recommend military intervention in behalf of repressive governments. Historically, realists have often failed to see that such interventions are seldom necessary to the state's interests, let alone its survival. But no tradition has a monopoly on political stupidity.[26]

Of course, many realists have not been liberals at all, even in the broad sense of the term I have been using. And realists who have been liberals have often grossly exaggerated the need for internal control within the liberal state. In my judgment, this willingness to accept the state on almost any terms is one of the weakest aspects of the realist perspective. By contrast, realism is at its strongest when it argues that internal necessities of state can sometimes exist for even relatively just states. Strong constitutional safeguards for internal dissent may not always permit the liberal state to defend itself against external and internal enemies in a just manner, especially when those enemies combine. In extreme cases, even liberal realists will argue that the state must sometimes suspend the rule of law.

Intention and Motive

Although it is difficult to say exactly how we should distinguish intention and motive, we do have an intuitive grasp of the distinction. Very roughly, intention is what a person aims at, as when a soldier shoots with the intention of killing an enemy in war; motive, on the other hand, is "perhaps expressive of the spirit" in which a person shoots, rather than descriptive of the end to which the shooting was a means.[27] Given this way of drawing the distinction, it appears possible to form the same intentions and perform the same actions from a variety of different motives. We may act with the intention of killing, for example, out of pity or hatred.

Instead of stressing philosophical difficulties in distinguishing between intention and motive, however, realists have historically tended to emphasize various practical problems. It is difficult to be certain of the intentions of others, and in particular, states do not always enjoy the luxury of trying to distinguish between the aggressive and defensive intentions of other states.[28] The attempt to set clear legal and moral limits on the defensive intentions of states must sometimes fail. The good intentions of moralists in foreign policy often lead to more suffering than happiness. And, as we shall see, some realists also think that just war theorists use the distinction between intending and foreseeing harm to disguise the hellishness of war.

Because realists think that political leaders and soldiers sometimes must intend what is wrong, the idea of motive tends to become more important in the realist tradition. Indeed, we might almost describe realism as an ethic of motivation. To a large extent, realism shifts our attention from the evils that we sometimes intentionally bring about to the spirit in which we bring them about. Some interpreters argue, for example, that St. Augustine was a "Christian realist" because he shifted the focus of our moral judgments about war from intentions to motives, and then argued that because we can neither be certain of motives nor act without sin, we must fall back on what is certain, namely, the laws of the state. On this interpretation, the real evil of war for Augustine is not that soldiers sometimes intentionally kill innocent people, but that soldiers sometimes intentionally kill innocent people out of motives of hatred and cruelty rather than reluctantly and in obedience to law.[29] Machiavelli stressed that a prince should not want to use cruelty for its own sake, and that motive is therefore one of the things that determines whether a prince has *virtù*.[30] More recently, Joel Rosenthal has argued that many American realists were influenced by Max Weber's notion of an "ethic of responsibility," which subordinates intentions to consequences and motives.[31] For Weber, the idea of motive seems to serve as a bridge between the ethical and political concerns of the statesman; in Weber's phrase, it determines "who can" have a true vocation for politics. According to Weber, the statesman who has such a vocation will do the responsible thing by getting his hands dirty, as he sometimes must, in the pursuit of higher ideals.[32] Reinhold Niebuhr also stressed that the statesman must act out of a sense of responsibility, although the exercise of responsible power brings moral guilt with it. In a famous passage on American foreign policy, Niebuhr noted that "the irony of our situation lies in the fact that we could not be virtuous (in the sense of practicing the virtues implicit in meeting our vast world responsibilities) if we were as innocent as we pretend to be."[33] Realists have often suggested that the goodness of motive redeems or at least limits the evil of intent.

The above quotation from Niebuhr raises two problems, however. First, it is hard to see from a realist perspective how the state can have any major "world responsibilities," at least in the sense of moral responsibility. For realists, the primary aim of foreign policy must be to preserve the state, or as Elihu Root said, to keep the state out of trouble. Whenever possible, a policy of isolation would seem to be more in keeping with realism than a policy of engagement (although historically, realists have often argued that a failure to impose world order will lead to world chaos, thus endangering domestic security). Second, how do we judge that the motives of American statesmen have been the "responsible" (that is, right or desirable) ones? In some cases, the answer to this question may be clear, but certainly not in all. If we are told that American statesmen have acted with desirable motives because they are responsible men of virtue, the answer will be circular if being virtuous depends on acting with the correct motives. If we are told that we can judge their motives by their actions, we seem to have left an ethic of motivation behind. Alternatively, the way we describe the actions of statesmen may contain an implicit and question-begging reference to motive—"this is mercy-killing, not murder," for example. Nevertheless, an ethic of motivation may often be the best we can do in international relations, or so some realists have argued.

Realists frequently see a sharp contrast between the motives of real politicians and the motives of the ideal leader with a "vocation" for politics. Real politicians are primarily motivated by a desire to acquire ("truly a very natural and ordinary thing," in Machiavelli's view).[34] In contrast, the ideal statesman wants to do the right thing and is morally anguished by some of the choices he faces. The first description of motives is cynical, the second has become banal. But the second description is so familiar precisely because political leaders so often embrace a realist ethic of motivation. Candidates for office often tell us that we want someone who can make "the tough choices," particularly in foreign policy. We might be pardoned for thinking that they sometimes mean by this to suggest that we want someone who can make immoral choices as well.

The Conduct of War

Historically, both just war theorists and realists have tended to focus on the causes and ends justifying war. Yet if the conduct of war is inherently unlimited, then many would argue that the issue of just cause becomes academic. Realism generally rejects the view that there are any inherent limits on the means that states may threaten or use to preserve themselves. In contrast, other ethical traditions, and particularly the natural law just war tradition, argue that there are such limits. The most important of these is a principle of discrimination that forbids intentionally attacking the innocent.

If ius in bello is to have any distinctive quality, the principle of discrimination cannot rest on some kind of appeal to the bad consequences that will result from failing to observe it. It cannot rest on the view that evil-doing inevitably corrupts the agent, or that the means of action are themselves the ends of action coming into existence.[35] Rather, the principle of discrimination must rest on the more basic principle that one may never do evil that good may come of it. For traditional accounts of ius in bello, what is evil about certain actions cannot be explained simply in terms of the negative value of certain consequences, but must be found in the intentions that give those actions their character. But according to some realists, this traditional understanding of the basis of ius in bello only illustrates its implausibility, because it rules out even the threat to do evil: "In this case, we are left with a position that an act which is unjust to commit ought never to be threatened, however remote the contingency that the act will ever be committed and whatever the consequences that may follow if the threat is abandoned. . . . When reduced to this pure form, the argument seems singularly unpersuasive. One may question whether the moralists themselves are prepared to accept it."[36]

Many moralists are quite willing to accept this view, however. More importantly, many moralists argue that the implications of this view will often not prove so radical, once we distinguish harm that is intended from harm that is foreseen but unintended. When combined with other moral considerations, such as proportionality, this distinction yields the principle of "double effect."

Although realists have usually rejected double effect, historically they have seldom paid much attention to the theory of action that the doctrine presupposes or to the other philosophical issues it raises. The most problematical aspect of the doctrine of double effect is the requirement that we should not intentionally harm the innocent as a means to our end. This requirement raises problems of interpretation, problems of consistency between the prescriptions it has been used to justify, and problems concerning the moral relevance of the distinction between side effects and what is intended. Attempts to deal with these problems have given rise to many different versions of the doctrine. Unfortunately, it is impossible to discuss all of the ways in which double effect has been criticized and defended.[37] Given the powerful and conflicting intuitions that people have about it, as well as the philosophical attention that it continues to command, it would be foolish to make any flat assertions about whether the doctrine can ultimately be defended. Instead, we should focus on how a realist rejection of the double effect alters our view of ius in bello.

Even if we think there is little moral difference between some of the harms we intend in waging war and some of the harms we merely foresee as a side effect of war, discrimination may continue to function as a subordinate principle of just warfare. If we can achieve the same military objective by killing soldiers or by killing both soldiers and civilians, for example, then obviously we can be blamed for not choosing the first, more discriminating alternative. If we reject double effect, motive will also remain important to our moral assessment of individual and state actors, since motive and intent differ. But if we reject double effect, it follows that "collateral" harm to the innocent must often be regarded as either deliberate or intentional. Absent some other justifying or excusing conditions, moral responsibility for such harm must be accepted, once we have done whatever we can to avoid such harm within the constraints of military necessity.

Furthermore, once we reject double effect, the wrong that is done in war will not involve merely the deliberate killing of noncombatants who are morally and technically "innocent," that is, "harmless." Many combatants appear to be innocent in both senses as well. Many soldiers have been forced to fight, and are therefore at least partly absolved of moral responsibility for the justice of their cause. But many soldiers are also harmless in the sense of not posing any immediate danger to other individuals and therefore not engaging their rights of self-defense. In war, soldiers often do not exercise rights of self-defense. Rather, they exercise rights of self-preservation by attacking soldiers who are green recruits, who are far behind the lines, or who otherwise present no immediate danger. If we may permissibly kill these soldiers, it may only be permissible because of a convention that allows us to treat them "as if" they are always dangerous.[38] Finally, on the basis of self-defense, it would also seem that soldiers may sometimes permissibly kill not only enemy soldiers who are not in fact dangerous, but also noncombatants who are not dangerous, who only shield a dangerous threat.[39] But if the normal conduct of war usually involves all of these kinds of killing, and if the rejection of double effect means that there is no necessary moral difference between intentional and foreseen harms, then it would appear that there is considerable support for the realist view that war constitutes a kind of activity that cannot be justified by common morality (without an appeal to some other excusing conditions).

In light of these criticisms of discrimination, the other basic principle of ius in bello, proportionality, obviously becomes much more important to our assessment of the conduct of war. Realists have argued amongst themselves and with their critics about how we should make judgments of proportionality and about how exact such judgments can be. They have acknowledged, or been forced to acknowledge, that such judgments must be quite crude. Nevertheless, all realists agree that there can be no statecraft without judgments of proportionality. Indeed, the idea of proportionality is of central importance to political realism. Even though realists are willing to accept the indiscriminate nature of nuclear deterrence, for example, they are generally unwilling to accept the idea that nuclear war could meet criteria of proportionality.

Though realists recognize the moral importance of impartial calculations of proportionality, they stress that states never in fact calculate proportionality in this way. As we shall see below, realists also hold that impartial calculations should not be of overriding importance to the state. They sometimes do make essentially utilitarian arguments, such as that it is in everyone's long-run interest for states to base their foreign policies strictly on self-interest. The argument that British terror bombing in the Second World War was justified because the Nazis posed a general threat to civilization can also be construed in a utilitarian or consequentialist way. But though the empirical assumptions of such arguments might be described as realist in character, there is nothing essentially realist about their moral assumptions. These arguments assume that we should be concerned about the welfare of humanity, not the welfare of a particular state or community. Distinctively realist arguments only begin to emerge when extreme measures are justified in terms of the interests of the members of a particular state.

A distinction is sometimes drawn between vulgar versions of realism that require everyday amorality or immorality from officials, and more sophisticated versions of realism that require only that officials be willing to override morality in rare situations involving communal survival or supreme emergency. This distinction presupposes that states usually have room to observe the traditional principles of ius in bello. It also presupposes that the traditional principles of ius in bello can be defended against philosophical criticism. If these standards cannot be justified, then even limited wars must violate a fundamental moral prohibition against intentionally harming the innocent (and may prove morally unacceptable in many other ways as well). This conclusion would not show that officials must always behave in amoral or immoral ways, but it would show that it is actually vulgar realism that best expresses the truth about the conduct of war.

Morality and Extremity

At the beginning of this essay, I noted that although historically, realism has sometimes been understood as the view that morality has no place in public life, it is better understood as the view that there are limits to the role of morality in public life. In other words, the central claim of realism is that morality should not *always* govern the conduct of states. States sometimes ought to be governed by considerations of self-preservation, and therefore ought at least sometimes to subordinate religious, moral, and utilitarian considerations to that end. But what is meant by saying that the state "ought" to preserve itself, if this is neither a religious nor a moral nor a utilitarian "ought"? Assuming we can make sense of this claim, what criticisms of religion, common morality, and consequentialism support it? Finally, if the state ought to ignore or override the demands of religion, morality, and utility sometimes, why not always? Can realists consistently maintain that the state should normally observe the constraints of morality but should violate those constraints in situations involving communal survival or supreme emergency? The realist outlook is compatible with many different answers to these questions, and we can consider only a few of them.

Before discussing these views, however, some cautionary remarks are in order. Obviously, morality comprises much of what makes an individual life go well: moral and prudential values, we might say, interpenetrate each other. Just as obviously, philosophers have disagreed not only about the relationship between prudence and morality, but also about how we should understand each independently. Given these complexities, the following schema is bound to be crude. Nevertheless, it may serve as one way of organizing our thoughts about a wide variety of views.

With this warning in mind, we can say that historically, realists have offered two views of the relationship between prudence and morality. The first *defines* the moral life in terms of the necessary conditions for the good life for individuals, which includes membership in the community. Various patriotic or communitarian realists present strong versions of this view; Hobbes, Niebuhr, and others present weaker versions that focus on the necessity of the state given the fact that people are often not moved to do what common morality seems to require. The second view defines the moral life and the good life independently, and argues that the good life always or sometimes *overrides* the moral life. Thrasymachus in the *Republic* presents a strong version of this view; those who defend a realist "escape clause" for supreme emergencies present a weaker version.

The purest example of patriotic realism is found in the speeches of Pericles in the *Peloponnesian War*. As David Grene puts it, "In the greatness of the thing created, the [Athenian] empire, there is a quality different from the qualities that created it; it is great in itself and for itself."[40] Robert Osgood faintly echoes this view when he writes that "so intimate is man's identification with his national group that national extinction, like the murder of own's family . . . would destroy a virtually indispensable source of personal security and happiness, as well as the sum of all those personal satisfactions derived from the nation's way of life."[41] These views treat the state as being of fundamental value, and lead to what I have called patriotic reason of state. Clearly, for patriotic reason of state there can be no radical conflict between prudence and morality, since the state is the most important value. Extreme measures in situations of supreme emergency present no special problem. Today, however, virtually no one is willing to regard the state as having transcendent value, and many are skeptical that the state is even the source of the most important values. Though human beings may be social by nature, many theorists reject the view that they are political by nature. Most theorists also reject any easy equation of the state with the community. Even if this equation were accepted, the values embodied in any particular community are often purportedly universal in character. They may also be deeply objectionable. For these and a variety of other reasons, it is difficult to equate the state with the community or to understand either as being of fundamental value. Nevertheless, patriotic reason of state has historically been an important part of the realist tradition.

More persuasive is the Hobbesian view that we should not devise abstract systems of morality that most people cannot consistently follow and that therefore have little or no relationship to social reality.[42] For Hobbes, it is a condition of any morality that individuals (and therefore collectives) be generally capable of complying with its demands.[43] In extreme situations, individuals are generally incapable of complying with moral demands for self-sacrifice. Such demands are generally ineffective and therefore unreasonable as moral requirements. Strictly speaking, this view does not hold that individuals and states should ignore or override the demands of morality in extreme situations, but rather redefines the demands of morality so that individuals and collectives have a *right* to take extreme measures for the sake of self-preservation. The importance of the state, on this view, is that it removes the necessity for individuals to exercise their right of self-preservation. The state becomes an indispensable condition of the most minimal and urgent prudential value, namely, physical survival. Of course, the notorious difficulty with this view is that it would seem to undercut demands to defend the state as often as it would justify extreme actions in defense of the state. According to Hobbes, as long as we have a state to protect us, any state will do, including a foreign one. But realists are generally committed not only to the view that the state has a right of self-preservation, but also to the view that the state ought to be defended, sometimes at a very high cost in individual life. Realists have sometimes argued in favor of appeasement, however. Thucydides' Melian dialogue, for example, suggests that the leaders of Melos acted foolishly and thus dishonorably in sacrificing their population to the Athenian sword.[44]

According to Reinhold Niebuhr, it is not individuals but collectives that are generally incapable of self-sacrifice. Unfortunately, although individuals are sometimes capable of self-sacrifice, their altruism is tainted by original sin and almost always expresses itself in a kind of patriotism that is nothing better than national egoism. Group relations "can never be as ethical as those which characterize individual relations," and therefore, Niebuhr argues, we need one morality for individuals and another for groups.[45] Niebuhr's argument explains how it might be possible to have a morality that effectively demands individual sacrifices for the state but that treats certain kinds of sacrifice by the state as unreasonably demanding. Yet from the higher perspective of Christian morality, both individuals and collectives are "covered in guilt." Political leaders cannot help doing wrong, particularly because they must exercise "responsible" power. For Niebuhr, whether power is exercised responsibly in turn depends largely on the motive for its exercise, since leaders sometimes cannot avoid intending and doing wrong. Aside from the theological or perhaps psychological assumptions that Niebuhr's argument requires, then, a great deal depends on the role of motive in public morality.

Realists have also argued that the good life always or sometimes *overrides* morality. A strong version of this view is expressed by some of the characters in Thucydides, for example, and in some of the Platonic dialogues. At times it is argued that a choice to preserve the state is "inevitable" because it is determined by a law of nature. This argument simply denies the possibility of choice and the significance of ethical discourse. A similar view sometimes appears in normative guise, however, in the argument that the strong ought to rule by a law of natural justice. Instead of Niebuhr's distinction between individual and collective morality, we are now presented with a distinction between the natural morality of the strong and the conventional morality of the weak. Thrasymachus, for example, does not object to conventional morality on the grounds that it sometimes conflicts with our well-being. Rather, common morality is always bad for our well-being. A few followers of Nietzsche notwithstanding, the difficulty with this view is simply that common morality seems to be a very large part of the good life, even if the two are not taken to be identical. Any radical opposition of the two seems unpersuasive.

Realists have often argued that political leaders are trustees who have a special prerogative, indeed a special duty, to take whatever measures are necessary to protect the community.[46] Since trustees can have no more right to act on behalf of their community than the community has to act for itself, this is not the best way of framing the issue. It is more helpful to ask whether the members of a community sometimes have a special prerogative to act in a way other than morality demands. The scope of such "agent-centered prerogatives" is currently of much interest in contemporary moral theory.[47] The justification and scope of such prerogatives is unclear, however. For example, it might be thought that individuals should only be exempt from various "imperfect" or "positive" duties of beneficence that seem too demanding, not from various "perfect" or "negative" duties against harming others. Yet philosophers who have argued for such a prerogative have also attacked these traditional distinctions, opening up the possibility that individuals might have a prerogative of doing some very nasty things to protect their fundamental personal commitments. This view is hard to accept. Yet if the claim that the state may act unjustly in extreme situations can be defended at all, this line of thought may prove suggestive.

The second point about the good life sometimes overriding the moral life is that so far we have discussed this view as a doctrine of justification, not as a doctrine of excuse. In other words, we have been considering the claim that the preservation of the state should sometimes override the demands of morality, not the claim that the state should always observe the demands of morality but may sometimes be excused for not doing so. This latter claim must also be briefly considered, however.

As Michael Walzer has observed, realists often use the term "necessity" in two different ways: certain policies are said to be necessary in the sense of being indispensable means to an end; and certain ends are said to be necessary in the sense of being inevitable or beyond choice.[48] As Walzer also observes, arguments about the indispensability of means often push us back to arguments about the inevitability of ends. But a strong claim of inevitability does not excuse; rather, it denies that moral terms like excuse have any application to our conduct. The question, then, is whether realists sometimes employ the idea of necessity in a third sense that does identify a set of excusing conditions.

According to some theorists, extreme actions are sometimes excused by "moral necessity." Unfortunately, so-called moral necessity is neither moral, since it involves immoral actions, nor necessary, since it involves choice. Nevertheless, we can see the point of using this oxymoron: though it may sometimes be clearly wrong for individuals to take innocent life in self-defense, for example, we might try to excuse such actions by pointing to the immense value of physical survival for most people. As Mill described the individual's claim to physical security: "*Ought* and *should* grow into *must*, and recognized indispensability becomes a moral necessity, analogous to physical, and often not inferior to it in binding force."[49] In some situations, there is a combination of elements that might excuse immoral conduct, namely, great psychological pressure, a partial transfer of responsibility to the attacker who has put the victim in a coercive situation, and the immense value that the victim assigns to his own survival. A similar combination of elements might also explain why the state should at least sometimes be excused for violating principles of morality when collective survival is threatened. Of course, just war theorists and pacifists are unwilling to assign such value to the survival of the individual, let alone of the state. Yet although individuals should not assign this sort of value to their own survival or to the survival of the state, we may be reluctant to blame them, or blame them fully. In choosing to act unjustly, we might say, they only do what anyone but a saint would do. This idea of necessity as a set of excusing conditions does seem to be expressed in many realist writings, although realists have seldom drawn a clear distinction between excuse and justification, much less explored the bearing of this distinction in any careful manner. This is unfortunate, since the idea of excuse might help us reconcile our judgments that certain actions are clearly wrong with our sense that such actions are sometimes necessary. Given a general lack of attention to these issues, it remains an open question whether the idea of necessity as a kind of excuse can be developed in a fruitful way.

Conclusion

According to realism, even internally just states sometimes face genuine moral and practical dilemmas in international relations. Yet realists have historically tended to focus on "the" state or all states, rather than on just states alone. This insistently state-centric emphasis is perhaps the most problematical feature of realism. Yet if just states must sometimes act unjustly in order to preserve themselves, we can see the point of this traditional emphasis on "the" state. The difference between just and unjust states diminishes once we accept the view that even just states must sometimes take the apparently self-contradictory course of acting unjustly abroad for the sake of preserving justice at home. Realism views states primarily from the external perspective of their relations with one another. From this perspective, states should perhaps be blamed for not working harder to achieve a more peaceful world, yet states are currently caught within the state system and should not be unduly blamed for responding to its necessities. Or so the realist argues.

This view tends to make most of us distinctly uncomfortable. Perhaps we should not be in too much of a hurry to refute realism, since a desire for comfort is unlikely to lead to clear thought. In considering the merits of realism, we should probably remember Mill's remark that "it is a far from frequent accomplishment, even among thinkers, to know both sides; and the weakest part of what everybody says in defence of his opinion is what he intends as a reply to his antagonists."[50] On the other hand, perhaps realism is a confused and pernicious view that should be rejected root and branch. Unfortunately, Mill's remark has proven all too true with respect to the critics of realism: realism has often been caricatured by its opponents. Realists have often caricatured other traditions of thought as well. The aim of this volume is to get beyond these caricatures in order to understand what is really at issue between various traditions of thought about the ethics of war and peace.

One caricature to avoid is the widespread view of realism as a doctrine that recognizes no role for morality in international relations. Some realists have taken this extreme position, but this is not the best way of understanding the challenge that realism presents to other traditions of thought. It is better instead to focus on the question of whether it is *always* reasonable to demand that a state be prepared to sacrifice itself for the sake of morality. This is itself an extreme demand; in contrast, realism might argue that it represents a position of moderation in international affairs.[51]

Notes

1. Of course, some realists do claim that there is a moral principle of national survival that entails that states have no right to pursue justice at the cost of security.

2. Thomas Hobbes, *Leviathan*, ch. 13.

3. Karl von Clausewitz, *On War*, ed. Michael Howard and Peter Paret (Princeton: Princeton University Press, 1976), 77.

4. Clausewitz, *On War*, 76.

5. Clausewitz, *On War*, 87.

6. Clausewitz, *On War*, 581.

7. Hedley Bull, *The Anarchical Society* (New York: Columbia University Press, 1977), 185.

8. Robert E. Osgood and Robert W. Tucker, *Force, Order and Justice* (Baltimore: The Johns Hopkins University Press, 1967), 221.

9. Thucydides *The Peloponnesian War* bk. 3, "Civil War in Corcyra."

10. As Ted Koontz explains at the beginning of Chapter 9 below, there are many different ways of understanding nonviolence and pacifism. This section of my chapter focuses on the kind of pacifism that condemns war as a particular kind of violence.

11. Machiavelli, *The Prince*, ch. 15.

12. For an influential presentation of the view that we must give up the state, see Jonathan Schell, *The Fate of the Earth* (New York: Alfred A. Knopf, 1982); for a retraction of much of this view, see Jonathan Schell, *The Abolition* (New York: Alfred A. Knopf, 1984).

13. Kenneth Waltz, *Theory of International Politics* (New York: McGraw-Hill, 1979), 111–13.

14. See Osgood and Tucker, *Force, Order and Justice*, 336–41.

15. For an example of this sort of criticism, see Robert Holmes, *On War and Morality* (Princeton: Princeton University Press, 1989), 159–63.

16. Michael Walzer, *Just and Unjust Wars* (New York: Basic Books, 1977), 8.

17. Yehuda Melzer, *Concepts of Just War* (Leyden: A. W. Sijthoff), 106–8.

18. Michael Howard, *The Causes of Wars* (Cambridge, MA: Harvard University Press, 1983), 16.

19. See Marshall Cohen, "Moral Skepticism and International Relations," in Charles Beitz, Marshall Cohen, Thomas Scanlon, and A. John Simmons, eds., *International Ethics* (Princeton: Princeton University Press, 1985), 8–11.

20. This passage repeats the criticisms of the doctrine of collective security presented by Robert W. Tucker and David C. Hendrickson in *The Imperial Temptation: The New World Order and America's Purpose* (New York: Council on Foreign Relations Press, 1989), 43–52. For a somewhat different critique of collective security, see Richard K. Betts, "Systems for Peace or Causes for War: Collective Security, Arms Control, and the New Europe," *International Security* 17 (1992), 5–43.

21. For some standard criticisms of the idea of the national interest, see Charles Beitz's discussion of Morgenthau in *Political Theory and International Relations* (Princeton: Princeton University Press, 1979), 24–25.

22. Kissinger, for example, offered this sort of rationale for pursuing detente with the Soviets.

23. David Grene, *Greek Political Theory: The Image of Man in Thucydides and Plato* (Chicago: University of Chicago Press, 1965), 90.

24. See Osgood and Tucker, *Force, Order and Justice*, 282–84. Tucker does not use the terms "patriotic" and "liberal" reasons of state and distinguishes these positions in a slightly different way.

25. Lincoln's general respect for civil liberties during the American civil war illustrates how a liberal realist might try to cope with internal political resistance (if one doubts that Lincoln was a "realist," consider his support for the way in which Grant and Sherman waged the war). Nevertheless, Lincoln felt compelled to suspend the writ of *habeas corpus* during the course of the war.

26. For an example of how a contemporary realist might approach the issue of intervention, see Hans Morgenthau, "To Intervene or Not to Intervene," *Foreign Affairs* 45 (Apr. 1967). According to Morgenthau, the United States has intervened "not wisely but too well" (p. 434).

27. G.E.M. Anscombe, *Intention* (Ithaca, NY: Cornell University Press, 1957), 18. Anscombe adopts a view of intention as the answer to a certain kind of "why" question. As she notes, the distinction between intention and motive is sometimes unclear. Here I am following Anscombe in giving an example of what she calls "motive-in-general": "To give a motive of the sort I have labelled 'motive-in-general,'" she suggests, "is to say something like 'See the action in this light.'" But "the question whether the light in which one so puts one's actions is a true light is a notoriously difficult one" (p. 21).

28. Since intentions may change, realists think states must also pay attention to "capabilities." Foreign-policy debates between realists have recently been linked to the intentions/capabilities issue through the introduction of a "democracies are peaceful" thesis. Nixon, for example, called for massive aid to the former Soviet states on the basis of this thesis; Kissinger worried about restoring Russian capabilities.

29. See Holmes, *On Morality and War*, 114–46.

30. Machiavelli, *The Prince*, ch. 8.

31. Joel H. Rosenthal, *Righteous Realists: Political Realism, Responsible Power, and the American Culture in the Nuclear Age* (Baton Rouge: Louisiana State University Press, 1991), 42–46.

32. "The Profession and Vocation of Politics," in Max Weber, *Political Writings*,

ed. Peter Lassman and Ronald Speirs (Cambridge: Cambridge University Press, 1994), 309–69.

33. Reinhold Niebuhr, *The Irony of American History* (New York: Scribner, 1952), 23.

34. Machiavelli, *The Prince*, ch. 3.

35. Osgood and Tucker, *Force, Order and Justice*, 304.

36. Robert W. Tucker, *The Nuclear Debate: Deterrence and the Lapse of Faith* (New York: Holmes and Meier, 1985), 54.

37. For a sample of the recent debate, see *Journal of Medicine and Philosophy* 16 (1991), an issue devoted to the doctrine of double effect. For some criticisms of the doctrine, see Jonathan Bennett, "Intended as a Means," in Sterling McMurrin, ed., *The Tanner Lectures on Human Values* (Cambridge: Cambridge University Press, 1981); and Nancy Davis, "The Doctrine of Double Effect: Problems of Interpretation," *Pacific Philosophical Quarterly* 65 (1984), 107–23.

38. According to some realists, states accept this convention because of its utility. The utility of the convention in turn rests on reciprocity: when one belligerent begins to violate the combatant/noncombatant distinction, other belligerents have less reason to observe it.

39. Authors differ over whether this is a matter of self-defense or self-preservation. For the first view, see Robert Nozick, *Anarchy, State, and Utopia* (New York: Basic Books, 1968), 35; for the second, see Paul Woodruff, "Justification or Excuse: Saving Soldiers at the Expense of Civilians," *Canadian Journal of Philosophy*, supp. vol. 8 (1982), 159–76.

40. Grene, *Greek Political Theory*, 84.

41. Robert E. Osgood, *Ideals and Self-Interest in America's Foreign Relations* (Chicago: University of Chicago Press, 1953), 11.

42. See Gregory Kavka, *Hobbesian Moral and Political Theory* (Princeton: Princeton University Press, 1986), xi–xv, 29–83.

43. It is difficult to formulate this Hobbesian condition precisely. According to James Griffin, "Moral principles must be such that one's believing or accepting them will, conjoined with the threats and inducements that both morality and the facts of human psychology permit, determine action." James Griffin, *Well-Being: Its Meaning, Measurement and Moral Importance* (Oxford: Oxford University Press, 1986), 350 n. 1.

44. Thucydides *The Peloponnesian War* 5.84–116.

45. Reinhold Niebuhr, *Moral Man and Immoral Society* (New York: Scribner, 1932), 83. In his later writings, Niebuhr modified his view that groups were incapable of self-sacrifice. See, for example, *Irony of American History*, 144–45.

46. Machiavelli and Hume have been interpreted as presenting versions of this argument. For this interpretation of Machiavelli, see Beitz, *Political Theory and International Relations*, 21–24; for this interpretation of Hume, see Cohen, "Moral Skepticism and International Relations," 33–50.

47. For the argument that impersonal ethical systems like utilitarianism and Kantianism are too demanding, as well as the suggestion that we may have a prerogative to act against the impersonal point of view, see Bernard Williams, "Persons, Character, and Morality," in Amelie Rorty, ed., *The Identities of Persons* (Berkeley and Los Angeles: University of California Press, 1976). For another ap-

proach, see Samuel Scheffler, *The Rejection of Consequentialism* (Oxford: Oxford University Press, 1982). Scheffler wants to modify consequentialist moral theory to make room for such a prerogative.

48. Walzer, *Just and Unjust Wars*, 8.

49. John Stuart Mill, *Utilitarianism*, 15th ed. (London: J. M. Dent and Sons, 1907), 81.

50. John Stuart Mill, *On Liberty*, in *Utilitarianism, On Liberty, Essay on Bentham*, ed. Mary Warnock (New York: New American Library, 1962), 172.

51. For comments on earlier drafts, thanks to Jackie Colby, David Goldfischer, David Hendrickson, Robert W. Tucker, and Terry Nardin.

CHAPTER 4

Realism, Morality, and War

Jeff McMahan

David Mapel has nicely distinguished the dominant strands of realist thinking on a variety of issues pertaining to the ethics of war.[1] I propose to carry his analysis further, drawing finer distinctions among several possible versions of political realism and indicating how certain common arguments apply to these different versions. This analysis will occupy the first part of the chapter. In the second part, I will examine more closely the idea, common to almost all traditional versions of realism, that there are circumstances in which states cannot be guided by the dictates of morality. I will argue that much of what realists have wanted to claim can be accommodated within a precisely characterized conception of commonsense morality.

My aim, then, is reconciliationist. In comparing different views of the ethics of war, it is important to discover what they have in common as well how they diverge. I will not, of course, try to show what realism has in common with all the viewpoints represented in this volume. I will be seeking a more limited reconciliation between certain strands of realist thought and a conception of morality that is dominant in contemporary Western societies. This conception derives from Jewish and Christian ethics, among other sources, and is neither systematic nor static. As applied to war, it is profoundly influenced by traditional theories of just war developed by Christian moralists and, in particular, by Catholic theorists of natural law. And, at least as applied to war, it is becoming increasingly influential across a wide variety of cultures. During the Gulf War, for example, George Bush and Saddam Hussein appealed to similar moral principles (like the impermissibility of attacking civilians) in criticizing each other's actions and attempting to justify their own. It does not seem overly optimistic to expect that as nations continue to debate the ethics of war, often in order to refine the international law of war, there will be an increasing convergence among the perspectives considered in this book.

Varieties of Realism

Some of the versions of realism I will distinguish may not appear in a pure form in the writings of those usually labeled "realists." They have a certain theoretical tidiness that is often absent in the work of the realists themselves. That should not disqualify them as genuine and interesting versions of realism. For historically, and especially during the twentieth century, what has unified realist writings is not a well-defined theory about the relation between morality and statecraft but a shared set of substantive views about what states are permitted or required to do. The views I will distinguish do, I think, capture this range of substantive views, so that distinguishing among them helps to illuminate the connections between the realists' substantive views and various conceptions of the relation of statecraft to morality.

Two further preliminary points should be made. First, realism is typically formulated as a view of how morality applies to the conduct of states. But nations, whose membership may not coincide with the citizenry of any one state, are also important agents in international affairs. And many nationalists have views about the application of morality to their nations that parallel realist views about morality and the state. Thus, though I shall continue to focus on the state, it is important to note that the versions of realism that I shall distinguish could be recast to take the nation rather than the state as the relevant unit.

Second, realists normally define their position in opposition to morality as they conceive it. Thus each of the views I will distinguish may be interpreted as an account of the conditions under which moral requirements may be disregarded. Yet some realists write not as if they are challenging the authority of morality, but as if they are advancing an unusually permissive conception of morality itself. And indeed, each substantive view I shall distinguish can also be interpreted as a theory of what states are morally permitted to do. I shall refer to these alternative interpretations as the nonmoral and moral interpretations of each view, respectively.

I refer to the most extreme, though by no means uncommon, version of realism as "Strong Realism." Interpreted nonmorally, Strong Realism holds that morality does not apply at all to the conduct of states in their relations with other states (though it may apply internally, to the relations between a state and its citizens). This version of the theory is sometimes supported by arguing that, because morality arises only from relations within a community, and because states inhabit a state of nature in which there is no community, relations among states cannot be governed by morality. Alternatively, some have claimed that the state is an altogether higher and more exalted entity than the individual and hence cannot be bound by the constraints that govern the conduct of individuals.

Interpreted as a moral view, Strong Realism holds that states *ought* to be guided solely by a concern for the national interest in their relations with other states. Various realist arguments might be invoked to support this view—for example, the argument that representatives of the state are morally obliged to do whatever is necessary to advance the interests of the state because they serve as agents who are required to act in behalf of their principals (namely, the citizens of the state).[2] Or it might be argued that the flourishing of the state is the supreme moral value, overriding all others. To support Strong Realism, however, this latter claim must take an agent-relative form. For no version of realism accepts the impartial view that one must do whatever promotes the flourishing of any state or all states. Rather, realism is normally universal in scope, though agent-relative in character: it holds that, for each person, it is only the flourishing of that person's own state that matters. According to some extreme versions of this view, the claim that the flourishing of one's own state is the supreme moral value implies that an individual's moral concern should extend only to the other citizens of his or her own state.[3]

The nonmoral version of Strong Realism has an analogue at the level of individual action—namely, moral skepticism, the view that individuals are not bound by the alleged demands of morality. Even Strong Realists tend to reject this view. More commonly, they claim that if individuals inhabited a state of nature analogous to that which characterizes relations among states, they too would be exempt from the demands of morality. But, since individuals in fact live in civil society, they are subject to the requirements of morality. (It is unclear, however, whether and how this view can accommodate the widely accepted judgment that relations between private citizens of different states are governed by morality.)

Proponents of the nonmoral interpretation of Strong Realism face a formidable task in defending this radical separation of the individual and the state.[4] Suppose that a father must, for whatever reason, intentionally kill an innocent stranger as a means of saving the lives of his wife and children. Can the Strong Realist plausibly claim that, though the state may intentionally kill innocent citizens in other states in order to promote even relatively trivial national interests, the father must obey the moral constraint that forbids the intentional killing of the innocent? It seems that, if the demands of loyalty and partiality are capable of suspending the constraints of morality in the case of the state, then they should also permit or even require the father to save his family, even if this necessitates intentionally killing the innocent. It is unconvincing to claim, as many realists do, that, whereas the state is exempt from the demands of morality, the father is bound by them by virtue of his membership in civil society. If anything, the demands of loyalty and partiality would seem to be *stronger* in the case of personal relations than for the largely impersonal relations among citizens of the same state.

The moral interpretation of Strong Realism also has an analogue at the level of individual action—namely, universalist egoism, the view that each individual ought to do what best promotes his or her own interests. Again, very few Strong Realists accept this view. But, rather than hold that there is a radical difference between states and individuals, the Strong Realist might accept an account of ethics that is compatible with both Strong Realism and the rejection of egoism. According to this view, what morality principally requires is keeping faith with those to whom one is committed by virtue of certain special relationships. Hence the father in the case just cited must save his family even if this requires intentionally killing the innocent. Common membership in a state is also a special relation; hence those who determine how the state shall act must never be led by other considerations, such as impartial concern for human welfare, to sacrifice the interests of the citizens of the state. In both cases, the partiality required by morality may dictate the intentional sacrifice of the innocent.

This conception of morality is, however, quite implausible. Although some special relationships do require loyalty and do legitimize a certain degree of partiality, the degrees of loyalty and partiality that are permitted vary with the character of the relationships—for example, one is permitted a greater degree of partiality toward one's child than toward a casual acquaintance, other things being equal. And even in the case of paradigmatically legitimate special relationships, partiality is constrained in various ways. Thus even if the father in the previous example is permitted to kill an innocent stranger to save his family, there is clearly a limit to the number of innocent strangers he may kill for this reason.[5] It seems wise, therefore, to retreat to a weaker version of realism that recognizes some constraints on the pursuit of the national interest.

At the level of individual action, commonsense morality holds that there are various factors, independent of considerations of consequences, that may contribute to determining the morality of action. Certain of these factors have been thought sufficiently significant to ground strong constraints on action. In particular, it is often held that there is a constraint against doing harm that does not apply to allowing harm to occur, as well as a constraint against intentionally doing harm (or allowing harm to occur) that does not apply to foreseeably but unintentionally doing harm (or allowing harm to occur).[6] As Mapel points out, realists tend to reject the moral significance of the distinctions between doing and allowing and between intending and merely foreseeing, at least in their application to the conduct of states. They are reluctant to recognize constraints based on considerations of agency (often called "deontological constraints") as opposed to consequences.

It is possible, however, to distinguish four positions on the issue of constraints that might be grouped together under the heading "Moderate Realism." (These are not the only possibilities. I am ignoring various less plausible positions.) First, there is the nonmoral view that, though there may be constraints that apply to individuals, states are not subject to these constraints (at least in their relations with one another) because states are relevantly different from individuals. To be distinguishable from Strong Realism, however, this view cannot hold that there are no restrictions whatsoever on the state's pursuit of the national interest. But instead of incorporating constraints based on either the distinction between doing and allowing or that between intending and foreseeing, this view acknowledges a restriction on the degree to which states are permitted to give priority to their own interests over the interests of other states. It holds that the priority of the national interest is not absolute; thus a state may not pursue a course of action if the extent to which it would be worse for other states exceeds by some fixed proportion the extent to which it would be better for the state itself. In short, this view endorses only limited national partiality and thus imposes a proportionality restriction on the amount of harm that a state is permitted to cause in pursuing the national interest.

Second, there is the view that morality itself, properly understood, does not recognize deontological constraints, either in the case of individuals or in the case of states. But morality does depart from consequentialism in allowing agents—individuals and states—to act on the basis of personal or national partiality. Again, however, the degree of permissible partiality is limited.[7]

A third variant of Moderate Realism holds that although moral constraints apply to the conduct of states, these constraints must sometimes yield to the imperatives of the national interest, not only in conditions of extremity or national emergency but whenever the interests of the state are seriously threatened. This third variant is sometimes defended by appealing to a conventionalist conception of morality, according to which it is in the interest of states to agree on and generally to adhere to certain rules or conventions. Since general conformity with the rules facilitates cooperation among states and reduces both the occasions for and the costs of war, each state ought generally to obey the rules in order to encourage reciprocal conformity. Nevertheless, because it is ultimately for reasons of national self-interest that the state gives its allegiance to the rules, it may default when the cost of compliance would be excessive.

A fourth variant holds that, although there are constraints that apply to the conduct of states, morality itself acknowledges that they are not absolute and thus may sometimes be overridden or suspended. Such a view might, for example, recognize the moral importance of loyalty and partiality within the state, allowing such considerations to override certain constraints in cases of conflict. Alternatively, a Moderate Realist who believes that moral constraints are mere conventions might argue that a state is released from its obligations vis-à-vis another state whenever that other state itself fails to comply with the constraint.

Realists often cite examples in which a state's survival would be imperiled if it were to do what morality seems to require. If there really are such cases, they provide the most compelling argument for the view that morality is excessively demanding. Though realists rely on these examples, most also hold that the situations in which a state is exempt from the demands of morality are more common than those in which the state's survival is threatened. Some theorists, however, believe that the requirements of statecraft diverge from those of morality only in conditions of extremity or national emergency, when what morality requires would imperil the continued existence of the state. I will refer to their view as the nonmoral interpretation of "Weak Realism."

There is also a moral version of Weak Realism according to which the constraints of ordinary morality are overridden by the state's duty of loyalty to its own citizens in conditions in which the survival of the state is threatened. Some realists recognize an analogous dispensation that permits individuals to violate constraints when this is necessary for self-preservation or for the preservation of those who are specially related to them (so that, for example, the father in our earlier example would be morally justified in killing the innocent to save his family).

In all these versions of political realism, the implications for what states may or must do with respect to war place realism at odds with morality as it is commonly understood. As Mapel points out, realists have claimed that there are occasions on which states either may or must resort to war in circumstances in which war is prohibited by the principles of *ius ad bellum*. And they have claimed that there are also occasions during war when states either may or must act in ways condemned by *ius in bello* constraints. The conflict between realism and morality, in other words, is between the realist's substantive intuitions and certain features that the realist attributes to morality. The realist view that a state is exempt from the demands of morality may therefore be challenged either by accepting that realist intuitions diverge from morality but arguing that these intuitions are wrong, or by arguing that there is in fact no divergence, since realist intuitions can be accommodated by morality. In the remainder of this chapter, I shall attempt to develop this second challenge. I shall argue that many of the substantive beliefs about war associated with realism are in fact compatible with ordinary morality. The intuitions of some realists diverge from morality only if morality is understood in an overly restrictive or rigid way.[8]

Just Cause and Aggressive War

The traditional doctrine of ius ad bellum encompasses six requirements: just cause, last resort, proportionality, reasonable hope of success, right intention, and competent authority.[9] In his discussion, Mapel focuses largely on the requirement of just cause, noting that realists reject the now common interpretation according to which only those wars fought in defense against aggression can be just. For realists hold that it can be justifiable to engage in a war of aggression—or at least that it can be justifiable to initiate the use of force—particularly when preemptive war, or perhaps even preventive war, is necessary to eliminate a serious threat to the security or survival of the state.

There is, certainly, a tendency among contemporary just war theorists to doubt the permissibility of all but self-defensive wars. But this tendency is more pronounced in the international law of war than it is in the views of moral theorists. Given the pervasiveness of wars of aggression throughout history, it is unsurprising that documents such as the UN Charter seek to achieve a dramatic change by announcing sweeping prohibitions of nondefensive war. Nevertheless, the principles that it is most useful to promulgate through international law do not necessarily coincide with the principles of morality. The latter may be too subtle, too complex, too difficult to enforce, or too likely to cause unnecessary conflict to serve the purposes of international law.[10]

Commonsense morality recognizes just causes for war other than self-defense against unjust aggression. There is, for example, a willingness to acknowledge the moral legitimacy of "humanitarian intervention"—that is, military intervention to stop a government from committing atrocities against its own population.[11] It might be said, of course, that this sort of nondefensive war is not the sort of war that the realist is interested in justifying, since the realist is distinguished by his concern for the national interest, not by his humanitarian concern for individuals in other states. But a war that has as its just cause the prevention of atrocities within another state need not be undertaken solely as an act of altruism. A war can be motivated primarily by a concern to advance the national interest and still be justified, in the same way that it can be justifiable to use force to stop a mugging, even though one may be motivated largely, or even exclusively, by the desire for a reward.

Commonsense morality also recognizes a right in some instances to go to war to redress past wrongs—in particular, to undo the effects of previous unjust aggression. Suppose, for example, that Iraq's invasion of Kuwait had initially gone unopposed and that a protracted occupation had become (as Israel's unjust occupation of the West Bank and Gaza has become) a settled feature of the international landscape. The passage of time and the eventual absence of resistance within Kuwait would have meant that a later war to reverse Iraq's aggression would itself have counted as an instance of initiating a war—perhaps as an instance of aggressive war. But, provided that the desire for self-determination remained strong among the Kuwaitis, it is hard to believe that the passage of time alone could nullify the justice of the cause of upholding the political independence of Kuwait.

Ordinary morality also recognizes that preemptive war, and even preventive war (which differs from preemptive war in that the threat it seeks to avert is temporally more remote), may sometimes be justified. Morality does, of course, assert a strong presumption against both types of war, for two reasons. One is that, just as we believe that a person must be guilty of some offense before it is justifiable to incarcerate him in order to prevent him from engaging in criminal activity in the future, so we believe that a state must normally be guilty of some actual offense before it is justifiable to go to war against it to prevent it from engaging in future aggression. Ordinarily, the offense that makes it permissible to disarm an adversary sufficiently to eliminate the threat of future aggression is actual, present aggression. That is, if a state engages in unjust aggression, it may be permissible to go to war against it, not only to stop the present aggression, but also to disarm it to prevent if from engaging in future aggression. But present aggression is not necessarily the only offense that can make it permissible to take belligerent action to eliminate a threat of future aggression. If, for example, a state is guilty of severe repression of its own citizenry, so that humanitarian intervention in behalf of the persecuted citizens is justified, then, if there is also strong evidence that the state poses a threat of aggression against other states, it may be permissible to continue belligerent action beyond that required to end the domestic repression in order to mitigate or eliminate the threat of future aggression.[12]

The second reason why there is a strong presumption against the permissibility of preemptive or preventive war is that a state's ability to understand the intentions and predict the future behavior of its adversaries is notoriously weak. If we were to permit a state to go to war against an adversary whenever it believed that the adversary would otherwise soon attack it, wars would be forever breaking out on the basis of unfounded fears and suspicions. Nevertheless, when the evidence that aggression will occur unless action is taken to prevent it is compelling and irrefutable, preemptive or even preventive war may be morally justifiable.

How can this conclusion be reconciled with the claim that, for war aimed at preventing future aggression to be justified, the target state must be guilty of some actual offense? There are two possibilities. One is to say that cases involving a near certainty of future aggression constitute exceptions to the claim that an offense is required in order for preemptive or preventive war to be justified. The other is to appeal to an analogy with domestic law. In Anglo-American law, some forms of evidence of future criminal behavior themselves constitute criminal offenses. Thus conspiracy in preparing to commit a certain type of crime is itself a crime. Similarly at the international level, preparations for war that constitute decisive evidence of an intention to engage in aggression may themselves constitute an offense that legitimizes the resort to war as a means of preventing future aggression. An *ex post* variant of this idea was in fact proposed at Nuremberg. It was argued there that the acts of Nazi officials prior to but in preparation for Germany's use of force beyond its borders exposed them to prosecution for the international analogue of criminal conspiracy.[13]

What these observations show is that, though there may be a tendency in international law to prohibit all but purely defensive wars, commonsense morality is not so restrictive. Although it is insufficiently permissive to satisfy the Strong Realist, morality may permit a sufficient variety of nondefensive wars to satisfy the Moderate or Weak Realist.

Proportionality and Last Resort

As usually understood, the ius ad bellum requirement of proportionality holds that, to be morally permissible, a war must not cause expected harm that exceeds the expected good it brings about.[14] Realists typically reject such a requirement. Although they believe that, to be rational, war must satisfy a prudential proportionality constraint (the war must advance, or at least not set back, the national interest), they also believe that a state may be justified in initiating a war that promises more harm than good, impartially considered, provided that the larger proportion of harm is suffered by the adversary whereas the state itself enjoys the larger proportion of benefit.

I believe that morality also rejects this crude conception of proportionality. There are at least two ways in which benefits and harms either may or must be weighted in the proportionality calculation. First, in a choice involving a conflict of interest between those who are morally innocent relative to that choice and those who are morally noninnocent, the interests of the innocent have priority. Suppose, for example, that one state ("Aggressor") is guilty of unjust aggression against another ("Victim"). To the extent that the soldiers fighting in behalf of Aggressor may be considered morally noninnocent, their interests do not weigh against those of either the soldiers or the civilians of Victim in the normal way. If Aggressor's forces are significantly morally culpable for their action, and if killing them is necessary to prevent them from causing significant harm to the morally innocent citizens of Victim (whether civilians or soldiers), their deaths may not figure in the proportionality calculation at all. In these conditions, the interests of the innocent have absolute priority—as they do in certain cases of individual self-defense in which the innocent victim is permitted to kill as many culpable attackers as is necessary to prevent the success of their murderous attack.

This is not to say that harms caused to the noninnocent never count at all in the proportionality calculation. Sometimes they do and sometimes they do not. It depends, among other things, on the degree of their noninnocence, the magnitude of the harm they might suffer, and the magnitude of the harm to the innocent that might be averted by harming them.

The details need not detain us here. The relevant point is simply that harms caused to the noninnocent must often be morally discounted relative to benefits to the innocent; and this allows for the possibility that a war may cause an amount of harm that is greater, when unweighted for moral innocence and noninnocence, than the amount of good it produces (which of course includes the harm it prevents) and still be morally justified.

Harms and benefits may also be weighted for national partiality in determining whether a war would be proportionate. Just as at the level of individual action, there are circumstances in which we are allowed (and perhaps, in some contexts, required) to give greater weight to the interests of those to whom we are specially related and about whom we specially care than to the interests of strangers. States are therefore permitted, at least in some contexts, to assign some degree of priority to the interests of their own citizens over those of the citizens of other states.

The permissibility of weighting harms and benefits for national partiality may depend both on considerations of innocence and noninnocence and on considerations of intention. It is not permissible, for example, to assign priority to the interests of one's own forces if one's cause is unjust and one's forces therefore cannot be regarded as wholly morally innocent. It is also doubtful that considerations of national partiality can affect the morality of intentionally harming morally innocent civilians in another country. Yet it may be permissible, other things being equal, to cause a somewhat greater amount of *unintended* harm to innocent civilians in a country with which one is at war in order to prevent one's own innocent citizens, civilians or soldiers, from suffering a lesser harm.

When both the priority of the innocent and the fact that some degree of national partiality is permitted are taken into account, it becomes clear that the proportionality requirement is much less restrictive than realists have supposed. Morality need not condemn a war that causes more harm than good, provided that the war is fought for a just cause and most of harm caused is suffered by those who are morally responsible for the wrong that the war is fought to prevent or rectify. Again, of course, even this more permissive interpretation will be excessively restrictive for Strong Realists and for many Moderate Realists as well. But some may be surprised to find that, with the refinements I have suggested, the requirement does not in fact rule out certain types of war of which they approve but that they think it condemns.

It is worth pointing out that recognizing the permissibility of a limited degree of national partiality also has the effect of mitigating the severity of the traditional requirement of last resort. A plausible interpretation of this requirement is that war is permissible only if there is no alternative, nonviolent means of pursuing the just cause that would have better expected consequences, considered impartially and taking into account the priority of the innocent. Imagine, however, a case in which there is such an alternative; yet, though both war and the alternative would be costly to the state, the burdens of the alternative would be even greater than the burdens of war. Assuming that there is a just cause, and assuming that the consequences of war would not be too much worse, impartially considered, than those of the alternative, it may be permissible for the state to resort to war rather than to adopt the impartially better nonviolent alternative. For partiality may permit it to spread the costs of achieving the just cause among others rather than absorbing them all itself.

Discrimination

The ius in bello requirement of discrimination has been variously interpreted. Mapel interprets it so that it "forbids intentionally attacking the innocent" and claims that it derives from the more basic Pauline principle that "one may *never* do evil that good may come of it."[15] This suggests that the principle is to be interpreted as an absolute prohibition—one that may never permissibly be violated, whatever the consequences. And indeed, the principle is often interpreted in this way.

At the formal level, the innocent are those who have done nothing to compromise or forfeit their moral immunity to attack. Different substantive conceptions of innocence correspond to different views about what makes a person morally vulnerable to attack or lowers moral barriers to attacking him. In both the just war tradition and international law, the innocent are sometimes said to be those who are not *nocentes*—that is, not engaged in causing harm. This conception of innocence is often referred to as "material innocence" to distinguish it from the more common notion of moral innocence. In the context of war, the materially innocent are usually identified with noncombatants, whereas only combatants are held to be materially noninnocent.[16]

If morality absolutely prohibits intentionally attacking the innocent, if noncombatants are relevantly innocent, and if civilians are noncombatants, then the requirement of discrimination rules out intentional attacks on civilians. Realists, however, typically claim that, in war, circumstances occasionally arise in which it is necessary intentionally to attack civilians. They therefore conclude that, on these occasions, morality must yield to the imperatives of prudence.

Again, however, it is a mistake to think that the realist's substantive intuitions are necessarily incompatible with morality. I shall argue that there are circumstances in which morality permits intentionally attacking civilians. The realist has been led to think otherwise by the fact that the just war tradition diverges from commonsense morality in two respects.

First, commonsense morality is not absolutist. It does, of course, recognize constraints on action that are independent of considerations of consequences, but it allows for the possibility that these constraints may be overridden in conditions of extremity. Thus it can recognize the permissibility of intentionally attacking civilians if the considerations that favor doing so are sufficiently urgent and compelling to be overriding. Yet the presumption against intentionally attacking the innocent in war, though not absolute, is extremely strong. Recall that commonsense morality recognizes two principal constraints on action that affects the innocent: one against *doing* harm and another against *intentional* harming. Both coincide in opposing intentionally attacking the innocent, and the strength of their opposition increases with the magnitude of the harm inflicted, which in war tends to approach the maximum that people are capable of inflicting on one another. So conditions in which the constraint against intentionally attacking the innocent in war may be overridden will be quite rare.

There remains, however, the second respect in which ordinary morality diverges from the just war tradition. Although that tradition holds that it is material noninnocence that compromises a person's immunity to attack, morality recognizes that both moral and material noninnocence may do so—indeed, that the effect of moral noninnocence in lowering moral barriers to intentional attack is clearer and more decisive than that of material noninnocence.[17] Thus there are cases in which material noninnocence alone does nothing to weaken a person's immunity. For example, a murderer has no right of self-defense against a police officer who attacks him to prevent his committing a further murder. Yet, because his action poses a threat of harm, the officer is materially noninnocent vis-à-vis the murderer. By contrast, moral noninnocence—in the form of responsibility for an unjustified threat—seems always to compromise a person's immunity, even when the person is materially innocent. Suppose, for example, that Romulus has maliciously tampered with the brakes of Remus's car. As the brakes fail, Remus realizes what has happened; for, as his car is about to go off the Palatine cliff, he sees Romulus in front of him, jeering triumphantly. Romulus is, however, an extremely large person, and Remus realizes that he can at least slow the car enough to jump to safety by steering it into Romulus. If that is the only way he can save himself, it seems clear that Remus may kill Romulus by running the car into him. But note that, in the relevant sense, Romulus is materially innocent. Although the threat to Remus's life was created by Romulus's past action, Romulus himself is now no part of the threat; hence Remus's running the car into him does not count as an act of self-defense, but rather as an act of self-preservation. Nevertheless, Romulus's moral noninnocence renders him liable; he cannot claim immunity simply by virtue of his material innocence.

This conclusion can be extrapolated to the case of war. It is often true that certain civilians contribute importantly to the initiation of war. In this respect, their relation to the victims of their country's war is analogous to that of Romulus to Remus: they set a threatening sequence in train but are not themselves the agents of the threat. Thus their moral noninnocence may render them liable to attack despite their current material innocence. Suppose, for example, that it is necessary intentionally to attack a certain number of morally noninnocent noncombatants in order to prevent their country's action from killing an equal number of morally innocent people—soldiers fighting in a just war or civilians on the side with the just cause, for example. In these conditions, morality would, it seems, permit attacking the noncombatants.

The case in which it is most obviously permissible intentionally to attack or kill a morally noninnocent noncombatant in war is that in which the assassination of a political leader who bears moral responsibility for his country's unjust aggression would be sufficient to stop that aggression, thereby eliminating the need to kill a large number of that country's soldiers. It might be argued, however, that such a political leader is not in fact materially innocent. Because of his position in the chain of command, he is in fact engaged in causing harm. On this understanding of causing harm, the distinctions between material innocence and noninnocence on the one hand, and noncombatancy and combatancy on the other, do not coincide. The problem with this suggestion, however, is that to separate material noninnocence from combatancy is to clear the way for the classification of a great many civilians as materially noninnocent—for example, the newspaper columnist and orator who effectively propagandizes and raises funds for a campaign of unjust aggression, or perhaps even all the voters and taxpayers who support and pay for the aggression.

Either way, therefore, it turns out that it may be permissible in war intentionally to attack certain civilians. If, on the one hand, we equate material innocence with noncombatancy, then it seems that material innocence is not sufficient for immunity, since morality concedes that certain morally noninnocent noncombatants, like the political leader who initiates an unjust war, may be attacked. If, on the other hand, we accept a broader understanding of causing harm, so that certain noncombatants (politicians, journalists, lobbyists, etc.) may be materially noninnocent, then many civilians will have forfeited whatever immunity is supposed to be afforded by material innocence.

There are, of course, problems with the idea that certain civilians may permissibly be attacked in war. For the constraint against intentional harming is relaxed only with respect to those civilians who are either morally or materially noninnocent. But civilian populations tend to be mixed, containing people who are morally and materially innocent as well as those who are either morally noninnocent, materially noninnocent, or both. And attacks on civilian populations in war normally cannot discriminate among these different groups.

I will not pursue this problem here, though I have done so elsewhere.[18] The important point is that commonsense morality does not, as realists have tended to believe, categorically prohibit all intentional attacks on civilians in war. Again, this will not satisfy the Strong Realist. Nor is it enough to satisfy those Moderate Realists who insist on a wider permission to attack civilians, the morally innocent as well as the morally noninnocent. But it may be enough for some.

Conclusion

If one accepts certain rigid or "moralistic" conceptions of morality—including that which underlies certain elements in the traditional theory of just war—then one may find that many versions of realism seem coherent and manage to avoid being intuitively repellent even though they claim that morality must occasionally be suspended or overridden. If, however, one explores the contours of ordinary morality more carefully, I believe that one will find that it contains subtleties and complexities that allow it to accommodate many of the substantive intuitions that lead some people to embrace realism. In particular, the substantive claims of Weak Realism and some variants of Moderate Realism seem to be compatible with commonsense morality, which is deontological but not absolutist in character. These versions of realism, therefore, may not really be distinctive doctrines at all; they may disappear as versions of realism, leaving only the more extreme versions that clearly diverge from morality. Of these latter, those that diverge from morality only slightly may not seem unreasonable, though they will diverge rather sharply from various rigid or oversimplified perceptions of morality (such as that which underlies the traditional theory of the just war). As the divergence from commonsense morality becomes more pronounced, however, the more extreme versions of realism become inescapably morally repellent, and it becomes more difficult to understand how people can defend them.[19]

Notes

1. David Mapel, Chapter 3 above.

2. This argument is cogently criticized in Marshall Cohen, "Moral Skepticism and International Relations," *Philosophy and Public Affairs* 13 (1984), 300.

3. For a view that verges on endorsing an extreme partiality of this sort, see Alasdair MacIntyre, "Is Patriotism a Virtue?" first published as The Lindley Lecture, University of Kansas, 1984; reprinted in Ronald Beiner, ed., *Theorizing Citizenship* (Albany: State University of New York, 1995).

4. In *Political Theory and International Relations* (Princeton: Princeton University Press, 1979), pt. 1, Charles Beitz argues that Strong Realism collapses into universal moral skepticism.

5. For further discussion, see McMahan, "The Limits of National Partiality," in Robert McKim and Jeff McMahan, eds., *The Ethics of Nationalism* (New York and Oxford: Oxford University Press, forthcoming).

6. I attempt to clarify the nature of the latter constraint in "Revising the Doctrine of Double Effect," *Journal of Applied Philosophy* 11 (1994).

7. See Samuel Scheffler, *The Rejection of Consequentialism* (Oxford: Clarendon Press, 1982). Scheffler is concerned entirely with individual morality, but the theory is easily extrapolated to the level of states.

8. Cf. Cohen, "Moral Skepticism and International Relations," 300 and passim.

9. These requirements and the relations among them are discussed by John Finnis in Chapter 1 above.

10. Compare my "Innocence, Self-Defense, and Killing in War," *Journal of Political Philosophy* 2 (Sept. 1994), sec. 4.1.2.

11. See, e.g., the otherwise strongly anti-interventionist theory developed in Michael Walzer, *Just and Unjust Wars*, 2d ed. (New York: Basic Books, 1992), pt. 2.

12. In "The Just War and the Gulf War," *Canadian Journal of Philosophy* 23 (Dec. 1993), sec. 2, Robert McKim and I argue that the aim of preventing future aggression can normally contribute to the justification for going to war only in the presence of another reason for going to war that by itself constitutes a just cause for war.

13. Telford Taylor, *The Anatomy of the Nuremberg Trials* (New York: Knopf, 1992), 36.

14. Although the restriction is seldom explicitly stated, the goods that weigh against the evils of war must be limited to those specified by the just cause; otherwise the achievement of certain goods would be allowed to count in favor of war when by hypothesis their realization is not part of the justification for going to war. See McMahan and McKim, "The Just War and the Gulf War," sec. 3.2.2.

15. Mapel, Chapter 3 above, emphasis added. Cf. Alan Donagan, *The Theory of Morality* (Chicago: University of Chicago Press, 1977), sec. 5.2.

16. John Finnis, who writes in Chapter 1 above that one "must not intend the death of innocents (noncombatants)," provides a representative discussion of the concept of innocence.

17. See my "Innocence, Self-Defense, and Killing in War," sec. 3; and also Jeff McMahan, "Self-Defense and the Problem of the Innocent Attacker," *Ethics* 104 (Jan. 1994), esp. secs. 2 and 6.

18. McMahan, "Innocence, Self-Defense, and Killing in War," sec. 4.2.3.

19. I am grateful to Terry Nardin and David Mapel for comments on an earlier draft, and to the John D. and Catherine T. MacArthur Foundation and the United States Institute of Peace for supporting my work on this chapter.

PART TWO

Expanding the Dialogue: Judaism and Islam

CHAPTER 5

War and Peace in the Jewish Tradition

Michael Walzer

THERE IS NO JEWISH theory of war and peace, and until modern times, there were no theories produced by individual Jews. Discussions of war and peace indeed find a place, though a very limited one, within the Jewish tradition. One might even say that there is an ongoing argument, and I will try to describe its central features in this chapter. But the argument is at best tangential to, and often at cross-purposes with, the topics proposed for this volume. Jewish writers argued almost entirely among themselves, in the peculiar circumstances of exile, without reference to any actually existing international society with its practices and codes.

It might be better to say that the only references are to the international society of the biblical period, but even these are highly indirect. For the text from which the arguments begin is Deuteronomy 20, written (so we are told by contemporary scholars) in the seventh century in a literary/religious genre that requires the pretense of Mosaic authorship. Hence the wars immediately referred to were fought, if they ever actually were fought, some five centuries earlier; the wars proposed, as it were, for the future had been fought some two or three centuries earlier; and it is impossible to say what impact King Josiah's wars, fought presumably in the lifetime of the Deuteronomist, had on the writing of his text. Present-mindedness is at no point a feature of Jewish writing about war. The crucial categories are rabbinic, but they are drawn from biblical experience and never adapted to the experience of the rabbis themselves. They are meant to explain the wars of Joshua and David. We have to guess at rabbinic attitudes toward, say, the Hasmonean wars or the wars fought by the Persians or the Romans.

In fact, Persian and Roman warfare does not figure in the tradition at all. That non-Jews fought wars, against the Jews and against one another, was a presupposition of the rabbis, the background but never the focus of their own arguments. Prophetic accounts of Assyrian or Babylonian imperialism are never picked up or developed in rabbinic legal discourse, and the crusading warfare of Muslims and Christians, despite its horrifying consequences for Jewish life in the diaspora, is rarely made the subject of critical reflection (it figures in dirges and laments, not in treatises or responsa). The concerns of the rabbis are particularist in the strong sense: they write about the wars that the Jews should or should not, can or cannot, will or will not fight and about the internal decision-making process and rules of conduct relevant to those wars.

But a Jewish war was, for almost two thousand years, a mythical beast. There are no examples; none of the rabbis after Akiba (who may have participated in the Bar Kochba revolt) had any experience of warmaking. This is one of the meanings of exile: Jews are the victims, not the agents, of war. And without a state or an army, they are also not the theorists of war. It might be worthwhile to try to imagine what a full-scale theory of war would look like written from the perspective of the victims, but nothing in Jewish literature comes near to this. What does exist is fragmentary and undeveloped—so much so that any account has to be a construction rather than an analysis. Since the establishment of the state of Israel, there have been a number of constructive efforts, but nothing on a large scale. This much has changed: whereas before 1948, the argument's typical form was that of the commentary—the Jewish version of an "academic" discussion—it now takes a form that resembles that of the legal responsa; that is, the argument now takes a practical form.

So, the literature that I shall be reporting on and explaining is extremely limited in its "real life" references, highly particularistic, and theoretically undeveloped. It is an interesting outcome of their exile that Jewish writers, religious and secular, played an important part in working out the idea of oppression but virtually no part at all in working out the idea of aggression. Their attention was focused on justice in domestic society, where they had an uncertain and subordinate place, not on justice in international society, where they had no place at all.

Conceptions

The Hebrew word for peace, *shalom*, derives from a root that indicates completion, wholeness, or perfection. As the derivation suggests, peace is not the normal state of the world in this historical age. In its fullest sense, it describes the achievement of the messiah (who must fight wars for the sake of this ultimate peace). It is obviously, then, a desirable and much-desired condition. The paean to peace is a fairly common literary genre, though peace among individuals figures more largely in it than political peace; prophetic visions of an end to war among nations, swords beaten into plowshares, are cited in rabbinic writings but not elaborated. *Shalom* also has a more local and immediate meaning, "not-war," as in the biblical command to "proclaim peace"—that is, to offer one's enemy the opportunity to surrender without fighting. Both surrender and victory bring peace, but this is a temporary condition, also associated with the idea of "rest," as in passages like, "And the land rested from war" (Josh. 11:23). One of the longer periods of rest was the reign of Solomon, whose name means peace and who was responsible for the building of the temple, called a "house of rest." David was not allowed to build the temple because he was "a man of war and hast shed blood" (1 Chron. 28:3). But the temple, once built, survived many years of unrest and war. Only the messiah, last of the Davidic line, can bring a permanent peace.

War, *milkhama*, seems always to have the local and immediate meaning, not-peace; it is a generalized term for "battles." There is no articulated conception of a state of war (like that described, say, by Thomas Hobbes and later political realists). But international society looks in most Jewish writing from the prophets onward very much like a state of war, where violence is the norm and fighting is continuous, or at least endemic. After the destruction of the temple, when Israel no longer figures as a member of international society, the sense of danger, of living always under the threat of violence, colors most Jewish perceptions of the gentile world. The idea that all the nations are hostile to Israel even plays a certain justifying role in arguments (entirely academic) about the legitimacy of preventive attacks. But this experience of generalized and prevailing hostility—conceptualized as *eivah*, enmity, and often given as a reason for prudential behavior—doesn't take on theoretical form, as in the contemporary idea of a "cold war."

The Jewish account of types or categories of war deals only with Jewish wars. So far as the rabbis are concerned, it is a theoretical, and in no sense a practical, typology. It is also an incomplete typology, for it has only two categories where three seem necessary. The first category includes all wars commanded by God; the list is very short, drawn from the biblical accounts of the conquest of the land, though it is subject to some modest rabbinic expansion for the sake of the subsequent defense of the land. The second category includes all "permitted" wars, and seems to be a concession to Israel's kings, since the only examples are the expansionist wars of David. These are the wars that disqualified David from temple-building, but they are permitted to him as king. If he fights, he cannot build, but there is no religious ban on fighting.

The missing third category is the banned or forbidden war. It cannot be the case that all wars not required are permitted, for it is fairly clear that there were wars of which the rabbis disapproved. But the disapproval is usually explained with reference to conditions of various sorts imposed on the permitted wars, not with reference to wars that are never permitted. Two kinds of warfare seem indeed to be ruled out by at least some Jewish writers, though without any generalizing argument. The first of these is the war of religious conversion, against which Maimonides may well be writing when he says that "no coercion to accept the Torah and the Commandments is practiced on those who are unwilling to do so."[1] His immediate reference is probably to non-Jewish residents of a Jewish state, not to foreign nations, but the general rule would seem to cover both. What are his sources? I do not know of any explicit rabbinic rejection of the forced conversion of the Idumeans by the Hasmonean king John Hyrcanus—a useful test case.

The second possibly prohibited war is what we might call the war for civilization or against barbarism—in Jewish writings, against idolatry, commonly understood to include all sorts of moral as well as spiritual "abominations." The biblical text on which the relevant discussion is centered is Genesis 34, which describes the campaign of the sons of Jacob against Shechem after the rape of Dinah. This campaign has much else to disrecommend it, but what is of interest here is whether the Shechemites were liable to attack by virtue of their idolatrous culture (even without regard to Dinah's rape). Nachmanides says flatly that "it was not the responsibility of Jacob and his sons to bring them to justice,"[2] and a number of major writers agree with him. There is probably a larger number of writers, including Maimonides (see the section on intention, below), who disagree. In any case, there is no theoretical follow-up to this discussion, and in no classical text are wars of conversion or wars against idolatry identified as forbidden wars.

So the rabbis work with only the two categories, commanded (*mitzvah*) and permitted (*reshut*, also translated as "optional" or "discretionary"). We might best think of these two with reference to monarchic politics, which is the assumed background of most rabbinic writing on military matters. In 1 Samuel 9:19–20, the elders of Israel ask Samuel for a king to "go out before us and fight our battles." The battles that need to be fought are against Midianite and Philistine invaders in defense of "the land of Israel," hence, in rabbinic terms, commanded wars. The "battles of the Lord" (to conquer the land) were the first commanded wars, and the elders' battles (to defend it) were the second. But the rabbis were tough-minded about politics: a king who fights "our battles" will also fight his own—in order, as Maimonides wrote, "to extend the borders of Israel and to enhance his greatness and prestige."[3] These battles are permitted: *his* battles, the price we pay for ours. The rabbis seem to believe that an Israelite king cannot be denied, as a matter either of principle or of prudence, the right to fight for reasons of state and dynasty. They attend instead to the legal conditions constraining the king's decision to go to war. Much of what they say is probably best read as an effort to make his battles, in practice, very difficult to begin or sustain.[4] But they do not prohibit them, or any set of them, and so the more standard dichotomy of just and unjust wars makes no appearance in their arguments.

Attitudes

The realism of the rabbis leads to an acceptance of the normality of war . . . in these days, before the messianic age. But the acceptance is grim. There is no value attached to war or to warriors in rabbinic literature; biblical passages that seem to celebrate military prowess are systematically reinterpreted to prove that "the mighty (*giborim*, also heroes) are none other than [those who are] strong in Torah."[5] Until the appearance of Jewish Nietzscheans in the early years of this century, no one wrote in praise of war. It was probably regarded as a gentile activity "in these days." At the same time, there is no critique of war comparable to the critique of capital punishment, where some of the rabbis are clearly abolitionists. And, although medieval Jews practiced passive resistance, *faute de mieux*, there was no defense of pacifism or nonviolence. The standard view was summed up in the talmudic maxim: "If someone comes to kill you, kill him first" (Sanhedrin 72a). Most of the rabbis assume that this means: you are permitted/enjoined to kill him only if there is no other way to stop him from killing you. But there is little desire to require risk-taking from the innocent victims of attack. This argument about self-defense carries over, as in other traditions, to arguments about defensive (and preemptive and preventive) war—and obviously works against any commitment to nonviolence.

The tradition is abolitionist only with reference to the messianic age. It has to be said that the messiah himself is often described as a warrior-king (though in some versions of the messianic story, God does all the fighting). There really are evil kingdoms in the story, which have to be forcefully overcome. But the messianic war is the classic case of a "war to end all wars," and it is, of course, necessarily successful: if the messiah does not win, he is not the messiah. His victory brings a genuine peace, which is also the perfection of the social world.

Grounds

Here and now, there are indeed grounds for war, though discussion among the rabbis, as I have already said, is focused mostly on procedural issues—the conditions that must be met before the king can actually fight. The immediate ground of a commanded war is the divine command, recorded in the Bible, to conquer the land. The same command is understood early on to include wars to defend the land, and it seems to be extended as well to defensive wars generally (which only means that if a Jewish kingdom were to be established outside the land, its wars of self-defense would also be "commanded"). I do not know of any explicit attempt to include the Maccabean or the Bar Kochba revolt in the category of commanded wars, but they would seem to fall well within the reach of the extended command. It does not follow, however, that every (Jewish) war of national liberation is religiously sanctioned. For the tradition clearly recognizes that God can grant (and at specific times has granted) legitimate power over the land of Israel to foreign emperors. Wars of preemption and prevention are even more problematic: although they are in principle defensive, they seem to be subject to all the conditions attached to permitted wars.

In the absence of a developed conception of prohibited wars, there is no limit to the grounds of permissibility. So far as the king's wars are concerned, any ground will serve, including, as we have seen, the glory of the royal name. Some rabbinic commentators were obviously made uncomfortable by such possibilities, and tried to avoid them by a radical reduction of all permitted wars to a single type. Since the nations of the world were assumed to be permanently hostile to Israel and forever plotting acts of aggression, any war against them, whatever its reasons in the king's mind, served in fact the purposes of prevention: "to diminish the heathen so that they do not come up against them [the Israelites]."[6] This reductiveness is all-inclusive, justifying all imaginable wars. At the same time, it suggests that any writer who holds that there might be nations not forever preparing to attack Israel could criticize (some of) the king's wars. Without the reductiveness, however, Maimonides' wars of expansion and prestige regain their independent standing—legitimate if all the conditions are met.

The clearest statement on preventive and preemptive attacks, and the only one I have found that attempts to distinguish between them, comes from the fourteenth-century sage Menachem Me'iri, who describes two kinds of permitted war: when the Israelites fight "against their enemies because they fear lest [their enemies] attack and when it is known by them that the enemies are preparing themselves [for an attack]."[7] The distinction does not seem to make a practical difference, but it follows from this account, as David Bleich has argued, that "absent clear aggressive design" (or, at least, a plausible fear that such a design exists), no military attack is permitted.[8] On the other hand, Me'iri does not claim here to exhaust the category of permitted war. If the "enemy" cannot be attacked on the assumption that he is preparing an attack of his own, he can be attacked for simpler and grosser reasons, "to extend the borders . . . ," and so on.

Ruling out these latter wars requires a more drastic move, giving up not only the assumption of universal hostility and the idea of "diminishing the heathens" but also the acceptance of monarchic ambition. The crucial text here comes from the hand of an eighteenth-century Italian rabbi, Samuel David Luzzatto, in a commentary on Deuteronomy 20:10–11. Luzzatto is working his way out of the commanded/permitted dichotomy, toward something like just/unjust.

> The text does not specify the cause for a permitted war or [say] whether Israel may wage war without cause, merely to despoil and take booty, or to expand our domain. [But] it seems to me that in the beginning of this section [20:1], in saying "When thou goest forth to battle against thine enemy," Scripture is determining that we may make war only against our enemies. The term "enemy" refers only to one who wrongs us; hence Scripture is speaking only of an invader who enters our domain in order to take our land and despoil us. Then we are to wage war against him—offering peace first.[9]

The repetition of the word "only" (three times) suggests that Luzzatto knows what he is doing, even if he seems to commit himself, imprudently, to fighting only against an invasion-in-progress. I cannot say, however, that he has had many followers within the *halakhic* community. Secular Jews commonly assume that the "Jewish tradition" allows only defensive wars, but the evidence for this is scant.

The more common rabbinic strategy is to retain the broad category of permitted war but to make the wars that fall within this category very difficult to fight. Before they can be fought, the king must meet a set of legal requirements. First, he must get the approval of the Sanhedrin, and he must consult the *urim* and *thumim*—two conditions that are literally impossible to meet in these latter days (and that were already impossible in talmudic times) since the Sanhedrin can no longer be convened and the priestly breastplate through which or on which the urim and thumim delivered their oracles is long lost. (The function of these two is disputed. Presumably, the Sanhedrin debates the legal issues and the urim and thumim foretell success or failure.) Then the king's officers must proclaim the exemptions from military service listed in Deuteronomy 20:5–8, sending home soldiers who have recently built a house or planted a vineyard or betrothed a wife as well as all those who are "fearful and faint-hearted." By the time the early rabbinic commentators finished expanding on this list, the king could count only on his mercenaries: effectively, there can be no conscription for permitted wars.[10] Finally, these royal wars can be fought only after the commanded wars, conquering and securing the land, have been won (God's battles and our battles come before *his*). All in all, permitted wars are only barely permitted; they are not, however, positively ruled out—probably because the Deuteronomic text seems to countenance territorial expansion—that is, military campaigns, against "cities which are very far off from thee" (20:15). Luzzatto deals with these cities by ignoring them, exercising the sovereign right of any commentator to choose his passages. But they seem to loom large in rabbinic consciousness.

Resistance

It is a commonplace of rabbinic thought that illegal commands of the king should be resisted—or at least disobeyed. "If the master's orders conflict with the servant's," says Maimonides, answering a rhetorical question in the Talmud, "the master's take precedence. And it goes without saying that if a king ordered [the] violation of God's commandments, he is not to be obeyed."[11] This is the minimalist position; the talmudic texts seem to require active "protest" against the king, though it is not clear exactly what this means, and there is, as usual, no explicit doctrinal elaboration of the duty involved. Interestingly, the cases, all of them biblical, are each connected to war or civil war: Saul's command to massacre the priests of Nob (in the course of his pursuit of David's rebel band), David's command to send Uriah to his death (in the campaign against Ammon), Joab's killing of Abner and Amasa (in different cases of civil war and rebellion).[12] Discussing the first two of these cases, the thirteenth-century commentator David Kimchi alludes also to what we now call the "superior orders defense"—and seems to acknowledge its possible legal, though not its moral, force:

> Even though it is always the case that "there is no agency for wrong-doing" . . . the case of Uriah is different: the text calls David the killer. Similarly with Saul, who ordered the massacre of the Nob priests—it is as though he killed them. Now it is true that in such a situation one should not execute the king's orders . . . but since not everyone is aware of this or knows how to construe [the relevant texts], punishment falls on the king.[13]

The Talmud also reports a philosophically (or theologically) more interesting discussion of disobedience of the immoral commands of God himself, once again in the context of a military campaign. The biblical starting point is Saul's war against the Amalekites, in which, say the rabbis, expanding on what is reported in 1 Samuel 15, the king refuses the divine command to slaughter the enemy, man, woman, and child (Yoma 22b). "If the adults have sinned," he asks God, "what is the sin of the children?" The rabbinic inventors of this story seem to have a clear sense of the rights of the innocent in war. But they must take God as they find him in the biblical text, even if, as the reply they put in God's mouth suggests, they take him with a touch of irony: "A heavenly voice came forth and said to him [Saul]: 'Do not be excessively righteous!'" There is no irony with kings, however, and no similar compromise. The story continues by reporting that when Saul ordered the killing of the priests of Nob, a heavenly voice came forth and said to him: "Do not be excessively wicked!" The servants of the king, who refused the order, are not charged with too much righteousness.

Challenging God may be excessive (unwise? imprudent? presumptuous? self-righteous?); challenging kings is not. No doubt, a certain aura of divinity attaches to the person of an anointed king, as David says when he lets pass an opportunity to kill Saul; the king's words, however, are human words, not divine commands. They can be refused. But the king himself, presumably because of his anointment, can only be challenged and overthrown with prophetic support. That seems to be the biblical doctrine, and the doctrine of the rabbis too, though they are not greatly interested in such matters. The gentile kings under whose rule they live must be disobeyed, exactly like Jewish kings, if they command violations of God's law (thus the stories in the book of Daniel), but there is no question of overthrowing them. Indeed, the focus of rabbinic literature, as of popular religious writing throughout the Middle Ages, is on martyrdom, not resistance or rebellion.

Modern Zionist writers have sought to reverse this order of interests, celebrating the Maccabean revolt, for example, as a legitimate and heroic military struggle against a foreign ruler.[14] The rabbis are surprisingly reluctant to offer a similar endorsement, even in their own terms: they would presumably describe the struggle as a commanded war (to defend the land and oppose idolatry within it). But they are more concerned to stress God's miraculous intervention (see, for example, the prayer *al ha'nisim*) than to describe the fight itself, more ready to celebrate Hannah and her seven martyred sons than the military heroes of the revolt.

Had the revolt been a "commanded" war, as Zionists would certainly argue (in their terms: just and necessary), everyone would have been obliged to fight: in commanded wars, the Talmud declares, "all go forth, even a bridegroom from his chamber and a bride from her canopy" (Sotah 44b). But none of the rabbis seems to have questioned the formal announcement of the biblical exemptions reported in 1 Maccabees 3:56 (did they know this text or have access to other historical accounts of the revolt?), even though rabbinic doctrine holds that individuals are to be sent home only in permitted (optional) wars.

It is important to recognize that those who return home from such a war are not protesting the war; they just have more important things to do (or they are cowards). What is involved here is nothing like the early modern Protestant idea of conscientious objection. Such an idea might have been developed out of the Deuteronomic exemptions had Jewish commentators been forced, over many years, to face the urgencies of military service. Instead, they merely expand upon the exemptions so as to make it very difficult, as we have seen, for the king to fight his "permitted" wars. Presumably, they would not have wanted to make difficulties for the Maccabees, but there is no engagement at all with such particular questions.

Two expansions of the list of individuals not bound to fight in permitted wars are of special interest. First, people engaged in religiously commanded activities are not required to give up those activities in order to join what will be, after all, a secular struggle. This is the source, or one of the sources, of the exemption of yeshiva students in Israel today (though this exemption can only be claimed by non-Zionists, who do not regard the defense of the present-day state as a "commanded" war). A more radical exemption is suggested by a singular, and until very recently unrepeated, interpretation of the biblical phrase "fearful and faint-hearted." It is a maxim of rabbinic interpretation that doublings of this sort must carry more than one message—since no word in the bible is superfluous. Hence Rabbi Akiba is quoted as saying that whereas "fearful" refers to the coward, "faint-hearted" must rather mean "soft-hearted" and refer to the compassionate. He goes on to argue that even a soldier who is a "hero among heroes, powerful among the most powerful, but who at the same time is merciful—let him return" (*Tosefta*, Sotah 7:14). This passage has been seized upon by modern commentators (particularly in the United States during the Vietnam War) as a possible foundation for a Jewish form of conscientious objection, though not, obviously, one focused on particular wars.[15] The effort suggests what might be done with the available texts, but it does not connect with anything actually done in the past.

Since commanded/permitted does not translate into just/unjust, there is nothing in the Jewish tradition that requires, or even that provides a vocabulary for, a moral investigation of particular Jewish wars. And since for almost two thousand years there were no wars that demanded investigation, and no political arena within which the investigation would be a relevant activity, questions of protest, objection, and opposition arise only marginally and indirectly with reference to the conduct of war, and not at all with reference to its overall character. There is no parallel in Jewish thought to the extensive Catholic discussions about whether individual soldiers should participate in wars they take to be unjust. (Whether they should participate in gentile wars was a question more frequently discussed, but, given the conditions of exile, what the rabbis have to say is self-censored and highly sensitive to the political needs of the communities they represent—not useful, then, for any sort of theory construction.)

Intention

Given the latitudinous ground on which permitted wars may be fought, one would not expect intention to be a central issue in Jewish discussions. It is certainly central to the tradition as a whole, playing its expected part in criminal and civil law, and figuring in what are, from a philosophical standpoint, very interesting discussions of prayer and the fulfillment of religious commands. But no one seems to have taken up the intentions of kings and warriors—except for Maimonides in one very strong, but also very odd, statement in his treatise on the Book of Kings. The statement is odd because its parallels are more easily found, as Gerald Blidstein has argued, "in the literature of crusade and *jihad* than . . . in the Talmud."[16] Maimonides seems to allow only commanded wars (though he has an expansive sense of that category, apparently including within it the war against idolatry—and the immediately following section of his treatise contains the more traditional, also rather expansive, account of permitted wars that I have already quoted). Indeed, only in commanded wars can a singular moral or religious intention be required. The king's "sole aim and thought," says Maimonides, "should be to uplift the true religion, to fill the world with righteousness, to break the arm of the wicked and to fight the battles of the Lord." His warriors are similarly enjoined: they should know that they are "fighting for the oneness of God."[17]

Perhaps Maimonides' purpose here is to rule out wars fought by the king for personal or dynastic reasons (despite his apparent permissiveness later on) and to admonish warriors who think only of plunder and booty. The only legitimate reason for fighting is religious: the elimination of idolatry from the world. I suppose that this can plausibly be described as one of the reasons (in the biblical text, the justifying reason) for the original conquest of the land: were it not for their "abominations," the Canaanites would never have been dispossessed. But the later wars to defend the land—what the elders of Israel called "our battles"—clearly had another reason: they were in no sense religious crusades, and there would have been no need and, presumably, no desire to fight them had Midianites and Philistines remained at home, worshiping their gods as they pleased. Nor were David's wars of expansion crusades: his subject peoples in the north and east were not, so far as we know, denied their idols. So Maimonides can hardly be describing these latter wars. His most likely purpose is to describe the intentions of the future king-messiah and the soldiers who join him. No contemporary wars would come under his purview. Even if he is borrowing from Muslim writers here, it would never have occurred to him that the *jihad* was a commanded war (but did he secretly admire the spirit with which it was fought?). In any case, by stressing the religious motives of the messiah, he is arguing against any kind of Jewish (national) triumphalism. The messiah will not fight so "that Israel might exercise dominion over the world, or rule over the heathens."[18] Intentions that may (or may not) be acceptable in the permitted wars of premessianic kings are clearly unacceptable in the days to come.

This is probably the best place to say a word about non-Jewish wars, like the jihad to which I have just referred. These are obviously not commanded wars; whether any of them are permitted is a matter of dispute among the rabbis. According to the Talmud (Sanhedrin 59a and Rashi's comment), wars of conquest against Jews and non-Jews alike are simply lawless, fought without authority or right—though these wars may nonetheless play a part in God's world-historical design. Even when they do, however, Jewish writers have nothing good to say about them. The rabbis acknowledge God's sovereignty but criticize the intentions of his gentile agents. The argument begins in the work of the prophet Isaiah, who recognizes God's hand in the wars of the Assyrians. The Assyrian king is "the rod of [God's] anger," sent into battle and charged to administer divine punishment.

> Howbeit he meaneth not so;
> Neither does his heart think so;
> But it is in his heart to destroy
> And cut off nations not a few.
>
> (Isa. 10:7)

So God's purposes are achieved, but the Assyrian king gets no credit for what he does, since his reasons are his own, aggressive and brutal. A post-biblical version of the same argument can be found in the talmudic tractate *Avodah Zara* (1a and b), where Roman and Persian imperialists claim before the heavenly court that their conquests brought peace to the world and freed Israel for the study of Torah. God replies, "All that you have done, you have only done to satisfy your desires"—and goes on to list the economic and political benefits they derived from their wars. But these examples should not be taken to suggest that the rabbis held some doctrine according to which wars could never rightly be fought for the sake of such benefits. Israelite kings fought for similar reasons, without embarrassment or (explicit) condemnation.

Conduct

Perhaps the surest sign of good intentions in war is restraint in its conduct. In the Jewish tradition, the moral necessity of restraint seems to have been widely assumed, but it is not so easy to find clear arguments. The rabbis labor, of course, under the burden of the biblical command to exterminate the Amalekites and the seven Canaanite nations. They cannot explicitly repudiate the command (though King Saul is allowed, as we have seen, to challenge it), but they do succeed first in limiting it and then in permanently bracketing it, so that it has no present or future application. The limiting argument, drawing on biblical texts and midrashic elaborations, is that these peoples are to be killed only if they persist in their abominations, not as a punishment for past behavior. If they abandon idolatry, they must be allowed to live in the land alongside the Israelites (they cannot be forced to adopt the religion of Israel). Nachmanides says flatly that many Canaanites did abandon their idols, and that is why, as the Bible makes clear, they survived in the land—still there, in fact, in the time of Solomon.[19]

The bracketing argument is probably best understood as a precaution against the messianic future, when Israel would come again into the land. Would it be bound to slaughter the inhabitants? No, says Maimonides, drawing on a text from the Mishna (*Yada'im* 4:4)—written, to be sure, with a different, though not unrelated, purpose: "Sennacharib came and put all the nations in confusion." Hence it is no longer possible to identify Amalekites or Canaanites, and so although in principle they are still subject to the ban (*herem*), in practice the ban is ineffective. I take this to mean that Maimonides, and presumably many of his predecessors, were not ready to countenance wars of extermination. But, again, he does not say that; nor do they.[20]

There is an alternative strategy to this uneasy engagement with the biblical text: to ignore entirely the commanded wars against the Amalekites and the seven nations of Canaan. And this may be the more direct path to a general argument for military restraint. The Alexandrian philosopher Philo, who is the first Jewish writer to make the general argument, addresses himself only to the biblical passages dealing with what the rabbis called permitted wars—though he writes without reference to, and presumably without knowledge of, the commanded/permitted dichotomy. Deuteronomy 20:13–14 holds that when a city has been conquered, "thou shalt smite every male thereof with the edge of the sword: But the women, and all the little ones, and the cattle, and all that is in the city, even all the spoil thereof, shalt thou take unto thyself." Philo's first interpretive move is to separate the women and children (all the commentators agree that "little ones" includes male children, up to arms-bearing age, despite the previous sentence) from the "spoil" or legitimate booty of war. He says simply that they must be spared. And then he gives the crucial reason:

> When [the Jewish nation] takes up arms, it distinguishes between those whose life is one of hostility and the reverse. For to breathe slaughter against all, even those who have done very little or nothing amiss, shows what I should call a savage and brutal soul.[21]

I doubt that this argument played much of a part in the great anti-Roman revolts of 68 and 132 C.E. But when the Jewish nation next "took up arms," in the 1930s and 1940s, Philo's distinction was incorporated into the official doctrine of the armed forces. The Zionist political leaders and publicists who defended *tohar ha'neshek*, purity of arms, claimed to be drawing upon the ethical teachings of the Jewish tradition as a whole. But when they argued that the use of force was only "pure" if it was directed specifically and exclusively against armed enemies, it was Philo, too hellenistic and too philosophical to play much of a part in the tradition, whose work they were echoing. The rabbis themselves have no such (explicit) doctrine. Why is it that we think them committed to humanitarian restraint? Why were the modern theorists of "purity of arms" so sure that theirs was the natural, with-the-grain reading of the tradition?

In fact, the tradition is rather thin, for the usual reason: there were no Jewish soldiers who needed to know what they could and could not do in battle. The law against murder would no doubt rule out direct attacks upon civilians, but the issue does not seem to have arisen (after the biblical period) until very recent times. Indirect attacks and unintended or incidental civilian deaths figure even less in the tradition. The only extended discussion by a major figure comes from the hand of Judah Loew of Prague, writing in the sixteenth century about the biblical encounter of Jacob and Esau (*Gur Aryeh* on Gen. 32:18).[22]

The argument begins from another rabbinic interpretation of a biblical doubling: "'Then Jacob was greatly afraid and distressed.'—R. Judah ben R. Ilai said: Are not fear and distress identical? The meaning, however, is that [Jacob] was afraid lest he should be slain and distressed lest he should slay [others]."[23] Loew takes Jacob's concern to be with the men accompanying Esau, since Esau himself was assumed to be an enemy whose obvious intention was to kill Jacob (so it would be lawful to "kill him first"). But perhaps Esau's men had been coerced to join his forces; perhaps they had no intention of participating in the attack. Loew concludes that Jacob would not be acting unlawfully to kill them in either case since, by accompanying Esau, they had taken on the guilt of his enterprise. Nonetheless, he is respectful of Jacob's scruples, and the whole passage suggests that it would indeed be a sin to kill innocent people, even in the course of a legitimate military engagement. The suggestion remains only that, however; it is not yet a developed argument, and it stands in the literature more as the resolution of a biblical difficulty than as a firm declaration of military policy. I am inclined, then, to accept with only minor reservations Bleich's claim that "there exists no discussion in classical rabbinic sources that takes cognizance of the likelihood of causing civilian casualties in the course of hostilities legitimately undertaken as posing a halakhic or moral problem."[24]

And yet the rabbis did deal fairly extensively with the law of sieges, in which this issue arises in paradigmatic form, and they seem to have written, if not with an explicit recognition of "a halakhic or moral problem," at least with the fate of the besieged civilians very much in mind. They may have won their reputation here, for their argument, picked up by Grotius, survived as the radical alternative to the standard version of international siege law.[25]

This is Maimonides' summary (based on a second-century teaching recorded in the *Sifre* to Numbers): "On besieging a city in order to seize it, we must not surround it on all four sides but only on three sides—thus leaving a path of escape for whomever wishes to flee to save his life."[26] Of course, a city surrounded on only three sides is not in fact surrounded. If people can leave, then the food supply inside the city can be stretched out, perhaps indefinitely; or other people can enter, bringing supplies and reinforcements. It is hard to see how the city could ever be taken given this rule, which seems clearly designed for the sake of the inhabitants, not of the army outside, though this is ostensibly a Jewish army. Nachmanides, writing a century after Maimonides, strengthened the rule and added a reason: "We are to learn to deal kindly with our enemy."[27] It is enemy civilians who are treated kindly here, for the ordinary or four-sided siege is a war against civilians. The radicalism of the Jewish law is that it pretty much abolishes siege warfare. But there is no acknowledgment of this, and other legal discussions (see Nachmanides on Deut. 20:19–20) assume the legitimacy of the siege and evince little concern with its impact on the civilian population.

Maimonides also proposes a general rule against the sorts of violence that commonly follow upon a successful siege: anyone "who smashes household goods, tears clothes, demolishes a building, stops up a spring, or destroys articles of food . . . transgresses the command *Thou shalt not destroy*."[28] This sort of thing the tradition is fairly clear about, and the clarity may help, again, to account for its reputation. What is missing is any analysis of underlying principles (like Philo's distinction between individuals whose life is one of hostility and all others) and any casuistic applications. These discussions have no cases—even the biblical cases are largely unmentioned. What, for example, would Maimonides have said about the prophet Elisha's call for an all-out war against Moab (2 Kings 3:19): "And ye shall smite every fenced city . . . and shall fell every good tree, and stop all wells of water, and mar every good piece of land with stones"? This sounds like an easy case, except that Elisha's advice could not easily be denounced. And how would besieged civilians fare when really hard choices had to be made, when the capture of the city was held to be militarily urgent or necessary?

Debate about such questions in contemporary Israel has not yet produced a major theoretical statement. A number of rabbis have criticized the official "purity of arms" doctrine, writing as if it were an alien ideology (secular, Kantian, absolutist) and demanding a relaxation of its ban on the killing of enemy civilians.[29] The critics do not argue that enemy lives are worth less than Jewish lives, for at least with regard to protection against murder, the tradition is basically egalitarian. Their argument seems to follow instead from a deep suspicion, learned in the centuries of exile and probably better remembered among religious than secular Jews, about the extent of the enmity of the others. Nor is the enmity—this is the concrete fear that goes with the generalized suspicion—reliably confined to soldiers; civilians, too, wait and plan to do us harm.

But if this argument has traditionalist roots, it is also very close to all the (secular, anti-Kantian, permissive) arguments that have been worked out in every contemporary nation whose soldiers have fought antiguerrilla or counterinsurgency wars. The guerrilla is hidden among the people, who thus become complicitous in his struggle; or he hides himself and is thus responsible for the civilian deaths we cause when we try to find and attack him. Anyway, war is hell: "For that is the nature of war," wrote Rabbi Shaul Yisraeli after the Kibiyeh incident in 1954, "that in it the innocent are destroyed with the wicked."[30] There exist both secular and religious responses to these arguments, but none of them seems to me specifically or in any strong sense Jewish. The resources of the tradition have not yet been fully mobilized and brought to bear in this (highly politicized) debate.

Extremity

Jewish discussions about overriding the law or setting it aside in wartime emergencies have focused on religious rather than moral law—sabbath observance above all. The first arguments took place during the Maccabean revolt when Jewish soldiers, attacked on the sabbath and refusing to fight, were massacred by their enemies (1 Macc. 2:32–38). Subsequently, a general decision was made to pursue the military struggle without regard to the sabbath laws. Josephus reports further debates and a similar decision some two centuries later during the Roman war. The rabbis endorsed these decisions, without any specific reference to them, on the grounds of "saving lives." The law was given, they argued, so that we might live by it, not die by it (Sanhedrin 74a). But to this general rule, they made three exceptions: Jews were to accept death rather than violate the laws against idolatry, murder, and incest. If noncombatant immunity rests on the second of these, then it would appear to be safe against emergency. Soldiers cannot deliberately take aim at and kill innocent people to save themselves or even to save the community as a whole. This would at least seem to be the Jewish position, though I do not think it has ever been stated with explicit reference to a military crisis.

All other prohibitions are probably subject to suspension in wartime emergencies: the rules against surrounding a city on four sides, for example, or cutting down fruit trees, or destroying property, can be overridden for the sake of "saving lives" (the Jewish version, perhaps, of military necessity). These prohibitions apply to both commanded and permitted wars, but they apply differently. Commanded wars must be fought even if it is known in advance that the prohibitions will have to be violated in their course, whereas permitted wars are permitted only if it is reasonable to assume that violations will not be necessary. The halakhic principle here is that one should avoid deliberately putting oneself in a position where it will be necessary (and permissible) to break the law. This is the only link that I know of in the Jewish tradition between ius ad bellum and ius in bello: in the case of permitted wars, one must think about how the fighting will be conducted before one can rightly begin it. But once the fighting has actually begun, there is no link at all. The rule about "saving lives" operates whatever the grounds of the war, and murder (now that it has become impossible to identify Canaanites and Amalekites) is everywhere and always ruled out.

Concluding Note

The clearest need in the tradition that I have been examining is to find some way to a comprehensive and unambiguous account of legitimate and illegitimate, just and unjust, warmaking. Would a category of "prohibited" wars open the way? Such a category would be symmetrical with "commanded" and "permitted," but who, at this late date, could issue the prohibitions? Commanded wars are specifically commanded by God, at least in the original cases, but he is not known to have announced any specific (or general) prohibitions. Nor, however, is he known to have commanded defensive wars; there is no record of such a command in the biblical texts. So, in principle, there could be prohibited wars of aggression in the same style as the commanded wars of defense—derived through interpretation and *s'vara* (common sense, reasonableness). And commands and prohibitions of this sort might also plausibly be "given" to Jews and Gentiles alike, in contrast to the original command, given to Israel alone. But would these divine commands and prohibitions be, in any sense, authentically *divine*? I cannot answer that question. Perhaps it is better to argue that after the original command, no longer operative, these matters are "not in heaven"—everything else is human work, though still carried on within a religious/legal tradition.

The category of "permitted" wars is well worth preserving, since it answers to certain difficulties in the just/unjust schema. Some just wars seem almost to be "commanded," that is, the goods at stake (the survival of the political community, say) seem urgently in need of defense. *They should be defended*, unless the defense is utterly hopeless, in which case the principle of "saving lives" might justify appeasement or submission. But some just wars are clearly "optional." They can rightly be fought, in response to some small-scale aggression, say, but political compromise, even if its terms are unjust, is also a permitted choice. Or, similarly, in the case of preemption: it is obviously permitted, though it may be imprudent, to wait for the enemy attack.

The hardest questions arise in the case of third parties in wars of aggression: they would be justified in coming to the rescue of the victim nation, but are they "commanded" to do that? International law recognizes a right of neutrality, a right that, for obvious reasons, makes many just war theorists uneasy. The issue is not taken up in classical Jewish texts—though individuals in analogous cases in domestic society are not permitted to "stand by the blood of [their] neighbor" (Lev. 19:16).[31] Might states have rights that individuals do not? A theory with three, rather than only two, possibilities at least facilitates the arguments that this question requires. So, once the category of prohibited wars is recognized and elaborated, it would be useful to divide the remaining wars into two kinds: those where the moral assumption is that they *should* be fought, and those where such an assumption is either weak or nonexistent (they *can* be fought). (It also seems plausible to suggest that exemptions from combat make more sense in wars of the second kind than in wars of the first kind.) Permitted wars are the king's wars in the sense that they depend upon a political decision, and so we ought to take an interest, as the rabbis did, in the complexities of the decision-making process.

A similar argument can be made with regard to the conduct of war, where there exists an urgent need to elaborate a full account of noncombatant immunity—a concept frequently intimated in the tradition, but nowhere developed—and to repudiate the moral nihilism of "War is hell." And in both these cases, with reference to the conduct and the classification of war, it is time to work the argument through and refine it out of a much larger number of examples than the Bible offers. After all, the Jewish encounter with war, in one form or another, reaches far across time and space: the Hasmonean wars, the Roman wars, the Crusades, the Christian conquest of Spain, the two world wars, and the Arab-Israeli wars. If the tradition is to serve contemporary uses, it must address itself to the full range of Jewish experience.[32]

Notes

1. Maimonides, *Mishneh Torah: Book of Judges*, trans. Abraham M. Hershman (New Haven, CT: Yale University Press, 1949), Kings 8:10.

2. Nachmanides, *Commentary on the Torah: Genesis*, trans. Charles B. Chavel (New York: Shilo, 1971), 419 (Gen. 34:13).

3. Maimonides, *Book of Judges*, Kings 5:1.

4. So argues Donniel Hartman, "The Morality of War in Judaism," *S'vara* 2, 1 (1991), 20–24.

5. *The Fathers According to Rabbi Nathan*, trans. Judah Goldin (New York: Schocken, 1974), 101.

6. See the argument on Maimonides, Kings 5:1, in *Lehem Mishneh*, a commentary on Maimonides' *Mishneh Torah*, untranslated; it is quoted in David Bleich, "Pre-emptive War in Jewish Law," *Tradition* 21, 1 (Spring 1983), 8–9.

7. *Bet ha-Behirah*, Sotah 43a. *Bet ha-Behirah* is a commentary on the Talmud, quoted in Bleich, "Pre-emptive War," 11–12.

8. Bleich, "Pre-emptive War," 12.

9. Luzzatto's biblical commentaries are not translated; Menachem Lorberbaum brought this text to my attention.

10. For a theoretically sophisticated account of the exemptions, see Geoffrey B. Levey, "Judaism and the Obligation to Die for the State," *AJS Review* (Journal of the Association of Jewish Studies) 12 (1987), 175–203.

11. Maimonides, *Book of Judges*, Kings 3:9.

12. I follow here the argument of Moshe Greenberg, "Rabbinic Reflections on Defying Illegal Orders: Amasa, Abner, and Joab," *Judaism* 19, 1 (Winter 1970), 30–37.

13. Kimchi, commentary on 2 Sam. 12:9, quoted in Greenberg, "Rabbinic Reflections," 35–36.

14. Anita Shapira, *Land and Power: The Zionist Resort to Force 1881–1948* (New York: Oxford University Press, 1992), 14 and passim.

15. For example, Samuel Korff, "A Responsum on Questions of Conscience," Rabbinical Court of Justice, Boston 1970 (mimeo).

16. Gerald Blidstein, "Holy War in Maimonidean Law," in Joel Kraemer, ed., *Perspectives on Maimonides* (Oxford: Oxford University Press, 1991), 209–20.

17. Maimonides, *Book of Judges*, Kings 3:10.

18. Maimonides, *Book of Judges*, Kings 12:4.

19. Nachmanides, *Commentary on the Torah: Deuteronomy*, trans. Charles B. Chavel (New York: Shilo, 1976), 238–41 (Deut. 20:10).

20. Maimonides, *The Commandments*, trans. Charles B. Chavel (London: Soncino, 1967), 200–201 (Positive Commandment 187).

21. *Philo*, Loeb Classical Library (London: Heinemann, 1940), vol. 8, "The Special Laws," 4.225.

22. This text was brought to my attention by Noam Zohar. The *Gur Aryeh* has never been translated into English.

23. Loew, *Midrash Rabah: Genesis*, trans. H. Freedman (London: Soncino, 1983), 2: 702 (Gen. 76:2).

24. Bleich, "Pre-emptive War," 19.

25. Hugo Grotius, *The Law of War and Peace*, trans. Francis Kelsey (Indianapolis: Bobbs-Merrill, 1963), bk. 3, ch. 9, sec. 14 (pp. 739–40).

26. Maimonides, *Book of Judges*, Kings 6:7.

27. Quoted in Maimonides, *The Commandments*, app. 1 to the Positive Commandments, 263.

28. Maimonides, *Book of Judges*, Kings 6:10.

29. See, for example, the responsum of Shimon Weiser, "The Purity of Arms—An Exchange of Letters," in David Hardan, ed., *The Moral and Existential Dilemmas of the Israeli Soldier* (Jerusalem: World Zionist Organization, 1985), 84–88.

30. Shaul Yisraeli, "The Kibiyeh Incident in Halakhic Light," *Torah and State*, vols. 5–6 (Tel Aviv, 1954), in Hebrew. But see also "After Kibiyeh," in Yeshayahu Leibowitz, *Judaism, Human Values, and the Jewish State* (Cambridge, MA: Harvard University Press, 1992), 185–90.

31. See the symposium on the talmudic discussion of this passage (Sanhedrin 73a) in *S'vara* 1, 1 (1990), 51–73.

32. I wish to express my thanks to Noam Zohar, who provided advice and support at every stage in the writing of this chapter.

CHAPTER 6

Prohibited Wars in the Jewish Tradition

Aviezer Ravitzky

Michael Walzer's chapter presents a comprehensive picture of the status of war, its limitations, and its manner of conduct, as reflected in central trends of the Jewish tradition. The chapter clearly explains the implications of the unique situation that has generated most of the relevant rabbinic literature—namely, a situation of exile (*galut*), in the absence of a sovereign Jewish state, in which Jewish communities had no political or military impact on international society. But Walzer's discussion also reveals possibilities immanent in the classical religious sources—even if what these sources have to say on the subject is partial and fragmented—for developing a contemporary Jewish ethic of war.

The sources in question, however, are in the nature of things quite diverse. They have been composed by representatives of many schools, both of *halakhah* and of Jewish thought, spanning the centuries from ancient times to the modern period and the contemporary State of Israel. Any generalization regarding these sources would therefore be open to criticism and unable to encompass all the manifold alternatives developed over the generations. This is all the more true when one is dealing with so crucial an issue as that posed in Walzer's discussion: just and unjust wars.

Types of Prohibited Wars

According to Walzer, Jewish religious tradition has not developed a concept of prohibited war. It distinguishes, indeed, between an "obligatory war" and an "optional war," imposing many restrictions upon the latter, but "it has only two categories [of war] where three seem necessary. . . . The missing third category is the banned or forbidden war." True, Walzer points out, Samuel David Luzzatto in the eighteenth century proposed such a view, but he did not have "many followers within the *halakhic* community." Walzer concludes by suggesting the need to formulate a clear halakhic distinction between permitted and prohibited wars, between legitimate and illegitimate warfare.

It seems to me, however, that one may point to several conceptions of forbidden war that have already been developed within the traditional halakhic community. Most of these were explicitly formulated only in recent generations, but all are based upon earlier Jewish sources and accept the religious authority of these sources.

Against What Kind of an Enemy May One Wage War?

According to one important halakhic approach, the permission to attack in war can only be applied against those nations which transgress the "seven Noahide commandments"—those minimal religious-ethical demands that make man human (according to Jewish religion). Civilized peoples, whose members refrain from bloodshed, incest, idolatry, robbery, and the like, are *ab initio* protected from any attack by a Jewish army.

Maimonides ruled: "One does not wage war against any human being, whether in an optional war or an obligatory war, until one calls for peace."[1] True, Maimonides' concept of "making peace" with an enemy includes political subjugation[2] as well as accepting the seven Noahide commandments. But what is the rule in the case of those nations which have long lived according to the universal religious-ethical code, and have not accepted it only from fear of war? "According to Maimonides . . . one is not allowed to make war against those who had previously fulfilled the seven commandments."[3] Thus states the "Hazon Ish" (Rabbi Avraham Yeshayahu Karelitz), the leading rabbinic figure of ultra-orthodox Jewry in prestate Palestine. Note that the traditional Jewish view conceives idolatry as directly connected with general ethical corruption. Maimonides excluded Muslims from the rubric of idolaters, and the thirteenth-century rabbi Menahem Hameiri likewise excluded Christians from this category.[4] Against whom then, according to the present view, would a Jewish army be allowed to wage an aggressive, discretionary war?

Furthermore, Rabbi Avraham Isaac Kook, the first chief rabbi of Palestine (d. 1935), believed that, already in ancient times, when the Sanhedrin was called upon to decide whether or not to allow the king to launch an optional war, a decisive criterion was the degree of ethical corruption of the potential enemy: "The matter was given over to the Court to examine the moral condition of those idolaters" against whom the king sought to declare war, "since not all [idolatrous] phenomena are alike."[5] That is to say, according to the former restriction (that of the Hazon Ish), a war against a civilized nation is forbidden a priori; whereas according to the latter restriction, that of Rabbi Kook, even a war against a pagan nation that is not utterly decadent, though not categorically prohibited, will also be ruled out by the Sanhedrin.

For What Ends Is It Permitted to Wage War?

Needless to say, Jewish law permits defensive wars, that is, wars "to deliver Israel from an enemy that attacks them."[6] Maimonides describes this kind of war as an obligatory one that does not need the approval of the Sanhedrin; all are called to participate in it, "even the bridegroom from his chamber and the bride from her canopy."[7] The same holds true regarding the biblical wars against the Canaanite and Amalekite peoples. But what of a war in order to conquer the Land of Israel in the present historical time? And what of a war of expansion intended "to augment the greatness and reputation" of a Jewish king? Can one point to halakhic writings that have developed a prohibited norm regarding such wars as well?

Nahmanides (writing in the thirteenth century) was the first to establish the commandment of conquering the Land of Israel as a formal, independent commandment, binding subsequent generations.[8] But what is the nature of this obligation of "conquest"? Nahmanides presents it as a permanent commandment, applicable to every Jew even during the time of exile. Did he mean to demand of his contemporaries that they declare private holy wars against the rulers of the land? Did any of the many sages who endorsed this approach over the generations approve such an option? In point of fact, halakhic language has always recognized a concept of "conquest" carried out, not by military means, but by collective settlement. Some authorities, among them Rabbi Shaul Yisraeli, a scholar of the highest authority among contemporary religious Zionists, have therefore claimed that in this case, too, one is not speaking of "a commandment of conquest through war, but of settling and inheriting the land." The commandment of military conquest was "of a singular nature. It referred to the time of Joshua only, where the master of the prophets [Moses] [had] himself expressed an explicit command." But no such command is applicable after that time.[9]

The question arises whether, if one is not in fact *commanded* to conquer the land in war, one is *permitted* to do so. Rabbi Nahum Rabinowitz, head of the Maaleh Adumim Yeshiva, is a leading spokesman for the prohibitory position. According to his interpretation of the tradition, there is no legitimate "conquest" of the Land of Israel save by "permitted means, and warfare *is not permitted to us* unless enemies threaten to attack or do attack" (that is, unless it is a case of either a preventive or a defensive war). Indeed, Rabinowitz infers from Nahmanides' text that even the biblical command to Joshua to conquer the Land of Israel by war reflected a deficient state of affairs, a temporary fate that befell the people of Israel as a punishment for their sins. One does not find in Nahmanides' writings, however,

> any basis for concluding that war is permitted [in the present era] for the sake of conquest of the Land. What is worse, such a reading entails indifference towards bloodshed. Such indifference undermines the very foundations of society and endangers the entire enterprise of the beginning of our redemption.[10]

Of course, not everyone will accept this interpretation of Nahmanides' teaching, even though it is based upon a careful analysis of the source.[11] In any event, this reading of Nahmanides reveals an additional possible aspect of the idea of prohibited war in Jewish tradition. As mentioned, the biblical command to wage war against the inhabitants of the Land is conceived here as being a consequence of sin. Similarly, Rav Kook in his day saw these biblical wars as a result of sin. Were it not for that,

> the nations who dwell in the land would have reconciled with Israel. . . . No war would have needed to have been conducted, and the [spiritual] influence of Israel would have emanated peacefully, as in the future Days of Messiah. . . . It was sin which caused [the realization of] this hope to be postponed for thousands of years.[12]

Already in the fourteenth century, Gersonides had argued that in the last days the people of Israel will inherit their land "in a manner that will not involve warfare."[13]

But what of the permitted wars of the kings of Israel? Did not Maimonides, as Walzer writes, permit an aggressive war of expansion by the king (at the advice of the Sanhedrin) only in order to augment the king's "greatness and reputation"? Not necessarily. "An optional war is not, God forbid, one which may be initiated arbitrarily or on the basis of purely pragmatic reasons," says Rabbi Aharon Lichtenstein, head of the yeshiva in Alon Shevut. "Launching an optional war requires deliberation, . . . ethical no less than political. . . . The decision should be guided by value considerations also, which even if not rooted in explicit *halakhot*, are obligatory as the law of conscience." The royal goal of the war may be political, but "the justification for the war" confronting the Sanhedrin cannot ignore the "ethical plane" (as we already found above in the remarks of Rav Kook).[14] As Yaakov Blidstein has remarked, the demand for an ethical justification of the optional war corresponds to the positive connotation of the term "optional" in Geonic literature.[15]

Moreover, Maimonides negates *ab initio* any secular activity on the part of a king—*any* king—that is not ultimately directed toward the religious and ethical perfection of the world ("to uplift the true religion, to fill the world with righteousness, to break the arm of the wicked, and to wage the battle of the Lord").[16] Here, according to many readings, an opening existed to introduce the demand for value considerations on the part of the king himself, considerations that restrict and overrule his practical goals.[17]

Is It Permissible to Conduct a War That Causes the Enemy Indefinite Losses?

According to one halakhic tradition, one may not conduct an aggressive war in which one anticipates killing more than one-sixth of the enemy. The Babylonian Talmud states: "A kingdom that killed one in six is not punished."[18] Who are these casualties? According to the interpretation offered by R. Samuel Edels (Maharsha) in the seventeenth century, this refers to enemy casualties during an optional war![19] In other words, if the casualties among the enemy reach the ratio of "one out of six," the Jewish king "is not punished"—but if the war causes the death of more, he *is* punished. It is superfluous to note that such a proscription against warfare causing large-scale death is particularly significant in light of the modern development of weapons of mass destruction. In the words of R. Moses Sofer (the Hatam Sofer), writing in the nineteenth century, "The king does not have the right to destroy an entire human genus."[20] Rabbi Yehudah Gershuni, a distinguished contemporary halakhic scholar, interprets this prohibition as applying not only to discretionary or "permitted" wars, but even to wars of self-defense. The prohibition is inapplicable only with regard to the biblical holy war launched against Amalek and the Canaanite nations.[21]

Prohibited War in Contemporary Rabbinic Discussion

The new Israeli reality brought in its wake a radical reinterpretation of the question of the limitations on wars. According to this new approach, the point of departure of the halakhah is that war as such is forbidden in principle: "For in every war there are two apprehensions: that one will be killed and that one will kill. . . . Both are related to violations of Torah."[22] Consequently, a special religious sanction (*heter*) is required in order to conduct any war, and in present times such concrete permission cannot be warranted save in the case of a clearly defensive war. From this point of view, we may find an interesting answer to the question of why Jewish tradition has developed only two categories (that is, optional and obligatory war) when a third category (prohibited war) seems necessary. The prohibition is the starting point for any specific discussion; it is the given norm, and only against this general background was it possible to develop two particular concepts of commanded and permitted war.

"There are *three kinds of war*," writes Rabbi Yehudah Shaviv:

> *prohibited war*, optional war, and obligatory war. The *halakhah* details the latter two cases only. It does not need to speak about the first, as any war which does not belong to the latter two is by definition prohibited: such a war involves

> the prohibition of bloodshed. For if an individual is prohibited by the Torah to spill the blood of another individual, how much more so for a people to spill the blood of another people![23]

Other rabbis have also made explicit statements about this question. For example: "Apart from the obligatory war, commanded to Moses by the Almighty, and the [optional] war conducted according to the counsel of the Great Sanhedrin, any war is prohibited"![24] These authoritative figures, like those mentioned above, are therefore likely to provide a direct answer to Walzer's question: "But who, at this late date, could issue the prohibitions [against 'prohibited war' . . . since God] is not known to have announced any specific (or general) prohibitions?"

Moreover, Rabbi Shaul Yisraeli makes the claim that the very halakhic force of the concept of permitted war is drawn from the conventions of war accepted among the nations.

> War is one of the means of solving disputes between one people and another. Only in our generations do they exert effort that war should be recognized as unlawful, but the generation is not yet ready and the nations are not prepared to enter into a mutual agreement of this sort.[25]

This is indeed a problematic approach, for if one assumes that warfare would be prohibited were it not for the existence of an international consensus, how can a general agreement make it permitted? Does a universal consensus to violate a religious or ethical prohibition (such as bloodshed) cancel the prohibition? One could support this argument, however, by the principle of self-defense. That is, it is not the consensus itself that renders warfare permissible, but its destructive consequences, the universal violence and aggression expressed by or stemming from it. As Rabbi Kook writes: "Regarding the question of war: at a time when all of their neighbors were literally desert wolves, it was utterly impossible for Israel alone to refrain from fighting; for then their enemies would gather together and Heaven forbid destroy all of our remnant."[26] In any event, may one not conclude that, should international conventions and behavior alter, the halakhic permissibility of engaging in voluntary wars will likewise change, without any need for new religious legislation?

Divine Authority and Human Response

Professor Walzer has drawn our attention to the problems involved in the need to obey an immoral divine command. He mentions the talmudic story about King Saul, who refused to carry out the command to destroy Amalek: "If the adults have sinned, what is the sin of the children?"[27] was Saul's question. As we know, the divine reply was, "Do not be excessively good." The human ethical protest receives no legitimization. But other midrashic sayings have exploited the Scriptures precisely to defend the status of an ethical opposition to war, conferring full legitimation upon that opposition. I will cite two such examples.

Midrash Tanhuma (*Zav*, ch. 3) states:

> You find that the Holy One, blessed be He, negated His edict for the sake of peace. When? At the moment that the Holy One said to Moses: "When thou besieged a city a long time" [Deut. 20:19], the Holy One told him to destroy them. . . . But Moses did not do so, but said, "Shall I now go and smite he that has sinned and he that has not sinned? Rather, I shall come to them in peace." . . . [Only] when the enemy did not come in peace, he beat them. The Holy One blessed be He said: "I said, 'You shall utterly destroy them' [Deut. 20:17], and you [at first] did not do so. By your life, as you said, so shall I, as is said: 'When thou comest nigh unto a city to make war against it, then proclaim peace unto it'" [Deut. 20:10].

That is to say, Moses, like Saul, lodged a moral protest against the command to smite innocent people. This time, however, the human protest not only received divine recognition, but was eventually given constitutional, legislative status, regulating the halakhah for future generations. From now on, "When thou comest nigh unto a city to make war against it, then proclaim peace unto it."

A similar response is related of another ideal figure, that of the messiah (*Midrash Tehillim*, 120):

> "I am for peace, but when I speak they are for war" [Ps. 120:7]. What is the meaning of "I am for peace"? Thus said the Holy One blessed be He to the Messiah: "Smash them with a rod of iron" [Ps. 2:9]. He said to Him: "Master of the Universe, no! Rather, I shall begin to speak to the nations with peace." Therefore it is said: "I am for peace, etc."

In these texts, the human conscience is granted an autonomous status vis-à-vis the divine imperative. Perhaps this is the difference between Moses and the messiah, on the one hand, and Saul, on the other: because God could not have answered the former, "Do not be overly wicked" (as in the talmudic story attributed to the latter), He could not have pushed them away with the ironical answer, "Do not be overly righteous."[28]

In any event, the tradition allows room for human ethical response even regarding obligatory war. It therefore should not be surprising that in the course of time, Rabbi Yitshak Aramah, a fifteenth-century Spanish sage, would come to argue that the commandment given by the Torah to proclaim peace does not simply refer to a formal call for the surrender of the enemy. Rather, it requires

> entreaties and supplications offered in the most conciliatory possible way, in order to turn their hearts . . . *for this follows necessarily from the human wisdom of peace, and the Divine will consent.* . . . For if we find that He commanded "You shall not destroy its tree [that is, that found in the city of the enemy], to lift against it an axe" [Deut. 20:19], all the more so should we take care not to commit damage and destruction to human beings.[29]

God invited, so to speak, the human initiative against warfare, and it is this initiative that underlies the primal notion of the "prohibited war" in halakhah—that is, any war in which one does not initially call for peace.

Spiritualization of War and Peace in the Jewish and Christian Traditions

Because of the historical situation of the Jews in their exile, Jewish sources tended to concentrate more on historical, theological, and anthropological reflections about war than on ethical guidelines for wartime. Jews speculated about the reasons leading mankind to take up the sword and asked whether war represents given human nature or a decline in that nature, but they were less concerned with the immediate political and practical questions concerning warfare.

Nevertheless, did Jews, rabbis included, really have no experience of warfare throughout the period of exile, as Walzer suggests? In the nature of things, such a generalization also has several interesting exceptions. For instance, many Jews in Spain were active in assisting the Muslim conquerors and later served as a home guard. In later generations as well, some of them were in the habit of bearing arms, to be involved in wars and to protect their cities. The best-known example is that of Rabbi Samuel ha-Naggid, the commander of the army of the kingdom of Granada, a warrior and officer whose military experience is preserved in poetry. Some Ashkenazic sages likewise report the battles fought by persecuted Jews against the Crusaders. Rabbi Solomon b. Samson depicted in a colorful way the army of the community of Mayence, who "wore armor and girded their weapons, from old to young,"[30] and rose up against their enemies. Rabbi Eleazar ha-Rokeah told of "an occasion when many great armies laid siege to the city of Worms on the Sabbath, and we permitted all the Jews to take up their weapons."[31] He portrays the heroes of Israel as feudal lords girding iron weapons. Even if we may doubt the accuracy of some of these claims, weight must be given to the self-consciousness and self-image regarding the fighting Jew.

Hence, among both Sephardic and Ashkenazic medieval sages, one occasionally encounters admiration of the Hasmonean rulers and their military accomplishments; Rabbi Abraham ibn Ezra, for example, writes of "the king Judah son of the Hasmoneans who was a warrior, whose hand was strong against the Hellenists, [even though] at the beginning he had neither wealth nor horses."[32] Rabbi Abraham ibn Daoud[33] in Spain and Rabbi Eliezer of Beaugency[34] in Franco-Germany express similar sentiments.[35]

These were the exceptions, however. Throughout the course of Jewish history, the wars of the Gentiles belonged to concrete historical reality, and that reality was the Jews' involuntary lot. The wars of Israel, in contrast, were a matter more for theology than for politics. They took place in scripture, either in the distant past or in the messianic era, in the distant future. The Jew waged concrete war against the evil inclination more than he did against any historical foe. Peace, too, was discussed primarily from a utopian perspective, in light of the biblical vision of the End of Days, and it, too, belonged mainly to the theological realm.

Thus, the course of history set the Jewish scholars an exegetical challenge that was the opposite of that faced by their Christian counterparts.[36] In the postbiblical Jewish sources, we find a distinct trend toward spiritualizing scriptural passages dealing with war, might, and the sword. The "sword and bow" mentioned in the Bible (Gen. 48:22; Ps. 44:7) are in fact "prayer and beseeching."[37] The "soldier and warrior" and "those who repel attacks at the gate" in the Book of Isaiah (3:2; 28:6) are not warriors in the literal sense, but "those who know how to dispute in the battle of the Torah."[38] The sword of the mighty is the Torah.[39] The generals of the Bible were transformed into scholars and heads of the Sanhedrin,[40] and even "David's warriors" (2 Sam. 23:8) were none other than manifestations of the might of his spirit "as he took part in the session [of scholars]."[41] This tendency to spiritualize scriptural verses dealing with might and war is prevalent throughout the aggadic (as opposed to the halakhic)[42] homiletical literature, and reappears in new and different guises in the philosophical and mystical literature of the Middle Ages: these verses are interpreted in the former as referring to the struggle between different faculties of the soul,[43] and in the latter as referring to divine attributes.[44]

There is a most illuminating converse parallel to the tendency we have described in the Christian exegesis of New Testament passages. Christianity started with a pacifist message. This message was expressed in several passages in the New Testament, particularly in the Sermon on the Mount, and it was as pacifists that the early Christians were depicted in their own time.[45] Later on, however, when Christianity had become the religion of the Roman empire, it developed the doctrine of the "just war." Augustine, the chief spokesman for this doctrine,[46] buttressed his arguments by citing sayings of the prophets in their literal, original senses; the pacifist verses in the New Testament, however, had to be given a new, nonliteral interpretation. Here, too, this was done by way of spiritualization—not, however, of texts that called to battle, but of those that rang with pacifism. The latter were interpreted as referring to man's inner state, to the depths of his spirit, and not to concrete historical reality.[47] Such was the way of a faith that had recently entered the political arena and become a power, in contrast to that of a faith long absent from that same arena.

A third stage in the Christian theory of war developed in the Middle Ages—that of the holy war, as manifested in the Crusades.[48] This, too, has a partial converse parallel in the development of Jewish tradition. The Jewish collective memory indeed recalls the biblical commandment to wage a holy war against the seven Canaanite peoples. The rabbinic sources had, however, neutralized this commandment with respect to the present and future day.[49] (Note also the story regarding the messages of peace sent by Joshua to the land's inhabitants.) Therefore, according to Maimonides, the notion of an obligatory war can refer today only to war waged to "deliver Israel from an enemy that attacks them"; this may be compared with the Christian concept of the "just war," but not with that of the "holy war."

The Zionist revolution has restored the Jewish people to the international arena and granted it political and military power. It has also fused national and religious motivations. Jewish religion has been called upon to demonstrate whether the process undergone by other cultures under these conditions has been an inevitable, deterministic one. That is, it remains to be seen whether the balance will now move from "just war" to "holy war" or, conversely, toward a sharper distinction between a just war of defense and prohibited war.

Notes

1. Maimonides, *Mishneh Torah, Hilkhot Melakhim* 6.1.

2. Cf. Shlomo Goren, *Meshiv Milhamah* (Jerusalem, 1986), 3: 259.

3. Yeshayahu Karelitz, *Hazon Ish: Be'urim ve-Hiddushim 'al ha-Rambam*. Printed in Maimonides, *Mishneh Torah* (Jerusalem, 1957), *Melakhim* 5.1.

4. Expressions of this approach already appear among the Tosaphists. See Jacob Katz, *Halakhah ve-Qabbalah* (Jerusalem, 1986), 291–310.

5. Rav A. I. Kook, *Iggerot ha-Re'ayah* (Jerusalem, 1966), 1: 140. Cf. Yehudah Amital, "The Wars of Israel According to Maimonides" [Heb.], *Tehumin* 5 (1987), 461.

6. Maimonides, *Mishneh Torah, Melakhim* 5.1.

7. Mishnah, Sotah 8:7; Maimonides, *Mishneh Torah* 7:4.

8. Ramban, *Hasagot 'al Sefer ha-Mizvot la-Rambam* (printed in Maimonides' *Sefer ha-Mizvot*), *Mitzvot 'Aseh she-hishmit ha-Rambam*, no. 3. For a detailed discussion, see Shaul Yisraeli, *Erez Hemdah* (Jerusalem, 1957), nos. 1–2; M. Z. Nehorai, "The Land of Israel in the Teachings of Maimonides and Nahmanides" [Heb.], in M. Halamish, ed., *Erez Yisrael be-Hagut ha-Yehudit bimei ha-beinayim* (Jerusalem,

1991), 129–36; Aviezer Ravitzky, *'Al Da'at ha-Maqom: Mehqarim be-Toldot he-Hagut ha-Yehudit* (Jerusalem, 1991), 42–46.

9. Shaul Yisraeli, "In Answer to a Query," in *Af Sha'al: Mizvah min ha-Torah?* (Jerusalem, 1978), 4; also Yisraeli, *Erez Hemdah*, no. 1. Rabbi J. J. Reines, the founder of the Religious Zionist movement, likewise advocated a stand unequivocally opposed to the conquest of the Land of Israel by warfare. However, his position was based upon the oath taken by the people of Israel (according to the Talmud and Midrash) that they would not rebel against the gentile nations during their period of exile! *Or Hadash 'al Zion* (Vilna, 1902), 18; also Rabbi Samuel Mohliver, *Sefer Shivat Zion* (Warsaw, 1900), 1: 9. This approach is deeply rooted within Jewish literature. It depends, however, not upon ethical but upon theological considerations, which go beyond the scope of our present discussion. Cf. Bahya ben Asher, *Perush 'al ha-Torah* (Jerusalem, 1958), to Gen. 32:7; R. Isaiah Horowitz, *Shenei Luhot ha-Berit* (Jerusalem, 1963), 3: 48. See the appendix to my book, *Messianism, Zionism and Jewish Religious Radicalism* (Chicago, 1995).

10. Nahum Rabinowitz, "The Approach of Nahmanides and Maimonides to the Commandment of Inheriting the Land" [Heb.], *Tehumin* 5 (1984), 184.

11. See, for example, the comment of Rabbi Yaakov Ariel, *Tehumin* 5 (1984), 174–79.

12. Rav A. I. Kook, *Orot* (Jerusalem, 1976), 14. Cf. the commentary of Rashi on Deut. 1:8.

13. R. Levi Gersonides, *Perush la-Torah*, to Deut. 7:9.

14. Aharon Lichtenstein, "Human Ethics and Divine Ethics" [Heb.], *'Arakhim be-Mivhan Milhamah* (Alon Shevut, 1982), 18. Cf. Yaakov Blidstein, *'Eqronot medini'im be-mishnat ha-Rambam* (Ramat Gan, 1983), 216–20.

15. Blidstein, *'Eqronot medini'im*, 220 n. 18. See the remarks of R. David Bonfil (thirteenth century): "It is not just to steal the portion of other nations; God did not give Israel their land save for the fact that it was in the hands of the Canaanites, who did not themselves merit it." *Hiddushim 'al Sanhedrin, ed. Lifschitz* (Jerusalem, 1968), to b. Sanh. 91a.

16. Maimonides, *Mishneh Torah*, *Melakhim* 4.10. Compare the above-mentioned papers by Rabinowitz (note 9) and Amital (note 5); also J. Blidstein, "Holy War in Maimonidean Law," in J. L. Kraemer, ed., *Perspectives on Maimonides* (Oxford, 1991), 209–20.

17. According to one interpretation of Maimonides, he permitted a deterrent war, not a war for expansion alone. See R. Abraham de Boton, *Lehem Mishneh* (printed in standard editions of Maimonides' *Mishneh Torah*), to *Melakhim* 6.1. Cf. Efraim Inbar, "War in Jewish Tradition," *Jerusalem Journal of International Relations* 9 (1987), 86–87.

18. *B. Shevuot* 35b.

19. Maharsha (R. Shmuel Edels), *Hiddushei Halakhot va-Aggadot*, ad loc. Cf. Naftali Zevi Berlin's Torah commentary, *Ha'amek Davar* (Jerusalem, 1984), to Gen. 9:5; Deut. 20:8.

20. Moshe Sofer, *Hatam Sofer* (Vienna, 1865), 1: 208; cf. Yehudah Shaviv, *Bezir Avi'ezer* (Alon Shevut, 1990), 102; Yosef Ahituv, "The Wars of Israel and the Sanctity of Life" [Heb.], in Y. Gafni and A. Ravitzky, eds., *Qedushat ha-Hayyim ve-Heruf ha-Nefesh* (Jerusalem, 1992), 263.

21. Yehudah Gershuni, "On Boundaries and on War" [Heb.], *Tehumin* 4 (1983), 59.

22. Amital, "The Wars of Israel According to Maimonides," 460.

23. Shaviv, *Bezir Avi'ezer*, 85 (emphasis added).

24. Rav Shlomo Zevin, *Le-or ha-Halakhah* (Jerusalem, 1978), 10.

25. Shaul Yisraeli, *'Amud ha-Yemini* (Tel-Aviv, 1966), 77. Cf. Ahituv, "The Wars of Israel and the Sanctity of Life," 265.

26. Rav Kook, *Iggerot ha-Re'ayah*, 1: 140. In the halakhic realm as well, Rav Kook understood the permission to shed blood in war as a temporary measure; see *Mishpat Kohen* (Jerusalem, 1966), 153–54. For this reason, all of the opinions presented in this section draw extensively upon him. Rav David Fraenkel, the great nineteenth-century exegete of the Jerusalem Talmud (author of *Qorban ha-'Edah*), linked the permissibility of war to the halakhic requirement that one protect an individual being pursued: if the Torah commanded one to save him from his pursuer, and in the absence of other options even permitted one to inflict mortal harm to the pursuer, how much more so to save an entire nation! See *Sheyarei Qorban* on *J. Sotah* 8:10; cf. Shemaryahu Arieli, *Mishpat ha-Milhamah* (Jerusalem, 1972), 13.

27. *Babylonian Talmud, Yoma* 22b.

28. Of course, this distinction is also related to the demonic image of Amalek and the commandment to obliterate him.

29. Yitzhak Aramah, *Aqedat Yizhaq*, nos. 81, 105.

30. A. M. Haberman, ed., *Gezerot Ashkenaz ve-Zorfat* (Jerusalem, 1960), 30, 97.

31. Eleazar ha-Rokeah, *Sefer ha-Roqeah* (Jerusalem, 1960), *Hilkhot 'Eruvin* nos. 196, 85.

32. R. Abraham ibn Ezra, Commentary to Zech 9:9–16.

33. Abraham ibn Daoud, *Divrei Malkhei Bayit Sheni* (Mantua, 1514), 62.

34. Eliezer of Beaugency, Commentary to Haggai 2:7–9.

35. The late historian H. H. Ben-Sasson reveals many interesting facts of this type in "The Singularity of the People of Israel According to Twelfth-Century Scholars" [Heb.], *Peraqim* 2 (Jerusalem, 1969), 166–68, 177, 214–16.

36. The following remarks are based upon my article "Peace in the Jewish Tradition," in A. Cohen and P. Mendes-Flohr, eds., *Contemporary Jewish Religious Thought* (New York, 1987), 691–92.

37. *Targum Onqelos* to Gen. 48:22; *Tanhuma*, *Beshalah*, ch. 9; cf. *Mekhilta de-Rabbi Yishma'el* 14.10; *Babylonian Talmud, Baba Batra* 123a.

38. *Babylonian Talmud, Hagigga* 14a; *Babylonian Talmud, Megilah* 15b.

39. *Midrash Tehillim* 45.4.

40. *Yalqut Shim'oni* 2: 141.

41. *Babylonian Talmud, Mo'ed Katan* 16b; Cf. Shlomo Goren, "Heroism in Jewish Teaching" [Heb.], *Mahanayim* 120 (1969), 7–13; Reuven Kimelman, "Nonviolence in the Talmud," *Judaism* 17 (1968), 316–34; D. S. Shapiro, "The Jewish Attitude towards Peace and War," in L. Jung, ed., *Israel of Tomorrow* (New York, 1946), 220ff.

42. Goren, "Heroism in Jewish Teaching."

43. See, for example, R. Ya'akov Antoli, *Malmad ha-Talmidim* (Lyck, 1866), fols. 22b, 31b, 85b; Moses Ibn Tibbon, *Perush 'al Shir ha-Shirim* (Lyck, 1874), fol. 14b, etc.

44. See, for example, Joseph Gikatilla, *Sha'arei Orah*, pts. 3–4 (interpretation of the name *zeva'ot*).

45. See G. F. Nuttal, *Christian Pacifism in History* (Oxford, 1958); John Ferguson, *War and Peace in the World Religions* (London, 1977), 101–22 and the extensive bibliography on 122–23.

46. Augustine *De civitate Dei* 19; see also the studies by L. B. Walters, *Five Classical Just-War Theories* (Hartford, CT, 1971), and J. B. Hehir, "The Just-War Ethic and Catholic Theology," in T. A. Shannon, ed., *War or Peace* (New York, 1980), 15–39.

47. See F. H. Russell, *The Just War in the Middle Ages* (London, 1977), 16–39; cf. Walters, *Five Classical Just-War Theories*, 61–62; Nuttal, *Christian Pacifism in History*, 106 (on parallels in Aquinas).

48. On the revival of the holy war approach among seventeenth- and eighteenth-century Protestants, see Michael Walzer, *The Revolution of the Saints: A Study in the Origins of Radical Politics* (London, 1966), 270ff.; Nuttal, *Christian Pacifism in History*, 115–16; and John Hick, "Christian Doctrine in the Light of Religious Pluralism," *International Religious Foundation Newsletter* 3 (1988).

49. See *M. Yadayim* 4:4; Maimonides, *Sefer ha-Mizvot, Mizvat 'Aseh*, no. 187; cf. Mordecai ha-Kohen, "Peace and the Wars of Israel" [Heb.], *Halakhah va-Halikhot* (Jerusalem, 1975), 180–203.

CHAPTER 7

War and Peace in Islam

Bassam Tibi

ISLAM IS A SYSTEM of moral obligations derived from divine revelation and based on the belief that human knowledge can never be adequate. It follows that believers must act on the basis of Allah's knowledge, which is the exclusive source of truth for Muslims. Ethics in Islam, though concerned with man's actions, always relates these actions to the word of God as revealed to the Prophet, Muhammad, and as collected in the Qur'an. This understanding of ethics is shared by all Muslims, Sunni or Shi`i, Arab or non-Arab.[1]

In this chapter, I first identify the Qur'anic conceptions of war and peace that are based on this ethical foundation. I then consider several Islamic traditions pertaining to the grounds for war, the conduct of war, and the proper relation of Islam to the modern international system. I conclude that the Islamic worldview is resistant to change and that there are many obstacles to the development of an ethic of war and peace compatible with the circumstances of the modern age.

The basic scriptures of Islam, the Qur'an and the Hadith, are written in Arabic. My effort here to understand Islamic thinking on war and peace focuses on the Qur'an and on interpretations of Islamic tradition in contemporary Sunni Islam. Because the most important trends in Sunni Islam have been occurring in the Arab world (all Sunni Muslims are, for example, bound by the *fatwas* of the Islamic al-Azhar university in Cairo), my references to the Arabic Qur'an, to the teachings of al-Azhar, and to authoritative sources for Islamic fundamentalism reflect not Arab centrism but the realities of Islam.

CONCEPTIONS OF WAR AND PEACE

The Qur'an chronicles the establishment of Islam in Arabia between the years 610 and 632 A.D. In early Meccan Islam, before the founding of the first Islamic state at Medina, in a Bedouin culture hostile to state structures, one fails to find Qur'anic precepts related to war and peace. Most Meccan verses focus on spiritual issues. Following their exodus (*hijra*) from Mecca in 622, the Prophet and his supporters established in Medina the first Islamic political community (*umma*). All Qur'anic verses revealed between

622 and the death of the Prophet in 632 relate to the establishment of Islam at Medina through violent struggle against the hostile tribes surrounding the city-state.

Most debate among Muslims about the Islamic ethics of war and peace is based on literal readings of the Qur'anic verses pertaining to early Medina. Muslims believe in the absolutely eternal validity of the Qur'an and the Hadith (the sayings and deeds of the Prophet). Muslims believe that human beings must scrupulously obey the precepts of the Qur'an. In addition, Muslims are generally reluctant to take a historical view of their religion and culture. Quotations from the Qur'an serve as the point of departure for discussions of war and peace.[2]

Qur'anic traditions of war are based on verses related to particular events. At times, they contradict one another. It is not possible, therefore, to reconstruct from these verses a single Islamic ethic of war and peace.[3] Instead, there are a number of different traditions, each of which draws selectively on the Qur'an to establish legitimacy for its view of war and peace.

The common foundation for all Islamic concepts of war and peace is a worldview based on the distinction between the abode of Islam (*dar al-Islam*), the "home of peace" (*dar al-Salam*) (Qur'an, Jon. 10:25), and the non-Muslim world, the "house of war" (*dar al-harb*).[4] This distinction was the hallmark of the Islamic system before the globalization of European society and the rise of the modern international system.[5] In fact, however, the division of the world in early Islam into the abode of peace and the world of unbelievers clashed with reality long before the intrusion of Europe into the Muslim world. Bernard Lewis, for example, argues that by the Middle Ages, the dar al-Islam was dismembered into a "multiplicity of separate, often warring sovereignties." Lewis also holds that "in international . . . matters, a widening gap appeared between legal doctrine and political fact, which politicians ignored and jurists did their best to conceal."[6] As we shall see, this refusal to come to terms with reality remains a hallmark of Islamic thought today.

The establishment of the new Islamic polity at Medina and the spread of the new religion were accomplished by waging war. The sword became the symbolic image of Islam in the West.[7] In this formative period as well as during the period of classical Islam, Islamic militancy was reinforced by the superiority of Muslims over their enemies. Islamic jurists never dealt with relations with non-Muslims under conditions other than those of "the house of war," except for the temporary cessation of hostilities under a limited truce.

The military revolution that took place between the years 1500 and 1800 signaled the start of modern times and, ultimately, the rise of the West and the concomitant decline of the world of Islam. Since the beginning of the seventeenth century, Muslims have tried to establish armies on the European model to offset the increasing weakness of the "abode of Islam."[8] The rise of the West as a superior military power ultimately led to the globalization of the European model of the modern state. The changed historical balance presented Muslims with a major challenge, for the dichotomy between dar al-Islam and dar al-harb is incompatible with the reality of the world of nation-states. Each of these changes created pressure for Muslims to rethink their holistic worldview and their traditional ethics of war and peace. But despite its incompatibility with the current international system, there has yet to be an authoritative revision of this worldview.

At its core, Islam is a religious mission to all humanity. Muslims are religiously obliged to disseminate the Islamic faith throughout the world: "We have sent you forth to all mankind" (Saba' 34:28). If non-Muslims submit to conversion or subjugation, this call (*da'wa*) can be pursued peacefully. If they do not, Muslims are obliged to wage war against them. In Islam, peace requires that non-Muslims submit to the call of Islam, either by converting or by accepting the status of a religious minority (*dhimmi*) and paying the imposed poll tax, *jizya*. World peace, the final stage of the da'wa, is reached only with the conversion or submission of all mankind to Islam.

It is important to note that the expression "dar al-harb" (house of war) is not Qur'anic; it was coined in the age of Islamic military expansion. It is, however, in line with the Qur'anic revelation dividing the world into a peaceful part (the Islamic community) and a hostile part (unbelievers who are expected to convert to Islam, if not freely then through the instrument of war). In this sense, Muslims believe that expansion through war is not aggression but a fulfillment of the Qur'anic command to spread Islam as a way to peace. The resort to force to disseminate Islam is not war (*harb*), a word that is used only to describe the use of force by non-Muslims. Islamic wars are not *hurub* (the plural of *harb*) but rather *futuhat*, acts of "opening" the world to Islam and expressing Islamic *jihad*.

Relations between dar al-Islam, the home of peace, and dar al-harb, the world of unbelievers, nevertheless take place in a state of war, according to the Qur'an and to the authoritative commentaries of Islamic jurists. Unbelievers who stand in the way, creating obstacles for the da'wa, are blamed for this state of war, for the da'wa can be pursued peacefully if others submit to it. In other words, those who resist Islam cause wars and are responsible for them. Only when Muslim power is weak is "temporary peace" (*hudna*) allowed (Islamic jurists differ on the definition of "temporary"). The notion of temporary peace introduces a third realm: territories under temporary treaties with Muslim powers (*dar al-sulh* or, at times, *dar al-'ahd*).[9]

The attitude of Muslims toward war and nonviolence can be summed up briefly: there is no Islamic tradition of nonviolence and no presumption against war. But war is never glorified and is viewed simply as the last resort in responding to the da'wa to disseminate Islam, made necessary by the refusal of unbelievers to submit to Islamic rule. In other words, there is no such thing as Islamic pacifism.

The Grounds for War

The Western distinction between just and unjust wars linked to specific grounds for war is unknown in Islam. Any war against unbelievers, whatever its immediate ground, is morally justified. Only in this sense can one distinguish just and unjust wars in Islamic tradition. When Muslims wage war for the dissemination of Islam, it is a just war (futuhat, literally "opening," in the sense of opening the world, through the use of force, to the call to Islam); when non-Muslims attack Muslims, it is an unjust war (*'idwan*).

The usual Western interpretation of jihad as a "just war" in the Western sense is, therefore, a misreading of this Islamic concept. I disagree, for example, with Khadduri's interpretation of the jihad as *bellum iustum*. As Khadduri himself observes:

> The universality of Islam provided a unifying element for all believers, within the world of Islam, and its defensive-offensive character produced a state of warfare permanently declared against the outside world, the world of war. Thus *jihad* may be regarded as Islam's instrument for carrying out its ultimate objective by turning all people into believers.[10]

According to the Western just war concept, just wars are limited to a single issue; they are not universal and permanent wars grounded on a religious worldview.

The classical religious doctrine of Islam understands war in two ways. The first is literal war, fighting or battle (*qital*), which in Islam is understood to be a last resort in following the Qur'anic precept to guarantee the spread of Islam, usually when non-Muslims hinder the effort to do so. The other understanding is metaphorical: war as a permanent condition between Muslims and nonbelievers. The Qur'an makes a distinction between fighting (qital) and aggression ('idwan) and asks Muslims not to be aggressors: "Fight for the sake of Allah against those who fight against you but do not be violent because Allah does not love aggressors" (al-Baqara 2:190). The same Qur'anic passage continues: "Kill them wherever you find them. Drive them out of places from which they drove you. . . . Fight against them until idolatry is no more and Allah's religion reigns supreme" (al-Baqara 2:190–92). The Qur'anic term for fighting is here *qital*, not *jihad.* The Qur'an prescribes fighting for the spread of Islam: "Fighting is obligatory for you, much as you dislike it" (al-Baqara 2:216). The qital of Muslims against unbelievers is a religious obligation: "Fight for the cause of Allah . . . how could you not fight for the cause of Allah? . . . True believers fight for the cause of Allah, but the infidels fight for idols" (al-Nisa' 4:74–76).

As noted above, Muslims tend to quote the Qur'an selectively to support their own ethical views. This practice has caused a loss of specificity in the meaning of jihad, as Saddam Hussein's use of the term during the Gulf War illustrates.[11] The current dissension about the concept of jihad dates from the rise of political Islam and the eruption of sectarian religious strife. Present-day Islamic fundamentalist groups—groups whose programs are based on the revival of Islamic values—often invoke the idea of jihad to legitimize their political agendas. The reason for this misuse of the concept is simple: most fundamentalists are lay people who lack intimate knowledge of Islamic sources and who politicize Islam to justify their activities. Before the Gulf War, for example, this occurred in Egypt, during the Lebanon War, and in the civil war in Sudan.[12] Through such overuse and misuse, the concept of jihad has become confused with the related Islamic concept of "armed fighting" (qital). Therefore, there is a great need for a historical analysis of the place of scripture in Islamic tradition. Although Islamic ethics of peace and war are indeed mostly scriptural, scriptural references can be adequately interpreted only in a historical context.

As we have seen, Islam understands itself as a mission of peace for all humanity, although this call (da'wa) can sometimes be pursued by war. In this sense, the da'wa is an invitation to jihad, which means fundamentally "to exert one's self" and can involve either military or nonmilitary effort.[13] Jihad can become a war (qital) against those who oppose Islam, either by failing to submit to it peacefully or by creating obstacles to its spread. Although Islam glorifies neither war nor violence, those Muslims who fight and die for the da'wa are considered blessed by Allah.

During the very beginnings of Islam (that is, before the establishment of the city-state at Medina in 622), the revealed text was essentially spiritual and contained no reference to war. In the Meccan chapter al-Kafirun ("the unbelievers"), the Qur'an asks supporters of the new religion to respond to advocates for other faiths in this manner: "You have your religion and I have mine" (al-Kafirun 109:6). In another Meccan chapter, the Qur'an simply asks believers not to obey unbelievers. Qur'anic verses from this period use the term *jihad* to describe efforts to convert unbelievers, but not in connection with military action. There is no mention of qital in the Meccan Qur'an. The Muslims then were, in fact, a tiny minority and could not fight. The verse "Do not yield to the unbelievers and use the Qur'an for your jihad [effort] to carry through against them" (al-Furqan

25:52) clearly illustrates this persuasive rather than military use of the word *jihad*: in Mecca, the only undertaking the Qur'an could ask of believers was the argument.

After the establishment of the Islamic state at Medina, however, the Qur'an comes gradually to offer precepts in which jihad can take the form of qital (fighting). Although the Qur'an teaches the protection of life as given by God and prohibits killing, this norm has an exception: "You shall not kill—for that is forbidden—except for a just cause" (al-An'am 6:151). But it is misleading to interpret this verse as a Qur'anic expression of just war because, as noted above, the distinction between just and unjust war is alien to Islam. Instead, the verse tells Muslims to remain faithful to morality during the qital.

The Conduct of War

When it comes to the conduct of war, one finds only small differences between Islam and other monotheistic religions or the international laws of war. Islam recognizes moral constraints on military conduct, even in wars against non-Muslims. As in other traditions, two categories of restrictions can be distinguished: restrictions on weapons and methods of war, and restrictions on permissible targets. And, just as other traditions sometimes permit these constraints to be set aside in extreme situations, in Islamic law (*shari'a*) we find the precept "Necessity overrides the forbidden" (*al-darura tubih al-mahzurat*). This precept allows moral constraints to be overridden in emergencies, though the criteria for determining whether an emergency exists are vague.

Islamic doctrine regarding the conduct of war developed in an age in which the destructive weapons of industrial warfare were not yet available. The Qur'anic doctrine on the conduct of war is also shaped by pre-Islamic tribal notions of honor. The Qur'an asks believers to honor their promises and agreements: "Keep faith with Allah, when you make a covenant. . . . Do not break your oaths" (al-Nahl 16:19). And: "Those who keep faith with Allah do not break their pledge" (al-Ra'd 13:19). It also prescribes that the enemy be notified before an attack.

Regarding permissible targets of war, Qur'anic doctrine is in line with the pre-Islamic norm of "man's boldness" (*shahama*) in strictly prohibiting the targeting of children, women, and the elderly. Consistent with this prohibition, as well as with the pre-Islamic tribal belief that it is not a sign of honor for a man to demonstrate his power to someone who is weaker, is the precept that prisoners be fairly treated (al-Insan 76:8–9). And because the goal of war against unbelievers is to force them to submit to Islam, not to destroy them, the rules of war forbid plundering and destruction.

Islam in the Age of the Territorial State

Like any text, Islamic scripture permits divergent readings or interpretations (*ta'wil*). I wish to turn now to a discussion of three divergent patterns of Islamic thinking about war and peace, each characteristic of a different period in Islamic history: the conformism of the Islamic scholar Ahmed Ben Khalid al-Nasiri; the more recent conformism of the al-Azhar; and finally, the contemporary fundamentalist reinterpretation of the concepts of jihad and qital. Conformism seeks to perpetuate, in an altered world, the traditional ethics and the religious doctrine on which it rests, whereas fundamentalism insists on the absolute truth of the religious doctrine.

The pattern of conformism is illustrated in Moroccan thought. Unlike most Islamic states, Morocco has been independent for more than three centuries. Moroccan dynastic history is state history, and is thus a good example of Islamic conformism. Morocco was the only Arab country the Turks failed to subordinate. Political rule in Morocco was legitimized by Sunni Islam in the Sultanate (*Makhzan*), just as Ottoman rule was legitimized by Sunni Islam in the Caliphate. Though nineteenth-century Muslim thinkers in general were confused by the changing global balance of power, those Muslim *'ulama* who stood in the service of the Moroccan sultan were in a better position to face the new reality. Ahmed Ben Khalid al-Nasiri (1835–97) was the first Muslim *'alim* (man of learning) of his age to acknowledge the lack of unity in the Islamic community (umma), as well as Islam's weakness in the face of its enemies.

Al-Nasiri provided the legitimizing device for the politics of his Moroccan sultan Hassan I, even though he was reluctant to legitimize the quasi-sovereign Moroccan state and to repudiate the duty of waging war against unbelievers. Conformism like that of al-Nasiri remains the typical pattern among Muslim statesmen and their advisors, many of whom do not even know of al-Nasiri. This pattern is characterized by submission to international standards of law and conduct and acceptance of peaceful relations with non-Islamic countries. But it retains the traditional Islamic belief in the superiority of Islam and the division of the world into Islamic and non-Islamic realms.[14] Al-Nasiri continually refers to the "abode of Islam" (dar al-Islam), even though he has only his own country, Morocco, in mind.

Al-Nasiri based his case on two arguments, one scriptural and one expediential. He selectively and repeatedly refers to the Qur'anic verse "If they incline to peace then make peace with them" (al-Anfal 8:61), which becomes the normative basis for the peace established between Morocco and Europe. Al-Nasiri's expediential argument pertains to the conditions of the Islamic community (umma):

> No one today can overlook the power and the superiority of Christians. Muslims . . . are in a condition of weakness and disintegration. . . . Given these circumstances, how can we maintain the opinion and the politics that the weak should confront the strong? How could the unarmed fight against the heavily armed power?[15]

Despite these insights, al-Nasiri maintains that Islam is equally a "shari'a of war" and a "shari'a of peace." He argues that the Qur'anic verse "If they incline to peace then make peace with them" rests on the notion of "Islamic interest" (*al-maslaha*). Under contemporary conditions, in al-Nasiri's view, the interest of Islam forbids Muslims to wage war against unbelievers:

> The matter depends on the Imam who is in a position to see the interest of Islam and its people in regard to war and peace. There is no determination that they must fight forever or accept peace forever. . . . The authority that cannot be contested is the opinion of the Imam [Sultan Hassan I]. . . . Allah has assigned him to fix our destiny and authorized him to decide for us.[16]

The neo-Islamic notion of maslaha is strongly reminiscent of the Western idea of the "national interest" of the modern state.

This pragmatic but submissive fatwa by a leading 'alim is reflected in the position of most contemporary 'ulama regarding war and peace. Their ethic of peace is implicitly determined by their view that non-Muslims are enemies with whom Muslims can, at best, negotiate an armistice (*muhadana*). The belief that true peace is only possible among Muslims persists, even though it runs counter to the idea of a pluralist, secular international society.

Today there are two contrary positions on the ethics of war and peace in Islam. The Sunni Islamic establishment, as reflected in the scholarship produced at the al-Azhar university, continues the tradition of Islamic conformism, reinterpreting the Islamic notion of jihad to discourage the use of force. In contrast to this peaceful interpretation of Islamic ethics, contemporary Islamic fundamentalists have emphasized the warlike aspect of jihad, while also emphasizing the dichotomy between the dar al-Islam and the dar al-harb.

The authoritative textbooks of al-Azhar contain an ethic of war and peace characterized both by selective use of the sacred text and by free interpretation. Al-Azhar does not offer either a redefinition or a rethinking of the traditional ethics of war and peace in Islam; it simply offers one variety of Islamic conformism.

In the most authoritative textbook of this school, Sheikh Mahmud Schaltut asserts that Islam is a religion for all mankind, but acknowledges that it is open to pluralism.[17] Schaltut quotes the Qur'anic verse "We have created you as peoples and tribes to make you know one another" (al-Hujrat 49:13) to support the legitimacy of interpreting scripture at the service of pluralism. He also rejects the notion that Islam must resort to war to spread its beliefs, again quoting the Qur'an: "Had Allah wanted, all people of the earth would have believed in Him, would you then dare force faith upon them?" (Jon. 10:99). War, he argues, is not a proper instrument for pursuing the call to Islam (da'wa). Because "war is an immoral situation," Muslims must live in peace with non-Muslims. Schaltut takes pride in the fact that centuries ago Islam laid the foundations for a peaceful order of relations among nations, whereas

> the states of the present [that is, Western] civilization deceive the people with the so-called public international law. . . . Look at the human massacres which those people commit all over the world while they talk about peace and human rights!

Peaceful coexistence should be sanctioned by treaties that "do not impinge on the essential laws of Islam."[18]

A two-volume textbook edited by the present sheikh of al-Azhar, Jad al-Haqq 'Ali Jad al-Haqq, continues the effort to establish the centrality of peace in Islamic ethics and offers a significant reinterpretation of the concept of jihad.[19] But, in line with Islamic tradition, there is no mention of states: at issue is the Islamic community (umma) as a whole on the one hand, and the rest of the world on the other.

In a chapter on jihad in the first volume of his textbook, Jad al-Haqq emphasizes that jihad in itself does not mean war. If we want to talk about war, he argues, we must say "armed jihad" (*al-musallah*), to distinguish between this jihad and the everyday "*jihad* against ignorance, *jihad* against poverty, *jihad* against illness and disease. . . . The search for knowledge is the highest level of *jihad*." Having made this distinction, the Azhar textbook downgrades the importance of armed jihad, since the da'wa can be pursued without fighting:

> In earlier ages the sword was necessary for securing the path of the *da'wa*. In our age, however, the sword has lost its importance, although the resort to it is still important for the case of defense against those who wish to do evil to Islam and its people. However, for the dissemination of the *da'wa* there are now a variety of ways. . . . Those who focus on arms in our times are preoccupied with weak instruments.[20]

Jad al-Haqq also avoids interpreting the da'wa as requiring the imposition of Islam on others: "The *da'wa* is an offer to join in, not an imposition. . . . Belief is not for imposition with force." Earlier Meccan verses are quoted again and again in an effort to separate the da'wa from any notion of qital or armed jihad. "Islam was not disseminated with the power of the sword.

The *qital* (fighting) was an exception only for securing and also for the defense of the *da'wa* (call) to Islam." Despite this substantial reinterpretation, however, the textbook insists on the traditional view of Islam as a mission for all of humanity, quoting the Qur'an: "We have sent you forth as a blessing to mankind" (al-Anbiya' 21:107).[21]

The Azhar believes that in the modern age, communication networks offer a much better medium than armed conflict for the pursuit of the da'wa. Jad al-Haqq does not work out the details, however. He does not resolve the question of treaties between Muslims and non-Muslims, nor does he mention territorial states. Jad al-Haqq quotes the classical al-Qurtubi commentary of the Qur'an.[22] According to this commentary, treaties creating an armistice (hudna) between Muslims and non-Muslims can be valid for a period of no more than ten years. The model here is the treaty of Hudaybiya, negotiated by the Prophet with the Quraysh in a state of war: it was a limited truce. If the Muslims are powerful, they may not hold an armistice for more than one year; if they are militarily inferior, an armistice of ten years is allowed. There is no discussion of what occurs after that time, which implies that it is seen as heretical to revise classical doctrine and that there is no desire to review this doctrine in the light of changed international circumstances. The result is conformity or acquiescence to the new international system, but no effort to alter the classic categories.

Unlike the al-Azhar conformists, who seek to read scripture in the light of present realities, Islamic fundamentalists are inclined to reverse the procedure: a true Muslim has to view reality in the light of the text. Islamic fundamentalism as a mass movement dates back to the 1970s, though its intellectual and organizational roots can be traced to 1928, when the Muslim Brotherhood (*al-Ikhwan al-Muslimun*) was created in Egypt.[23] The leading authorities on the political thought of Islamic fundamentalism are Hasan al-Banna, the founder of this movement, and Sayyid Qutb, its foremost ideologue. But they speak only for fundamentalism, which, because it is a recent trend within Islam, cannot be seen as representative of Islam as a whole—a mistake often made in the Western media.

In his treatise on jihad, Hasan al-Banna makes literal use of the Qur'an and Hadith to support conclusions opposed to those of the Islamic conformists quoted above. According to al-Banna, the jihad is an "obligation of every Muslim" (*farida*).[24] *Jihad* and *qital* are used interchangeably to mean "the use of force," whether in the pursuit of resistance against existing regimes or in waging war against unbelievers. Fundamentalists follow the Islamic tradition of not considering states in the context of war and peace; the term "war" is used here to mean fighting among loose parties of believers and unbelievers, no matter how they are organized politically. And in contrast to traditionalists, who distinguish between the use of force to further Islam and wars of aggression ('idwan), fundamentalists apply the word *jihad* indiscriminately to any use of force, whether against unbelievers or against fellow believers whom they suspect of being merely nominal Muslims.

Al-Banna begins his treatise by quoting the al-Baqara verse referred to above: "Fighting is obligatory for you, much as you dislike it" (2:216). He continues with another quotation from the Qur'an: "If you should die or be slain in the cause of Allah, his mercy will surely be better than all the riches you amass" ('Imran 3:158). And, "We shall richly reward them whether they die or conquer" (al-Nisa' 4:74). These and similar quotations serve as the basis for al-Banna's glorification of fighting and death in "the cause of Allah."

But al-Banna does not cite the tolerant Qur'anic verse from al-Kafirun, "You have your religion and I have mine," preferring instead to extend the obligation of the qital even against the "people of the book" (*ahl al-kitab*)—Christians and Jews—with the verse "Fight against those who neither believe in Allah nor in the Last Day . . . until they pay tribute out of hand and are utterly subdued" (al-Tauba 9:29). Allah, he concludes, "has obliged Muslims to fight . . . to secure the pursuit of *al-da'wa* and thus of peace, while disseminating the great mission which God entrusted to them."[25]

With a few exceptions, the al-Azhar textbook does not treat the armed jihad (*jihad al-musallah*) as a duty for Muslims in the modern age. It downgrades the status of fighting (qital) while it upgrades the nonmilitary jihad against such evils as ignorance, poverty, and disease. In contrast, al-Banna draws a distinction between "low jihad" (*al-jihad al-asghar*) and "high jihad" (*al-jihad al-akbar*), ridiculing those Muslims who consider the qital to be a "low jihad." He considers this denigration of qital to be a misunderstanding of qital as the true essence of jihad: "The great reward for Muslims who fight is to kill or be killed for the sake of Allah." Al-Banna's treatise is in fact permeated with rhetoric glorifying death, which seems to legitimize the suicidal terrorist acts often committed by Islamic fundamentalists:

> Allah rewards the *umma* which masters the art of death and which acknowledges the necessity of death in dignity. . . . Be sure, death is inevitable. . . . If you do this for the path of Allah, you will be rewarded.[26]

It is clear that for al-Banna, peace is possible only under the banner of Islam. Non-Muslims should be permitted to live only as members of protected minorities under Islamic rule. In all other cases, war against unbelievers is a religious duty of Muslims.

The other leading fundamentalist authority, Sayyid Qutb, has revived the dichotomous Islamic division of the world into "the house of peace" (dar al-Islam) and "the house of war" (dar al-harb). He employs this dichotomy to establish that war against "unbelievers" is a religious duty for

Muslims. Giving the old dichotomy a new twist, he coins the expressions "the world of believers" and "the world of *neo-jahiliyya*" (*jahiliyya* is the Islamic term for the pre-Islamic age of ignorance). For Qutb, modernity is nothing more than a new form of jahiliyya. Qutb claims that "the battle lying ahead is one between the believers and their enemies. . . . Its substance is the question *kufr aw iman?* (unbelief or belief?), *jahiliyya aw Islam?* (ignorance or Islam?)."[27] The confrontation, then, is "between Islam and the international society of ignorance"[28]—a confrontation in which victory is reserved for Islam.[29]

The large number of pamphlets industriously produced by Islamic fundamentalists during the past two decades seldom go beyond quoting passages from al-Banna and Qutb. Contemporary fundamentalists often cite passages like this from Qutb:

> The dynamic spread of Islam assumes the form of *jihad* by the sword . . . not as a defensive movement, as those Muslim defeatists imagine, who subjugate to the offensive pressure of Western orientalists. . . . Islam is meant for the entire globe.[30]

Qutb's repudiation of the mainstream conformist view that Islam resorts to war only for the defense of Muslim lands is central to fundamentalist thinking.

Qutb's influence is illustrated in Muhammad Na'im Yasin's 1990 book on jihad. The book develops an understanding of war between believers and unbelievers as a gradual process in which, in the last stage, "regardless of an attack of the Muslim lands by unbelievers, . . . fighting of Muslims against them ought to take place." Yasin then quotes the Qur'anic verse "Fight against the unbelievers in their entirety as they fight against you in your entirety" (al-Tauba 9:36), commenting on the verse as follows: "The duty of *jihad* in Islam results in the necessity of *qital* against everyone who neither agrees to convert to Islam nor to submit himself to Islamic rule." He concludes that the ultimate "return to Allah cannot be pursued through wishful thinking but only through the means of *jihad*."[31] According to Colonel Ahmad al-Mu'mini, an officer in the Jordanian army, this offensive view of jihad must determine the military policies of all Islamic states.[32] Al-Mu'mini's views have been widely circulated.

As we have seen, some Muslims have made the effort to adapt Islamic doctrine to the modern international system, but many go only so far as to make pragmatic adjustments to the doctrine that mankind must either accept Islam or submit to Muslim rule. It is true that Islamic states subordinate themselves to international law by virtue of their membership in the United Nations. But although international law prohibits war, Islamic law (the shari'a) prescribes war against unbelievers.[33] Does the recognition of international law by Islamic states really indicate a revision of Islamic ethics regarding war and peace? Or does this recognition indicate no more than outward conformity of the Muslim world to international society?

Most Western authors on war and peace in Islam overlook the fact that there is no concept of the territorial state in Islam.[34] Therefore, Islamic thinkers view war as a struggle, not between states, but between Muslims as a community (umma) and the rest of the world inhabited by unbelievers (dar al-harb). In contrast, the classic treatise on Islamic "international law" by the Muslim legal scholar Najib Armanazi acknowledges that the international order established by the treaty of Westphalia—in which relations among states are organized on the basis of the mutual recognition of each other's sovereignty—is contradicted by the intention of the Arab conquerors to impose their rule everywhere. But despite this contradiction, Armanazi argues, Muslims do in practice recognize the sovereignty of states with whom they conduct relations on the basis of "the *aman*, customary law or the rule of honoring agreements (*'ahd*, *'uhud*)." Nevertheless, "for Muslims war is the basic rule and peace is understood only as a temporary armistice. . . . Only if Muslims are weak [are their adversaries] entitled to reconciliation." And, he continues, "for Muslim jurists peace only matters when it is in line with the *maslaha* (interest) of Muslims."[35] Between Muslim and non-Muslim, peace is only a temporary armistice and war remains the rule.

In short, Muslim states adhere to public international law but make no effort to accommodate the outmoded Islamic ethics of war and peace to the current international order. Thus, their conduct is based on outward conformity, not on a deeper "cultural accommodation"—that is, a rethinking of Islamic tradition that would make it possible for them to accept a more universal law regulating war and peace in place of Islamic doctrine. Such a "cultural accommodation" of the religious doctrine to the changed social and historical realities would mean a reform of the role of the religious doctrine itself as the cultural underpinning of Islamic ethics of war and peace.[36] If this is correct, then Mayer's conclusion that "Islamic and international legal traditions, long separated by different perspectives, are now starting to converge in areas of common concern"[37] is far too optimistic. The convergence is limited to practical matters and does not reach to basic conceptions of war and peace.[38]

On the contrary, what we have seen, instead of convergence with Western ideas, is a revival of the classical doctrine of the dichotomy between dar al-Islam and dar al-harb. Muslim writers today commonly describe all the wars involving Muslim lands since 1798 (when Napoleon invaded Egypt) down to the Arab-Israeli wars and the Gulf War as "unjust wars" undertaken by the "crusaders" against the world of Islam.[39]

For Muslims, the modern age is marked by a deep tension between Islam and the territorial state.[40] In fact, there is no generally accepted concept of the state in Islam; the "community of believers" (umma), not the state, has always been the focus of Islamic doctrine. With a few exceptions, Islamic jurists do not deal with the notion of the state (*dawla*). As the Moroccan scholar 'Abdullatif Husni writes in his study of Islam and international relations, recent defenders of the classical Islamic division of the world

> confine themselves to quoting classical Islamic jurists. In their writings we do not even find the term "state." This deliberate disregard indicates their intention to ignore the character of the modern system of international relations. They refuse to acknowledge the multiplicity of states which are sovereign and equal in maintaining the notions of *dar al-Islam* and *dar al-harb*.[41]

Though the Islamic world has made many adjustments to the modern international system,[42] there has been no cultural accommodation, no rigorously critical rethinking of Islamic tradition.[43]

Conclusion

In discussing the basic concepts of the Islamic tradition of war and peace, and their understanding by Muslims at the present, my focus has been on Muslim attitudes toward war. The ground for war is always the dissemination of Islam throughout the world. And in conducting war, Muslims are to avoid destruction and to deal fairly with the weak. Muslims do not view the use of force to propagate Islam as an act of war, given their understanding of the da'wa as an effort to abolish war by bringing the entire world into the "house of Islam," which is the house of peace. For this reason, as we have seen, Islamic conquests are described by Islamic historians not as wars (hurub) but as "openings" (futuhat) of the world to Islam.

Despite the universal religious mission of Islam, the world of Islam was a regional, not a global, system.[44] The only global system in the history of mankind is our present international system, which is the result of the expansion of the European model. As we have seen, this modern international system has placed strain on the ethics of war and peace in Islam, generating the divergent responses of conformism and fundamentalism.

Islamic war/peace ethics is scriptural and premodern. It does not take into account the reality of our times, which is that international morality is based on relations among sovereign states, not on the religions of the people living therein. Though the Islamic states acknowledge the authority of international law regulating relations among states, Islamic doctrine governing war and peace continues to be based on a division of the world into dar al-Islam and dar al-harb. The divine law of Islam, which defines a partial community in international society, still ranks above the laws upon which modern international society rests.

The confrontation between Islam and the West will continue, and it will assume a most dramatic form.[45] Its outcome will depend on two factors: first, the ability of Muslims to undertake a "cultural accommodation" of Islamic religious concepts and their ethical underpinnings to the changed international environment; and second, their ability to accept equality and mutual respect between themselves and those who do not share their beliefs.

Notes

1. George Makdisi, "Ethics in Islamic and Rationalist Doctrine," in Richard G. Hovannisian, ed., *Ethics in Islam* (Malibu, CA: Udena Publications, 1985), 47. On the concept of knowledge in Islam, see Bassam Tibi, *Islamischer Fundamentalismus, moderne Wissenschaft und Technologie* (Frankfurt am Main: Suhrkamp Verlag, 1992), 80–93; and Tibi, "Culture and Knowledge," *Theory, Culture, and Society* 12 (1995), 1–24.

2. Representative of this method, and equally authoritative, is a book by the former sheikh of al-Azhar, 'Abdulhalim Mahmud, *Al-jihad wa al-nasr* (Cairo: Dar al-Katib al-'Arabi, 1968). This work is the point of departure for the other books published in Arabic that are cited here.

3. On this point, I disagree with Muhammed Shadid, *Al-jihad fi al-Islam*, 7th ed. (Cairo: Dar al-tawzi' al-Islamiyya, 1989), the most widely known and authoritative study in Arabic on this topic, and with Majid Khadduri, *War and Peace in the Law of Islam* (Baltimore: The Johns Hopkins University Press, 1955). Both authors suggest, though from different points of view, that a consistent concept of jihad can be found in the Qur'an. My reading of the Qur'an does not support this contention.

4. Qur'anic references are to the Arabic text in the undated Tunis edition published by Mu'assasat 'Abdulkarim ben 'Abdullah. I have checked my translations against the standard German translation of Rudi Paret (Stuttgart: Kohlhammer Verlag, 1979), the new German translation by Adel Th. Khoury (Gütersloh: Gerd Mohn Verlag, 1987), and the often inadequate English translation by N. J. Dawood, 4th ed. (London and New York: Penguin, 1974).

5. See Bernard Lewis, "Politics and War," in Joseph Schacht and C. E. Bosworth, eds., *The Legacy of Islam*, 2d ed. (Oxford: Clarendon Press, 1974); Marshall G. S. Hodgson, *The Venture of Islam*, 3 vols. (Chicago: University of Chicago Press, 1974); Adam Watson, *The Evolution of International Society* (London: Routledge, 1992), 113ff.; and Hedley Bull, "The Revolt against the West," in Hedley Bull and Adam Watson, eds., *The Expansion of International Society* (Oxford: Clarendon Press, 1984), 217–28.

6. Lewis, "Politics and War," 173, 176.

7. See, for example, Beate Kuckertz, ed., *Das Grüne Schwert: Weltmacht Islam* (Munich: Heyne Verlag, 1992).

8. See David B. Ralston, *Importing the European Army: The Introduction of European Military Techniques and Institutions into the Extra-European World, 1600–1914* (Chicago: University of Chicago Press, 1990), esp. chs. 3 and 4.

9. See Sabir Tu'aymah, *Al-Shari'a al-Islamiyya fi 'asr al-'ilm* (Beirut: Dar al-Jil, 1979), 217, 223ff.

10. Khadduri, *War and Peace*, 63–64. Khadduri concludes, I think prematurely, that "at the present it is not possible to revive the traditional religious approach to foreign affairs. . . . The jihad has become an obsolete weapon" (p. 295). See the more recent survey by John Kelsay, *Islam and War: A Study in Comparative Ethics* (Louisville, KY: Westminster/John Knox Press, 1993).

11. See the Arabic text of the first call by Saddam Hussein to jihad in *Al-Muntada* (Amman) 5 (Sept. 1990), 21–22. The concept of jihad is considered by Kenneth L. Vaux, *Ethics and the Gulf War: Religion, Rhetoric, and Righteousness* (Boulder, CO: Westview Press, 1992), 63–86. See also James Piscatori, ed., *Islamic Fundamentalisms and the Gulf Crisis* (Chicago: American Academy of Arts and Sciences, 1991), esp. the entry for jihad in the index (p. 259). Earlier, Islamic jihad had been interpreted in Western terms as a war of liberation grounded in the right of self-determination against colonial rule. On this topic, see Rudolph Peters, *Islam and Colonialism: The Doctrine of Jihad in Modern History* (The Hague: Mouton, 1979); Bassam Tibi, "Politische Ideen in der 'Dritten Welt' während der Dekolonisation," in Iring Fetscher and Herfried Münkler, eds., *Pipers Handbuch der politischen Ideen*, vol. 5 (Munich: Pipers Handbuch, 1987), 363–402; and Jean-Paul Charney, *L'Islam et la guerre: De la guerre juste à la revolution sainte* (Paris: Fayard, 1986).

12. On Egypt, see Nabil 'Abdulfattah, *Al-mashaf wa al saif* (Cairo: Madbuli, 1984), and Nu'mat-Allah Janinah, *Tanzim al-jihad* (Cairo: Dar al-Huriyya, 1988); on Lebanon, see Martin Kramer, "Hizbullah: The Calculus of Jihad," in Martin Marty and Scott Appleby, eds., *Fundamentalisms and the State* (Chicago: University of Chicago Press, 1993); and on Sudan, see Bassam Tibi, *Die Verschwörung: Das Trauma arabischer Politik* (Hamburg: Hoffmann and Campe, 1993), 191–208.

13. See Shadid, *Al-jihad fi al-Islam*.

14. The work of al-Nasiri has been republished in nine volumes: Namudhaj Ahmed ben Khalid al-Nasiri, *Al-Istiqsa' fi akhbar al-Maghreb al-Aqsa* (Casablanca: Dar al-Kitab, 1955). I am relying on the comprehensive study by 'Abdullatif Husni, *Al-Islam wa al-'alaqat al-duwaliyya: Namudhaj Ahmed ben Khalid al-Nasiri* (Casablanca: Afriqya al-Sharq, 1991), which examines al-Nasiri's work in its entirety. See also Kenneth Brown, "Profile of a Nineteenth-Century Moroccan Scholar," in Nikki Keddie, ed., *Scholars, Saints, and Sufis: Muslim Religious Institutions in the Middle East since 1500* (Berkeley and Los Angeles: University of California Press, 1972), 127–48.

15. Quoted in Husni, *Al-Islam*, 141.

16. Quoted in Husni, *Al-Islam*, 149, 150.

17. Mahmud Schaltut, *Al-Islam 'aqida wa shari'a*, 10th ed. (Cairo: Dar al-Shuruq, 1980).

18. Schaltut, *Al-Islam*, 404, 409, 406.

19. Jad al-Haqq 'Ali Jad al-Haqq, for al-Azhar, *Bayan ila al-nas*, 2 vols. (Cairo: al-Azhar, 1984–88).

20. Jad al-Haqq, *Bayan ila al-nas*, 1: 277, 278–79.

21. Jad al-Haqq, *Bayan ila al-nas*, 1: 281; 2: 268; 1: 280.

22. Jad al-Haqq, *Bayan ila al-nas*, 2: 371.

23. See Richard Mitchell, *The Society of Muslim Brothers* (Oxford: Oxford University Press, 1969).

24. Hasan al-Banna, *Majmu'at Rasa'il al-Imam al-Shahid Hasan al-Banna*, new legal ed. (Cairo: Dar al-Da'wa, 1990), 275.

25. Al-Banna, *Majmu'at Rasa'il*, 275, 287.

26. Al-Banna, *Majmu'at Rasa'il*, 289, 291.

27. See Sayyid Qutb, *Ma'alim fi al-tariq*, 13th legal ed. (Cairo: Dar al-Shuruq, 1989); the quotation is from p. 201. For a commentary on Qutb's view, see Tibi, *Islamischer Fundamentalismus*.

28. Sayyid Qutb, *Al-Islam wa mushiklat al-hadarah*, 9th legal ed. (Cairo: Dar al-Shuruq, 1988), p. 195. See also his *Al-Salam al-'alami wa al-Islam*, 10th legal ed. (Cairo: Dar al-Shuruq, 1992).

29. Sayyid Qutb, *Al-Mustaqbal li hadha al-din* (Cairo: Dar al-Shuruq, 1981).

30. Sayyid Qutb, *Ma'alim fi al-tariq*, 72.

31. Muhammad N. Yasin, *Al-Jihad: Mayadinahu wa asalibahu* (Algiers: Dar al-Irschad, 1990), 76, 77, 81.

32. Colonel (al-Muqaddam) Ahmad al-Mu'mini, *Al-Ta'bi'a al-jihadiyya fi al-Islam* (Constantine, Algeria: Mu'asasat al-Isra', 1991).

33. For an interpretation of the shari'a, see Ann E. Mayer, "The Shari'a: A Methodology or a Body of Substantive Rules?" in Nicholas Heer, ed., *Islamic Law and Jurisprudence* (Seattle: University of Washington Press, 1990), 177–98; and Bassam Tibi, *Islam and the Cultural Accommodation of Social Change* (Boulder, CO: Westview Press, 1990), 59–75.

34. The concept of an "Islamic state" (*dawla islamiyya*) is not found in the classical sources; it is a new idea related to the concerns of Islamic fundamentalism. See, among others, Muhammad Hamidullah, *The Muslim Conduct of State* (Lahore: Sh. Muhammad Ashraf, 1977); Abdulrahman A. Kurdi, *The Islamic State* (London: Mansell Publishers, 1984); and Bassam Tibi, *Die fundamentalistische Herausforderung: Der Islam und die Weltpolitik* (Munich: C. H. Beck, 1992). A more detailed discussion of the confusion between the terms "community" (umma) and "nation" may be found in Tibi, "Islam and Arab Nationalism," in Barbara F. Stowasser, ed., *The Islamic Impulse* (Washington, DC: Center for Contemporary Arab Studies, 1987), 59–74.

35. Najib al-Armanazi, *Al-Shar' al-duwali fi al-Islam*, reprint of the 1930 edition (London: Riad El-Rayyes Books, 1990), 226, 157, 163.

36. See Tibi, *Islam and Cultural Accommodation*.

37. Ann E. Mayer, "War and Peace in the Islamic Tradition: International Law," mimeo, ref. no. 141 (Philadelphia: University of Pennsylvania, Wharton School, Department of Legal Studies, n.d.), 45.

38. Because the Islamic perception of non-Muslims either as *dhimmi* (Christians and Jews as protected minorities) or as *kafirun* (unbelievers) is untenable in the international system, there is an urgent need to revise the shari'a in the light of international law. See Abdullahi Ahmed an-Na'im, *Toward an Islamic Reformation: Civil Liberties, Human Rights and International Law* (Syracuse, NY: Syracuse University Press, 1990). This Islamic view of non-Muslims is incompatible with the idea of human rights, as an-Na'im clearly shows; on this point, see Ann E. Mayer, *Islam and Human Rights: Tradition and Politics* (Boulder, CO: Westview Press,

1991); and Bassam Tibi, "Universality of Human Rights and Authenticity of Non-Western Cultures: Islam and the Western Concept of Human Rights" (review article), *Harvard Human Rights Journal* 5 (1992), 221–26.

39. See Bassam Tibi, *Conflict and War in the Middle East* (New York: St. Martin's Press, 1993); and *Die Verschwörung*, 273–326.

40. For a different view, see James Piscatori, *Islam in a World of Nation-States* (Cambridge: Cambridge University Press, 1986), 40ff. I discuss this view in the introductory chapter of *Arab Nationalism: A Critical Inquiry*, 2d ed. (London: Macmillan Press, 1990).

41. 'Abdullatif Husni, *Al-Islam*, 59.

42. See the discussion above of the conformism of al-Nasiri and al-Azhar.

43. Bassam Tibi, *The Crisis of Modern Islam: A Preindustrial Culture in the Scientific-Technological Age* (Salt Lake City: University of Utah Press, 1988); Fazlur Rahman, *Islam and Modernity* (Chicago: University of Chicago Press, 1982); and W. Montgomery Watt, *Islamic Fundamentalism and Modernity* (London: Routledge, 1988).

44. Watson, *Evolution of International Society*, 112–19 and 214–18.

45. See Samuel P. Huntington, "The Clash of Civilizations?" *Foreign Affairs* 72 (1993), 22–49; and Bassam Tibi, *Der Krieg der Zivilisationen* (Hamburg: Hoffmann and Campe, 1995), esp. ch. 4.

CHAPTER 8

Interpreting the Islamic Ethics of War and Peace

Sohail H. Hashmi

If their discourse on the recent Persian Gulf War is any indication, Muslims are hopelessly divided on the Islamic ethics of war and peace. One graphic indication of this division is found in the deliberations of the People's Islamic Conference, a group of Muslim activists and scholars from several countries originally convened to find a resolution for the Iran-Iraq War. During January 1991, in the weeks immediately before the Gulf War air campaign against Iraq, the conference was meeting simultaneously in Baghdad and Mecca, with the Baghdad group demonstrating sympathy with the Iraqi position and the Meccans supporting the anti-Iraq coalition. In the end, both groups issued communiques declaring their side's cause to be a "just" war, that is, *jihad.*

Muslim writers of many intellectual persuasions have long argued that Westerners hold an inaccurate, even deliberately distorted, conception of jihad. In fact, however, the idea of jihad (and the ethics of war and peace generally) has been the subject of an intense and multifaceted debate among Muslims themselves. So diffusely defined and inconsistently applied has the idea become in Islamic discourse that a number of religious opposition groups have felt compelled to differentiate their cause from competing "false" causes by naming themselves, tautologically, "Islamic" jihad.

Nevertheless, when the contemporary Islamic discourse on war and peace is studied in the context of recent historical events, including decolonization and the many conflicts in which Muslims have been involved, one can discern an emerging consensus among Muslim intellectuals on the current meaning of jihad. This consensus is by no means universal, and given the diffuse nature of religious authority in the Islamic tradition, debate on the ethics of war and peace is likely to continue. But as I hope to demonstrate, the concept of jihad in contemporary Islam is one that is still adapting to the radical changes in international relations that have occurred since the medieval theory was first elaborated. We are witnessing a period of reinterpretation and redefinition, one characterized by controversy and confusion about how the concept should be applied to contemporary events, but also by movement toward wider agreement on the essential points of an Islamic ethic of war and peace.

This chapter, in contrast to Bassam Tibi's presentation of the "basic religious doctrine," seeks to place the traditional legal discussion of war and peace within a broader ethical context. I begin by considering the conceptions of war and peace outlined in the two essential sources for any Islamic ethics, the Qur'an and practice (*sunna*) of the Prophet Muhammad. These sections are necessarily to some extent exegetical, for my main contention is that a comprehensive ethical framework for addressing the question of violence in human society is present in the Qur'an and elaborated by the traditions of the Prophet. In the remaining two sections, I consider issues relating to the grounds for war and the means of war as treated by the medieval Muslim jurists. But my main purpose in these sections is to consider how these two categories of moral evaluation of war are today being reinterpreted by Muslim thinkers representing a wide spectrum of cultural and ideological backgrounds. The proper conclusion, I believe, is that Islam has more in common with the Western ethical traditions considered in this volume than Tibi allows. Regarding the issue of the relationship between the Islamic tradition of jihad and the Western tradition of just war, I shall suggest that there is a growing convergence in conceptions of jihad and just war that permits a cross-cultural dialogue on the ethics of war and peace.

Much of the controversy surrounding the concept of jihad among Muslims today emerges from the tension between its legal and ethical dimensions. This tension arises because it is the juristic, and not the philosophical or ethical, literature that has historically defined Muslim discourse on war and peace. With the rise of the legalistic tradition, ethical inquiry became a narrow and secondary concern of Islamic scholarship. What we find from the medieval period are legal treatises propounding the rules of jihad and discussing related issues, but few ethical works outlining a framework of principles derived from the Qur'an and sunna upon which these rules could be based. With increasing political instability in the central Islamic lands beginning in the twelfth century, even legal development became moribund. The results have been particularly deleterious in the political realm. As Fazlur Rahman has observed, the stagnation of formal legal theory resulted in the increasing "secularization" of Islamic administrative law. As the dictates of the medieval Islamic law (*shari'a*) became anachronistic according to the demands of various Muslim states, jurists increasingly appealed to the notions of *maslaha mursala* (general interest) and *darura* (necessity) as justifications for various state practices.[1] The result has been the continual erosion of the ability of Islamic law to address contemporary political concerns and the reduction of Islamic ethics to the ad hoc application of principles to specific situations in a chaotic and unsatisfactory manner. One of the central dimensions of the current controversy concerning the shari'a that is raging in the Muslim world—although it is not often phrased in this manner—is the need for a comprehensive Qur'anic ethics as a precursor to the reform of law.

Conceptions of War and Peace in the Qur'an

Ibn Khaldun observes in the *Muqadimma*, his celebrated introduction to a history of the world composed at the end of the fourteenth century, that "wars and different kinds of fighting have always occurred in the world since God created it." War is endemic to human existence, he writes, "something natural among human beings. No nation and no race is free from it."[2] Ibn Khaldun's brief comment summarizes rather well the traditional Islamic understanding of war as a universal and inevitable aspect of human existence. It is a feature of human society sanctioned, if not willed, by God Himself. The issues of war and peace thus fall within the purview of divine legislation for humanity. Islam, Muslims like to say, is a complete code of life, and given the centrality of war to human existence, the moral evaluation of war holds a significant place in Muslim ethical/legal discussion. The Islamic ethics of war and peace is therefore derived from the same general sources upon which Islamic law is based.

The first of these sources, of course, is the Qur'an, which is held by Muslims to be God's final and definitive revelation to humanity. The Qur'anic text, like other revealed scriptures, is not a systematic treatise on ethics or law. It is a discursive commentary on the actions and experiences of the Prophet Muhammad, his followers, and his opponents over the course of twenty-three years. But as the Qur'an itself argues in several verses, God's message is not limited to the time and place of its revelation; it is, rather, "a message to all the worlds" (81:27) propounding a moral code with universal applicability (39:41). From this commentary emerge broadly defined ethical principles that have been elaborated throughout Islamic history into what may be termed an Islamic conception of divine creation and man's place in it. In other words, although the Qur'an does not present a systematic ethical argument, it is possible to derive a consistent ethical system from it.[3]

Why is humanity prone to war? The Qur'anic answer unfolds in the course of several verses revealed at various times, the essential points of which may be summarized as follows.

First, man's fundamental nature (*fitra*) is one of moral innocence, that is, freedom from sin. In other words, there is no Islamic equivalent to the notion of "original sin." Moreover, each individual is born with a knowledge of God's commandments, that is, with the essential aspects of righteous behavior. But this moral awareness is eroded as each individual encounters the corrupting influences of human society (30:30).

Second, man's nature is to live on the earth in a state of harmony and peace with other living things. This is the ultimate import of the responsibility assigned by God to man as His viceregent (*khalifa*) on this planet (2:30). True peace (*salam*) is therefore not merely an absence of war; it is the elimination of the grounds for strife or conflict, and the resulting waste and corruption (*fasad*) they create. Peace, not war or violence, is God's true purpose for humanity (2:208).

Third, given man's capacity for wrongdoing, there will always be some who *choose* to violate their nature and transgress against God's commandments. Adam becomes fully human only when he chooses to heed Iblis's (Satan's) temptation and disobeys God. As a result of this initial act of disobedience, human beings are expelled from the Garden to dwell on earth as "enemies to each other" (2:36, 7:24). Thus, wars and the evils that stem from them, the Qur'an suggests, are the inevitable consequences of the uniquely human capacity for moral choice.

The Qur'an does not present the fall of man as irrevocable, however, for God quickly returns to Adam to support and guide him (2:37). This, according to Islamic belief, is the beginning of continuous divine revelation to humanity through a series of prophets ending with Muhammad. God's reminders of the laws imprinted upon each human consciousness through His prophets are a manifestation of His endless mercy to His creation, because all human beings are potential victims of Iblis's guile, that is, potential evildoers, and most human beings are actually quite far from God's laws (36:45–46). When people form social units, they become all the more prone to disobey God's laws through the obstinate persistence in wrongdoing caused by custom and social pressures (2:13–14, 37:69, 43:22). In this way, the individual drive for power, wealth, prestige, and all the other innumerable human goals becomes amplified. Violence is the inevitable result of the human desire for self-aggrandizement.

Fourth, each prophet encounters opposition from those (always a majority) who persist in their rebellion against God, justifying their actions through various self-delusions. One of the principal characteristics of rejection of God (*kufr*) is the inclination toward violence and oppression, encapsulated by the broad concept *zulm*. When individuals choose to reject divine guidance, either by transgressing against specific divine injunctions or by losing faith altogether, they violate (commit zulm against) their own nature (fitra). When Adam and Eve disobey the divine command in the Garden, the Qur'an relates that they cry out in their despair not that they have sinned against God, but that they have transgressed against their own souls (7:23).

When an entire society rejects God, oppression and violence become the norm throughout the society and in relations with other societies as well. The moral anarchy that prevails when human beings abandon the higher moral code derived from faith in a supreme and just Creator, the Qur'an suggests, is fraught with potential and actual violence (2:11–12, 27, 204–5; chapter 7, *al-A'raf*, deals with this theme at length).

Fifth, peace (*salam*) is attainable only when human beings surrender to God's will and live according to God's laws. This is the condition of *islam*, the conscious decision to acknowledge in faith and conduct the presence and power of God. Because human nature is not sufficiently strong to resist the temptation to evil, it is necessary for man to establish a human agency, that is, a state, to mitigate the effects of anarchy and enforce divine law.

Sixth, because it is unlikely that individuals or societies will ever conform fully to the precepts of islam, Muslims must always be prepared to fight to preserve the Muslim faith and Muslim principles (8:60, 73).

The use of force by the Muslim community is, therefore, sanctioned by God as a necessary response to the existence of evil in the world. As the Qur'an elaborates in an early revelation, the believers are those "who, whenever tyranny afflicts them, defend themselves" (42:39). This theme of the just, God-ordained use of force for legitimate purposes is continued in several other verses. In the first verse, which explicitly permits the Muslim community to use armed force against its enemies, the Qur'an makes clear that fighting is a burden imposed upon all believers (not only Muslims) as a result of the enmity harbored by the unbelievers:

> Permission [to fight] is given to those against whom war is being wrongfully waged, and verily, God has indeed the power to succor them: those who have been driven from their homelands against all right for no other reason than their saying: "Our Sustainer is God!"
>
> For, if God had not enabled people to defend themselves against one another, monasteries and churches and synagogues and mosques—in all of which God's name is abundantly extolled—would surely have been destroyed. (22:39–40)

A subsequent verse converts this permission to fight into an injunction. The rationale given for using armed force is quite explicit: "Tumult and oppression (*fitna*) is worse than killing" (2:191).

These two verses clearly undermine the possibility of an Islamic pacifism. One verse in particular offers an implicit challenge to an ethical position based on the renunciation of all violence: "Fighting is prescribed for you, even though it be hateful to you; but it may well be that you hate something that is in fact good for you, and that you love a thing that is in fact bad for you: and God knows, whereas you do not" (2:216). There is, thus, no equivalent in the Islamic tradition of the continuing debate within Christianity of the possibility of just war. There is no analogue in Islamic texts to Aquinas's Question 40: "Are some wars permissible?" The Islamic discourse on war and peace begins from the a priori assumption that some types of war are permissible—indeed, required by God—and that all other forms of violence are, therefore, forbidden.

In short, the Qur'an's attitude toward war and peace may be described as an idealistic realism. Human existence is characterized neither by incessant warfare nor by real peace, but by a continuous tension between the two. Societies exist forever in a precarious balance between them. The unending human challenge is *jihad fi sabil Allah* (struggle in the way of God) to mitigate the possibility of war and to strengthen the grounds for peace. The resulting human condition may bear out the truth of the angels' initial protest to God that his decision to create man will only lead to corruption and bloodshed in the world. But the Qur'anic message is, if anything, continually optimistic about the human capacity to triumph over evil (5:56; 58:19, 22). God silences the angels, after all, not by denying their prognostication, but by holding out the possibility of unforeseen potential: "I know what you know not" (2:30).

Conceptions of War and Peace in the Sunna

The second source for the Islamic ethics of war and peace is the practice (sunna) of the Prophet Muhammad. It is impossible to comprehend the Qur'an without understanding the life of the Prophet and impossible to comprehend the life of the Prophet without understanding the Qur'an. As the Prophet's wife, 'Aisha bint Abi Bakr, is reported to have said: "His character (*khuluqhu*) was the Qur'an."[4]

Muhammad was born into a milieu characterized by internecine skirmishes (*ghazwa*) among rival tribes. These were seldom more than raids undertaken for petty plunder of a neighboring tribe's flocks. If the conflict had any "higher" purpose, it was usually collective reprisal for an injury or affront suffered by a single member of the tribe according to the prevailing *lex talionis*. Larger confrontations for higher stakes, such as the actual conquest of territory, were rare, although not unknown. The Qur'an itself alludes in the 105th chapter to a full-scale invasion of the Hijaz by an Abyssinian army a few months prior to the birth of the Prophet in 570 C.E.

Naturally, tribal loyalty was the cornerstone of this society's ethos, and virtue was often equated with martial valor. It would, however, be incorrect to view pre-Islamic Arab culture as glorifying war. Imru'l-Qays, the renowned poet of the pre-Islamic period known as the *Jahiliyya*, compares war before it is started to a young and alluring girl. But once a war begins, it quickly becomes like an old woman, hideous in appearance, unable to find any young suitor to embrace her.[5] Moreover, as Fred Donner points out, the ghazwa was often viewed by its participants as a sort of ongoing game, a struggle to outwit the opponent with a minimum of bloodshed. The aim was not to vanquish the foe but to demonstrate the qualities of courage, loyalty, and magnanimity—all components of masculine nobility included in the term *muruwwa*. Implicit in the Arab martial code were "rules of the game" that prohibited, among other things, fighting during certain months, the killing of noncombatants, and unnecessary spoliation.[6]

The conceptions of warfare existing in the Jahiliyya undoubtedly influenced the Prophet's approach to the subject. In particular, many of the qualities of muruwwa were incorporated into Islam within a new ethical context, and the Prophet became the new exemplar of Arab chivalry.[7] But it would be false to suggest, as have some Western writers, that the Prophet's approach to war was largely an extension of the pre-Islamic Arab approach to the ghazwa.[8] Such a contention is not borne out by either the Prophet's practice or his (and the Qur'an's) self-image as a reformer of pagan Arab values.

We can construct an outline of the Prophet's approach to the ethics of war and peace not only by referring to the Qur'an, but also by making use of the large body of literature comprising the Prophet's sayings and actions (hadith) and biography (*sira*) compiled between the second and fourth Islamic centuries. It is clear from these records that from an early age, Muhammad was averse to many aspects of the tribal culture in which he was born. In particular, there is no indication that he ever showed any interest in affairs of tribal honor, particularly in the ghazwa. Throughout the Meccan period of his prophetic mission (610–22 C.E.), he showed no inclination toward the use of force in any form, even for self-defense. On the contrary, his policy can only be described as nonviolent resistance. This policy was maintained in spite of escalating physical attacks directed at his followers and at him personally. And it was maintained in spite of growing pressure from within the Muslim ranks to respond in kind, particularly after the conversion of two men widely considered to embody traditional Arab virtues, the Prophet's uncle Hamza and 'Umar ibn al-Khattab. Some Qur'anic verses reflect the growing tension among the Meccan Muslims over the use of force (16:125–28, 46:35). Nevertheless, the Prophet insisted throughout this period on the virtues of patience and steadfastness in the face of their opponents' attacks. When the persecution of the most vulnerable Muslims (former slaves and members of Mecca's poorer families) became intense, he directed them to seek refuge in the realm of a Christian king, Abyssinia.

The Prophet's rejection of armed struggle during the Meccan period was more than mere prudence based on the Muslims' military weakness. It was, rather, derived from the Qur'an's still unfolding conception that the use of force should be avoided unless it is, in just war parlance, a "last resort." This ethical perspective is clearly outlined in the continuation of a verse (42:39) cited earlier, which defines the believers as those who defend themselves when oppressed:

> The requital of evil is an evil similar to it: hence, whoever pardons [his enemy] and makes peace, his reward rests with God—for, verily, He does not love evildoers.
>
> Yet indeed, as for any who defend themselves after having been wronged—no blame whatever attaches to them: blame attaches but to those who oppress [other] people and behave outrageously on earth, offending against all right: for them is grievous suffering in store!
>
> But if one is patient in adversity and forgives, this is indeed the best resolution of affairs. (42:40–43)

The main result of these early verses is not to reaffirm the pre-Islamic custom of lex talionis but the exact opposite: to establish the moral superiority of forgiveness over revenge. The permission of self-defense is not a call to arms; military force is not mentioned, although neither is it proscribed. Instead, it should be seen as a rejection of quietism, of abnegation of moral responsibility in the face of oppression. Active nonviolent resistance and open defiance of pagan persecution is the proper Muslim response, according to these verses, and was, in fact, the Prophet's own practice during this period. Because the Meccan period of the Prophet's mission lasted almost thirteen years, three years longer than the Medinan period, it is absolutely fundamental in the construction of an Islamic ethical system. Clearly, jihad in this extended period of the Prophet's life meant nonviolent resistance. For potential Muslim nonviolent activists, there are many lessons to be learned from the Prophet's decisions during these years. But, regrettably, the Meccan period has received scant attention, either from Muslim activists or from jurists, historians, and moralists.[9]

The period that has been the traditional focus of Muslim and non-Muslim concern in discussing the Islamic approach to war and peace is the decade during which the Prophet lived in Medina (622–32 C.E.). It was in Medina that the Muslims became a coherent community, and it was here that jihad acquired its military component.

According to the early Muslim historians, the Prophet enacted a new policy toward the Quraysh, the ruling tribe of Mecca, within a year of settling in Medina: war aimed at redressing Muslim grievances. He authorized small raids against specific pagan targets, in particular caravans proceeding along the trade route to Syria. These raids, according to many orientalist accounts, were intended specifically to be a means of collecting booty in order to alleviate the financial distress of the immigrants to Medina as well as to provide an added incentive for potential converts. The raids, it is suggested, signaled a fundamental shift in the Prophet's approach to an emphasis upon violent struggle, a shift sanctioned by increasingly belligerent Qur'anic verses of the Medinan period.

Both the early historians' accounts and the subsequent orientalist speculations have been challenged by contemporary Muslim biographers of the Prophet. Muhammad Haykal, for example, argues that the early forays were not military expeditions but only small raids intended to harass the Meccans, impress upon them the new power of the Muslims, and demonstrate the necessity for a peaceful accommodation with the Muslims.[10]

Both positions in the debate are obviously speculative. The uncertainty regarding any shift in the Prophet's attitude toward the employment of violence is compounded by the uncertainty regarding the actual date of the Qur'anic revelation permitting fighting (22:39). Haykal himself implies that the Qur'anic permission to fight had already been revealed before these expeditions: "This peaceful show of strength by Islam does not at all mean that Islam, at that time, forbade fighting in defense of personal life and religion, or to put a stop to persecution. . . . What it did really mean at that time, as it does today or will ever do, was to condemn any war of aggression."[11]

Thus the Prophet's first year in Medina may rightly be characterized as a transition period in the evolution of his new policy toward the Meccans. The event that signals a clear break with pre-Islamic custom was the outcome of the third expedition, led by 'Abdallah ibn Jahsh during the prohibited month of Rajab in the second year A.H. (after *hijra*, the Prophet's flight to Medina in 622 C.E.). According to the Prophet's instructions to 'Abdallah, he and his companions were simply to reconnoiter Qurayshi positions outside Mecca. But when they came upon a Meccan caravan, the temptation to attack it overcame them. In the process they killed one man, took two others captive, and returned to Medina with the booty. Realizing that 'Abdallah had violated his instructions as well as the prohibition against fighting in that month, the Prophet rebuked 'Abdallah and refused to take any share of the booty. The incident also touched off an anti-Muslim propaganda campaign led by the Quraysh, making 'Abdallah and his compatriots even more unpopular with their fellow Muslims. It was upon this occasion that the following Qur'anic verse was revealed:

> They ask you concerning fighting in the prohibited months. Answer them: "To fight therein is a grave misdeed. But to impede men from following the cause of God, to deny God, to violate the sanctity of the holy mosque, to expel its people from its precincts is with God a greater wrong than fighting in the prohibited month. Tumult and oppression are worse than slaughter." (2:217)

This verse is indicative of the continuing Qur'anic exposition of the Islamic ethics of war and its "appropriation" of certain pre-Islamic Arab values, now, in the context of the Medinan city-state, placed within an altered, more coherent moral framework. Fighting continues to be viewed as undesirable, and in some months is to be avoided altogether. In extremis, however, it is a legitimate response to injury and aggression already received at the hands of oppressors of religion. Even at this point it remains the less desirable choice and is to be exercised, the Qur'an repeatedly urges, with restraint and brevity (2:190, 193, 194; 8:61). Subsequent verses subject other pre-Islamic customs, including the ban on fighting near the Ka'aba, to the same moral evaluation (2:191).

Open warfare between the Muslims and the Quraysh was begun with the battle of Badr, fought in the month of Ramadan in 2 A.H. In the eight years following, the Prophet personally led or authorized over seventy military encounters, ranging in intensity from pitched battles in defense of Medina, to sieges, raids, and skirmishes against enemy targets. Such an astounding number of military engagements could only have had profound implications for the Prophet personally as well as for the nascent Muslim community. The preaching of Islam and the conducting of the community's day-to-day activities had to occur within a milieu characterized by outright warfare against a range of enemies: Quraysh, bedouin tribes, the Jewish tribes of Medina, and the Byzantine empire. The Muslims of this period, according to one report, "did not sleep or wake except with their weapons."[12] Qur'anic verses of the period exhorting the Prophet and his followers to fight suggest the strain that the constant threat of war must have imposed upon the community (8:24, 65).

The battle of Badr was fought when the Prophet was fifty-four years old. And although it is clear that he personally conducted several key campaigns afterward, the combined evidence of the sources indicates that he remained a reluctant warrior. On several occasions he urged the use of nonviolent means or sought an early termination of hostilities, often in the face of stiff opposition from his companions. At the same time, consonant with Qur'anic revelation, he seems to have accepted as unavoidable fighting in defense of what he perceived to be Muslim interests. The essence of his approach to war is crystallized in the following words ascribed to him: "O people! Do not wish to meet the enemy, and ask God for safety, but when you face the enemy, be patient, and remember that Paradise is under the shade of swords."[13]

The Grounds for War

Ibn Khaldun continues his discussion of war in the *Muqadimma* by distinguishing four types of war. One arises from petty squabbles among rival families or neighboring tribes, another from the desire for plunder found among "savage peoples." These two types he labels "illegitimate wars." Then, reflecting the prevailing medieval approach, he divides legitimate wars into two types: jihad and wars to suppress internal rebellion.[14] This latter division of legitimate wars is the logical outgrowth of the medieval juristic bifurcation of the world into two spheres, dar al-Islam (the realm where Islamic law applied) and dar al-harb (all other lands). According to the Sunni legal schools, jihad properly speaking was war waged against unbelievers. Because all Muslims were understood to constitute a single community of believers, wars between Muslim parties were usually classed in a separate category, *fitna* (literally, a "trial" or "test"). Like Plato, who has Socrates declare that Greeks do not make war on one another,[15] the Muslim jurists viewed intra-Muslim disputes as internal strife that should be resolved quickly by the ruling authorities. This approach to war among Muslims, important in medieval theory, has assumed greater significance in modern controversies about the definition of jihad.

The descriptions of jihad in the medieval texts reflect the historical context in which legal theory was elaborated. Because the medieval juristic conception of jihad provided legal justification for the rapid expansion of the Islamic empire that occurred in the decades following the Prophet's death, its connotations are offensive rather than defensive. Relatively little consideration was given to jihad defined as "defensive struggle," that is, war undertaken strictly to safeguard Muslim lives and property from external aggression. It was considered obvious that Muslims may wage war in self-defense, according to the Qur'anic verses cited earlier. This defensive war was *fard 'ayn*, a moral duty of each able-bodied Muslim, male or female.

More detailed discussion of jihad comes in the context of offensive struggles aimed at expansion of Islamic hegemony, an expansion aimed ultimately at the universal propagation of Islam. In the twelfth century, Ibn Rushd (Averroes) wrote a legal treatise that deals at some length with the conditions of jihad.[16] His treatise is representative of the medieval theory for two reasons. First, as one of the later medieval writers, he incorporates into his work the views of earlier scholars. Second, his treatise is typical of the methodology applied by earlier jurists in reconciling apparently conflicting verses of the Qur'an or actions of the Prophet.

Because the ultimate end of jihad is the propagation of the Islamic faith, not material gain or territorial conquest, Ibn Rushd, like other medieval writers, implicitly, if not always explicitly, separates the grounds for jihad from the grounds for war (harb or qital). Because Islam is viewed as a universal mission to all humanity, jihad is the perpetual condition that prevails between dar al-Islam and dar al-harb. Participation in the jihad to overcome dar al-harb was a *fard kifaya*, a moral obligation only for those capable of assuming it, namely able-bodied and financially secure adult males. Actual warfare, qital, arose only as the final step in a "ladder of escalation." The first step in any contact between the Muslim state and a foreign power was an invitation to allow the peaceful preaching of Islam. This was consonant with the practice of the Prophet, who had sent letters to the rulers of Byzantium, Iran, and Egypt for precisely this purpose. If a foreign ruler refused this invitation, he was to be offered the incorporation of his people into the Islamic realm as a protected non-Muslim community governed by its own religious laws, but obliged to pay a tax, the *jizya*, in lieu of performing military service. Only if the non-Muslims refused these conditions were there grounds for active hostilities. At this point, the Muslim ruler was not only permitted but required to wage war against them.

According to Ibn Rushd, the medieval jurists disagreed most on the question of when it was permissible to suspend jihad. The basis of the controversy was the apparent discrepancy between the Qur'an's "verses of peace" and "verses of the sword." In the eighth chapter, for example, is the following verse: "If they incline toward peace, incline you toward it, and trust in God: verily, He alone is all-hearing, all-knowing" (8:61). In the ninth chapter, however, we encounter the following commands: "And so, when the sacred months are over, slay the polytheists wherever you find them, and take them captive, and besiege them, and lie in wait for them at every conceivable place" (9:5); and

> Fight against those who—despite having been given revelation before—do not believe in God nor in the last day, and do not consider forbidden that which God and His Messenger have forbidden, and do not follow the religion of truth, until they pay the *jizya* with willing hand, having been subdued. (9:29)

As Ibn Rushd observes, some jurists held the opinion that the sword verses must be read in context with the peace verses, and that the ruler (*imam*) was therefore entitled to suspend jihad whenever he deemed it appropriate. Others read the sword verses as requiring continual warfare against unbelievers (both polytheists and the recognized "peoples of the book," that is, Jews, Christians, Sabaeans, and Zoroastrians) until they had been incorporated within dar al-Islam. They invoked the interpretive principle of "abrogation" (*naskh*) to support their conclusion: because the sword verses had been revealed *after* the peace verses, the command to wage jihad against non-Muslims supersedes the permission to engage in peaceful relations.[17]

Thus, as Ibn Rushd's discussion makes apparent, the medieval juristic literature is characterized by fundamental disagreements on the grounds for war. But most of the legal scholars agree that the object of jihad is not the forcible conversion of unbelievers to the Islamic faith. This object would contradict several clear Qur'anic statements enjoining freedom of worship, including "Let there be no compulsion in religion; the truth stands out clearly from error" (2:256), and "If your Lord had so willed, all those who are on earth would have believed; will you then compel mankind, against their will, to believe?" (10:99). With regard to verse 9:5 (quoted above), which seems to sanction a war of mass conversion of all polytheists to Islam, most acknowledge that the full context in which the verse occurs limits its application to the pagan Arabs who were so implacably opposed to the earliest Muslim community at Medina. The object of jihad is generally held by these writers to be the subjugation of hostile powers who refuse to permit the preaching of Islam, not forcible conversion. Once under Muslim rule, they reason, non-Muslims will be free to consider the merits of Islam.

The medieval theory of an ongoing jihad, and the bifurcation of the world into dar al-Islam and dar al-harb upon which it was predicated, became a fiction soon after it was elaborated by medieval writers. The "house of Islam" disintegrated into a number of rival states, some of whom found themselves allied with states belonging to the "house of war" in fighting their co-religionists. Nevertheless, the idea that "Islam" and the "West" represented monolithic and mutually antagonistic civilizations underlay much Muslim and European writing, particularly during the heyday of European imperialism in the eighteenth and nineteenth centuries. Shades of this viewpoint are very much apparent in our own day.

In his discussion of recent Muslim thinking on the grounds for jihad, Bassam Tibi outlines two contending approaches, the "conformist" and the "fundamentalist." He suggests that the reinterpretation of the medieval theory of jihad by modernists (as the conformists are more commonly known) is half-hearted and that, in the end, it is the fundamentalists' resurrection of the medieval dar al-harb/dar al-Islam distinction that best characterizes the current Muslim view of international relations generally and issues of war and peace in particular. His presentation, I think, does not adequately acknowledge the significance of modernist challenges to the medieval theory or real differences in how fundamentalists employ medieval terms like dar al-harb.

It is important to recognize that modernists as well as fundamentalists believe that Islamic thought must be revived by returning to the "true sources," that is, the Qur'an and sunna. This approach leads the modernists to challenge many aspects of medieval legal doctrine regarding war and peace, beginning with the division of the world into separate spheres. As they point out, this rigid bifurcation is nowhere to be found in the Qur'an or the traditions of the Prophet. Although the Qur'an's division of mankind into believers and unbelievers lends support for such a view, modernist writers argue that the Qur'anic verses cannot be interpreted to suggest a perpetual state of war between the two, nor any territoriality to the "house of Islam," when these verses are taken in the full context of the Qur'anic message. In one of the leading modernist expositions of Islamic international law, Mohammad Talaat al-Ghunaimi dismisses the dar al-Islam/dar al-harb distinction as an idea introduced by certain medieval legal thinkers in response to their own historical circumstances, but having no basis in Islamic ethics.[18]

Having undermined the medieval dichotomy, the modernists proceed to challenge the medieval conception of "aggressive jihad." Again, their method is to return to the "sources." When the Qur'anic verses and the Prophet's traditions on warfare are studied in their full context, they argue, jihad can only be a war of self-defense. As the influential Egyptian scholar Muhammad Abu Zahra writes, "War is not justified . . . to impose Islam as a religion on unbelievers or to support a particular social regime. The Prophet Muhammad fought only to repulse aggression."[19]

Turning to the fundamentalists, we do find a much more assertive, militant, violent interpretation of jihad. This is not surprising, given that most of the writers labeled "fundamentalist" are involved in revolutionary movements seeking to overthrow entrenched and militarily superior nationalist regimes. Yet if we probe even superficially beneath the rhetoric of the fundamentalists' polemics, we find real differences between their ideas and those of medieval legal theory, and real similarities uniting them with the modernists. It is true that there remains a large gap between the modernists and the most militant fundamentalist groups operating in the Muslim world today, but these groups, despite the media attention they receive, represent only the fringes of Islamic activism.

First, with respect to the fundamentalists' use of the expressions dar al-Islam and dar al-harb, there is a substantial difference between the notion of the new Jahiliyya, as it appears in the works of such writers as Hasan al-Banna and Sayyid Qutb, and medieval conceptions of dar al-harb. Jahiliyya is used by the fundamentalists as a sweeping condemnation of cultural norms and political corruption that has only the vaguest connection with medieval ideas. Fundamentalist writers do argue that the origin of this anti-Islamic culture is Western, but their polemics are equally, if not mainly, focused on allegedly hypocritical Muslim rulers and other "Westernized" elites who actively propagate *jahili* culture in their own societies. Thus, the fundamentalist attack on Western values is not a resurrection of the medieval dichotomy between Islam and the rest of humanity. It is, I believe, the Muslim version of the attack on "neoimperialism" that characterizes many Third World polemics against the current international order. The dar al-Islam/dar al-harb dichotomy developed by medieval jurists was predicated on the moral and military superiority of Islamic civilization. When twentieth-century writers such as al-Banna, Qutb, Maududi, and Khomeini depict international politics as a struggle between Islam and the West, they are governed more by their understanding of the history of European colonialism and American policies in the Muslim world than by medieval notions of dar al-harb. They are motivated by faith in the moral superiority of Islam, but also by a painful awareness of the technological and military weakness of the Muslim world compared to the West.

Second, regarding the use of jihad by fundamentalist writers, there is again a substantial difference between recent and medieval works. The thrust of the medieval jihad is outward into the dar al-harb. Central to medieval theory is the issue of right authority. A war is jihad, that is, lawful, only when it is declared by a legitimate ruler, the imam, who bears responsibility for assessing the war's right intent and right conduct. Sunni writers discuss at considerable length the characteristics of a legitimate ruler, but devote almost no attention to illegitimate rulers. The medieval political theory favors acquiescing to any ruler who can maintain order and enforce the law, regardless of the means he has used to assume power. Thus, on the topic of political rebellion, the medieval theorists are generally quite conservative. Rebellion threatened the established order of dar al-Islam and the resulting anarchy undermined the religious life of the community. As a result, there is a strong bias against any right of rebellion and an emphasis on the need to speedily reincorporate rebels into the body politic.

With the emergence of postcolonial Muslim states, political legitimacy and the rights of the people in the face of oppressive regimes have emerged as central issues in Islamic discourse. These issues figure prominently, of course, in all fundamentalist literature.

Fundamentalists view themselves as a vanguard of the righteous, preparing the way for the elimination of jahili values from their societies and the establishment of a just "Islamic" order. The details of this order remain vague in the fundamentalist tracts. What is clear from these works is the view, supported by experience, that the secular, nationalist regimes ruling most Muslim countries today, backed by their Western supporters, will not willingly cede power, even if the majority of the population does not support them. They will maintain power by any means, including the violent repression of dissent. In other words, it is argued that these regimes have declared war on Islam within their countries, and that it is incumbent upon all true believers to respond by whatever means are necessary, including violence, to overthrow them. The fundamentalist writings are therefore focused on combating the social ills and international oppression that they believe faces the Muslim community (umma) everywhere. Jihad is for the fundamentalists an instrument for the realization of political and social justice in their own societies, a powerful tool for internal reform and one required by the Qur'an's command that Muslims "enjoin the right and forbid the wrong" (3:104). The thrust of the modern jihad is thus very much inward. Warfare on the international level is considered only to the extent that Western governments are viewed as archenemies who impose corrupt and authoritarian regimes upon Muslims. Jihad as an instrument for the imposition of Islamic rule in non-Muslim states today hardly figures in fundamentalist works. Such views would be absurd given the fundamentalist position, which they share with many other Muslim writers, that most of the Muslim countries themselves do not at present have Islamic governments.

One area in which modernists and fundamentalists are tending to converge is upon the argument that jihad is an instrument for enforcing human rights. For example, the Iranian revolutionary leader Ayatollah Murtaza Mutahhari argues that "the most sacred form of jihad and war is that which is fought in defense of humanity and of human rights."[20] Similarly, the Indian/Pakistani scholar Maulana Abu'l-A'la Maududi writes that jihad is obligatory for Muslims when hostile forces threaten their human rights, which in his analysis includes forcibly evicting them from their homes, tampering with their social order, and obstructing religious life.[21]

To some extent these arguments are a response to Western writings on the international protection of human rights. But it is interesting to note that whereas there is continuing debate in the West on the legality of humanitarian intervention against sovereign states, continuing ambivalence toward the territorial state in Islamic thought lends weight to the argument in favor of such intervention among a broad range of Muslim writers.[22]

The Conduct of War

Because the goal of jihad is the call to Islam, not territorial conquest or plunder, the right conduct of Muslim armies has traditionally been an important concern within Islam. The Qur'an provides the basis for *ius in bello* considerations: "And fight in God's cause against those who wage war against you, but do not transgress limits, for God loves not the transgressors" (2:190). The "limits" are enumerated in the practice of the Prophet and the first four caliphs. According to authoritative traditions, whenever the Prophet sent out a military force, he would instruct its commander to adhere to certain restraints. The Prophet's immediate successors continued this practice, as is indicated by the "ten commands" of the first caliph, Abu Bakr:

> Do not act treacherously; do not act disloyally; do not act neglectfully. Do not mutilate; do not kill little children or old men, or women; do not cut off the heads of the palm-trees or burn them; do not cut down the fruit trees; do not slaughter a sheep or a cow or a camel, except for food. You will pass by people who devote their lives in cloisters; leave them and their devotions alone. You will come upon people who bring you platters in which are various sorts of food; if you eat any of it, mention the name of God over it.[23]

Thus, the Qur'an and the actions of the Prophet and his successors established the principles of discrimination and proportionality of means. But as Ibn Rushd's treatise makes clear, the elaboration of these broad principles created serious divisions among medieval jurists.

The legal treatises generally focus on a number of issues raised by the Qur'an itself: the treatment of prisoners, both combatants and noncombatants (47:4, 8:67); the granting of quarter or safe passage (*aman*) to residents of dar al-harb (9:6); and the division of booty (8:41). In addition, the jurists also dealt with the traditional concerns of ius in bello: the definition and protection of noncombatants and restrictions on certain types of weapon.

The legal discussions address three issues: Who is subject to damage in war? What types of damage may be inflicted upon persons? What types of damage may be inflicted upon their property? Underlying the differing opinions on these issues once again are the apparent contradictions between the peace verses and the sword verses. The jurists who contend that the sword verses provide a general rule superseding earlier revelation argue that belief is the decisive factor in establishing immunity from attack. Since verse 9:5, in their view, commands Muslims to fight all polytheists, only women and children (who were specifically designated by the Prophet as immune) are prohibited targets. All able-bodied polytheist males, whether actually fighting or not, may be killed.

Other jurists, who do not consider the peace verses to have been abrogated, maintain that capacity to fight is the only appropriate consideration, and therefore include old men, women, children, peasants, slaves, and hermits among prohibited targets.[24] The prohibition against direct attack, however, does not establish the absolute immunity of noncombatants, because, according to most jurists, all of these persons (except for hermits) are subject to the laws pertaining to prisoners of war. They may be enslaved or ransomed by the Muslim forces.

During the fighting, Muslims are permitted to inflict damage on the property of their enemies to the extent necessary to overcome them. Most jurists do not permit the unnecessary slaughter of animals, the destruction of homes, the cutting down of fruit trees, or the use of fire.[25] However, the eighth-century jurist Shaybani reports that Abu Hanifa, the founder of one of the four Sunni legal schools, allowed these tactics as well as the use of catapults and flooding to defeat the enemy. These methods may be employed against an enemy target even when women, children, and old men will be killed. If the enemy uses Muslims as shields, even then the Muslim forces may attack them. The reason given by Abu Hanifa is that if Muslims stopped attacking their enemies for fear of killing noncombatants, they would not be able to fight at all, "for there is no city in the territory of war in which there is no one at all of these . . . mentioned."[26]

Abu Hanifa's justification summarizes the medieval approach to noncombatant immunity. Muslim forces should exercise discrimination in war, but if "collateral damage" is inflicted, then the blame lies with the enemy, who made protection of noncombatants impossible. In general, the medieval theory views damage to the enemy as self-incurred harm. If Muslim forces violate the normal restrictions on conduct, it is because of provocation by the enemy. Yet strict reciprocity has never been established as a principle of the Islamic ethics of war: wanton disregard for humane treatment of combatants and noncombatants by the enemy does not permit Muslim armies to respond in kind.

In current Muslim discourse on war and peace, ius in bello issues receive very little attention. This is true despite the vast changes that have occurred in both the international law and the technology of warfare. The discussion that does occur is usually undertaken by modernists seeking to reinterpret the Qur'an and sunna so that Islamic injunctions correspond to current international practice.[27] Invariably these works concentrate on demonstrating the obsolescence of various aspects of medieval theory, such as the killing or enslavement of prisoners or the distribution of enemy property. More contemporary issues, such as the definition of noncombatant immunity and the use of terrorist methods by some Islamic groups, have yet to be treated systematically.

Far more relevant and interesting discussion of right conduct in war occurs in the context of specific conflicts. During the "war of the cities" toward the end of the Iran-Iraq War, for example, Mehdi Bazargan and the Liberation Movement of Iran (LMI) repeatedly protested that Khomeini was violating Islamic prohibitions against targeting civilians when he authorized missile strikes against Baghdad in retaliation for Iraq's Scud missile attacks against Teheran. In one "open letter" to Khomeini, the LMI wrote:

> According to Islam, it is justifiable retribution only if we, with our own missiles, hit the commanders or senders of the Iraqi missiles rather than hitting civilian areas and killing innocent people and turning their homes and communities into ghost towns and hills of rubble, all in the name of striking military targets.[28]

But the LMI never developed its argument. Issues raised by its criticism, such as "double effect," "reciprocity," and "proportionality of means," were never fully addressed.

More systematic discussion of just means occurred during the Persian Gulf War. In fact, ius in bello rather than ius ad bellum concerns dominated Muslim debates on the ethics of the conflict. Among the points raised by opponents of the anti-Iraq coalition's policies was that the conflict should be treated as fitna, that is, a dispute among Muslims. The rules concerning fitna developed by medieval jurists do not permit Muslims to ally themselves with non-Muslims, particularly when military decision-making is in non-Muslim hands. The prohibition was based on the belief that unbelievers would not apply the stricter code of conduct incumbent upon Muslims when fighting other Muslims. Critics of the Gulf War have argued that the conduct of the war by the coalition validates the medieval jurists' concerns. The massive air bombardment of Iraq's governmental and industrial facilities, they charge, was disproportionate to the Iraqi provocation and insufficiently discriminated between military and civilian targets. Moreover, the slaughter of Iraqi troops fleeing Kuwait City on the "highway of death" directly contravened one of the central points of Islamic law, namely that the goal of all military campaigns against other Muslims should be to rehabilitate and not to annihilate the transgressing party.

The most glaring area of neglect in contemporary Islamic analyses of ius in bello concerns weapons of mass destruction. So far, no systematic work has been done by Muslim scholars on how nuclear, chemical, and biological weapons relate to the Islamic ethics of war. This is an astonishing fact in light of the development of nuclear technology by several Muslim countries and the repeated use of chemical weapons by Iraq. In discussing the issue with several leading Muslim specialists in international law, I have found a great deal of ambivalence on the subject. Most scholars cite the Qur'anic verse "Hence, make ready against them whatever force and war mounts you are able to muster, so that you might deter thereby the enemies of God" (8:60) as justification for developing nuclear weaponry. Muslims must acquire nuclear weapons, I have been repeatedly told, because their enemies have introduced such weapons into their arsenals. There is unanimous agreement that Muslims should think of nuclear weapons only as a deterrent and that they should be used only as a second-strike weapon. But Islamic discussion of this topic remains at a very superficial level. There is little appreciation of the logistics of nuclear deterrence and of the moral difficulties to which a deterrence strategy gives rise.

Conclusion

Is the Islamic jihad the same as the Western just war? The answer, of course, depends upon who is defining the concepts. But after this brief survey of the debates that have historically surrounded the Islamic approach to war and peace and the controversies that are continuing to this day, I think it is safe to conclude that even though jihad may not be identical to the just war as it has evolved in the West, the similarities between Western and Islamic thinking on war and peace are far more numerous than the differences.

Jihad, like just war, was conceived by its early theorists basically as a means to circumscribe the legitimate reasons for war to so few that peace is inevitably enhanced. Jihad, like just war, is grounded in the belief that intersocietal relations should be peaceful, not marred by constant and destructive warfare. The surest way for human beings to realize this peace is for them to obey the divine law that is imprinted on the human conscience and therefore accessible to everyone, believers and unbelievers. According to the medieval view, Muslims are obliged to propagate this divine law, through peaceful means if possible, through violent means if necessary. No war was jihad unless it was undertaken with right intent and as a last resort, and declared by right authority. Most Muslims today disavow the duty to propagate Islam by force and limit jihad to self-defense. And finally, jihad, like just war, places strict limitations on legitimate targets during war and demands that belligerents use the least amount of force necessary to achieve the swift cessation of hostilities.

Both jihad and just war are dynamic concepts, still evolving and adapting to changing international realities. As Muslims continue to interpret the Islamic ethics of war and peace, their debates on jihad will, I believe, increasingly parallel the Western debates on just war. And as Muslims and non-Muslims continue their recently begun dialogue on the just international order, they may well find a level of agreement on the ethics of war and peace that will ultimately be reflected in a revised and more universal law of war and peace.

Notes

1. Fazlur Rahman, "Law and Ethics in Islam," in Richard G. Hovanissian, ed., *Ethics in Islam: Ninth Giorgia Levi Della Vida Biennial Conference* (Malibu, CA: Undena Publications, 1985), 9.

2. Ibn Khaldun, *The Muqadimma: An Introduction to History*, trans. Franz Rosenthal (Princeton: Princeton University Press, 1981), 223.

3. The Qur'an argues in several places for the inner consistency of the moral code elaborated within it. See 4:82, 25:32, and 39:23. These verses are part of an extended debate contained in the Qur'an against the Meccan polytheists as well as Christians and Jews who argued that the Qur'an was Muhammad's own agglomeration of disparate scriptures and moral codes.

4. Ahmad b. 'Abdallah Abu Nu'aim al-Isfahani, *Dala'il al-Nubuwwa* (Hyderabad: Da'irat al-Ma'arif al-'Uthmaniyya, 1977), 139.

5. Cited in M. Abu Laylah, *In Pursuit of Virtue: The Moral Theology and Psychology of Ibn Hazm al-Andalusi* (London: TaHa Publishers, 1990), 51.

6. Fred Donner, "Sources of Islamic Conceptions of War," in John Kelsay and James Turner Johnson, eds., *Just War and Jihad: Historical and Theoretical Perspectives on War and Peace in Western and Islamic Traditions* (New York: Greenwood Press, 1991), 34.

7. See the valuable study by Toshihiko Izutsu, *Ethico-Religious Concepts in the Qur'an* (Montreal: McGill University Press, 1966), 74–104.

8. Montgomery Watt, for example, writes: "It was essentially from the lighthearted razzia [the corrupted form of ghazwa] that the Islamic idea and practice of the jihad or holy war developed." W. Montgomery Watt, "Islamic Conceptions of the Holy War," in Thomas Murphy, ed., *The Holy War* (Columbus: Ohio State University Press, 1976), 142.

9. There are, however, some significant modern examples of Muslim advocacy and practice of nonviolent resistance. See Ralph E. Crow, Philip Grant, and Saad E. Ibrahim, eds., *Arab Nonviolent Political Struggle in the Middle East* (Boulder, CO: Lynne Rienner Publishers, 1990).

10. Muhammad Husayn Haykal, *The Life of Muhammad*, trans. Ismail Ragi al-Faruqi (Indianapolis: North American Trust, 1976), 204.

11. Haykal, *Life of Muhammad*, 208.

12. Jalal al-Din al-Suyuti, *Asbab al-Nuzul* (Cairo: Dar al-Tahrir li'l-Tab' wa'l-Nashr, 1963), 128.

13. Imam Bukhari, *Sahih al-Bukhari*, trans. Muhammad Muhsin Khan (Beirut: Dar al-Arabia, 1985), 4: 165.

14. Ibn Khaldun, *Muqadimma*, 224.

15. Plato, *The Republic*, trans. Allan Bloom (New York: Basic Books, 1968), 150.

16. Ibn Rushd, *Bidayat al-Mujtahid*, in Rudolph Peters, ed. and trans., *Jihad in Medieval and Modern Islam* (Leiden: E. J. Brill, 1977), 9–25.

17. Ibn Rushd, *Bidayat al-Mujtahid*, 22–23.

18. Mohammad Talaat al-Ghunaimi, *The Muslim Conception of International Law and the Western Approach* (The Hague: Martinus Nijhoff, 1968), 184.

19. Muhammad Abu Zahra, *Concept of War in Islam*, trans. Muhammad al-Hady and Taha Omar (Cairo: Ministry of Waqf, 1961), 18.

20. Ayatollah Murtaza Mutahhari, "Defense: The Essence of *Jihad*," in Mehdi Abedi and Gary Legenhausen, eds., *Jihad and Shahadat: Struggle and Martyrdom in Islam* (Houston: Institute for Research and Islamic Studies, 1986), 105.

21. Abu'l-A'la Maududi, *Jihad fi Sabil Allah* (Lahore: Idara Tarjuman al-Qur'an, 1988), 55–56.

22. For a more detailed discussion of this issue, see Sohail Hashmi, "Is There an Islamic Ethic of Humanitarian Intervention?" *Ethics and International Affairs* 7 (1993), 55–73.

23. Quoted in John Alden Williams, ed., *Themes of Islamic Civilization* (Berkeley and Los Angeles: University of California Press, 1972), 262.

24. Ibn Rushd, *Bidayat al-Mujtahid*, 16–17.

25. The prohibition against using fire in warfare was based on a tradition of the Prophet: "No one is free to punish by means of fire, save the Lord of the Fire"—that is, God. Ibn Rushd, *Bidayat al-Mujtahid*, 18.

26. Muhammad ibn al-Hasan Shaybani, *Siyar al-Kabir*, trans. Majid Khadduri, *The Islamic Law of Nations* (Baltimore: The Johns Hopkins University Press, 1966), 101–2.

27. Two important modernist discussions of the means of war are Abu Zahra, *Concept of War in Islam*, 44–68, and Muhammad Hamidullah, *The Muslim Conduct of State*, 7th ed. (Lahore: Sh. Muhammad Ashraf, 1977), 202–54.

28. Liberation Movement of Iran, "A Warning Concerning the Continuation of the Destructive War" (Houston, TX: Maktab, 1988), 14.

PART THREE

Critical Perspectives: Christian Pacifism and Feminism

CHAPTER 9

Christian Nonviolence: An Interpretation

Theodore J. Koontz

I HAVE FOUR AIMS in this chapter. The first is to describe briefly something of the range of views that may fit under the heading "Christian nonviolence." The second is to give an account of the context out of which it makes sense to be committed to a certain kind of Christian nonviolence ("pacifism"). The third is to note how, from this pacifist perspective, the questions posed to the contributors to this volume are not the central questions about peace and war, and how focusing on them in fact distorts our thinking. The fourth is to attempt, nevertheless, to deal with these questions from this pacifist perspective. Needless to say, a discussion that includes all of these issues will be rather sketchy.

Varieties of Christian Nonviolence

There are a number of ways to classify views that might be seen as belonging to the "family" of Christian nonviolence. John H. Yoder presents over twenty different "pacifist" views, and Peter Brock, the dean of historians of Christian pacifism, identifies six pacifist views, all of which are essentially subsets of the first tradition I outline below.[1] Each of these views has a somewhat different basis, rationale, and perspective, and each might approach the questions addressed in this book in a somewhat different way.

For our purposes, I note three versions of Christian nonviolence—pacifism, abolitionism, and nonviolent resistance. None of these is exclusively "Christian." Historically, however, the first view is more closely tied to Christian thought in the West than the other two views, whose advocates have been more diverse.[2]

A comment on terminology is in order. Language here is confusing. "Pacifism" originally meant something closer to what I am calling "abolitionism," and people who are what I am calling "pacifists" previously often called themselves "nonresistants" and sharply differentiated themselves from "pacifists," that is, abolitionists.[3] The term "pacifism" has evolved in ways parallel, perhaps, to the term "liberalism" in politics, with parallel confusions. I use the term the way I do because I think this is closer to common usage today. There is also no agreement on what to call what was formerly called "pacifism." Essentially, what was called "pacifism" is what

I am calling "abolitionism." The same basic perspective has been described by other authors and given different labels: "pacific-ism" by Martin Ceadel and "utopian pacifism" by James Turner Johnson, for example.[4] The first form of nonviolence, pacifism, is also the oldest. It is—minimally—the view that it is *morally* wrong for *me* to participate *directly* in *killing* in *all war*. Each of the italicized terms is important in carving out a minimal definition of pacifism. Pacifists often make larger claims (it is morally wrong for *everyone*, *all* killing is wrong, etc.), and the definition includes persons making such larger claims also. The term "pacifism" is, however, sometimes used to refer to those who have a strong desire for peace or aversion to war, but who are not necessarily committed to personal nonparticipation in all wars. This view is not included in my usage.

Pacifism, as understood here, was the dominant (though by no means only) position of Christians for the first three centuries of the Christian movement, the position of the early Waldensians, the early Unity of the Czech Brethren, and the Anabaptists. It has been and is the predominant (and official) position of Mennonites (and the related Amish), Quakers (Friends), and the Church of the Brethren.[5] In recent centuries, especially, one also finds an increasing number of individuals and subgroups within nonpacifist denominations who are pacifists. I will focus here primarily on the historical pacifist groups.

In the West, pacifism typically has been rooted in specifically Christian theological claims. It focuses on the need for *Christians* to live and act on Christian standards, rather than on what often seem to representatives of this tradition like less-than-Christian standards. It focuses on creating a new society, made up of believers who are committed to governing their lives together by those standards. It does not necessarily claim to offer readily applicable policy advice to public officials on matters of war and peace. It typically stresses the need for conversion in order to enable persons and communities to live nonviolently, defenselessly, and is most often pessimistic about the prospects of peace in a world that does not know Christ. Although pacifists know that sometimes turning the other cheek is effective in transforming the enemy, they tend to stress readiness to accept suffering as an essential part of the disarmed life.

The second tradition I call "abolitionism." Within this tradition, there is a commitment to abolish the evil of war, in a way somewhat parallel to the way in which there developed a commitment to abolish the evil of slavery. War in this view is no more an inherent part of life or a necessary evil than slavery was. There is a moral mandate to set up a world system that will make war obsolete. There is a great moral revulsion against war, and a skepticism about its utility that is typically absent from "realist" and just war writings. At the same time, there is an optimism about getting rid of war that is typically absent from just war and realist thought, and from much pacifist thought. And, in contrast to pacifists, abolitionists do not *necessarily* (though some do) firmly refuse to participate in all wars. There is a focus on transforming the whole world (not on living a new life in an alternative society made up of those who have voluntarily chosen to follow Christ's way), and there is a confidence in human nature (apart from conversion) and in education—helping people see the evident follies and costs of war as a means of settling conflicts—that is quite different from the most typical expressions of Christian pacifism.

The abolitionist tradition goes back at least to Erasmus and is not as exclusively Christian in its membership as the pacifist tradition. Nor is it as necessarily Christian, meaning it depends less upon uniquely Christian theological claims. Immanuel Kant's scheme for perpetual peace, along with other world-peace plans propounded by figures such as William Penn (among others), reflect this perspective.[6] Various peace societies that emerged in the nineteenth century in England and the United States came to have predominantly this coloring.[7] This was the dominant mode of American and British "liberal pacifists" in the early part of this century.[8] In a less nearly pacifist form, it also was behind the internationalism and idealism that led to the formation of the League of Nations and the United Nations. Throughout the last two decades or so, this viewpoint finds embodiment in its more radical form in much of the "peace movement," and in a less radical form in groups like the World Policy Institute that press for a more effective international community, often including removal of military force from the hands of independent states.

It is worth noting that although the tone and ethos of these first two "types" of Christian nonviolence are quite different, they are not incompatible in a fundamental sense: one could be (many have been) a pacifist—one personally refusing service in all wars—and an abolitionist. Thus, though it is helpful to differentiate them, they should not be separated too sharply.

The third member of this "family" we might best call "nonviolent resistance." Though the name stresses *resistance*, and though this perspective has been developed most fully in settings where the need for resistance to unjust political power is a primary motivating factor, the perspective also includes efforts to find ways of *defending* relatively just political systems from aggression (or, to make this compatible with our terminology, ways of *resisting* aggression).

This perspective is characterized, especially in relation to "pacifism" as portrayed here, by its insistence that there are normally (if not always) pragmatically effective nonviolent means of "fighting" that are viable alternatives to war and military conflict and that can achieve or protect crucial values. Although its chief practitioners can be, and often have been, pacifists in the sense of renouncing all use of arms on ethical grounds, this position does not necessarily rely on a theological/ethical argument, though such an argument is often part of the case made for this view. What distinguishes it from "pacifism" is its stress both on the effectiveness of nonviolent action and on the need for active involvement in the pursuit of justice. The Gandhian movement in India and the civil rights movement in the United States led by Martin Luther King, Jr. have been the chief inspirations for this viewpoint. The chief intellectual architect of this position in the contemporary secular Western world is Gene Sharp of the Albert Einstein Institution in Cambridge, Massachusetts, which is probably the major research center devoted specifically to "advancing the study and use of strategic nonviolent action in conflicts throughout the world." Central to this view is the claim that power depends upon the consent—or acquiescence—of the governed. This means that the tyranny of governments can be overcome through nonviolent resistance and that countries can be defended against aggression nonviolently. Adherents to this view do not necessarily hope that threats, including military threats, will disappear as better conflict-resolution mechanisms evolve and as people and groups become more internationalist in outlook (as abolitionists seem to hope). Instead they argue that there are effective nonviolent means for dealing with such threats—as the first view often does not assume.

As the mention of Martin Luther King, Jr. suggests, there are important bridges between "pacifist" commitment (as defined above), Christian theological understanding and commitment, and certain strands of nonviolent resistance to evil. King's own writings reflect these bridges, combining a theologically based commitment to nonviolence and an activist commitment to the pursuit of justice. Thus, as he shows, Christian "pacifism" and Christian "nonviolent resistance" belong together, even though intentionally moving to confront evil, as King did, often has not characterized pacifist groups. In its Christian versions, "nonviolent resistance" relies less on pragmatic claims about effectiveness, stressing especially both the need to identify with the poor and marginalized and the cost of doing so.[9] Nevertheless, those holding such views do generally seem to have a greater hope for the transformation of entire societies through effective nonviolent struggle than is typical of most pacifist groups historically.

The overthrow of communist regimes in Eastern Europe and the former Soviet Union is seen by advocates of nonviolent resistance as providing recent and dramatic evidence in favor of this perspective. From this vantage point, it is striking in light of recent events in Eastern Europe, the Philippines, and Iran (to mention only the places where "revolutions" have taken place essentially along lines advocated by persons like Sharp) that the power of nonviolence is not reflected more in the essays here. Surely it is the case that such power does not always "win," as Tiananmen Square shows. But the same is true of violence. Don't these events challenge some of the basic assumptions of realism and just war theory, or at least raise questions about when we have reached last resort? What would it mean to take these experiences seriously as we seek to rethink our views about ethics and war?

I hope this brief description is useful in showing that these pacifist views are different in significant ways. At the same time, it is important to note that they are not necessarily opposed to one another in important respects. In fact, they often overlap and intermingle. One could, for example, be a pacifist who promoted strengthening international institutions and who advocated nonviolent defense. These three members of the Christian nonviolence "family" share, in contrast to most realist or just war views, an understanding of power that is not easily correlated with the ability to coerce or force others to do one's bidding through military means. Even though pacifists stress the power of persuasion and example (rooted for Christian pacifists in the power of suffering love and God's overarching power or control), abolitionists emphasize the power of reason and common interests, and advocates of nonviolent resistance underscore the power of withdrawing consent through nonviolent actions, each group in its own way disputes the claim that power grows out of the barrel of the gun. Thus these viewpoints are less inclined to see the "necessity" of war than are most other views "outside the family."

Understanding Christian Pacifism

In this section, I am intentionally narrowing the focus to the first of the three views outlined in the previous section, and to one version of that view. Even so, the task is not an easy one. How does one make Christian pacifist commitment intelligible to the wise of the world? I frankly doubt that it can be done. But if it can, I believe the only possible way to proceed is by seeking to show how reality looks from within the world of those (or some of those—there is diversity) who hold this view, not by arguing for it.[10]

"Showing how reality looks" from this Christian pacifist perspective requires challenging some assumptions that we commonly make, and that are made in this book. One such assumption is that we come to know the truth primarily through intellectual argument and exchange, and, perhaps, that there is something like "neutral" ground on the basis of which to judge alternatives. A closely related assumption is that a conference or a classroom is the primary venue though which we come to know the truth. I do not intend to argue here that these assumptions are wrong. I do not know how to make such an argument. But I do want to claim that these are not the assumptions that Christian pacifists make, and that if one wants to understand why some people are Christian pacifists, one must suspend these assumptions and enter their (our) world on their (our) terms. In making this claim, I do not mean to say that such activities are illegitimate, or to claim that we Christian pacifists do not engage in them (I make my living, after all, standing in front of a class and attending conferences), or to put what I say beyond the reach of criticism. But I do mean to say that when we engage in intellectual arguments with those outside the Christian pacifist tradition, we are speaking, as it were, a "second language," and we are doing so in a context that is not our "home."

Worship, it seems to me, is where Christian pacifists are most deeply at home, where they (we) come to know the truth, where we speak our first, our deepest, language. It is in this context of worship, with its "language" of hymns, prayers, sermons, stories, testimonies, confession, praise, celebration, and communion, that Christians come to know God's will. One might well state it even more forcefully. It is worship that in fact constitutes and defines the community. It is worship that creates and sustains it. Worship is not mainly an activity the community undertakes, but its reason for being, that which makes it a community.[11]

Thus much of what gives power and vitality to the tradition of Christian pacifism cannot be perceived in a book like the one you are reading. Our "truth" is apt to be invisible here, or in an academic conference. Nevertheless, I can seek to open a small window onto the world of Christian pacifism by bringing a part of our "worship" before you. I have chosen to do so through an excerpt from a sermon I preached one Palm Sunday. There is nothing exceptional about the sermon. Indeed, that is the point. In important respects it is typical of the viewpoint that Christian pacifists hold and that shapes their (our) understandings of ethics, war, and peace. It was titled, "Blessed Is the King!"

I began the sermon by noting that in two important respects Palm Sunday is a Sunday of false hope: first, because it proclaimed a victory before it was won—Jesus, the one who was proclaimed messiah on Palm Sunday, was arrested and crucified within the week; and second, because Jesus was not the kind of messiah the people wanted. He did not break the power of Rome and restore the glory of the Davidic kingdom. Yet the Christian Gospel claims that he is king, messiah, that he is victorious, powerful. How can this be?

> His is a strange victory, a strange power. Victory came, and can come, but in a radically different way than the Palm Sunday crowds expected. The victory of Jesus is not a popular, political, national liberation victory. It is a victory that is realized when it takes root in the hearts and minds of people who have eyes to see and ears to hear and who form communities to celebrate the victory they see and hear. It is a victory that the powers that rule in the capitals of the world can, if they choose, simply pretend is not real, at least for a very long time. It is

a victory that conquers no one except as they open themselves to it. Yet it is a victory that is extremely hard to resist if one does open one's eyes to see, and does unstop one's ears to hear. And it is a victory that freed and empowered those frightened first disciples when they finally saw it, heard it, even while the structures of Roman power remained unshaken. While it is a victory that threatens, and ultimately overcomes, the resistance of the enemy, it is a victory that can be experienced, celebrated, lived, even while the enemy still sits smugly on his throne.

The victory of Jesus is also strange because it is not the work of a dedicated band of revolutionaries who seized the reins of power in order to remake human history. Rather, the victory of Jesus, confirmed in his resurrection, is one that comes by Another's hand. Whatever else Christian faith may mean, it surely has something to do with affirming this kind of surprising, powerful, renewing action by God. It means not finally resting our hopes on ourselves or on other humans, although we surely have our part.

If the shape of the victory of Jesus is strange, so too is the power that wins the victory. I think it is their failure to recognize this strange power as *true* power that causes Jesus to say of the people of Jerusalem as he overlooks the city, "If only you had recognized the things that make for peace" (Luke 19:42). One way to describe this power that makes for peace is to call it the power of vulnerability. It is the power that comes when defenses fall, when fear of being hurt or killed disappears, when one is no longer interested in defending oneself, but in doing God's will. When we no longer seek to protect or defend ourselves, when we make ourselves fully vulnerable, we are free. Of course we can be killed. But nothing can deter us from doing or saying what we believe is true. When we accept vulnerability, literally nothing has power over us.

For many years I had puzzled over what it might mean to say, as Paul does in Colossians 2:15, Jesus "disarmed the principalities and powers and made a public example of them, triumphing over them in it (the cross)."

How did Jesus disarm the powers, or make a public example of them through the cross? What is the nature of the power that this King Jesus exercises, the nature of the power that he offers to us?

I was helped to understand this by remembering the story of "The Emperor's New Clothes" by Hans Christian Andersen. . . . The emperor in the story is not that different from many modern "emperors," who won't admit to mistakes or sins for fear that doing so will undermine their authority. They would rather pretend they are not naked—stripped of the moral right to rule—and punish those who point out that they are, than to change their ways.

More important, the people around Andersen's emperor are not that different from many modern people, who, fearing punishment or loss of position, go along with their emperor's pretensions. There is a powerful incentive for officials, and for ordinary citizens, to pretend they don't see the emperor's nakedness because emperors often torture and kill those who expose them.

But despite this, the power or authority of emperors is still dependent on the people being willing to go along with emperors' claims to "legitimacy" (the emperor's moral *right* to rule). If ever there has been a historical moment when the truth of this claim ought to be evident, it is now. Within the last fifteen years we have witnessed the fall of incredibly powerful regimes that could not withstand the power of people who were willing to say, "The emperor is naked!" From Iran, to the Philippines, to Eastern Europe, to the Soviet Union, change that was unimaginable, and that could not be brought about by force of arms, has taken place. As my colleague Walter Sawatsky and others have shown, central to the changes in the East was a commitment of a few to begin speaking and living the truth, a commitment to refuse participation in the lie, a commitment to begin living now "as if" honesty, freedom, and human decency were already the norms by which society ran.[12] It is simply true, to turn to another source of authority for Americans, the US Declaration of Independence, that governments derive their "powers from the consent of the governed." When enough people, despite fear of repression, see and *say* of illegitimate regimes, with the child in Andersen's story, that the emperor is naked, then his power is gone, because his power is based on fear. What is most remarkable about governments is not their incredible capability to repress dissent but their fragility when their moral nakedness is exposed.

This, I think, is what Jesus showed us. Jesus had power over the powers that be because their power *is*, finally, dependent on the acquiescence of the people—and Jesus refused to acquiesce. Jesus stripped the emperor's power over him because he did not let fear of what the authorities could do to him force him to pretend the emperor was clothed. Since, when consent is absent, terror is the only kind of power left to emperors, Jesus did, in fact, "disarm" the powers that be, he "made a public example of them" showing not only their illegitimacy but also their literal "powerlessness" in the face of those who refuse to be terrorized. Thus he "triumphed over them," precisely "in the cross."

The key to this triumph, though, is overcoming fear, accepting vulnerability. So long as we are ruled by fear, we can be neither free nor powerful. How can we overcome fear, accept the possibility of the cross, live lives that are, paradoxically, both fully vulnerable, and wonderfully powerful? I believe that the key lies in really seeing, in really *believing*, that Jesus is King. Though we take for granted the Kingship of Jesus and, unlike the people of his time, understand that his Kingship is radically different from that of worldly kings, I wonder if we *really* understand, I wonder if we *really* believe.

I remember the power of Martin Luther King, Jr., and how that power required overcoming fear. He lived with constant threats, and survived a number of attacks aimed at him. Perhaps a small sense of the pressure under which he lived can be gained by recalling the story told by Joan Baez of a meeting with King in 1964, four years before he was killed. King, Baez, and another friend went to a restaurant at an odd hour for a quiet conversation. At a table nearby in the nearly empty restaurant there was a group of men sitting, watching them. Curious about what they were doing, she went over and asked them. Sheepishly, they answered that they were reporters who had been assigned to follow King wherever he went. Their purpose was to be there so that they would have the scoop when the inevitable happened and King was assassinated. Shaken, but seeking to act normal, Baez returned to King's table and sat down. Before she could say anything, King said quietly and matter-of-factly, "They are waiting for me to be killed, aren't they?"

Now King, like Jesus, is a heroic, larger-than-life figure. We may not be called to live with such radical vulnerability. Their examples may seem irrelevant to us. Yet I think we often fail to choose the power of vulnerability, even though we have a very small amount to lose by choosing *that* power instead of the power of self-protection, the power of hiding behind the emperor's clothes. If you are like me, you often have refused to speak to someone with whom you disagree and have allowed a barrier to grow between you, because of fear of confrontation. If you are like me, you have sometimes failed to speak to friends about things that trouble you concerning their behavior. If you are like me, you have sought to block potential criticism by issuing a quick and superficial "I'm sorry," or simply by avoiding one who may have reason to admonish you. If you are like me, you often do not speak of that which matters most to you, about your faith, about your fears, about your dreams, about your failures, yes, even about your sins. If you are like me, you often do not reach out deeply to those near you who face struggles, because entering deeply into their struggles may mean exposing and facing your own struggles. Behind all these failures to live freely, powerfully, vulnerably, lies fear, fear growing out of our desire to protect ourselves. And to the extent that our lives are shaped by fear, to that extent we testify that we, like the people of Jesus' time, do not understand, do not believe, that Jesus is really King. Have we, any more than the disciples, really seen the new thing that Jesus did?

In this regard, I was struck by the text, "Do not remember the former things, or consider the things of old. I am about to do a new thing; now it springs forth, do you not perceive it?" (Isa. 43:18–19). We all have been well trained to see the "old things," to understand, and use, the kind of power that the Kings of this world use, though, of course, on our own modest scale. It is a power that seeks to perpetuate and solidify our ability to make ourselves *invulnerable*. It is the kind of power that has dominated the writing of history. A challenge to this view of power, this view of how history moves, is at the center of Christian faith. It is an illusory power, as Jesus' defeat of the powers shows, yet it is an illusory power that has a tenacious grip on us. When we can open ourselves to the Kingly, yes, even the Godly power of Jesus, when we can say "Blessed is *this* King," when we can overcome fear with love because we know that God is love and that God is all-powerful, when we can see the new thing that the Kingship of Jesus teaches us—when we can do these things we will become strangely powerful, we will be

> blessed with the power of God. Of course, exercising this kind of power sometimes will be costly. But when we truly see the power of Jesus, we also will see that the risk is worth it, for it is through accepting the power of vulnerability that we find abundant life. It is, after all, our servant-King, Jesus, the one who reveals to us God's nature, who promised, "Those who find their life will lose it, and those who lose their life for my sake will find it" (Matt. 10:39). We have nothing essential to lose in choosing to live by relying on Jesus's sort of power. And we have authentic life itself to find.

If one enters into the world of a people shaped by this kind of sermon, one will note that some additional widely held assumptions come into question. These include the assumption that we have a "right" to violently defend ourselves from harm, the assumption that we have a responsibility to ensure that we and our neighbors are not harmed by enemies if it is within our physical ability to do so, the assumption that we have the responsibility to provide an ethic for rulers that they can use and still maintain their domineering power, and the assumption, which seems to lie behind the idea that war is sometimes "necessary," that the most powerful power is the ability to force others, by physical threat or force, to do what we want them to do. Of course, the cross symbolizes the fact that Jesus's sort of power is not without cost. But then, neither is the power of war.

Topics

> The nature of the questions we raise is as important as the answers to our questions. Which questions guide our lives? Which questions do we make our own? . . . Finding the right questions is as crucial as finding the right answers.[13]

Before addressing directly the questions assigned that provide the point of departure for the essays in this volume, I want to reflect on them a bit more. A helpful place to begin is with Henri Nouwen's devotional book, *Lifesigns*. He observes the extraordinary degree to which fear drives us, controls us, and how this fear is rooted in accepting fear-full questions as our own.

> We are often seduced by the fearful questions the world presents to us. Without fully realizing it, we become anxious, nervous, worrying people caught in the questions of survival. . . . Once these fearful survival questions become the guiding questions of our lives, we tend to dismiss words spoken from the house of love as unrealistic, romantic, sentimental, pious, or just useless. When love is offered as an alternative to fear we say: "Yes, yes, that sounds beautiful, but. . . ." The "but" reveals how much we live in the grip of the world, a world which calls Christians naive and raises "realistic" questions. . . .

> When we raise these "realistic" questions we echo a cynical spirit which says: "Words about peace, forgiveness, reconciliation, and new life are wonderful but the real issues cannot be ignored. They require that we do not allow others to play games with us, that we retaliate when we are offended, that we are always ready for war. . . .
>
> Once we accept these questions as our own, and are convinced that we must find answers to them, we become more and more settled in the house of fear. When we consider how much of our . . . lives are geared to finding answers to questions born of fear, it is not hard to understand why a message of love has little chance of being heard.
>
> Fearful questions never lead to love-filled answers. . . . Fear engenders fear. Fear never gives birth to love.[14]

I sense that the questions we are to address are questions coming from "the house of fear." I am convinced that "defensive" or "justifiable" war is one of the deepest expressions of fear in human life, despite the undoubted courage of many who fight such wars. The questions, and "good" wars, are expressions of fear because they suggest that, unless we at least hold open the option of engaging in the carnage that war brings, what we care about will be destroyed.

This is, of course, a "realistic" fear. Yet Nouwen suggests that when we allow such a fear to dominate us, "we are back again in the house of fear." And he holds the conviction that "love is stronger than fear, though it may often seem that the opposite is true. 'Perfect love casts out all fear,' says St. John in his first letter." The question, he suggests, is this: "Is it possible in the midst of this fear-provoking world to live in the house of love and listen there to the questions raised by the Lord of love? Or are we so accustomed to living in fear that we have become deaf to the voice that says: 'Do not be afraid.'"[15]

What questions pertinent to our topic would we claim as our own if we lived in "the house of love," if we listened to the questions raised by the Lord of love? I do not have the answer to that. Some of my thinking on it, however, is reflected in the section below, "Morality in Extremity." Surely our questions would focus our attention much more on building peace than on asking when we may go to war. Generally, the key questions for Christian pacifists would be like these, I think: "How can we be conformed to the mind of Christ, enflesh his power? How can we incarnate God's radical, enemy-loving compassion, revealed in Jesus, in this case, in that situation? How can we break down the dividing walls of hostility?" More specifically, the questions may take these forms, as they have for particular friends and colleagues of mine in the last several months: "Should I leave my wife and two small children to return to Somalia for more peace-building talks, even though the last time I was there for that purpose I lost my leg and almost my life?" "Should I uproot my family with school-aged children so that I can work with other Christians to strengthen commitment to reconciliation in Serbia, Croatia, and Bosnia?" "Should we postpone or forego our plans for graduate school in order to volunteer for three years as teachers in an isolated West Bank village?" "Should we move our family to Mozambique so we can work with churches there in rebuilding, development, and reconciliation after more than a decade of war?" "Hearing" such questions surely requires us to hear the words of one who tells us, "Do not be afraid." Yet questions such as these seem to me to be the questions we will ask as we live in the house of love.

Nevertheless, even though the questions addressed in this volume seem to me to lead us into the house of fear, and thus to be the wrong questions, I am obliged to attempt a response. In what follows, I will speak to them primarily from the Christian nonviolence perspective I sketched in the previous section. Though at points I will suggest how other perspectives within the "family" might address an issue, I cannot be comprehensive or systematic.

Conceptions of War and Peace

For many Christian pacifists, war is understood as rooted most deeply in our "natural" (since the fall) sinful human impulses. Although the use of the term "war" is not limited, at least metaphorically, in this tradition to organized violence between large groups, our sinful human impulses spill over into group egoism, and into organized violence between groups—war. "What causes wars, and what causes fightings among you? Is it not your passions that are at war in your members? You desire and do not have; so you kill. And you covet and cannot obtain, so you fight and wage war" (James 4:1–2a, RSV). This description of war—war as the greedy grasping of selfish egos—sounds more realistic to many advocates of Christian nonviolence than do most moral justifications.

This perspective leads many Christian pacifists to a focus on the need for a voluntary, personal decision to accept the lordship of Christ and to allow God's power to begin transforming one so that it becomes possible to really love one's neighbor as oneself, so that it becomes possible even to love one's enemy, and thus, finally, so that it becomes possible to live nonviolently—without fear, in the house of love. This necessarily involves not only a personal experience, but participation in a community that undergirds and sustains such a commitment. The questions that are asked, the stories that are told, the conceptions of reality, including of God and God's power, that are communicated, have the effect of creating certain dispositions and orientations of persons within the community that foster a tendency to see things in a way that sustains nonviolent commitment and undergirds nonviolent living.

For Christian pacifists, then, peace would be understood broadly and positively (not simply as the absence of war), like the biblical term *shalom*, "a state of well-being, an all-rightness, an okayness."[16] This state refers to prosperity and security in the physical realm, to just and healthy relationships in the interpersonal or intergroup realm, and to honesty and integrity in the moral realm.[17] The tradition has been committed to finding ways to live in shalom concretely, here and now, within the community of faith and, as much as possible, in relation to the wider world. Though this has never been achieved fully even within the community, many ways of seeking to do so have evolved, including various kinds of mutual aid and sharing (barn-raisings are perhaps the most conspicuous example, though persons in a part of the tradition, Hutterites, have held all property in common, and many other kinds of mutual assistance have developed), and immigration when military service was demanded or when lack of land threatened to impoverish permanently some members of the community. Traditionally, elders within the many pacifist churches would visit members before communion to make certain that all serious hurts and conflicts were dealt with so that the body could be united in its celebration of the Lord's Supper. These practices, and many others, have been designed to foster shalom in a full sense, especially within the faith community.[18] Though Quakers have long engaged in "positive peacemaking" in the wider world, in the twentieth century this shalom-building in the world (not withdrawal or passivity) has increasingly typified the orientation of other Christian pacifist groups as well.[19]

Yet although the vision of peace is broad, encompassing, positive, the tradition has also held that one can be "at peace" with one's enemies, in situations that are far from shalom. One will not always be treated rightly, justly, no matter how much one seeks to treat others that way. In such cases, this tradition has encouraged injured persons (and others knowing of the injury) to seek redress by confronting the party doing wrong (following the model of Matt. 18:15–17, for example, in cases involving other believers). Pacifism is not passive acceptance of abuse. Yet the tradition has also stressed the need to forgive repeated offenses (Matt. 18:21–22), to let go of hurt, anger, animosity, to forego retaliation.

> You have heard it said, an eye for an eye and a tooth for a tooth, but I say unto you, do not resist one who is evil. But if any one strikes you on the right cheek, turn to him the other also. . . . You have heard that it was said, "You shall love your neighbor and hate your enemy." But I say to you, Love your enemy and pray for those who persecute you. . . . For if you love those who

> love you, what reward have you? Do not even the tax collectors do the same? (Matt. 5:38–46)

With the enablement of God's transforming love, one need not either hate or return evil to one who does harm. Again, the tradition is full of stories that illustrate this, and that undergird commitment to live this way, the foremost being Jesus on the cross: "Father, forgive them, for they do not know what they are doing" (Luke 23:34). Another central story from the Anabaptist Mennonite tradition is that of Dirk Willems. Dirk's story is retold in *The Martyrs Mirror*, a book second in importance only to the Bible in Mennonite homes for generations. It is a bloody, 1,100-page account of Christians being martyred for their faith, often at the hands of other Christians. Dirk, the court record shows, was apprehended and confessed to his crimes: that

> he was rebaptized in Rotterdam . . . and that he, further, in Asperen, at his house, at divers hours, harbored and admitted secret conventicles and prohibited doctrines, and that he also has permitted several persons to be rebaptized in his aforesaid house; all of which is contrary to our holy Christian faith, and to the decrees of his royal majesty, and ought not to be tolerated, but severely punished, for an example to others.

Therefore, the judges condemned Dirk to be "executed with fire, until death ensues." Dirk escaped from prison and ran across some thin ice to get away from the "thief-catcher" who was sent after him.

> The thief-catcher following him broke through, when Dirk Willems, perceiving that the former was in danger of his life, quickly returned and aided him in getting out, and thus saved his life. The thief-catcher wanted to let him go, but the burgomaster, very sternly called to him to consider his oath, and thus he was again seized by the thief-catcher, and . . . put to death at the lingering fire."[20]

Shalom living in the midst of a sinful world demands the ability to forgive and love even when an enemy continues to treat us as an enemy, to continue to repay evil with good even in the face of injustice. "Heroes" exemplifying this, like Dirk, shape character in rather different ways than heroes like Rambo.

Attitudes toward War and Nonviolence

As is clear from what has been said previously, there is a very strong presumption against war within the tradition of Christian nonviolence. For most within this tradition, we might say that the presumption is absolute, allowing no exceptions. It may be worth reiterating, however, that although Christian pacifism has generally been rooted in a theological/ethical framework that interprets Christian ethics as requiring renunciation of violence in order to conform to the mind of Christ, other grounds for a presumption against violence are present in other strands of the tradition of Christian nonviolence.

These grounds include the claim that other structures can and should be put into place that would provide alternative means for resolving conflicts in more orderly and less destructive ways than war offers (abolitionism), and the claim that there are other more effective means for overthrowing unjust regimes or for defending against aggression that are less costly and thus are to be preferred on pragmatic grounds to war (nonviolent resistance). There is nothing logically inconsistent about holding all three arguments for the presumption against war, and many standing within this tradition do so. It might also be worth noting that although the arguments in favor of abolitionism and nonviolent resistance are often made on the grounds of pragmatic considerations (perhaps at least in part in order to appeal to others who seem to base decisions on pragmatic considerations), those who have advanced such arguments or have found them most compelling are frequently committed to nonviolence as an ethical principle. Whether this is a matter of wishful thinking, wanting to "have one's cake and eat it too," or whether it is a case where commitment to an ethical principle enables one to "see" viable alternatives that are not visible from perspectives that typically dominate ethical thought in the West cannot be resolved here.

One further note. Persons standing within the tradition of Christian nonviolence generally respond to wars with a deep feeling of sadness. War represents for Christian pacifists an ultimate symbol of human fallenness. This sense of war's sinfulness sometimes leads to angry denunciations of it or to a sinful smugness ("we" are not sinful like "they" are), but more deeply and authentically it leads to soul-searching for both the roots of war and conflict within oneself and one's community, for ways to act concretely to relieve the suffering that wars bring, and increasingly, in modern times, for ways to facilitate the avoidance of and/or ending of wars. I have in mind here, of course, the various abolitionist projects one associates with the figures described in the section on abolitionism, but also particularly Quaker (though not exclusively Quaker) efforts to foster dialogues between conflicting groups in contexts where options for settling differences can be explored informally and off the record.[21]

The Grounds for War

Though the tradition of Christian nonviolence recognizes many *reasons* for war, often running along the lines noted above under "Conceptions of War and Peace," all those within the tradition would claim that there are virtually never "legitimate grounds" for war, and most would hold that there are never such grounds. As noted earlier, some abolitionists are not opposed to personal participation in all wars. Historically, the willingness of abolitionists to sanction war has come mainly when a war is seen as necessary in order to end war. The First World War as the war to end war is the prime example.[22] In a somewhat related way, abolitionists have sometimes been willing to approve of wars that are deemed necessary in order to create a situation of "justice" that is seen as a prerequisite for peace in a positive (shalom-like) sense. Thus some whom I have called "abolitionist" (in relation to abolishing war) sanctioned the American civil war as a necessity to abolish the injustice of slavery.[23] Also, in recent times, some abolitionists have sanctioned, or at least have been unwilling to criticize, wars of "national liberation" or wars against "oppressive" regimes.[24] In addition, there have been apocalyptic groups who were committed to pacifism in the present age, but who were also ready to pick up the sword to help usher in the kingdom of God upon Christ's return. Some of these groups have decided that the time to fight has arrived, and have therefore abandoned their pacifism in favor of a righteous war.[25]

It is also the case that a certain "particularism" in a "typical" Christian pacifist perspective (this particularism has been less true of Quakers than of most other pacifist groups) that expects those committed to the way of Christ to live in ways that are different from what can be expected in the world has left open the possibility of persons from this perspective providing a certain "quasi-legitimate ground" for wars, not by "Christians," but by the state. It has been clear from within the tradition of Christian pacifism that *Christians* are called to live by the standards outlined, for example, in Romans 12:

> Bless those who persecute you; bless and do not curse them. . . . Do not repay anyone evil for evil. . . . No, "if your enemies are hungry, feed them; if they are thirsty, give them something to drink; for by doing this you will heap burning coals on their heads." Do not be overcome by evil, but overcome evil with good.

But the central text for the state for many Christian pacifists has been Romans 13:1–7, in which Christians are told to "be subject to the governing authorities," to "do what is good" because "rulers are not a terror to good conduct, but to bad." Although it has not been worked out systematically, since the focus has been on ethics for the Christian community, sometimes there has been a reluctance to condemn for the state certain wars of the state. This reluctance has its roots in an understanding of the state as given by God to maintain order, to protect the good, and to punish the wicked.

A classical formulation of this view for the Mennonite tradition is stated in the Schleitheim Confession dating from the beginning of the movement in 1527: "The sword is an ordering of God outside the perfection of

Christ. It punishes and kills the wicked, and guards and protects the good."[26] This view recognizes the state's ordering function, its calling to protect the good and restrain the evil; sometimes it even tacitly admits that the state's ordering function may entail the use of violence, perhaps even war. This recognition perhaps accounts for the fact that although pacifists have opposed participation in wars, some of them have not condemned a government's waging of certain of those wars (for example, American participation in the Second World War). This position seems to rest, at least in part, on a differentiation between the "vocation" or "calling" of Christ's disciples and that of the state. This differentiation has not necessarily been seen as meaning that Christians must reject all "governing," but it has meant that "governing," as well as everything else, must be done in ways compatible with Christ's teaching and example—and it has often meant much skepticism about the possibility of governing nations in a Christian manner.[27]

Having said all this, however, it must also be said that there has been no developed theory that seeks to argue exactly when wars might be "justified" for the state. In fact, "justified" must be in quotation marks, because war and violence are never finally, ultimately, "justified," from a Christian pacifist perspective. God's ultimate, final will for everyone is nonviolence. At best, war and violence are penultimately "justified" for persons who do not follow Jesus (as pacifists understand the meaning of that) and who are mandated to carry the ordering function of the state in a fallen world where "ordering" may require war or violence. If pressed on when wars might be "justified" for the state, pacifists within this tradition would perhaps utilize something like just war criteria. More generally, they might be inclined to argue that the appropriate standard for the state in international conflict, as well as in domestic law enforcement, could be derived from the concerns outlined in Romans 13, focusing especially on the state's responsibility to "protect the good." Such pacifists would also want to insist that this be done with the least possible degree of violence or coercion.[28] It is worth noting that the particularistic perspective reflected in this discussion, although it has deep roots in the Christian pacifist tradition, has increasingly been questioned by those who emphasize that the "lordship of Christ" extends not only over the church (where it is recognized) but over the world (even though it is not recognized there), and that there can therefore be no difference in ethical norm for the state as compared to the church. Persons holding this perspective would be more ready to condemn forthrightly all wars by the state, as well as all Christian participation in wars, while at the same time often being more ready to accept for Christians some "coercion" and "police" functioning than many more "particularistic" pacifists would be. Duane Friesen's work would be an example of this.[29]

Resistance to Political Authority

Christian pacifists have been quite ready to resist political authorities on points where they feel obeying political authorities would mean compromising obedience to God. The central text has been, "We must obey God rather than any human authority" (Acts 5:29). This resistance has taken various forms among those within the pacifist tradition, including, obviously, refusal of military service, but also sometimes including refusing to pay taxes used for military purposes, refusal to swear oaths, and refusal to engage in other practices that appear idolatrous. Sometimes pacifists have also seen nationalism, and the human sacrifices made in wars to the "gods" of the nations, as a kind of idolatry to be resisted.[30] In recent decades, resistance has also taken the form of pacifist agencies working against government restrictions that prevent them from carrying out their humanitarian programs. A case would be shipping medical supplies to North Vietnam in the early 1970s, thereby violating or circumventing the US policy outlawing "trading with the enemy." Resistance to authority within the Christian pacifist tradition has normally taken the form of "civil disobedience" rather than revolutionary attempts (either violent or nonviolent) to overthrow regimes. Christian pacifists have generally seen Jesus's approach either as nonpolitical or as following a different model of "politics" than that adopted by the revolutionaries of his time, the Zealots.[31] Often citing a text like Romans 13, they typically have had a rather high regard for the legitimate authority of government (even when it must be disobeyed because of a higher loyalty to God), and also typically have had a low view of what one might hope for from governments. Thus, generally, they have not been inclined to revolutionary activity. The Quakers, however, often have been more hopeful of changing governments than most other pacifist groups have been, and they have thus been more politically active, though still not revolutionary.[32]

The "nonviolent resistance" perspective has often been supportive of efforts toward "nonviolent revolution" in oppressive situations and has sought to provide mechanisms for overthrowing oppressive regimes that do not represent the will of the people. A kind of "democratic" standard seems to operate from within this perspective: governments are legitimate when they have the support of the population, and are legitimately overthrown (nonviolently) when they lack such support.

In earlier centuries, Christian pacifists faced with military service generally just sought some way to avoid that service, since it violated their convictions. As more democratic notions about government and citizenship (that is, the notion of being citizens rather than simply subjects) have become more widely prevalent among pacifist groups, pacifists have become active in advocating the "rights" of conscientious objectors, including the rights of objectors to particular wars. Some pacifists have seen conscientious objection as a means to resist the government and its warmaking machinery, and have therefore sought to upset that machinery by refusing to cooperate with a conscription system. Other pacifists have accepted conscription as a "legitimate" part of a state system of which they do not necessarily approve and in which they do not exercise power, but to which they are subject. Such pacifists have typically not resisted conscription when alternatives to military service are provided, but rather have been grateful that the government has shown respect for their religious convictions. Despite the variations, it is probably fair to say that most Christian pacifist groups have had an underlying attitude of some suspicion or mistrust of governments.

Motive or Intention

The Christian pacifist tradition does focus on motivation or intention when it stresses love of neighbor and love of enemy. Love is certainly a motive and an intention, a desire to seek the best for the other out of compassion. At the same time, pacifists are typically deeply skeptical of views that emphasize that actions should be judged on the basis of motives or intentions when the actions themselves seem to belie the stated motive or intention, or that do not attend to the destructiveness of the actions themselves. Augustine, for example, sometimes focuses on the effects of war on the person waging it in a way that seems to downplay excessively what it means in itself or to its victims:

> What is the evil in war? Is it the death of someone who will soon die in any case, that others may live in peaceful subjection? This is mere cowardly dislike, not any religious feeling. The real evils of war are love of violence, revengeful cruelty, fierce and implacable enmity, wild resistance, and the lust of power, and such like.[33]

Specifically, pacifists have found it difficult to take very seriously views that, in the case of war, stress that one can really "love" a person and at the same time kill him or her. The point is not that no one could ever kill and still feel compassion for the one being killed, but that this is a mistaken understanding of what Christian love is. Love is not mainly a sentiment or a feeling (though proper motivation is surely a part of it), but an action that concretely seeks the best for the one being loved. In this sense, pacifists have wanted to focus on the inherent quality of actions, as well as intentions or motives. Just as the Book of James argues that "faith by itself, if it has no works, is dead" (James 2:17), pacifists tend to hold that motivations or intentions that do not take the form of *action* understandable by those *receiving* the action as reflective of the motive or intention are dead.

It is as important to focus on the meaning of the action for its recipient as on the meaning of the action for its giver, for our actions are a central part of one of our most fundamental tasks, that of witnessing to, *communicating*, God's love.

All of this does not mean that pacifists have absolutely no interest in differentiating various motives or intentions related to warfare. But pacifists are deeply aware of the human heart's ability to deceive itself and, as a rule, tend to trust actions that are "inherently right" more than motives or intentions that are said to be "good"—even though the actions resulting from these motives or intentions violate normally accepted standards. It also means that pacifists often put more weight on not harming, and less weight on righting the evils of the world through the use of armed force, than many nonpacifists. This issue of self-deception, and of justifying actions that may be harmful to others on the basis of good intentions or good motives, is a central part of pacifists' problems with just war. From a pacifist standpoint, it seems that just war serves almost always to justify or legitimize *our* nation's war (rather than to call it seriously into a "court" where it must bear the burden of proof in showing that the normal presumption against war should be overridden), and to condemn *their* nation's war. And, of course, for "them," it works the same way in reverse.

The story of Dirk Willems calls to mind an additional reason for a typical pacifist skepticism about appeals to motives or intentions that then justify killing others out of love for them. Many of the torturers and killers of Anabaptist and other Christian martyrs claimed (I suspect sincerely) to be acting in love for them—and for other innocent souls who might be misled by them—as they cut off their fingers or put them on the pyre to burn them alive. In the discussions in Jerusalem that are part of the background of this book I was struck by the fact that representatives of some groups that have been relatively powerless (Jews and pacifists) argued for a focus on actions, and that some of those who have been powerful (Catholic advocates of natural law) argued for a focus on intentions and motives. Is such a focus on intentions and motives a luxury of the powerful—or even a way of rationalizing to themselves their hurtful behavior—that the weak cannot afford?[34]

The Conduct of War

I noted earlier that some abolitionists give up their opposition to war when war seems especially necessary to achieve some crucial end. This can also result in an uncritical attitude regarding the conduct of war. The same has sometimes been true of apocalyptic groups.

Christian pacifists generally have been skeptical of the possibility of moral restraint in warfare once it has begun. In this sense many pacifists have been "realists." The violence of warfare has seemed to have its own, escalating, often senseless, logic. It is partly for this reason that pacifists have insisted that the line should be drawn between "war and no war" instead of between "just and unjust war."

This does not mean that pacifists are committed to the view that war *ought* not be limited by moral constraints. Pacifists would typically side with just war theorists in hoping that wars can be so restrained, though they would be skeptical of the realism of that happening. Some pacifists have in fact tried to take just war seriously and engage it on its own terms in an attempt to strengthen the moral constraints on war. These attempts to take just war seriously have often been disappointing because of being disqualified before the discussion starts (as Paul Ramsey does[35]), or because it seems very difficult to get many within the just war tradition to define the tradition in such a way that it is even theoretically possible for it to yield a *clear* negative judgment about a specific war, or because so many seem unable to apply a theoretically possible negative judgment to one's own country's wars.[36]

Morality in Extremity

From a Christian pacifist perspective, it is vitally important to begin doing ethics from the "center." It is always a temptation in ethics to become fixated on "the hard cases," and in doing so to lose sight of the central affirmations that make the cases hard. From a pacifist perspective, this frequently happens in discussion about war, and just war theory is part of the problem. Just war theory can be viewed (when it is not dismissed as a rationalization for wars, as some pacifists tend to do) as an elaborate system for controlling exceptional resort to war and as thus recognizing the norm of nonviolence that regulates everyday human life. So far so good. Yet the structure of the theory focuses our attention wrongly, on the periphery instead of on the center, on the hard case instead of on the normal case. From the pacifist perspective, the central question relative to international conflict would be something like, "How can we live together without killing each other?" not, as it is in just war thought, "When can war be legitimately waged, and how?" From a pacifist perspective, in other words, this elaborate theory too often has the effect of making war look "normal," rather than like an exception, and therefore has the effect of almost automatically justifying a nation's wars, and distracting us from what is most important—finding ways to hold to our key convictions rather than figuring out when we have to make exceptions to them. From a pacifist perspective, just war theory is a case of the tail wagging the dog. If the accuracy of this assessment is doubted, consider the following questions. Why is it that we have an enormously elaborated and nuanced moral theory about "just war," but no similarly elaborated and nuanced moral theory of "just diplomacy" or "just international relations" or "just peace"? Why is it that in this book, called "The Ethics of War and Peace," the great bulk of our time is spent focusing on *war*—if, when, and how to engage in it—rather than on *peace*—how to build and maintain it? Even more concretely (if more removed from just war theory and this book), why do we spend, in the United States, more than $250 billion annually on our military, and a tiny fraction of that on diplomacy, economic aid, support for the United Nations, etc.? The point is that if we attended to the central question (from a pacifist perspective) and put both our theoretical and our financial resources into addressing it, we might well have far fewer situations where we need to address the "exception" that just war is designed to address.

Thus pacifists are skeptical of approaching ethics through the extreme cases rather than through the ordinary cases, where, often enough, we do not act ethically anyway. From this viewpoint, the most basic problem of ethical living is failing to do what we know we should do because it may be costly to do so, not deciding when to make exceptions to the normal rules that govern our lives.

All of this is not to deny that pacifists face awkward questions when asked things like, "How can you just stand by and let Muslim women be raped and murdered in Bosnia?" There are things for pacifists to say to response to such questions. These include noting that pacifist prescriptions for policy have normally been ignored in the years leading up to the crisis and then, suddenly, we are asked for a solution to a problem caused by someone else's policies. They include observing that often pacifists are not just "standing by" but are deeply involved in working to solve such problems in ways compatible with their convictions, often at considerable cost or risk to themselves. They include pointing to other options that may not have been attempted. And they include simply confessing that we have often not done what we could have done. Other responses could be added. But I grant that they are hard questions. And I grant that perhaps, in theory, just war theory may have more satisfying answers (from many perspectives) to them. But even if one is convinced that something like just war theory can yield a theoretically more satisfactory answer to a hard question about a hard case like Bosnia, are we really farther ahead morally by building an elaborate moral system to deal with the hard case? Might we not be farther ahead if we learned to say simply, "Killing is wrong," and refused to systematize war morally (and therefore legitimize it morally)? After all, it must be the case, simply on statistical grounds, that less than half of the world's wars can be objectively just according to just war criteria themselves. From the just war perspective, no war can be just objectively on both sides, and many wars (colonial wars where countries fight each other to take over someone else's territory, wars waged out of desire to satisfy the vanity of rulers, etc.) are just on neither side. In this light, and in light of the consistent tendency of persons in opposing countries to justify their own country's wars, pacifism seems a safer moral wager than trying to guess the rightness of wars.

This does not mean that pacifists can avoid the question of extremity. But, as should by now be evident, for pacifists, indeed for all within the tradition of Christian nonviolence, the issue of "extremity" arises at a different point (in one sense) than it does for those within the tradition of just war thinking. From the pacifist perspective, the question of extremity is not whether the normal rules of warfare can in certain extreme cases be overridden, but whether the presumption against any and all war can ever be overridden in an extreme case. Despite this difference, however, it is worth noting that it is not only the pacifist who is faced with the uncomfortable choice of holding to his or her moral principles or abandoning them in the face of what seems to be an overriding necessity. Like pacifists, just war theorists, if they hold to a "strict constructionist" view of just war theory, sometimes will need to choose between their moral principles and seeming "effectiveness" in reaching their (ostensibly just) goals. Indeed, any moral view that does not yield finally to a purely consequentialist perspective faces the same apparent collision between morality and necessity.

It is crucial to note, however, that from a Christian pacifist perspective, there is no such thing as "absolute necessity." There is only "necessity" in relationship to achieving certain ends that are deemed more important than holding to one's ethical commitments. Near the very root of Christian pacifist commitment is the freedom from the "necessity" to value my life, or the lives of my friends, above the lives of others, since my life, and the lives of my friends, are "safe" in God's hands. In like manner, Christian pacifists are also freed from the burden of "making history come out right."[37] Such pacifists insist that history is finally in God's control, and that it is our responsibility to act as Jesus teaches us to act, and that as we do so, God will bring about the outcome of history that God intends. We are simply not smart enough to know what the outcomes of our various actions will be. (In a certain way, a realistic appraisal of our limitations in forecasting outcomes itself is a strong argument for pacifism). We have no "responsibility" to violate standards revealed to us in order to help God out. This does not mean, of course, that we do not calculate consequences or that we ought not use our human intelligence to achieve good instead of evil. Yet the conviction that we do not bear the burden of history's outcome alone frees us from a compulsiveness about stopping what we perceive as evil or achieving what we perceive as good that, in the final analysis from a Christian pacifist perspective, reflects a kind of functional atheism. There are, after all, many evils that we simply, physically, *cannot* prevent, many goods we *cannot* bring about—because we are not God. Why should we feel compelled to try (with varying and unknown probabilities of success) to prevent those evils or bring about those goods if the only way we can do so involves violating our moral commitments? From this perspective, our responsibility for "making history come out right" is limited not only by our power to influence history's outcome (which pacifists often feel is much more modest than that of those who are used to ruling the world), but also by our higher responsibility to live in ways consonant with God's revelation to us in Jesus Christ.

There is one more approach to the issue of "extremity." In contrast to most politicians and many moralists, Michael Walzer argues for a stringent criterion to govern "extremity," what he calls (following Churchill) "supreme emergency." He says, in effect, that we should not be like Chicken Little, always contending that the sky is falling, thus rationalizing immoral action on the basis of "necessity." Unlike Chicken Little, we should only violate the rules of war when "the heavens are (really) about to fall."[38]

One way for a Christian pacifist to respond to Walzer's view is to ask, "Will the heavens fall? Can the heavens fall?" Another way is to ask, "Have the heavens fallen?" when nations have lost wars. In responding to these questions, much, obviously, depends on what one means by the "heavens." Walzer's way of putting the issue makes it evident that, for him, the "heavens" means something like, "my nation, or some political community with important moral commitments, good political institutions, etc." If this falls, the heavens fall. A view like this seems implicit in all views that defend the rightness of violating normal norms in war in the face of extremity, if only because wars are fought to defend political communities, nations.

A Christian pacifist response to these questions might go like this. On the one hand, the heavens surely *will* fall, no matter what we do to hold them up—we are not God—if we identify the heavens with our political community or ideology. No political community will last forever, whatever we do to preserve it. There is simply no way to hold the heavens up in the long run. If that time frame seems too grand, note also that it is the very thing that makes a political community most worth defending that is destroyed first when that community violates its own standards of right under the pressure of "necessity." Are the "heavens" the physical continuity of a certain nation or of its moral commitments?

On the other hand, I would insist that the heavens *cannot* fall. The heavens did not fall when Athens fell, when Rome fell, when . . . fell. They will not fall when the United States falls. They will not even fall when, in one way or another, the earth is destroyed. These are claims, I take it, that Christians make when we speak of God's providence, power, goodness, eternity, and of our ultimate destiny as being somehow with God. And they are claims that deny that any nation or political ideology or system amounts to "the heavens."

These observations about extremity get us back to the central claims of the pacifist position that I represent, a position that is finally dependent upon a conviction about God and God's action in the world (and its implications for our action) that is known to us in Jesus Christ. In the absence of faith in the God of Jesus Christ, this sort of pacifism is certainly foolishness. But, "to those who are called, both Jews and Greeks, Christ [is] the power of God and the wisdom of God. For God's foolishness is wiser than human wisdom, and God's weakness is stronger than human strength" (1 Cor. 1:24–25).

Epilogue

Earlier in this chapter, I told the story of Dirk Willems. His death was part of a "debate" over religious truth. In sixteenth-century Europe it was believed, functionally at least, that questions of truth could be settled by torture and killing. I am personally grateful that in the conference at Jerusalem we sought to find the truth in a different way! This other way of seeking truth is not uncommon in our world today. In a way, this rightly can be interpreted as a triumph of toleration. But we might also interpret this in a slightly different way. Someone has said, "We are all Marxists now," in the sense of recognizing that material interests are important shapers of action. I believe it is fair to say that in a similar way, in relation to questions of religious and philosophical truth claims, "We are all pacifists now." This is to say that Christian pacifists are committed to the propositions that our only "weapons" are words (and the way we live), that the most powerful power is finally the power of truth, and that one can only convince someone of something by . . . well, by *convincing* them, not by forcing them. Most intellectuals are now committed to this same proposition when it comes to understanding the truth. This "triumph" of pacifism is a cause for rejoicing—at least for those of us who are pacifists!

It is ironic—no, sad—however, that we in late twentieth-century Western culture do not believe that the "right" thing in relationships between peoples and nations must also be determined by using nothing other than words as "weapons," by relying on nothing other than the power of truth, the power of moral appeal. In settling questions of right between nations, we are still in the equivalent of the sixteenth century—we still use the methods used in that century to settle questions of religious truth. Is this because we simply have not "seen" in relation to political conflicts what we have "seen" in relation to the quest for philosophical or religious truth? Or is it because what matters to us now is not "true" religion, but our own and our nation's ideologies and interests? I frankly think it is probably mainly the latter. If this is true, there is less reason for rejoicing from a Christian pacifist perspective. If this is true, it means that we no longer take God seriously enough to fight over religion, but now as much or more than ever, we bow before idols of our own making—nations, and political ideologies and interests—and we make sacrifices on their altars, human sacrifices by the millions in the form of wars' victims. One of the hard theoretical questions put to me during the conference was whether I would not act violently to prevent the takeover of a civilized country by "barbarians," barbarians who even went so far as to practice human sacrifice. A good question. But I fear that the barbarians are not out there. We are the barbarians, complete with human sacrifice.

As long as we believe that the power that "wins" by dominating others, by cowing others into submission—the kind of power symbolized best by military force—is the strongest power, we will remain barbarians. As long as we believe that, we will be doomed to wars and more wars. But when we come to see that the power of truth, spoken and lived, is finally more powerful—when we come to see and accept the power of the cross through which Jesus disarmed the principalities and powers—then we will be free. The truth will set us free. Free from the need to compel others to conform to our visions of the right. Free from the fear that makes us submit to injustice. Free from the fear of death. And free from war.

Notes

1. See John H. Yoder, *Nevertheless: Varieties of Religious Pacifism*, rev. ed. (Scottdale, PA: Herald Press, 1992), and Peter Brock, *Pacifism in Europe to 1914* (Princeton: Princeton University Press, 1972), 472–76.

2. Brock has suggested essentially the same three viewpoints, in embryonic form, in the preface to *Freedom from War: Nonsectarian Pacifism, 1814–1914* (Toronto: University of Toronto Press, 1991), vii–viii.

3. John H. Yoder, *Christian Attitudes to War, Peace, and Revolution* (Elkhart, IN: Associated Mennonite Biblical Seminaries, 1983), 372–401.

4. Martin Ceadel, *Thinking about Peace and War* (New York: Oxford University Press, 1987), and James Turner Johnson, *The Quest for Peace: Three Moral Traditions in Western Cultural History* (Princeton: Princeton University Press, 1987).

5. This is by no means an inclusive list. Similar pacifist movements have appeared in many other times and places, though the pacifism of such movements has often been short-lived. This happened, for example, in nineteenth-century America. See Yoder, *Christian Attitudes*, 299–317, for a brief description. Also see the forthcoming book tentatively titled *Proclaim Peace: Voices of Christian Pacifism in America Outside the Historic Peace Churches*, edited by Richard Hughes and Theron F. Schlabach. For additional examples, see both 1991 volumes by Brock: *Freedom from Violence: Sectarian Nonresistance from the Middle Ages to the Great War* and *Freedom from War: Nonsectarian Pacifism, 1814–1914* (Toronto: University of Toronto Press).

6. Roland H. Bainton, *Christian Attitudes toward War and Peace* (Nashville, TN: Abingdon Press, 1960), 178–84.

7. Brock, *Freedom from War.*

8. Cf. Yoder, *Christian Attitudes*, 319–40.

9. For additional expressions of Christian nonviolent resistance perspectives, see Philip McManus and Gerald Schlabach, eds., *Relentless Persistence: Nonviolent Action in Latin America* (Philadelphia, PA: New Society Publishers, 1991), and Dominque Barbé, *Grace and Power: Base Communities and Nonviolence in Brazil* (Maryknoll, NY: Orbis, 1987).

10. As I understand it, this is one central point of Stanley Hauerwas's essay, "Can a Pacifist Think about War?" (in Hauerwas, *Dispatches from the Front* [Durham, NC: Duke University Press, 1994]), a point I wish to illustrate here and to make concrete.

11. There is literature exploring the connection between worship and ethics of which I became aware after drafting this chapter. See, for example, Vigen Guroian, "Seeing Worship as Ethics: An Orthodox Perspective," *Journal of Religious Ethics* 13 (1985), 332–39.

12. Walter Sawatsky, "Truth Telling in Eastern Europe: The Liberation and the Burden," *Journal of Church and State* 33 (1991), 701–29, and Timothy Garton Ash, *The Magic Lantern: The Revolution of '89 Witnessed in Warsaw, Budapest, Berlin and Prague* (New York: Random House, 1990).

13. Henri J. M. Nouwen, *Lifesigns: Intimacy, Fecundity, and Ecstasy in Christian Perspective* (Garden City, NY: Doubleday, 1986), 18.

14. Nouwen, *Lifesigns*, 17–20.

15. Nouwen, *Lifesigns*, 20–21.

16. Perry B. Yoder, *Shalom: The Bible's Word for Salvation, Justice, and Peace* (Newton, KS: Faith and Life Press, 1987), 12.

17. The term "positive peace," used frequently in the modern peace studies movement, has a similar meaning. See, for example, the introductory text by David P. Barash, *Introduction to Peace Studies* (Belmont, CA: Wadsworth Publishing Company, 1991), 9–11.

18. Although it speaks to a somewhat different time and setting, for a fleshing out of what this has meant concretely from within this tradition, see Guy F. Hershberger, *The Way of the Cross in Human Relationships* (Scottdale, PA: Herald Press, 1958).

19. For an overview of what one Christian pacifist organization is doing to make the peace commitment an active and positive movement, rather than simply a passive refusal to participate in war, see the annual "Workbook" of the Mennonite Central Committee, Akron, PA 17501.

20. Thieleman J. van Braght, *The Bloody Theater or Martyrs Mirror of the Defenseless Christians* (Scottdale, PA: Herald Press, 1968 [original in Dutch, 1660]), 741–42.

21. See the book on Quaker conciliation efforts by C. H. Mike Yarrow, *Quaker Experiences in International Conciliation* (New Haven, CT: Yale University Press, 1978). There is also growing involvement of Mennonites in conciliation efforts, both locally and internationally. See the newsletter *Conciliation Quarterly*, published by the Mennonite Central Committee, Akron, PA 17501, for regular reporting of Mennonite and related activity in this area.

22. Cf. Ray H. Abrams, *Preachers Present Arms* (Scottdale, PA: Herald Press, 1969 [original 1933]), esp. 161ff.

23. Cf. Peter Brock, *Freedom from War*, 117ff.

24. At least, this is a key criticism of some who are called "pacifists." Cf. Guenter Lewy, *Peace and Revolution: The Moral Crisis of American Pacifism* (Grand Rapids, MI: Eerdmans, 1988), but also various objections to Lewy's interpretation in Michael Cromartie, ed., *Peace Betrayed? Essays on Pacifism and Politics* (Washington, DC: Ethics and Public Policy Center, 1990).

25. Cf. James M. Stayer, *Anabaptists and the Sword*, 2d ed. (Lawrence, KS: Coronado Press, 1976), chs. 4 and 11–12.

26. *The Schleitheim Confession*, trans. and ed. John Howard Yoder (Scottdale, PA: Herald Press, 1973), 14. "Sword" here refers to the coercive, order-maintaining function of the government. It does not refer specifically to warmaking (28 n. 44).

27. For a sampling of sixteenth-century Anabaptist views, see Walter Klaassen, ed., *Anabaptism in Outline: Selected Primary Sources* (Scottdale, PA: Herald Press, 1981), 244–64.

28. Cf. Ted Koontz, "Mennonites and the State: Preliminary Reflections," *Essays on Peace Theology and Witness: Occasional Papers*, no. 12 (Elkhart, IN: Institute of Mennonite Studies, 1988), 35–60.

29. Duane K. Friesen, *Christian Peacemaking and International Conflict* (Scottdale, PA: Herald Press, 1986).

30. Cf. Dale Aukerman, *Darkening Valley: A Biblical Perspective on Nuclear War* (Scottdale, PA: Herald Press, 1989). The activities of people like the Berrigans provide an example.

31. Cf. John Howard Yoder, *The Politics of Jesus* (Grand Rapids, MI: Eerdmans, 1972), esp. ch. 2.

32. Peter Brock, *The Quaker Peace Testimony: 1660–1914* (York: Sessions Book Trust [distributed in the US by Syracuse University Press], 1990), is the best recent overview of Quaker pacifism.

33. Quoted in Arthur F. Holmes, ed., *War and Christian Ethics* (Grand Rapids, MI: Baker Book House, 1975), 64.

34. For a perceptive discussion of some roots of Christian religious "coercion" of other Christians, see Peter Brown, *Religion and Society in the Age of St. Augustine* (New York: Harper and Row, 1972), 260–78, 301–31.

35. Paul Ramsey, *The Just War: Force and Political Responsibility* (New York: Scribner, 1968), 259ff.

36. John Howard Yoder's book, *When War Is Unjust* (Minneapolis: Augsburg, 1984), is one example of a pacifist attempt to engage just war theory on its own terms. On the Gulf War, see also Yoder, "Just War Tradition: Is It Credible?" *Christian Century* (13 Mar. 1991), 295–98.

37. John Howard Yoder, *Politics of Jesus*, 233–50.

38. Michael Walzer, *Just and Unjust Wars* (New York: Basic Books, 1977), 231.

CHAPTER 10

Conflicting Interpretations of Christian Pacifism

Michael G. Cartwright

THOUGH HE DISCUSSES Christian nonviolence with scholarly care, Ted Koontz remains a passionately committed Christian. By insisting that the questions nonviolent Christians ask about the ethics of war and peace are different from the questions asked by those who approach the topic from other directions, he reminds us of the importance of religious convictions, or the absence of such convictions, in shaping how we understand war/peace ethics.[1] Moreover, his forthrightness in articulating the conceptions of truth and power that arise from the tradition of Christian pacifism, and especially from the practices of Christian worship, opens the way for a fuller assessment of the possibilities and limits of conversation between ethical traditions.

Koontz's chapter also evokes a number of critical questions, however. How adequate is the typology of Christian nonviolence he presents? Which conceptions of war and peace are omitted from his discussion? Given the differences he identifies between "the house of fear" and "the house of love," has Koontz exaggerated the contrast between Christian nonviolence and just war thinking? And if so, what are the implications of this exaggeration for assessing the particular understanding of truth and power he wishes to defend? Finally, might not his portrayal of the conversation between Christian pacifists and others distort, and thereby impede, this conversation?

No matter how we answer questions like these, Koontz has brought into view a set of concerns that, though not often examined in comparative ethics, are essential to understanding the moral logic of Christian nonviolence.

INTERPRETING TYPOLOGIES OF WAR/PEACE ETHICS

Koontz acknowledges that his chapter offers no more than "an interpretation" of Christian nonviolence. There are good reasons for such hermeneutical modesty. Christian ethicists—pacifist and nonpacifist—have struggled for many years with a broad array of hermeneutical issues,[2] and there remain significant and unresolved disagreements between the various forms of pacifism, abolitionism, and nonviolent resistance, as well as opposition to arguments outside the family of Christian nonviolence. Christian pacifists today have no choice but to take seriously the fact that "peacemaking" has become a kind of linguistic umbrella under which a diversity of theological approaches now collect. Nor can they ignore the fact that many nonpacifists regard their views as at best quaint and at worst dangerous.

Calling attention to the hermeneutic self-consciousness of Koontz's chapter opens the way toward assessing the other, more significant, interpretive issues he raises. To begin with, we need to examine the typology on which he relies. Some typologies are designed to characterize precisely each identified position,[3] others to identify "family resemblances" linking an unresolved diversity of positions. Koontz's typology is of the latter sort, though he is concerned to avoid misrepresenting the different positions that cluster under the label "Christian nonviolence." Nevertheless, how we define alternative types of ethical thinking about war and peace can significantly structure the ensuing conversation. Different typologies of pacifism project different conversations about war and peace.

If the conversation is framed as one between just war thinking and Christian pacifism, it is likely to proceed with advocates for just war focusing attention on Christian pacifists—as if *they* were the problem—while neglecting the challenge posed by other kinds of thinking about war and peace, such as "holy war" thinking, political realism, and Rambo-style militarism. But one can also frame the war/peace conversation in terms of a quite different typology, one designed to clarify the areas of theological agreement and disagreement that exist within a given tradition of Christian nonviolence.[4] In the former case, the conversation will be one that is focused on the responsibilities of citizen-leaders in relation to the state. In the latter, the typology points toward a conversation in which the identification of different types of peace theology is preliminary to developing a theological consensus (within the religious tradition) that can, in turn, lead to more articulate ways of representing Christian pacifism in ecumenical and political contexts.

In short, the usefulness of a typology of the ethics of war and peace depends upon which conversation is in view and which kind of conflict of interpretations is being assessed. It is a mistake to assume that there is one principle of classification that will sort everything out for us. The interpretive conflicts internal to particular traditions of moral thinking generate one kind of moral argumentation and disputation; conflicts between ethical traditions generate another. For this reason, Koontz's discussion, which seeks to represent Christian nonviolence in a book concerned with dialogue between different perspectives, is less nuanced, theologically speaking, than were he to address the topic in the context of a debate about Mennonite peace theologies. But the conversation with other viewpoints implicit in Koontz's chapter has its own coherence insofar as it allows for honest disagreements over how to characterize the similarities and differences between perspectives.

Given his assignment, it is hardly an accident that Koontz has structured the conversation as he has. The threefold typology of Christian nonviolent perspectives—pacifism, abolitionism, and nonviolent resistance—serves several purposes in his argument. First, he uses it to describe an array of approaches, some explicitly grounded in theological conceptions and others more pragmatically or politically grounded. He does not attempt to identify conceptual differences within an array of historical categories. Instead, the typology merely describes a number of positions that have taken shape in relation to one another. In doing so, it hides important differences. In the case of abolitionism, for example, Koontz's formulation mixes two conceptually distinct approaches, one represented by what might be called "world order visionaries" like Erasmus, the other by the isolationist abolitionism of many liberal Protestant pacifists during the 1920s and 1930s. The moral arguments relied upon in each case are logically separable, however much these approaches may resemble each other in other ways.

Second, Koontz explicates the theological context of a single position within this typology—what he calls "Christian pacifism." But the typology permits him to include all three types of Christian nonviolence in answering the topic-related questions—questions that are particularly awkward to address from within the theologically grounded perspective of Christian pacifism.

It is important to be clear about what Koontz is and is not doing with his typology of Christian nonviolence in relation to his larger argumentative strategy. He does not use it to present certain categories as universally applicable and thus to delegitimize all forms of pacifism as "irresponsible." What he is doing is more nearly the opposite of such a strategy. Implicit in his chapter, however, and coinciding with his use of the typology, is a bid for respect from various interlocutors whom he identifies in relation to the questions around which this book is constructed. By arguing that if one wants to understand why some people are Christian pacifists, one must enter their world and on their own terms, Koontz appeals to his audience to set aside their assumption that pacifists are irrelevant or dangerous characters. Here we see him engaging in a subtle form of apologetic argument. In effect, Koontz is saying to his readers: "I want you to understand why it is that you cannot understand what I am talking about."

Must One Be a Pacifist to Understand Pacifist Arguments?

Had the conversation in which Koontz finds himself been structured by a different set of questions, he might not have felt the need to employ this kind of indirect apologetic. But the questions the contributors to this volume were asked to address do not lend themselves to providing a "thick description" of his own theologically based pacifism. Accordingly, Koontz prefaces his discussion of these questions with a brief commentary on the significance of the kinds of question we permit to guide our thinking about the issues of war and peace. And he is right to do so, because, too often, the discussion of war and peace is conducted without awareness of how the questions we ask provide an overriding authority for some modes of ethical inquiry while they reject others. There is, for example, a tendency to assume that "consequentialist" questions are somehow definitive, and that moral viewpoints that reject consequentialist reasoning are, for that reason, defective.

But it is one thing to contest the adequacy of the questions being asked, and quite another to present the case for Christian nonviolence in a way that implies that one must be a pacifist to understand pacifist arguments. In this respect, Koontz appears to have overstated the incommensurability, philosophically speaking, of pacifist and nonpacifist conceptions of peace. It is unfortunate that he largely ignores the historical character of those conceptions of war and peace that are part of the wider family of Christian nonviolence, because the very shape of the conversation in which these conceptions have emerged has changed. To be precise, several changes have occurred during the past century in the way moral arguments about war and peace are engaged—changes in moral thinking and social analysis that also inform Koontz's own argument. Though no single factor has determined these changes, there is a sense in which Christian pacifists have repeatedly had to face interpretations of their stance that are unfavorable, even if not always tendentious. Nowhere is this more true than in the North American context, where Christian nonviolence is frequently seen as irresponsible unless its advocates assent to the interpretation of their conception of peace as apolitical.

Let us consider an example. On the eve of the Second World War, Reinhold Niebuhr provided an influential argument for "Why the Christian Church Is Not Pacifist."[5] As John Howard Yoder has noted, the impact of Niebuhr's argument that nonviolence is morally and politically irresponsible can be illustrated in the ways that Christian pacifists began to articulate their position at mid-century. Many Christian pacifists simply accepted the Niebuhrian distinctions between nonresistance and nonviolence without raising questions about the theoretical basis of such classifications. Although Niebuhr's conception of politics and its corollary dichotomy between "moral man and immoral society" have been criticized, theologically as well as politically, his "Christian realism" remains potent enough to inform a number of recent attacks upon Christian pacifists.[6]

Those Christian pacifists who have contested Niebuhrian-style polemics have shifted the burden of proof back to those in the just war and realist camps who characterize Christian nonviolence as irresponsible. Yoder, for example, has avoided conceding the authority of just war reasoning, and instead has used particular wars to test the adequacy of the idea of the "justifiability" of warmaking.[7] Others have adopted what might be called a "contrarian" approach, one that presumes that just war arguments mask ends other than that of restoring peace and that such arguments reflect an unannounced political agenda. This approach is contrarian, not only because of the combative way it rejects the legitimacy of just war arguments, but also because it questions the very framework within which the discussion of war and peace proceeds.

This contrarian tendency has been particularly noticeable in the wake of the 1991 Persian Gulf War. Stanley Hauerwas's "Whose Justice? Which Peace?" is illustrative.[8] Dissenting from the just war premises of the other essays on the morality of the Gulf War in the collection in which his appears, Hauerwas argues that "there is much more to the question of the moral evaluation of war than the question of whether a war conforms to just war criteria" and calls attention to assumptions that have dictated what are "widely regarded as the relevant questions for assessing the morality of the Gulf War." Having raised the issue of meta-ethical criteria, he goes on to argue that

> it makes all the difference who is asking questions about the "justice" of war and for what reasons. When questions of who and why are ignored, the history that has shaped just war reflection as well as the conflicting histories of the Gulf War are assumed irrelevant.

The Gulf War was fought by those for whom it was actually a kind of holy war, but who "found it useful to justify it on just war grounds."[9]

Though Koontz avoids Hauerwas's combative tone, he, too, adopts a contrarian strategy. Both argue that Christian identity is not only important for grasping the moral significance of Christian nonviolence, but further, that it is necessary for understanding. At their best, these arguments invite nonpacifist readers to consider the possibility that "the emperor has no clothes," but they also say, "I want you to understand why you cannot understand me." Though provocative, this stance does not invite further conversation—unless the nonpacifist reader is already disposed to convert to this position! Arguably, then, the contrarian style of argument can be taken to suggest that there is no reason for nonpacifists to engage in conversation with Christian nonviolence. By assuming antipathy on the part of the conversational partner, the contrarian overstates the incommensurability of moral arguments and thereby (prematurely) suggests that various kinds of dialogue, which may or may not develop, will *not* occur.

Oddly enough, Koontz's rhetoric stresses incommensurability while it appears to offer his readers a hermeneutical key to unlock the mystery that lies at the heart of Christian pacifism. Though he invites conversation to explore its disagreements with other viewpoints, Koontz severely limits that conversation by offering an account of Christian pacifism that itself presumes an ethical dualism based upon a "two kingdoms" political ethic. His argument differs from Hauerwas's inasmuch as Koontz identifies with the reader's incredulity instead of indicting the opponent's integrity. At the same time, Koontz goes beyond inviting the reader to consider the possibility that "the emperor has no clothes" to offer a theological assessment of the difference between those who inhabit the "house of love" (Christian pacifists) and those who dwell in the "house of fear" (realists and just warriors).

Nowhere is this tension between inviting conversation and rejecting it more prominent than in his sermon, "Blessed Be the King." The sermon provides outsiders with a glimpse of the theological conceptions underlying Christian pacifist discourse by illuminating the difference between what (from a Christian point of view) is the "false hope" that sees political and social progress narrowly in terms of the application of the power of the state, and what is an authentically *Christian* hope that condemns as false and even idolatrous conceptions of power that presume to eliminate the necessity of suffering.

When Koontz turns to the topic-related questions, it is clear that the sermon not only has served the purpose of elucidating the theological warrants that underlie Christian pacifist claims about war and peace, but also has revealed the ideological conflicts that make it difficult for these claims to be registered as politically significant. For, he argues, the claim of "necessity" makes sense only in relation to ends that are deemed more important than keeping one's moral commitments. Unlike the political realist—or indeed, anyone else holding a consequentialist ethic—the Christian pacifist is free of the necessity of worrying about what is in God's hands, free from the burden of making history come out right. We can have no duty to "help God out" by violating God's moral standards.

In this context, Koontz's use of Henri Nouwen's image of inhabitants of the "house of fear" versus those of the "house of love" provocatively juxtaposes alternative worldviews. But it is not obvious that the contrast between the "house of love" and the "house of fear" is as sharp as this would imply. It may be true that "fearful questions never lead to love-filled answers," but there are many kinds of "fearful questions," and not all such questions are necessarily prompted by the same kinds of fear. To refine the image of the two houses, then, we might agree that not all rooms in the house of fear are equally well-furnished, morally speaking. Whatever may be said about the differences between just war and pacifism, for example, in contrast to *realpolitik* or "the blank check," just warriors and pacifists agree that the burden of proof is upon those who choose war. Both reject the primacy of consequentialist reasoning in making political as well as personal decisions. By putting political realism and just war thinking in the same house, Koontz exaggerates the moral differences that separate natural law and Christian pacifism while he neglects the differences between natural law and political realism. Because Koontz's image of the two houses exaggerates the contrast between pacifist and anticonsequentialist moral outlooks, it arbitrarily limits the possibilities for conversation between their adherents.

Conflicting Interpretations of Christian Nonviolence

The bold contrast that Koontz draws between those who have converted to the Christian position and those who have not reflects a broader conception of dualist ethics, one that sharply distinguishes the moral obligations of the Church from those of the (unconverted) world. According to the dualist conception, Koontz argues, those "committed to the way of Christ" are expected to live differently from those in "the world." The dualist conception therefore leaves open the possibility of a certain "quasi-legitimate" justification for war, provided it is chosen and waged not by Christians but by the state. This view of the "higher responsibility" of Christians has its origins in another ongoing conflict of interpretations within a number of Protestant traditions. As Koontz observes, the conflict arises out of two closely related scriptural passages, St. Paul's Letter to the Romans 12:9–21 and 13:1–7, and is dramatically evident in the 1527 Schleitheim Confession: "The sword is an ordering of God outside the perfection of Christ. It punishes and kills the wicked and protects the Good."

According to some historians of Christianity, the idea that there are different expectations for those who are part of the covenant of Christianity and those "outside the perfection of Christ" crystallized only at Schleitheim in 1527; others hold that the idea emerged long before this time. But even the "Schleitheim interpretation" has not always been articulated with the same political assumptions in mind, either by Christian pacifists in the Anabaptist-Mennonite tradition or by those in the broader tradition of Protestant Christianity. Just as not all American Mennonites have articulated their peace witness within the rhetoric of "nonresistance"—some nineteenth-century Mennonites preferred the older vocabulary of "defenseless" (*wehrlos*) witness, for example—not all Christian pacifists have felt it necessary to adopt ethical dualism as part of the rationale for their Christian pacifist stance.

Christian pacifists both inside and outside the Anabaptist tradition who have adopted some version of ethical dualism with respect to the state often cite the Schleitheim formulation as if it were applicable to every situation of pacifist engagement with the state. But Yoder has cautioned Christian pacifists about the conceptual error of "solidifying the dualism" of the Schleitheim statement, arguing that the Schleitheim formulation should not be treated as if it were a "systematic or comprehensive political ethic."[10] On the contrary, the Schleitheim formulation represents a "tense missionary dualism" that became necessary in a situation marked by a refusal to tolerate the witness of Anabaptists in the world in which they found themselves at the time. And, as Yoder goes on to argue elsewhere, this particular response needs to be seen in light of the "variety of logically possible positions which could be taken on the question of the sword in the context of the Reformation debates."[11]

When this kind of historical analysis is performed, it becomes clear that the "two kingdoms" dualism later generations have articulated in relation to the Schleitheim Confession is not the only kind of response consistent with the Christian Bible. The dualistic interpretation also overlooks some of the most salient features of the political situation the Anabaptists who gathered at Schleitheim were facing. An excessive focus on Schleitheim can distort the conversation that Christian pacifists have with nonpacifists precisely to the degree that it assumes that the Christian witness to the state always takes shape within one kind of conversation. But this is not the case, as the existence of other kinds of Christian nonviolence demonstrates.

The writings of James Douglass, a Catholic lay theologian and antinuclear peace activist, offer a version of Christian nonviolence that is not structured by ethical dualism and that therefore illustrates wider possibilities for conversation between Christian nonviolence and the nonpacifist traditions. Douglass's reflections on peace grow out of his training in natural law and his subsequent conviction that the prospect of nuclear war has made warfare pointless as a mode of settling differences. Douglass therefore bases his argument in *The Non-Violent Cross* in part on just war grounds. But he also anchors it in the more elastic conception of peace found in the papal encyclical *Pacem in terris* of John XXIII, which Douglass admires for its pervasive, though admittedly undefined, conception of nonviolence. As he notes, though the encyclical is addressed to the Church, it is also "addressed far beyond the visible church," that is, to the larger world it may eventually help to transform.[12] Douglass acknowledges the many criticisms of *Pacem in terris*, including those of Protestant moralists like Reinhold Niebuhr, but he resists Niebuhr's complaint that the encyclical lacks realism, and he even provides natural law arguments for what he sees as a coming "revolution of peace" through Gandhian nonviolence.

In retrospect, Douglass's arguments for the "transformation of man" and the "revolution of peace" seem careless and overstated. They do, however, provide an interesting specimen of a conception of Christian nonviolence that is not determined by the kind of ethical dualism to which Koontz is committed. For though Douglass's chapter on "Christians and the State" discusses the issues presented by Romans 13:1–7, it is clear that his conception of peace is not determined by the interpretation of this passage. There are two reasons why this is the case. First, Douglass sharply distinguishes between applying such a passage in Paul's time and the various "two kingdoms" interpretations of the passage articulated by Protestants like Martin Luther. Second, following Karl Rahner, he contends that the Church can be both catholic and in diaspora at the same time. Therefore, the Church's sphere of peacemaking is not confined to the community of belief, but takes the form of a "decisive confrontation" with the world in which the Church embodies the "cross of suffering redemptive love." In the end, then,

> there can be no ethical justification even for the governing authorities bearing the sword, because the only valid ethic is that revealed by Christ in the Gospel, a love that does no wrong to a neighbor.[13]

Thus, though tension between the peace of the Christian community and the so-called peace of the world continues, it is a mistake to attribute to St. Paul a "responsibility ethic" based on Romans 13:1–7.

Most observers would agree that Douglass's conception of peacemaking is not representative of contemporary Catholic thinking on war and peace. This may be more true of American Catholicism than of the Vatican itself, however. According to a 1992 editorial in *La civiltà Cattolica*, the Jesuit magazine published in Rome, the transformation of warfare in the modern era "obliges us to consider arguments for war from a completely new perspective." The editorial argues that Roman Catholic thinking on the ethics of war and peace has shifted significantly during the course of the century. The Catholic Church has formally condemned war in four important documents between 1920 and 1991. More and more, the Church "has absolutely condemned war and moved beyond the old arguments for the 'just war' or 'holy war' in defense of the faith," and "this attitude indicates an advance in Christian conscience regarding the absolute immunity of war." The editorial discusses the 1991 Persian Gulf War as the principal example of the way an "ideology of war" has co-opted just war theory in the midst of the transformation of modern warfare. The author concludes:

> The theory of the just war is indefensible and has been abandoned. In reality—with the sole exception of a purely defensive war against acts of aggression—we can say that there are no "just wars" and there is no "right" to wage war.

Accordingly, Roman Catholics are called upon to "unmask" warmaking, even as they engage in positive efforts to make peace between individuals and nations.[14]

Like Douglass's argument in *The Non-Violent Cross*, that put forward in *La civiltà Cattolica* posits no ethical dualism. The Church's pastoral concern is addressed not only to its own members but also to non-Christian citizens and governments, for whom it is presented as normative, on natural law grounds. In this respect, the editorial remains squarely within the mainstream of Roman Catholic moral theology. But by historicizing the debate about the justifiability of war and thereby going beyond secular interpretations of just war thinking, the editorial reasserts a broadly and distinctively Christian way of thinking about the ethics of war and peace. Clearly, both these examples of Catholic revisionism converge with the concerns of Christian pacifism, even though they are argued from within a version of natural law ethics. Both share Koontz's wish to articulate an ethic of peace that does not rest on worldly conceptions of truth and power, but they do not share Koontz's ethical dualism. This dualism disallows the possibility, yet to be fully explored, of a convergence between pacifism and natural law.

Kingship and Martyrdom

These disputes about ethical dualism raise further questions about the alternative conceptions of truth and power implicit in Koontz's treatment of the "kingship" of Christ in his Palm Sunday sermon. Recall that, in this sermon, Koontz poses a question to his congregation: "How can we overcome fear, accept the possibility of the cross, live lives which are, paradoxically, both fully vulnerable, and wonderfully powerful?" The answer he offers is specified in terms of discovering the reality of the kingship of Christ:

> I believe that the key lies in really seeing, in really *believing*, that Jesus is King. Though we take for granted the Kingship of Jesus and, unlike the people of his time, understand that his Kingship is radically different from that of worldly kings, I wonder if we *really* understand, I wonder if we *really* believe.

As we have already noted, Koontz here attempts to identify the heart of the mystery of Christian pacifism for his readers while he also stresses the ultimate difference between those who "really believe" and those who do not.

The Acts of the Apostles suggest that the earliest Christian communities really did believe that Jesus Christ was their king (Hebrew "messiah"). Christians were characterized by the officials of the Roman empire as those "who have turned the world upside down . . . acting against the decrees of Caesar, saying there is another king, King Jesus" (Acts 17:6, 7). The early Christians were viewed with suspicion precisely because their witness (Greek *martyria*) called into question the political conceptions of truth and power upon which the Roman empire was built. Christian witness was often mistaken for atheism by those who did not recognize the King to whom they bore witness.

The example of Dirk Willems, the Dutch martyr, which Koontz discusses at two points in his chapter, also illustrates the alternative conceptions of truth and power toward which Koontz gestures. From the perspective of natural law, Willems's martyrdom seems unnecessarily heroic, an act of supererogation, and therefore not the kind of thing that should be regarded as a duty for everyone.[15] But his act becomes morally significant when placed in the context of a Christian understanding of the conduct required of those who bear witness to "King Jesus"—an understanding that places the meaning of history *not* in the progression of political actions, narrowly understood, but in the acts of God in the world in behalf of God's people, the Church.

But even more important than the striking difference in assessments evoked by this particular example of martyrdom is the overriding question of the relationship between conceptions of war and peace and conceptions of truth. As Koontz notes at the end of his essay, Dirk Willems's martyrdom cannot be detached from the broader framework of sixteenth-century theological disputes, as these disputes were handled in the political sphere. As he pointedly observes, Willems's death "was part of a 'debate' over religious truth" in a society in which people believed that truth could be discovered through torture. Pushing his point even further, Koontz asserts that with regard to how we go about settling questions of right between nations, we have hardly progressed beyond this level.

Koontz also calls attention to the presumptions about power in the conflict of truth claims between the "defenders of civilization" and "barbarians." His eloquent homiletic conclusion demonstrates the difference that is made when one's analysis of human conflict is framed by the theological and historical vision of "the power of the cross through which Jesus disarmed the principalities and the powers." But when Koontz concludes dramatically that the barbarians are not "out there," that "we are the barbarians," he seems to have lost sight of the difference he previously posited between those who really believe and those who do not. If we are all barbarians, it would appear that even those who inhabit the "house of love" are possessed by fear.

This point brings us back to nonpacifist suspicions about the legitimacy of conceptions of truth and power embedded in the claims of Christian nonviolence. The presence of such suspicions cannot help but have implications for conversations between Christian pacifists and those whose thinking about war and peace is shaped by other ethical traditions. Yet, as different as Koontz's conceptions of truth and power are from those implicitly or explicitly present elsewhere in this volume, there is no reason to believe that the other contributors (or the readers of this book) cannot grasp the point Koontz is making in his sermon. Whether they will be persuaded to convert to Christianity (or to Christian pacifism) is another question! The point, however, is not to suggest that such an illustration must persuade. It is enough merely to show that the moral action embodied in Dirk Willems's martyrdom can be made intelligible. In this as in other matters, advocates of Christian nonviolence have little choice but to be patient as well as persistent in offering their nonviolent witness to the state.

Conversation Despite Interpretive Conflict

It is characteristic of the Christian pacifist understanding of itself that it should seek conversation with "the world" for the purpose of converting the world to the way of Christ. Once this purpose is understood, we are in a better position to assess the claim that pacifist and nonpacifist arguments are incommensurable.

As we have already observed, one of the conceptual tensions at the heart of Koontz's chapter is the relationship between the ideas of truth and power as these are understood within "the house of love" and "the house of fear." Here it may help to call attention to the practical and theological importance of the relationship between the *evangelical* practice of "speaking truth to power" as a way of engaging the world nonviolently, and the *ecclesial* practice of peacemaking between Christians, a practice identified in the writings of sixteenth-century radical reformation as "The Rule of Christ." Explicating these practices in relation to one another will help us see how the conversation between Christian pacifists and others might be structured in a way that escapes Koontz's overly hermeneutical contrast.

Most adherents to the tradition of Christian nonviolence agree that "speaking truth to power" is an integral part of Christian witness to the state. But there is disagreement about whether Christians can ever legitimize particular instances of violence by the state. Christians, it sometimes urged, should focus their efforts on "living at peace with all people" insofar as this is possible (and here, as in so many things, we have to confront the limits of our moral imaginations), leaving vengeance as well as "making history come out right" in the hands of God (Rom. 12:9–21). In this respect, I would agree with Yoder's rather sparse, untheorized account of Christian witness to the state, which assumes that there is no such thing as "the state" per se.[16] There are simply states as we encounter them in particular historical situations. Just as we do not have to regard the Church's situation before the world to be, in all cases, like that presumed by the Schleitheim Confession, so we are not stuck with the "worldly authorities" described in Romans 13:1–7 or, for that matter, with "the beast" of Revelation 13:1–18.

Christian engagement with political authority must allow for other possibilities, including the possibility (however unlikely it may be in most instances) that the principalities and powers might join in acknowledging the Lordship of Jesus Christ and alter their practices accordingly. After all, according to the vision of the end of history described in Revelation 5:1–14, the procession of Christian worship will ultimately include every creature on earth. Christian pacifists should therefore not underestimate the political power of celebrating the Lordship of Christ. After all, this is the truth to which a story like that of Dirk Willems's attests.

Meanwhile, Christian pacifists have more than enough to do making a different kind of peace, one structured by a different set of questions, than the kind of peace sought by most governments most of the time. Here, too, I would join with Yoder in arguing that it is possible to "translate" or render intelligible "before the eyes of the watching world" specifically Christian conceptions of peace by focusing on particular practices.

Space permits only one illustration of how this works. The early Anabaptists received their name because they rebaptized people as an act of resistance to the Constantinian alliance between Church and State. But it is arguably the practice of "the Rule of Christ" that was more provocative politically because it located the source of authority in God's will as manifested in the practices of the community of Christian believers rather than in those of the "tax collector." "The Rule of Christ" is also known as "binding and loosing," after Matthew 18:15–20:

> If another member of the church sins against you, go and point out the fault when the two of you are alone. If the member listens to you, you have regained that one. But if you are not listened to, take one or two others along with you, so that every word may be confirmed by the evidence of two or three witnesses. If the member refuses to listen to them, tell it to the church; and if the offender refuses to listen even to the church, let such a one be to you as a Gentile and a tax collector. Truly I tell you, whatever you bind on earth will be bound in heaven, and whatever you loose on earth will be loosed in heaven. Again, truly I tell you, if two of you agree on earth about anything you ask, it will be done for you by my Father in heaven. For where two or three are gathered in my name, I am there among them.

These practices concretely embodied a different kind of political power and a different kind of truth-telling, both of which were intelligible only in relation to the life, ministry, death, and resurrection of Jesus.

The confidence of Christian pacifists in the face of religious repression, including the implied or actual threat of martyrdom, is perhaps best summed up in the sixteenth-century epigram "Truth is unkillable."[17] The immediate context of at least one famous use of this provocative declaration was an explication in the 1520s by Balthasar Hubmaier of "binding and loosing" as a practice of dialogue and discipline, centered in a congregation of Christians, that includes the possibility both of forgiveness and absolution (where repentance is present) and of excommunication (where there is no repentance).[18] This practice, which over time has taken several different shapes, is central to the tradition of Christian discipleship identified with the Anabaptists and with the Mennonite Church in particular.

More recently, Stanley Hauerwas has called attention to the moral significance of the ecclesial virtue of "peacemaking" described in Matthew 18:15–22. As the following passage suggests, this practice of peacemaking projects conceptions of truth and power that differ dramatically from those presupposed by nonpacifists:

> If peacemaking as a virtue is intrinsic to the nature of the church, what are we to say of those outside the church? First, I think we must say that it is the task of the church to confront and challenge the false peace of the world which is too often built on power more than truth. To challenge the world's sense of peace may well be dangerous, because often when sham peace is exposed it threatens to become more violent. The church, however, cannot be less truthful with the world than it is expected to be with itself. If we are less truthful we have no peace to offer to the world.
>
> Secondly, Christians are prohibited from ever despairing of the peace possible in the world. We know that as God's creatures we are not naturally violent nor are our institutions unavoidably violent. As God's people we have been created for peace. Rather, what we must do is to help the world find the habits of peace whose absence so often makes violence seem like the only alternative. Peacemaking as a virtue is an act of imagination built on long habits of the resolution of differences. The great problem in the world is that our imagination has been stilled, since it has not made a practice of confronting wrongs so that violence might be avoided. In truth, we must say that the church has too often failed the world by its failure to witness in our own life the kind of conflict necessary to be a community of peace. Without an example of a peacemaking community, the world has no alternative but to use violence as a means to settle disputes.[19]

Hauerwas's way of making the point is useful for spelling out another set of conceptual problems embedded in Koontz's ethical dualism. First, whatever we may make of various attempts to provide empirical assessments of human disorder, theologically speaking, Christians have a stake in arguing that human beings are not naturally violent. Accordingly, while we recognize the "fallenness" of the world, we must nevertheless call the world to be that which God has created it to be, and part of what it means to communicate this more positive assessment of "the world as it was created to be" is to avoid resigning ourselves to the "fallenness" of the world.

Second, had Koontz paid even more attention than he does to the *prac-*

tices of peacemaking, he would not have overstated the hermeneutical contrast between Christian pacifism and other ethical perspectives. For political practices like "the rule of Christ" ("binding and loosing") can provide, as Yoder puts it, "analogies for conflict resolution, alternatives to litigation, and alternative perspectives on 'corrections.'"[20] In other words, the kind of ecclesial practice described in Matthew 18:15–20 can "function as a paradigm for ways in which other social groups may operate. . . . People who do not share the faith or join the community can learn from them."[21]

Finally, as Hauerwas suggests, the absence of alternative forms of peacemaking helps to explain why many people "in the world" find the Christian pacifist understanding of war/peace ethics implausible. In the end, conceptions of war and peace can only be fully explicated in relation to the practices that embody these conceptions. From a Christian pacifist perspective, the resolution of interpretive conflicts is ultimately subject to the persuasion that may or may not occur when Christian pacifists encounter those who understand the ethics of war and peace differently. Following Hauerwas's argument about the political significance of the practice of peacemaking, the best way to begin the conversation with the adherents of nonpacifist traditions as they encounter Christian pacifists may be to point to practices like "the rule of Christ." If in the process these other traditions are able to understand the connection between this practice and the theological claim that the Lordship of Jesus Christ applies not only over the Church but over "the principalities and powers," and over history itself, then we will have succeeded in starting a conversation about Christian peacemaking in the midst of Christian pacifism's ongoing conflict of interpretations.[22]

Notes

1. The best discussion of the ethical significance of religious convictions is James William McClendon, Jr. and James M. Smith, *Convictions: Defusing Religious Relativism*, rev. ed. (Valley Forge, PA: Trinity Press International, 1994).

2. Awareness of the importance of interpretive issues occurs as early as Reinhold Niebuhr's *An Interpretation of Christians Ethics* (New York: Harper and Brothers, 1935). For discussion of the many ways in which the question of hermeneutics haunts contemporary Christian ethics, see William B. Schweiker's essay, "Interpretation, Teaching and American Theological Ethics," *Annual of the Society of Christian Ethics 1990* (Washington, DC: Georgetown University Press, 1990), 284.

3. See, for example, John Howard Yoder, *Nevertheless: Varieties of Religious Pacifism* (Scottdale, PA: Herald Press, 1971; rev. ed. 1992).

4. See, for example, the collection of articles in *Mennonite Peace Theology: A Panorama of Types*, edited by John Richard Burkholder and Barbara Nelson Gingrich and available from the Mennonite Central Committee Peace Office in Washington, DC.

5. See the first essay in Reinhold Niebuhr's *Christianity and Power Politics* (New York: Charles Scribner's Sons, 1940), 1–32.

6. The most recent of these Niebuhrian attacks on Christian pacifism is Guenter Lewy's *Peace and Revolution: The Moral Crisis of American Pacifism* (Grand Rapids, MI: Eerdmans, 1988).

7. See, for example, Yoder's *When War Is Unjust: Being Honest in Just War Thinking* (Minneapolis: Augsburg, 1984), and his "Just War Tradition: Is It Credible?" in *Christian Century* 108 (13 Mar. 1991), 295.

8. Stanley Hauerwas, "Whose Justice? Which Peace?" in David DeCosse, ed., *But Was It Just?* (New York: Bantam Doubleday Dell, 1992), 83–105.

9. Hauerwas, "Whose Justice? Which Peace?" 83, 84, 88.

10. John Howard Yoder, *Christian Attitudes to War, Peace and Revolution: A Companion to Bainton* (Elkhart, IN: Associated Mennonite Biblical Seminaries, 1983), 193.

11. See Yoder's "Anabaptism and the Sword Revisited: Systematic Historiography and Undogmatic Nonresistance," *Zeitschrift für Kirchengeschichte* 85 (1974), 270–83. I am indebted to John Richard Burkholder for calling this comment to my attention. See Burkholder's "Mennonite Peace Theology: Reconnaissance and Exploration," *Conrad Grebel Review* 10 (1992), 264, esp. n. 13.

12. James W. Douglass, *The Non-Violent Cross: A Theology of Revolution and Peace* (London: Macmillan, 1966), 83.

13. Douglass, *Non-Violent Cross*, 205, 207.

14. An English translation of "Modern War and the Christian Conscience," originally published in *La civiltà Cattolica*, has been published in DeCosse, *But Was It Just?*. The quoted passages are from pages 118, 121, and 123 of this edition. Although the editorials published in *La civiltà Cattolica* are not official statements of the Vatican, they are reviewed by the Vatican Secretariat of State. According to the Rev. GianPaolo Salvini, editorial director of this journal, the article is "not contrary to the mind of the Vatican."

15. Although realists usually regard religious martyrdom as politically irrelevant, on occasion the martyr may be seen as dangerous. In 1993, for example, an exhibit of martyrs' stories scheduled to open at the Smithsonian Institution in Washington, DC, was abruptly cancelled. The reason? According to museum officials, the public display "threatened national security." The proposed exhibit was to have included life-size illustrations made from surviving copperplate etchings from the 1685 edition of *The Martyrs Mirror of the Defenseless Christians*, among them a picture of Dirk Willems. For an account of the controversy, see Tom Price, "Mennonites Off the Wall," *Christian Century* (14–21 Jul. 1993), 200.

16. John H. Yoder, *The Christian Witness to the State* (Newton, KS: Faith and Life Press, 1964), 78, esp. n. 5.

17. For a discussion of the background of this epigram (*Die Warheit ist untödlicht*) and a justification of the way it has been translated, see John H. Yoder and Wayne Pipkin, *Balthasar Hubmaier, Theologian of Anabaptism* (Scottdale, PA: Herald Press, 1989), 76–77 n. 10.

18. Balthasar Hubmaier was one of the most articulate sixteenth-century Anabaptists. A theologian whose learned efforts to refute the charges lodged against the Anabaptists led to his own martyrdom on 10 March 1528, Hubmaier argued

that Christians should forego violence "for the present," but he also appears to have expected the saints to wield the righteous sword of judgment on their behalf. Yoder and Pipkin, *Balthasar Hubmaier*, 18.

19. Stanley Hauerwas, *Christian Existence Today* (Durham, NC: Labyrinth Press, 1988), 95.

20. See John H. Yoder's "Sacrament as Social Process: Christ the Transformer of Culture," *Theology Today* 48, 3 (Apr. 1991), 33, 41.

21. Yoder, "Sacrament as Social Process," 41.

22. I am grateful to Ted Koontz, Richard Miller, and Terry Nardin for conversations related to this project that helped to clarify several conceptual issues. I am also grateful to John Richard Burkholder, Stanley Hauerwas, and John H. Yoder, each of whom supplied me with materials used in this chapter.

CHAPTER 11

Is There a Feminist Tradition on War and Peace?

Jean Bethke Elshtain

THERE IS NO SEPARATE feminist tradition on war and peace. A recent work on *Traditions of International Ethics* includes no chapter on a "feminist tradition."[1] For good reason: each articulated feminist position represents either an evolution within or a break-out from a previous historic discourse. Thus one finds feminist Hobbesians and feminist pacifists, liberal internationalists, and nationalistic isolationists. Which feminist position a particular thinker or advocate endorses will depend upon the tradition in which her feminism is lodged or out of which it emerges. Although feminist antiwar pacifism (variously grounded) is perhaps the best known and most prevalent of feminist positions, it does not stand alone. In this chapter, I shall offer a sense of the landscape of feminist discourse, historically and currently, on matters of war and peace. To say that it is difficult to assess "a feminist tradition" in matters of war and peace is to understate. Do not expect a tidy picture. Despite the often doleful pleas of feminists for women to unite, women and feminism remain divided on every important war and peace question. There is no clear-cut "feminist way" to discuss how war and peace have been understood. There is, however, a rather rough-and-ready feminist outlook that serves as a backdrop to current controversies. I will begin there.

Feminism emerged in the West as one feature of liberalism, indebted to Enlightenment presuppositions and the doctrine of the "rights of man." I refer, of course, to feminism as a self-conscious enterprise, an enterprise announced by the publication in 1792 of Mary Wollstonecraft's *A Vindication of the Rights of Woman*. Wollstonecraft sought to extend the French Revolution's proclamation of the rights of man to women. She insists that women must be active citizens if they are to pass civic virtue on to their young. She effaces the distinction between men and women, where bodily strength is concerned, by calling for identical educations for boys and girls. What would emerge from educational symmetry, she hoped, was a decisive strike against what she took to be Jean-Jacques Rousseau's misidentification of virtue—his embrace of what I have called "armed civic virtue." For Wollstonecraft, there is no honor in the soldier, past or present, for the vast majority of soldiers are a mass swept along by coercion and command. Thus a standing army is "incompatible with freedom." She condemns Rousseau for exalting "to demi-gods [those] who were scarcely human—the brutal Spartans, who, in defiance of justice and gratitude, sacrificed, in cold blood, the slaves who had shewn themselves heroes to rescue their oppressors."[2] Yet, in general, she endorses many of the ends and aims of civic republicanism—civic virtue and autonomy first and foremost, shorn of its martial dimensions. But she nowhere addresses what the grounds, if any, for war might be. Nor does she spend any time exploring wartime conduct.

Wollstonecraft simply assumes a national identity, paying no attention to the violent manner in which the revolutionary French molded that identity by yanking young men out of their local identities, disciplining their bodies to armed purposes, scraping off the insignia of their particularity by the visible sign of putting diverse human elements into identical uniforms. A supporter of the Revolution, she does not engage the presiding revolutionary images. These included paintings of the militant Spartan Mother and of liberty as represented by Marianne, a young female militant with one breast bared.[3] The civic republican world, for all its female icons, was strongly male-dominant. Wollstonecraft endorses this tradition but hopes that, somehow, if men and women receive the same education, a softening will follow. This tension—endorsing "the same" but expecting "the different"—is by no means limited to Mary Wollstonecraft; indeed, if there is a tradition of feminist thought on war and peace, one feature of it is an ongoing repetition of a fundamental ambivalence: should women "fight" men or join men in fighting? There is also a near-silence on the most salient war/peace issues as they emerged in the writings of Western theorists, moralists, and war-fighters: What is a justified war? What should or should not be done in fighting a war? What are the grounds for resistance to political authority, and what is permissible by way of resistance? What is most strikingly displayed, as one surveys the history and literature of feminism, is the continuing manifestation of an abiding (one is almost tempted to say, Ur-) ambivalence.

Mary Wollstonecraft inherited a tradition in which women were tied to diverse conceptions of war and peace. One, the historically grounded, legendary, and prototypical Spartan Mother, offers up the woman as a civic militant who bears children "that they might die for Sparta and this is what has come to pass for me." She is one of the prefeminist exemplars who helps to frame later feminisms. For the Spartan Mother, war is the consequence of the existence of an external "other" who poses a threat to one's city, civic republic, or polity. Her identity is entangled with war's honor and the valor of husbands and sons. War is justified for patriotic reasons of state. Later civic republicans, like Rousseau, recalling the glories of Sparta, insisted that the potent love of mother country, the willingness to serve and protect her, would shrivel on the civic vine if mothers no longer figured overpoweringly in the affections and civic upbringing of their children. There are so many continuing evocations of the Spartan Mother tradition that it would take volumes to catalog all of them. This much, however, should be noted: for the Spartan Mother, any serious threat to civic freedom is a justified *causus belli*. I know of no systematic discussion in the Spartan Mother image, past or present, of the conduct of war. Presumably, war is hell, a sometimes necessary hell. Here Spartan Mothers would vary depending upon the traditions of their own society. No doubt the mother of historic Sparta and the mother of the United States during the Second World War would take different tacks on this matter, though even here I am not so sure. Eighty to eighty-five percent of Americans endorsed dropping the atomic bombs on Hiroshima and Nagasaki, with no significant gender difference at the time. Women were by no means exempt from a perfervid nigh-exterminationist rhetoric where the Japanese were concerned.

My claim is not that the Spartan Mother is a feminist exemplar but that she embodies a version of women's history in relation to war and peace with which all feminists must grapple. In her civic determination and fortitude, she shines with the sort of civic identity that many feminists were later to endorse as preeminent among the familial verities and loyalties. When the crunch comes, she sacrifices private loyalties to overriding public purposes. For the Spartan Mother, there is no presumption against war save on the level of a hope that her country's freedom will never be threatened, from within or without. The grounds for war, or for crushing the oppositional forces that appear to threaten the polity from within, are primarily those of security—for her family and her nation.

For contemporary feminists whose worldview begins with an inexorable division between men and women, the Spartan Mother can only represent a retrograde "male-dominated" perspective and force. Ironically, hard-line "realist" feminists, who believe men and women are ontologically akin to different species and are, as well, in a state of perpetual war, are often far more unrelenting in their views of the necessity for a "sex war" than Spartan Mothers ever were in defense of their country's wars. Yet such feminists see in the Spartan Mother's loyalty to her polity and her willingness to see young men die in its defense a false-consciousness that they disdain to admit into the category "feminist"—despite the fact that they, too, anticipate the triumph of "public" over "private" values. Also, to make this sort of dismissive move requires jettisoning much of a tradition that, historically, often shifts uneasily between Spartan Mother and Beautiful Soul poles. Because we are all historically shaped, such wholesale dismissal is never possible.

The second main female exemplar, the Beautiful Soul, enters history—or, perhaps better put, is secured within the history of the West—with the triumph of Christianity, hence with a presumption against violence and a dream of a peaceable kingdom. For there is what I am tempted to call a "feminization" of ethics associated with Christianity. Finding in the "paths of peace" the most natural as well as the most desirable way of being, Christian pioneers exalted a pacific ontology. Violence must justify itself before the court of nonviolence. Over time, within this broad tradition, men were constituted as just Christian warriors, fighters, and defenders of righteous causes whose violence required (at least in principle) elaborate justification. Women, unevenly depending upon social location, became solidified into a culturally sanctioned vision of virtuous, nonviolent womanhood I call the "Beautiful Soul." It is important to note here that, although the Christian pacifist and just war streams parted historically, they nonetheless remain tied genealogically. Both put violence on trial, placing the burden of proof on those who take up arms.

For the Beautiful Soul, this presumption plays out as a nigh-absolute interdiction on female violence coupled with a mingling of regret and resoluteness should her society embark on a course of war. If there is one dominant feminist tradition before the twentieth century, it lies in a politicized version of the Beautiful Soul (of which more below). Once again, the tale is by no means simple, but by the late nineteenth century, "absolute distinctions between men and women in regard to violence" had come to prevail.[4] The female Beautiful Soul is pictured as frugal, self-sacrificing, and, at times, delicate. Although many women empowered themselves to think and to act according to this ideal of female virtue, the symbol slides easily into sentimentalism. To "preserve the purity of its heart," writes Hegel, the Beautiful Soul must flee "from contact with the actual world."[5] In matters of war and peace, the female Beautiful Soul cannot put a stop to suffering, cannot effectively fight the mortal wounding of sons, brothers, husbands, fathers. She continues the long tradition of women as keepers of the flame of non-warlike values even as, in the nonpacifist versions of Beautiful Souldom, it is the woman on the home front who makes the war effort itself sustainable over time. It is important to note that, in times of war, the Beautiful Soul exemplar often merges with the Spartan Mother as women are identified, and identify themselves, as heroines of the home front and upholders of a more or less total *levée en masse* associated with French Revolutionary civic republicanism.

Nineteenth-century suffragists appropriated both Spartan Motherhood and Beautiful Souldom for their cause. Votes for women were justified on the grounds of ontological equality between the sexes on the one hand, *and* female difference on the other. Some suffragist supporters trafficked in such sentiments as: "For the Safety of the Nation to the Women Give the Vote/For the Hand that Rocks the Cradle Will Never Rock the Boat!" Here an argument for votes for women on the grounds of utility ("for the safety of the nation") and stability ("will never rock the boat") prevails. Presumably, giving women the vote will not disturb the existing, and justified, habit of entrusting war/peace decisions to men. During America's Civil War, the leading suffragists supported the war effort even as they condemned war. They chided men for having brought the country into war, yet praised the fervent and spontaneous patriotism war engenders—a reaction frequently repeated, most recently in the United States in the Persian Gulf War of 1991. Suffragists decried war's terrible cost, yet celebrated and legitimized the many campaigns fought by women in sanitary commissions, as suppliers, nurses, buriers of the dead. Elizabeth Cady Stanton extolled the "multitude of delicate, refined women, unused to care and toil, thrown suddenly on their own resources" during the war, and she used this story of wartime loyalty and sacrifice as further ammunition in behalf of the suffrage effort once the war was concluded.[6] Stanton supported the Civil War, but she also thundered against "male wars" in other contexts, proclaiming that a "new evangel of womanhood" would put a decisive end to chaos and destructiveness. Here are her words:

> The male element is a destructive force, stern, selfish, aggrandizing, loving war, violence, conquest, acquisition, breeding in the material and moral world alike discord, disorder, disease and death. See what a record of blood and cruelty the pages of history reveal! Through what slavery and slaughter, and sacrifice, through what inquisitions and imprisonments, pains and persecutions, black codes and gloomy creeds, the soul of humanity has struggled for the centuries, while mercy has veiled her face and all hearts have been dead alike to love and hope! The male element has held high carnival thus far, it has fairly run riot from the beginning, overpowering the feminine element everywhere, crushing out the diviner qualities in human nature until we know but little of true manhood and womanhood, of the latter comparatively nothing, for it has scarce been recognized as a power until within the last century. . . . The need of this hour is not territory, gold mines, railroads, or specie payments, but a new evangel of womanhood, to exalt purity, virtue, morality, true religion, to lift man up into the higher realms of thought and action.[7]

This is a tall order. It reminds me of the sentiment so often inscribed by one's friends in one's senior yearbook (if you graduated high school in the late 1950s in the United States, as I did): "Stay as Sweet as You Are!"—an expression often coupled to admonitions to be successful in life. How the suffragists thought to pull this one off remains murky, but there is little doubt they did intend it. All the problems of war and peace would somehow melt away once the epiphany of the new society was attained. In the meantime: condemn war, either absolutely or strategically; condemn men, either in principle or provisionally; extol women, both for their wartime loyalty and contribution—as Spartan Mothers—and for their general outlook and principled opposition to violence—as Beautiful Souls.

A similar fusion of disparate imperatives and identities emerged in the era of the First World War with one group of solid Spartan Mothers—like Britain's famous (or infamous) "Little Mother," who trashed all pacifists, male and female. The "Little Mother" wrote a letter, published in the London *Morning Post* in 1916, denouncing pacifists and whiners and declaring that she herself was delighted to send her son off to war—the "sacred trust of motherhood" demands no less, for "women are created for the purpose of giving life, and men to take it."[8] Less violently, one Mrs. F. S. Hallowes in her 1918 book, *Mothers of Men and Militarism*, noted women's equally "passionate love of mother-country. . . . Though we loathe slaughter we find that after men have done their best to kill and wound, women are ever ready to mend the broken bodies, soothe the dying, and weep over nameless graves!"[9] The Connecticut Congress of Mothers issued a "Ten Commandments of Womanhood," which called for Mothers to "Hearten Thy Men and Weep Not" and to "Keep Thou the Faith of Thy Mothers, for in the years of thy country's sacrifice for Independence and Union they served valiantly and quailed not."[10]

In this same era, thousands of politicized women who were suffragists agitated for their country's entrance into the war and proclaimed themselves ready to serve. Women of the Triple Entente often justified the war on liberal internationalist grounds: the world will be safe only when democracy defeats autocracy. (This argument, a bit tricky to square with Romanov Russia's alliance with the British and French democracies, is expressive nonetheless of the liberal internationalist view that the world will be safe only when democracy defeats autocracy, for only then will the breeding ground for war be vanquished.) In line with such patriotic identification and in the wider cause of destroying the breeding ground of political evil (autocracy, militarism), when the Women's Emergency Corps was created in Britain, women queued up in long lines waiting for the doors to open so they could sign up. For such women, the war was becoming a crusade. In this era, thousands of politicized women agitated for peace and proclaimed themselves in opposition to the war on the grounds of a new internationalism and humanism that would one day trump particularistic national loyalties as well as "militarism," a generic term for the evil of arms, armies, and war.

The feminist antiwar stance in the era of the First World War is perhaps best summed up in the notion that there is an "eternal opposition," in Jane Addams's words, between feminism and militarism. Women have been linked to peace campaigns at least since the Middle Ages, to antiwar sentiment since the Greeks: I have in mind *The Trojan Women*, for example, although here, as always, things are tricky. It is well to recall that the maternal Hecuba, mourning the death of Andromache and Hector's son, her grandson, Astyanax, decries the latter's "wretched death"—he has been thrown from the top of the city wall of Troy by its conquerors—and adds, "You might have fallen fighting for your city," anticipating, with this line, an honorable Spartan Mother resolution.[11] The traditional distinction between peace women and war women made sharply visible a prewar division between militant suffragists (more prevalent in Britain than in the United States), who were prepared to use violent methods ("the argument of the thrown stone") to achieve their ends, and the greater number of women who were opposed to all forms of violence, including violence against property. With the war, the militant suffragists tended toward Spartan Motherhood of the most jingoistic sort; the antiviolence suffragists, in their most visible incarnation, surfaced as that uneasy amalgam of Spartan Motherhood and Beautiful Souldom noted above. But there was a third alternative—opposition to the war as a logical continuance of the suffrage campaign. To such advocates, this meant humanizing governments by extending the suffrage to women. Women peace activists who embraced this idea discovered the causes of war in the maladjustment of industrial relations and the failure to pacify states by extending the suffrage. For many, women's nonviolence was a logical extension of maternalism. For others, particularly those associated with a socialist vision, peace meant the day when the causes of war (capitalism, imperialism) had been eliminated and men as well as women could embrace this vision.

My aim here is not to recall a well-documented history but to make explicit the markers of social identity and structures of discourse deployed by antiwar feminists in the era of the First World War. A Women's Peace Party was formed. At its height in the United States there were 165 group memberships totaling some 40,000 women. The American party was one section of the Women's International Committee for Permanent Peace—the Kantian echoes are apt—which had branches in fifteen countries. Antiwar feminists, in line with what Michael Howard calls "the liberal conscience," pushed for continuous arbitration, for a negotiated peace short of total victory, and for a peace settlement shorn of vindictiveness. In this and other ways, feminists in this period located themselves within the larger frame of pacifist/just war discourse. Women peace campaigners promulgated internationalism as a worldwide concatenation of peace-loving peoples, especially of women, to bring into being the conditions for permanent peace. After the war, women were influential in pressing for the Kellogg-Briand Pact of 1928 declaring war illegal, and were on the National Committee on the Cause and Cure of War, which collected ten million signatures on a disarmament petition in 1932. Contemporary feminist and women's peace efforts look back to these and other instances of female activism, much of it under a feminist imprimatur, as historic warrant for their own efforts. Beautiful Soul presumptions against violence are dominant in these and similar efforts: violence is always terrible; women are the special keepers of non-warlike values; war is the breakdown of a natural condition of harmony and equilibrium, realizable and restorable yet again once the various "enemies" of this humane condition and vision are bested.

This version of feminism emerges, as I have already indicated, primarily as a variant of liberal internationalism. But the hope remains that if women ran things, the things they ran would look much different and be much better (more peaceful) than at present. At this point, feminism turns into pacifism—a pacifism grounded less on a Christian nonviolent ethic than on an often essentialist argument for women's inherent peacefulness. All the questions having to do with war and peace historically—What are the grounds for war? What grounds are justifiable and what are not? Are there limits to fighting a war, even a "good war"?—melt away if one assumes that once women take over, war itself will disappear. This is a very old idea, continually refurbished as feminist ideology. For example, one of the first discursive moments in the history of feminism (retrospectively constructed, for the author in question was not self-consciously feminist) is Christine de Pizan's *The Book of the City of Ladies*. Three goddesses—Rectitude, Reason, and Justice—found the author's city. Noteworthy in this "mirror of princes" utopia is the falling away of any nastiness, any dilemma that might implicate the Wise Princess in the perennial dilemma of "dirty hands." Wars are dramatic by their absence in the City of Ladies. Christine repeats the story of the Amazons, noting their "delight in the vocation of arms" and their merciless policy of vengeance; they were women whose skills demonstrated that they were "fit for all tasks."[12] Accepting Amazonian escapades as historic truth, Christine nonetheless denies this narrative of female ferocity and martial vigor any contemporary clout. Her own vision of the "lady" and the Wise Princess bars such appropriations.

Christine thus anticipates later humanists, liberals, and rationalists who shared her fondness for Rectitude, Reason, and Justice and found war irrational, stupid, wasteful, and atavistic. This, at least, is a principled version of feminist antimilitarism and antiwar activity, and it is one variant of liberal internationalism. The major difference, perhaps, is that feminists are less likely than historic internationalists to justify military intervention on humanitarian grounds, finding in the means a collision with preferred ends. This tendency toward "purism" also provides an escape from the problem of "dirty hands." Women scholars and activists prepared to talk about the latter problem fall between the stools of contemporary feminist discourse on war and peace.

This brings me to the turbulent present in feminist thinking on war and peace. To draw together this chapter's themes, I will concentrate on feminism's uncertain trumpet—and I say this not to condemn but to reinforce the picture of competing feminist viewpoints and to offer a reminder of their often contradictory endorsements. For from its inception, feminism has not quite known whether to fight men or to join them; whether to lament sex differences and deny their importance or to acknowledge and even celebrate such differences; whether to condemn all wars outright or to extol women's contributions to war efforts. At times feminists have done all of these things, with scant regard for consistency.[13] Thus one finds "right to fight" feminists who are endorsed by integrationist feminism incarnated in the United States by the National Organization for Women; revolutionary Marxist feminism prepared to approve "Third World revolutionary struggles" as well as to sanction a teleology of violence (if necessary) as part of their own struggle against the bourgeois order; pacifist feminism, sanctified by a plethora of old and new efforts. At the antiwar end of the spectrum, military women become explicable only as "clones of the male model." At the "right to fight" end, pacifist women are construed as "wimps" and regarded as antifeminist because they find women less capable of soldiering than men.

It is impossible to survey the whole of contemporary feminist discourse in a few pages; it is, however, possible to situate feminist arguments on questions of war and peace inside one of several frames. Interestingly, feminism reproduces many assumptions that structure the historic discourses of realism and just war, recreating prototypical characters and arguments. Contemporary feminism has its "Machiavellian moment" as well as its Beautiful Soul reiterations of just war and pacifist ideas. One aspect of feminist argumentation is its often totalizing character: women must wage a total war against every aspect of patriarchal society, or women must struggle for world peace, total disarmament, and the like. That is, for radical feminist "realists" who presume men and women are, and have been, in a perpetual state of war, "anything goes" to achieve the overthrow of patriarchy. For feminist pacifists, means must be limited and constrained—not just "anything goes," but anything is possible, including perpetual peace, once the conditions for war have been eliminated.

This is how feminist "realism" of a separatist variety works: Separatists declare the very condition of humankind to be one of undeclared but total war between men and women. They endorse a Hobbesian social ontology and construe politics as a continuation of this war. They advise women to "fight dirty" and make generous use of military metaphors (Who is the Enemy? Where is he located? How can you best defeat him?). Politics becomes a paradigm case of Oppressor and Oppressed, and there is a lot of tough talk about the sex war and the need for women to take over the extant power structure, even to wear uniforms and carry guns, as the only way to end their "colonization."[14] Others in this mode turn to the language of pathology and disease. Men are the carriers of a taint. They have a need to oppress women. The pathology must be destroyed, by taming men or eliminating them. This is an argument for revolutionary violence that can, at best, produce an uneasy truce in the sex war—unless the enemy has actually been eliminated, through either unconditional surrender or a policy of actually reducing the number of men in the human race.[15] Women who are not "pawns of men" must be in charge of all the changes.

The following is a pretty standard summary of a hard-core feminist "realism" in the present situation—all-out war, an ontology of violence governing relations between all men and all women everywhere—coupled with an apocalyptic utopian insistence that women, naturally pacifistic, will one day rule in peace:

> Why weren't we prepared for this?—the imminence of nuclear holocaust; the final silencing of life; the brutal extinction of the planet. . . . We have lived with violence so long. We have lived under the rule of the fathers so long. Violence and patriarchy: mirror images. An ethic of destruction as normative. Diminished love of life, a numbing to real events as the final consequence. We are not even prepared. . . . Wars are nothing short of rituals of organized killing presided over by men deemed "the best." The fact is—they are. They have absorbed in the most complete way the violent character of their own ethos. . . . Women know and feel the lies that maintain nuclear technology because we have been lied to before. We are the victims of patriotical lies. . . . To end the state of war, to halt the momentum toward death, passion for life must flourish. Women are the bearers of lifeloving energy. Ours is the task of deepening that passion for life and separating from all that threatens life, all that diminishes life; becoming who we are as women.[16]

Oddly, the triumph of the Beautiful Soul is anticipated in these often remorseless narratives. The rhetoric of total war dominates; but, ultimately, the victims will vanquish their oppressors. More plausible versions of feminist realism and its Beautiful Soul variants include, first, the stance of the National Organization for Women and, by extension, all versions of feminism based on rights absolutism. NOW has argued (in an amicus brief in a case involving the constitutionality of the all-male draft) that military service is central to the concept of citizenship. It follows that if women are to gain first-class citizenship, they, too must have the right to fight. In some instances this is coupled with the hope that women will "humanize" the armed services. Equal-opportunity feminism, then, walks an uneasy line between a presumption against war and the insistence that women fight wars.

The grounds for war are not discussed in any systematic way save for a tendency to favor wars for "liberation" and to oppose American intervention for almost any purpose, anywhere, at any time. This latter predisposition was strained during the Gulf War, where some 6 percent of the deployed American force were women. Replaying a familiar hand, a number of prominent feminist politicians and activists condemned the war as an overreaction (at best), yet used the war as an occasion to push for total abrogation of the few remaining statutory limits to women in combat for the American All-Volunteer Force. Unsurprisingly, many military women—especially reservists—told feminist activists to mind their own business: they did not want to fight. But others, primarily officers, often from military families themselves, were delighted at the opportunity to test their mettle.

My own favorite testimony along these lines is Major Rhonda Cornum's postwar ("as told to") memoir. Cornum, who was taken prisoner by the Iraqis when her helicopter crashed, writes of the fact that she didn't want "to go home without seeing action" for she was prepared to "go to war. . . . Fly and fight. I loved it."[17] She had chosen to go to a military medical school rather than a civilian one (she is a flight surgeon), and she and her husband "feel the same way about the big things: duty, honor, country, loyalty. . . . [My daughter] would have thought that I was a wimp if I stayed home."[18] She, for one, wasn't afraid of dying—much worse would be to dishonor her uniform and her country. This is a stance that feminist pacifists, whether Christian or the strategic sort whose pacifism comes and goes with the occasion, find well-nigh inexplicable. Cornum, needless to say, sees herself as a women's rights egalitarian.

For remember, emerging from the historic discourse surveyed above is a version of the Beautiful Soul grounded in a pacific, not a violent, ontology. Men may be oppressors, but the condition of society is not "war"; it is injustice to be fought by nonviolent means. Analysts in this mode insist that women do have insights to bring to bear on the public world. Women are located as moral educators and political actors. This discourse struggles to forge links between what Sara Ruddick has called "maternal thinking" and nonviolent theories of conflict without assuming that it is possible to translate, easily, maternal imperatives into a public good.[19] This view differs from celebrations of a peaceful matriarchy. Its proponents recognize that people must grow up, must become citizens. A citizen is not guaranteed nurture but is sure, instead, to find disagreement and conflict short of war, save for truly extreme instances (Nazism, genocide). The pitfalls of this feminism are linked to its intrinsic strengths. By insisting that women are in and of the social world, its framers draw explicit attention to the context within which their subjects act. But this wider context is one that continues to bombard women and mothers with the formulation that "doing good" means "being nice." Thus, even as stereotypical maternalism exerts pressure to sentimentalize, it is repudiated by competing feminisms that find in any evocation of "maternal thinking" a trap and a delusion.

In her book *Is the Future Female?* Lynne Segal finds much to praise and to challenge in contemporary evocations of "maternal thinking" tied to a wider set of hopes for peaceful arbitration of disputes. Those who evoke this hope (she includes Ruddick and Elshtain in this company) reject the biological reductionism of many eco-feminists and feminist pacifists (like the late Petra Kelly or Dr. Helen Caldicott, for example, who make much of wombs, harmony, inner peace, and so on). But the maternalist view is compatible, Segal argues, with many other positions—both radical and conservative. Unsurprisingly, she finds that real flesh-and-blood women (the majority!) more often than not express patriotism as well as "humanitarian revulsion from war." Her case rests on a series of interviews with women who wire up weapons for the big arms industry (notice the Spartan Mother imagery lurking in the statement):

> Our attitude [says one such woman] was that although it was unfortunate we were involved [in the Falklands War, in this case], once it was upon us we had to get on and do everything to back our boys. People were very willing to work overtime and do whatever was necessary, whether you've got a son involved or not, when it's the English, it's your boys, isn't it? I mean it could be your boy next time.[20]

I am reluctant to conclude on such an uncertain note. But it is one that aptly reflects the vagaries of the many "feminist" traditions in the matter of war and peace. Perhaps a story will help the reader to better appreciate my frustration. When I was putting together a collection on just war theory, I searched high and low for articles by feminists—indeed, by female scholars—lodged securely in the just war tradition and exploring either feminism or war and peace more generally inside that framework. I turned up almost nothing. Perhaps because women have not been history's war fighters, it has been easier for them—and feminists, too—to treat the matter in one of two often extreme ways: either everything is war and ordinary life is construed as a state of "supreme emergency" with men trying, quite literally, to kill and coerce women, or the concrete realities and limits of the world in which we live are overcome discursively by working toward and arguing in behalf of some Kantian (or more feminized) version of perpetual peace. (I refer, of course, to feminists who are not specifically Christian or ethical pacifists. To the extent they are, their feminism seems less dominant than their pacifism, and that is explored by Ted Koontz in his chapter.)

At this point, I would go in the direction of a version of Christian realism in the Niebuhrian tradition. Here's why: I cling to no shibboleth that women, if drafted in large numbers, would somehow transform the military and war-fighting. We are not well served by the abstract language of civic obligation and rights here. One example would be the ways in which theories of justice modeled on macroeconomics, if given a feminist turn and applied internationally, often lead to the imposition on other societies of a vision of justice and a norm of gender relations that is distinctly Western, even North American. I recall the unsettling experience of hearing a feminist scholar, herself indebted to such models of justice, justifying the Soviet invasion of Afghanistan on the grounds that the Afghans were a patriarchal, sexist people—somehow the Soviets would bring them up to speed! Such abstract conceptions of justice suggest that we will have a just society or a just international order only when messy human life and lives conform to a more or less formal model, one that is by definition a static snapshot rather than a theory supple enough to come to grips both with the ebb and flow of human affairs and with differences, sexual, political, and cultural. If anything, the post–Cold War world should disabuse us of the idea that people (women included) will, when the crunch comes, prove more devoted to an abstract ideal of some future perfect society than to defending their own very specific cultures and "places"—often coupled with a rough-and-ready notion of human rights as a minimal standard, a set of restrictions on what governments or opponents or enemies should do to their own or other people.

The realism toward which I gesture has more in common with just war thinking than it does with Hobbesianism or Machiavellianism. I call my prototypical civic character a "chastened patriot," one who modulates the rhetoric of high patriotism (and hence repudiates the Spartan Mother as a dominant identity), keeping alive the distancing voice of ironic recognition of how patriotism can shade into the excesses of nationalism, recognition of the fact that patriotism in the form of armed civic virtue is a dangerous chimera. The chastened patriot is both committed and detached: enough apart so that he or she can be reflective about civic ties and loyalties, cherishing many loyalties rather than one alone. This version of civic identity is not only compatible with but helps to sustain a "minimalist universalism" without falling into the abstract, juridical naiveté of so much liberal internationalism. How such a character—who might or might not be a feminist, although a feminist variant would be apt—sorts out conceptions of war and peace would be complex, drawing upon the many traditions and currents that have shaped and continue to shape Western life and thought.

Notes

1. Terry Nardin and David R. Mapel, *Traditions of International Ethics* (Cambridge: Cambridge University Press, 1992).

2. Mary Wollstonecraft, *A Vindication of the Rights of Woman* (New York: W. W. Norton, 1967), 75.

3. In *Women and War* (New York: Basic Books, 1987), I introduce several prototypes exemplifying particular perspectives. The Spartan Mother—the woman who

places the civic above the private and is prepared (even eager) to sacrifice her sons on the altar of civic necessity—is one. The Just Warrior and the Beautiful Soul are the other dominant collective representations in the Western story of war and peace.

4. Natalie Zemon Davis, "Men, Women, and Violence: Some Reflections on Equality," *Smith Alumnae Quarterly* (Apr. 1975), 15.

5. G.W.F. Hegel, *The Phenomenology of Spirit*, trans. A. V. Miller (Oxford: Clarendon Press, 1977), 399–400.

6. Elizabeth Cady Stanton, Susan B. Anthony, and Matilda Joslyn Gage, eds., *History of Woman Suffrage*, vol. 2 (Rochester, NY: Charles Mann, 1887), 1–2.

7. Stanton et al., *History of Woman Suffrage*, 2: 785.

8. For a full discussion, see Elshtain, *Women and War*, 192–93.

9. *Mothers of Men and Militarism* (London: Headley Brothers, Bishopsgate, 1918), 24–25.

10. As cited in Elshtain, *Women and War*, 147.

11. David Grene and Richmond Lattimore, eds., *Greek Tragedies*, vol. 2 (Chicago: University of Chicago Press, 1960), 272, 288.

12. Christine de Pizan, *A Book of the City of Ladies*, trans. Earl Jeffrey Richards (New York: Persea Books, 1982), 40–42.

13. In discussing contemporary feminism, I draw freely on *Women and War*.

14. These quotations are from "early" (1970s) feminist texts, but the presumptions are widely shared, as I note, to the present moment. The sources are Ti-Grace Atkinson, "Theories of Radical Feminism," in Shulamith Firestone, ed., *Notes from the Second Year: Women's Liberation* (n.p., 1970), 37, and Susan Brownmiller, *Against Our Will: Men, Women and Rape* (New York: Simon and Schuster, 1975), 388.

15. "The proportion of men must be reduced to and maintained at approximately 10% of the human race." Sally Miller Gerheart, "The Future—If There Is One—Is Female," in Pam McAllister, ed., *Reweaving the Web of Life* (Philadelphia: New Society Publishers, 1982), 266–84.

16. Barbara Zanotti, "Patriarchy: A State of War," in McAllister, *Reweaving*, 16–19.

17. Rhonda Cornum (as told to Peter Copeland), *She Went to War* (Novato, CA: Presidio Press, 1992), 4.

18. Cornum, *She Went to War*, 21.

19. See Ruddick's essays, "Maternal Thinking" and "Preservative Love and Military Destruction," in Joyce Trebilcot, ed., *Mothering: Essays in Feminist Theory* (Totowa, NJ: Rowman and Allanheld, 1983), 213–30 and 231–62 respectively. See also "The Rationality of Care," in Jean Bethke Elshtain and Sheila Tobias, eds., *Women, Militarism and War* (Totowa, NJ: Rowman and Littlefield, 1990), 229–54.

20. *Is the Future Female?* (London: Virago Press, 1987), 198.

CHAPTER 12

Toward a Feminist Ethic of War and Peace

Sarah Tobias

JEAN ELSHTAIN BEGINS her chapter by asserting that "there is no separate feminist tradition on war and peace." According to Elshtain, feminist approaches to international relations theory are largely derivative, reflecting familiar themes from within the mainstream literature. Yet she finds enough in the "rough-and-ready feminist outlook" to merit an extended discussion of the relationship between feminism and issues of war and peace. Furthermore, although she notes that feminism is heterogeneous, Elshtain suggests that most feminist scholarship on war and peace falls into one of two polar categories, symbolized by either the bellicose Spartan Mother or the pacifist Beautiful Soul.

I will consider Elshtain's claims in relation to contemporary feminist scholarship. Her account is problematic because she approaches feminist writings on war and peace primarily as an exercise in historical exegesis rather than as an exploration in international ethics. Although she occasionally alludes to conceptions of value, ends, and moral judgment, and to familiar paradigms in international ethics, Elshtain does not delve beneath the surface of feminist discourse to address the ethical positions elaborated in these writings. In particular, she fails to distinguish between normative and descriptive elements in the arguments she considers—both those of realism and natural law theory, on the one hand, and those of feminist theory, on the other. This conflation of norms and description effectively undermines the analytical power of the Spartan Mother/Beautiful Soul dichotomy. The complexity of feminist arguments about war and peace cannot adequately be captured by polar categories that are simultaneously amorphous and reductionist.

Many of the difficulties that beset Elshtain's discussion stem from her insistence that "each articulated feminist position represents either an evolution within or a break-out from a previous historic discourse." Spartan Motherhood, she suggests, is a variant of political realism, while Beautiful Souldom is a hybrid of the natural law and pacifist traditions. The prevailing paradigms in international ethics are not, however, the primary influences on feminist writings on war and peace. Rather, feminists who address these topics draw upon their own traditions of moral and political thought. Feminism is a political movement dedicated to ending the subordination of women by challenging the existence and implications of gender distinction. In so doing, feminists have developed new understandings of domination and subordination, authority and resistance, violence and peace. Feminists' ontological and epistemological claims are drawn from women's experience, and they neither replicate nor simply refurbish familiar philosophical concepts. These claims have enabled feminists to develop alternative approaches to questions of reason, motivation, and moral obligation to those found in conventional discourses.

Some elaboration is necessary to clarify the character of ethics and to assess the impact of applying feminist ethics to international affairs. In this chapter, I define ethics broadly to include considerations of value, judgment, and the good life.[1] Thus ethics both incorporates and transcends a narrow focus on morality. Diverse references to ethics pervade most feminist texts, regardless of the political propensities of their authors. Radical feminists, like Andrea Dworkin, Mary Daly, and Susan Brownmiller, do not present these references systematically, and they must therefore be carefully extricated from the complex arguments in which they are embedded.[2] Other feminists, such as Nel Noddings, Virginia Held, and Joan Tronto, draw upon the empirical studies of the psychologist Carol Gilligan to develop systematic interpretations of the ethics of care.[3] These feminists do not conceive of morality as consisting of abstract and universal standards; rather, they maintain that morality entails responsiveness to particular relationships in specific contexts. When the ethics of care is applied to international affairs, the result is an approach to war and peace that differs qualitatively from the principled rationalism of natural law theory and the self-interested consequentialism of political realism. Despite some serious and unresolved theoretical problems, the ethics of care therefore poses a fundamental challenge to the dominant perspectives on international ethics.

Radical Feminism

To reveal the flaws in Elshtain's argument, I will consider in turn the perspectives of radical and care-oriented feminists. Before assessing the radical feminist discussion of war and peace, however, it will be useful to recall Elshtain's characterization of feminist realism. She argues that this approach to international affairs derives from the prefeminist conception of Spartan Motherhood. The Spartan Mother's main concern is with the security of her family and country. Accordingly, reasons of state are sufficient to justify a military response to threats of violence or incursion. Clearly, Elshtain's account of Spartan Motherhood reflects political realism's preoccupation with self-interested justifications for using force. Although Elshtain does not address this preoccupation directly, her discussion of feminist realism's Hobbesian character implies the importance of self-interest. Feminist realists, she suggests, see social life as an "undeclared but total war between men and women" and "advise women to 'fight dirty.'" For such feminists, "'anything goes' to achieve the overthrow of patriarchy." Although she stresses the similarities between feminist realism and political realism, Elshtain hints at one major difference between the two perspectives. Whereas political realists see peace as an unstable condition, constantly threatened by the security dilemma, feminist realists share the conviction that "naturally pacifistic" women will ultimately triumph and govern in peace. Thus Elshtain implies that essentialism anomalously undercuts the radical feminist adherence to realist premises.

A striking feature of Elshtain's treatment of feminism's "Machiavellian moment" is her reluctance to distinguish between the larger radical feminist tradition and radical feminist *realism*. The ensuing confusion between two quite different outlooks is compounded by her claim (in note 14) that the presumptions of feminist realism are widely shared. Although some of the earliest, most polemical works of radical feminist theory reflect a ruthless disregard for customary moral constraints, most radical feminist arguments only superficially resemble those of political realists.[4] Radical feminists draw upon their own analyses of the politics of women's oppression to subvert conventional archetypes.

This is particularly evident in the radical feminist approach to war. Radical feminists dispute the realist definition of war as "organized violence carried out by political units against each other."[5] Instead, they suggest that the global oppression of the gender class women by the gender class men is also a kind of war. In this war, men use physical and psychological violence to control women's labor and sexuality. Men thereby intimidate women into universal submission.

Since women are subject to varying intensities of violence, Andrea Dworkin and other radical feminists distinguish between war and what Dworkin calls "primary emergency."[6] Dworkin describes three particularly horrific instances that illustrate this kind of extremity: the thousand years during which Chinese men bound and crippled Chinese women's feet, the mass burnings of women as witches by European and American men, and the raping of Bengali women by male soldiers. To these examples Mary Daly adds the ritualistic brutality of African "genital mutilation" and the abuse American women suffer at the hands of gynecologists and mental health professionals.[7] By asserting that war is a global and gendered phenomenon rather than a state-centric one, radical feminists like Dworkin and Daly challenge the association between war and national interest that is central to realist thought. In so doing, radical feminists project a conception of international relations that is based on women's shared personal and political experiences of oppression instead of on the diplomatic and military maneuvering of states.[8]

Radical feminists do not merely define war in broader terms than those acknowledged by realists. They also counter the realist claim that war "represents the abandonment of policy."[9] Indeed, radical feminists suggest that war is synonymous with patriarchy, that is, the consolidation of policy under "institutionalized male supremacy."[10] They therefore assert that the war of men against women entails both order and hierarchy. Clearly, the radical feminist analysis of war diverges fundamentally from the "Hobbesian social ontology" that Elshtain ascribes to radical feminism. According to Hobbes, the state of nature is inhabited by men who are equally prudent and rational, hopeful and powerful—and thus likely to compete for scarce resources on equal terms. War, for Hobbes, entails a kind of equality. Radical feminists insist that women are the *victims* of a violent war waged against them by men. War, for them, implies *inequality*. Women are coerced into modifying their hopes and expectations to fit the constraints of life in a male-dominated society.

Radical feminists posit an alternative to patriarchy that challenges the realist reluctance to countenance "any equation of peace with justice."[11] Freedom and justice are central to the radical feminist vision of a postpatriarchal world. The radical feminist understanding of freedom, which resembles Berlin's conception of positive liberty,[12] reflects a desire for "self-determination, self-enrichment, the freedom to live one's own life, set one's own goals, the freedom to rejoice in one's own accomplishments."[13] At the same time, radical feminists distinguish between justice and social equality. Recognizing that the latter might be attainable without a fundamental transformation of patriarchal institutions, they maintain that this outcome can never be "a proper, or sufficient, or moral, or honorable final goal."[14] Justice requires the eradication of patriarchy in general and of culturally constructed gender roles in particular. As one radical feminist remarks:

> We believe that the male world as it now exists is based on the corrupt notion of "maleness vs. femaleness," that the oppression of women is based on this very notion and its attendant institutions. . . . We must eradicate the sexual division on which our society is based. Only then do men and women have a hope of living together as human beings.[15]

Given this emphasis on the eradication of sexual polarities, it is clear that not all radical feminists envisage a future tied to images of pacifistic womanhood ruling according to the dictates of their nature. Although some radical feminists do endorse a kind of pacifist essentialism, many of the most sophisticated theorists within this tradition argue instead that androgyny is a crucial component of peace. That Elshtain does not comment on the importance of androgyny for radical feminists suggests that her characterization of their thought is selective and incomplete.

Radical feminists have little loyalty to the state because it functions as an instrument of patriarchal oppression. There are, however, divergent opinions within radical feminism about how best to resist patriarchy. Some radical feminists describe resistance primarily in psychological terms. According to Mary Daly, for example, it is important for women to destroy the "patriarchal Lie" by "burning/melting/vaporizing the constricting walls imposed upon the Self."[16] For Daly, resisting patriarchy ultimately involves separatism. Susan Brownmiller, in contrast, argues that women can resist patriarchy in a variety of ways. Thus she argues that women should learn self-defense to protect themselves from attack. It is only within this context that she stresses the importance of learning to "fight dirty." Contrary to Elshtain's implication, Brownmiller never advocates a violent or militaristic strategy "to take over the extant power structure." Indeed, Brownmiller condemns "premeditated murder" and other violent crimes. She suggests instead that the best way for women to oppose patriarchy is through the criminal justice system.[17]

The most significant account of resistance from within the radical feminist canon is provided by Andrea Dworkin. Dworkin argues that patriarchy will ultimately be overthrown by a "revolutionary sisterhood." The sisterhood will refuse to perform domestic chores for men. It will also campaign for equal political rights and demand the integration of more women into the criminal justice system. To address the problem of rape, the sisterhood will campaign for new laws, refuse to "participate in the dating system which sets up every woman as a potential rape victim," "publicize unprosecuted cases of rape," and "make the identities of rapists known to other women."[18] Clearly, the strategy that Dworkin advocates to overthrow patriarchy is a far cry from the admonition to "fight dirty" that Elshtain finds typical of feminist realists.

When Dworkin advises women to press for political change by challenging current law, and ultimately by renouncing all forms of male control, she insists upon the application of stringent ethical standards to conduct. These standards militate overwhelmingly against the "anything goes" approach that Elshtain ascribes to radical feminists. Thus Dworkin argues that the revolutionary sisterhood will be guided in its struggle against patriarchy by the "values which originate in sisterhood." These values dictate an absolute commitment to nonviolence. For women to "betray . . . the worth of human life," she argues, would be for them to "internalize . . . [male] values and . . . replicate [male] crimes."[19]

Dworkin's discussion of the ethics of resistance emphasizes the reductionism inherent in Elshtain's account. As we have seen, by suggesting that "anything goes" when radical feminists contend with the enemy, Elshtain implies that radical feminists ignore moral constraints in conflict. Thus Elshtain plays on a variant of "vulgar" realism that is a recurrent motif in international relations theory. Yet in equating radical feminist arguments with realist ones, Elshtain not only distorts radical feminism but maligns the realist tradition as well. For political realists do not necessarily advocate an amoral approach to international affairs. More frequently, realism involves juggling the competing claims of morality and self-interest. Realists differ dramatically in determining when, precisely, moral constraints should be ignored. For some, it is only in extremity that self-interest requires abandoning moral constraints to secure the survival of the state and the community it embodies.[20] Indeed, from an ethical perspective, this state-centric consequentialism is perhaps the defining characteristic of political realism.

It is abundantly clear from Dworkin's writings that she does not advocate a consequentialist approach to war and peace. By insisting on women's absolute allegiance to nonviolent principles, Dworkin endorses an approach to resistance that is antithetical to realism. Since Elshtain fails to distinguish between the normative and descriptive elements of political realism and radical feminism, her account obscures the importance of deontological reasoning in the radical feminist canon.

Yet despite Dworkin's deontological emphasis, her account is no closer to Elshtain's description of the Beautiful Soul than it is to feminist realism. Dworkin rejects Elshtain's claim that for the Beautiful Soul, "the condition of society is not 'war'; it is injustice to be fought by nonviolent means." Moreover, Dworkin's stress upon androgyny is at odds with the Beautiful Soul's desire "to translate . . . maternal imperatives into a public good." Elshtain's Spartan Mother/Beautiful Soul dichotomy is, in short, far too simplistic to capture the nuances of radical feminist thought.

The Ethic of Care

Although radical feminists contest many of the definitions that are central to realist accounts of war and peace, they neither challenge the distinction between deontological and consequentialist reasoning in international ethics, nor question the way in which political realists and natural lawyers interpret this distinction. I want to consider how a fully developed feminist ethic of war and peace would transcend the conventional construction of the deontological/consequentialist distinction.

The consequentialism advocated by realists is distinguished by its focus on self-interested justifications for using force. Yet the realist conception of morality is nevertheless a principled one. Realists acknowledge "the moral importance of impartial calculations" about various rules of war, such as those concerning proportionality, even if they ultimately fail to abide by them.[21] Indeed, Morgenthau insists that when statesmen act immorally to promote the national interest, their acts may still be judged by universal moral principles.[22] Natural law theorists are, of course, even more insistent than realists that morality should be understood as a set of principles. The recognition by both realists and natural law theorists that moral principles are embedded in a complex ethical system, and that they are neither simple nor unambiguous, does not sever the close link between morality and principle that exists in these traditions.

Both realism and natural law theory have their antecedents in Western traditions of moral and political philosophy. Feminists have recently begun to argue that these traditions are gender-biased, reflecting the ontological and epistemological concerns of men. Some feminists have responded to this assertion by drawing directly from women's moral experience to construct an alternative approach to ethics: the ethics of care.

Among the commonalities shared by feminists working on the ethics of care is the propensity to define morality as a practice. Unlike Michael Oakeshott, for whom morality is a noninstrumental practice, "without any extrinsic purpose,"[23] these feminists argue that morality is a practice directed toward a concrete end: providing for the care of specific others in particular contexts. They differ from one another, however, in how they delineate the ethical aspects of care. Joan Tronto, for example, identifies four types of caring practice, each of which has an ethical component: attentiveness, responsibility, competence, and responsiveness. In contrast to Tronto, Nel Noddings distinguishes between natural caring, "that relation in which we respond as one—caring out of love or natural inclination," and ethical caring. The latter entails acting to protect another person or to promote his or her welfare in accordance with an ethical ideal: a "memory of our own best moments of caring and being cared for."[24] However feminists define the ethics of care, they understand it to be a way of sustaining the tenuous social ties that bind individuals to one another. Care-oriented feminists thus reiterate Carol Gilligan's claim that moral practice primarily entails a focus on "responsibility and relationships."[25]

The feminist approach to the ethics of care, with its stress on benevolence, seems at first glance to reflect the natural law tradition's emphasis on *caritas*, *concordia*, and *societas*. Yet care-oriented feminists reject the natural lawyer's assertion that moral conduct is synonymous with "an unconditional adherence to the truth about what reason requires."[26] Since the contexts in which individuals need care are diverse and always changing, many care-oriented feminists eschew truth claims for an appreciation of the indeterminate character of moral obligations. They reject the tendency to equate reason with "abstract and hypothetical" logic, since this excludes women's experience of thought linked to the emotive and the concrete. Whereas some feminists argue that the connection between rationality and morality should therefore be severed altogether, others attempt to construct alternative conceptions of rationality that link reason with emotion in a "contextual and narrative" mode.[27] By depicting morality as a practice in which reason and emotion are intertwined, feminists deflect many of the questions that theorists often pose to differentiate motive (spirit) and intention (aim).

The feminist preoccupation with an ethic of context results in an approach to judgment that differs procedurally from natural law theory and substantively from realism. In contrast to natural law theory, the ethics of care stipulates that it is not necessary to establish an action's "practical reasonableness" before deeming it morally correct. The rectitude of an act is determined largely by its consequences. Whereas the philosophical forebears of realism, like Machiavelli, endorse a self-interested consequentialism, feminist advocates of the ethics of care stress that the relevant consequences are predominantly those that concern the impact of care-giving on particular others.[28] Unlike Hobbes, another realist forebear, feminists argue that moral practices cannot be codified into universal imperatives without misrepresenting their character. Thus Tronto notes that "care is distorted if we separate the principles of care—that care is necessary—from the particular practices of care in a given situation."[29] Some feminists therefore discard the moral significance of principles altogether. In this spirit, Noddings asserts that "to care is to act not by fixed rule but by affection and regard."[30] Even those feminists who acknowledge the need for some general principles stipulate that these must "be compatible with particular judgments based . . . on feelings of empathy and on caring concern rather than on rational calculation or abstract reasoning."[31]

Given that the care-oriented approach to ethics differs substantively from approaches based on rational principles and procedural justice, it is not surprising that even the most problematic applications of the ethics of care to international affairs do not "reproduce . . . [the] assumptions that structure the historic discourses of realism and just war."[32] Rather, care-oriented feminism raises important questions about the paradigms currently used to analyze issues of war and peace. Many of these questions are considered in the work of Sara Ruddick. Although other feminists have attempted to apply the ethics of care to international affairs, Ruddick contributes the first sustained feminist discussion of international ethics. Ruddick's argument is therefore indicative of how feminists might proceed to develop their own ethics of war and peace.

Ruddick's approach to the ethics of war and peace is derived from the practice of mothering. According to Ruddick, "men can be mothers." Yet because motherhood has generally been the responsibility of women, and as "in most cultures the womanly and the maternal are conceptually and politically linked," the ethical outlook derived from maternal practice is strongly associated with gender.[33] Maternal practice involves the formation of strong bonds between mother and child. The relationship that develops between them challenges the liberal conception of autonomous man, whose competitive impulses are constrained by rules and rights. Rather, mother and child are interdependent, mutually responsive, and motivated by the responsibility of care. The ties that connect a mother and her child inspire and are reflected in a particular type of thinking. Ruddick argues that "maternal thinking" involves a style of judgment and a set of values and ends that differ significantly from "dominant public ones."[34] That is to say, maternal thinking constitutes a unique system of feminist ethics.

A central characteristic of maternal ethics is that it defines the right in terms of the good. Maternal conduct is virtuous to the extent that it furthers the preservation, growth, and social acceptability of a child. A mother struggles to achieve the virtues of humility ("a metaphysical attitude one takes toward a world beyond one's control") and of clear-sighted cheerfulness ("a matter-of-fact willingness . . . to welcome life despite its conditions").[35] Most importantly, a mother strives to cultivate the "capacity" and "virtue" of attentive love. Such love requires the coincidence of empathetic attention and love in a way that serves to "keep . . . [a child] safe and help her grow." A mother whose thought is guided by attentive love will ask her child the question, "What are you going through?" and listen carefully to the response. Yet a mother's empathy should never be so all-consuming that it confuses the identities of mother and child. Attentive love functions most appropriately when a "mother really looks at her child" and "tries to see him accurately rather than herself in him."[36]

Attentive love encourages mothers to make ethical judgments in a "concrete" fashion. Ruddick argues that because mothers respond to particular children, their judgments are nuanced and context-bound. Thus she observes that "concreteness requires inventing alternatives even when there seem to be none, looking closely at what is happening, [and] . . . asking hard questions." Ruddick contrasts concreteness with the tendency to think abstractly and to simplify the complexities of moral life into "dichotomous choices."[37] She claims that abstract rules can even encourage war because, so often, those who fight do so out of loyalty to an abstract cause. Ruddick is particularly hostile to just war theory because its abstractions invite soldiers and civilians "to turn away from the details of suffering, to see instead the just causes and conventional rules of war."[38] By contrast, Ruddick suggests that there will be "greater safety, pleasure, and justice in a world where the values of care are dominant."[39] Ruddick's own approach to international ethics is derived from maternal thinking and is constructed as a concrete alternative to both just war theory and political realism.

Ruddick argues that because mothers experience conflict with children, families, and external authorities as part of their daily lives, resistance is a part of maternal practice. Concomitantly, mothers require an ability to restore peaceful relationships with those whom they care about. Ruddick suggests that maternal responses to conflict could easily be extended to international politics. "Nonviolent peacemaking," her approach to international affairs, is governed by four ideals: "renunciation, resistance, reconciliation, and peacekeeping." The first of these, the "renunciation of violent strategies and weapons," is particularly important for Ruddick's attempt to apply maternal thinking to global politics. She notes that because mothers are generally weaponless, they often try to achieve their goals by adopting strategies like "prayer, persuasion, appeasement, self-suffering, negotiation, bribery, invocation of authority, ridicule, and many other sorts of psychological manipulation." Since most of these tactics can on occasion be injurious, Ruddick suggests that mothers make special efforts "to distinguish permissible hurt from damaging harm."[40] Nonviolent peacemaking therefore requires an ability to evaluate thoroughly the specific circumstances that might warrant conflict, and to appreciate that different ways of fighting will be appropriate in different struggles.

In an early essay, Ruddick argues that maternal thinking, like pacifism, requires "the renunciation of violence even if—and where—violence seems the only means to achieve a desired end."[41] Although she retains a preference for nonviolent action, her later writings modify the absolutism of her earlier stance. In these writings she acknowledges that sometimes, in an international context, it will be necessary to use force. Thus she asserts that "it is unnecessary and divisive to require of all peacemakers an absolute commitment not to kill."[42] Nevertheless, like mothers, those committed to peacemaking will avoid fighting if they can and, if they cannot, will strive to limit all battles. When the fighting is over, peacemakers publicize criminal acts, holding those who have committed them accountable. Ultimately, however, a peacemaker will endeavor to forgive her enemies. She will therefore act in the recognition that her relationship with her neighbors must continue long after the fighting is over.

There are many problems with Ruddick's approach to war and peace. Her attempt to define a care-oriented international ethic is incomplete because she never develops a comprehensive account of motivation, moral judgment, or obligation in international affairs. Moreover, Ruddick fails to explain why mothering is the most appropriate practice from which to develop an international ethic of care. This is especially important since a mother's concern for her own children can prevent her from attending to the needs of others. If maternal imperatives are transplanted into an international context, the result is potentially a very parochial ethic. Guided by the ethics of care, governments might seek to foster the preservation and growth of the states with which they are most closely linked while ignoring those that are geographically or culturally distant. Even more problematically, Ruddick sometimes uses the mother-child relationship as an analogy for the ideal conduct of states in the international system, thereby raising awkward questions about the relationship between power and order. Whereas a mother is often very powerful compared to a child—she can exert her will to direct and discipline her offspring—there is no disciplinary mother figure in the international system, nor is there any other effective form of common government. Ruddick's mother-child analogy therefore seems fundamentally at odds with a decentralized international system in which order cannot be imposed from above.

Despite the difficulties in Ruddick's account, her approach suggests that a fully developed feminist ethic of war and peace would be significantly different from both natural law theory and political realism. Since Ruddick shuns any uniform and abstract commitment to moral principles, and eschews all Kantian-style claims of duty, she clearly rejects the principle-oriented approach of natural law theory. Her emphasis on contextual judgment therefore permits a more flexible approach to international conduct than is permitted by natural law. Yet although Ruddick is a consequentialist, she is not a realist. Many realists argue that the rules of war should be observed when useful, but ignored when they conflict with reasons of state. Implicit in this position is the assumption that when statesmen reject the rules of war, they also reject moral claims. By denying the moral force of principles and endorsing a radically contextualized morality, Ruddick articulates a conception of international ethics that defies classification in conventional terms, and that owes more to Gilligan than to Aquinas, Suarez, Machiavelli, and Hobbes.

Given that Ruddick's approach to the ethics of war and peace differs from realism and natural law theory, it is not surprising that it also eludes the confines of Elshtain's Spartan Mother/Beautiful Soul dichotomy. Elshtain describes Ruddick's account of war and peace as an example of Beautiful Souldom. According to Elshtain, the Beautiful Soul acquires her moral convictions from the natural law and Christian pacifist traditions and therefore counsels "a nigh-absolute interdiction on female violence." Yet, as we have seen, Ruddick's peacemaker is neither a pacifist nor a deontologist. If the ethical aspects of Elshtain's categories are defining, then Elshtain misclassifies Ruddick's work.

Conclusion

Much contemporary feminist theory has sought to challenge inappropriate dichotomies in political philosophy. Feminists have addressed a series of distinctions, such as those between man and woman, public and private, and nature and culture, in an attempt to reveal their biased and exclusionary character. I have tried in this chapter to show how feminist approaches to the ethics of war and peace challenge the dominant dichotomies of international ethics. Both radical feminism and the ethics of care differ from the self-interested consequentialism of political realism and the dutiful adherence to rational principle so central to natural law. Elshtain is therefore mistaken in claiming that feminism reproduces the "prototypical characters and arguments" of realism and natural law theory. Feminists subvert rather than reiterate these arguments and themes.

Since the application of feminist ethics to international affairs is a relatively recent phenomenon, many issues remain to be resolved. Feminists have yet to engage in many of the debates that concern international ethicists. Those who adopt a care-based approach to ethics need to address the problem that care in particular relationships provides little guidance on how to treat persons or communities outside those relationships. Furthermore, an emphasis on contextual morality threatens to reduce feminist ethics to state-centrism, and to ignore the international aspects of women's subordination. Finally, going beyond issues of war and peace, feminists have barely begun to address questions of global distributive justice. As we have seen, even the nascent feminist discussion of the ethics of war and peace challenges and subverts conventional analyses. A comprehensive feminist approach to these and other issues could contribute significantly to the ongoing discourse in international ethics.

Notes

1. For a similar definition of ethics, see Elizabeth Frazer, Jennifer Hornsby, and Sabina Lovibond, eds., *Ethics: A Feminist Reader* (Oxford: Blackwell, 1992), 1–3.

2. Some lesbian feminists discuss ethics systematically. Alongside their own arguments, they sometimes develop particular radical feminist ideas specifically for application in the lesbian community. See Sarah Lucia Hoagland, *Lesbian Ethics* (Palo Alto, CA: Institute of Lesbian Studies, 1988).

3. Carol Gilligan, *In a Different Voice* (Cambridge, MA: Harvard University Press, 1982).

4. For an example of a kind of radical feminist amoralism, see Valerie Solanis, "Excerpts from the SCUM (Society for Cutting Up Men) Manifesto," in Robin Morgan, ed., *Sisterhood Is Powerful* (New York: Random House, 1970).

5. David Mapel, Chapter 3 above.

6. Andrea Dworkin, *Woman Hating* (New York: Plume Books, 1974), 23–24.

7. Mary Daly, *Gyn/Ecology* (Boston: Beacon Press, 1978).

8. This perspective is also adopted by scholars who are trying to develop a feminist approach to the empirical study of international relations. See, for example, Cynthia Enloe, *Bananas, Beaches, and Bases: Making Feminist Sense of International Politics* (Berkeley and Los Angeles: University of California Press, 1989).

9. Mapel, Chapter 3 above.

10. Marilyn French, *The War against Women* (New York: Ballantine Books, 1992), 16.

11. Mapel, Chapter 3 above, under "War and Peace."

12. Isaiah Berlin, *Four Essays on Liberty* (New York: Oxford University Press, 1969), 118–72.

13. Chicago Women's Liberation, "Statement by Chicago Women's Liberation" in Morgan, *Sisterhood Is Powerful*, 531.

14. Dworkin, *Our Blood* (London: The Women's Press, 1982), 11.

15. Bonnie Kreps, "Radical Feminism 1*," in Anne Koedt, Ellen Levine, and Anita Rapone, eds., *Radical Feminism* (New York: Quadrangle Books, 1973), 239.

16. Daly, *Gyn/Ecology*, 20, 380.

17. Susan Brownmiller, *Against Our Will: Men, Women and Rape* (New York: Bantam Books, 1975), 453, 436, 426. Elshtain bases her characterization of the separatist strand of feminist "realism" in part on Brownmiller's book.

18. Dworkin, *Our Blood*, 20, 19, 43–44.

19. Dworkin, *Our Blood*, 65, 72, 65, 48.

20. This is the position taken by Michael Walzer in *Just and Unjust Wars* (New York: Basic Books, 1977).

21. Mapel, Chapter 3 above.

22. Hans J. Morgenthau, *Politics among Nations*, brief ed. rev. by Kenneth W. Thompson (New York: McGraw-Hill, 1993), 12.

23. Michael Oakeshott, *On Human Conduct* (Oxford: Oxford University Press, 1975), 62.

24. Nel Noddings, *Caring* (Berkeley: University of California Press, 1984), 5, 79.

25. Gilligan, *In a Different Voice*, 19.

26. John Finnis, Chapter 1 above.

27. Sara Ruddick, "Remarks on the Sexual Politics of Reason," in Eva Feder Kittay and Diane T. Meyers, eds., *Women and Moral Theory* (Savage, MD: Rowman and Littlefield, 1987), 240.

28. It is important to note, however, that many feminists who advocate an ethic of care challenge the traditional dichotomy between egoism and altruism by arguing that the self is socially constituted rather than "antecedently individuated." As Marilyn Friedman writes: "If the self is inherently social, then a concern for other persons is fundamental to the self and is not reducible to a mere variety of self-concern. Indeed, the conception of the social self tends somewhat to blur the distinction between self and other. If my relationship to someone or to some group is internal to who I am, then she or they are somehow a part of me. . . . I [therefore] show a moral attitude that is neither egoism nor self-denying altruism." See Marilyn Friedman, *What Are Friends For?* (Ithaca, NY: Cornell University Press, 1993), 68–69.

29. Joan C. Tronto, *Moral Boundaries* (New York and London: Routledge, Chapman, and Hall, 1993), 153.

30. Noddings, *Caring*, 24.

31. Virginia Held, *Feminist Morality* (Chicago: University of Chicago Press, 1993), 35.

32. Jean Elshtain, Chapter 11 above. The feminist conception of the self, together with the feminist rejection of conventional understandings of reason and justice, differentiate the ethics of care from other contextual theories. The ethics of care does not replicate Christian "situation ethics," for example. Although they

regard the obligation to care as paramount, situation ethicists also assert that love is synonymous with justice and accept the natural lawyer's conviction that reason is "the instrument of moral judgment." See Joseph Fletcher, *Situation Ethics* (Philadelphia: Westminster Press, 1966), 26. Nor is the ethics of care a kind of utilitarianism. For ethics based upon the "principle of utility," whether defined in terms of welfare, the greatest happiness, or satisfaction, stands in stark contrast to the ethics of care's rejection of formulaic responses. Moreover, adherents of the ethics of care would probably endorse Rawls's concern that utilitarianism fails to "take seriously the distinction between persons" (John Rawls, *A Theory of Justice* [Cambridge, MA: Harvard University Press, 1971], 27). They would therefore criticize an approach to ethics in which the good of the majority always prevails over the good of the few as one in which particular relationships are depreciated.

33. Sara Ruddick, *Maternal Thinking* (New York: Ballantine Books, 1989), 41.

34. Sara Ruddick, "Maternal Thinking," in Joyce Trebilcot, ed., *Mothering* (Totowa, NJ: Rowman and Allanheld, 1983), 214.

35. Ruddick, "Maternal Thinking," 217–18.

36. Ruddick, *Maternal Thinking*, 119, 123, 121.

37. Ruddick, *Maternal Thinking*, 95.

38. Ruddick, "Preservative Love and Military Destruction: Some Reflections on Mothering and Peace," in Trebilcot, *Mothering*, 250.

39. Ruddick, *Maternal Thinking*, 135–36.

40. Ruddick, *Maternal Thinking*, 161, 165–66, 168.

41. Ruddick, "Preservative Love," 245.

42. Ruddick, *Maternal Thinking*, 138.

PART FOUR

Comparative Overview

CHAPTER 13

The Comparative Ethics of War and Peace

Terry Nardin

THE PURPOSE OF THIS comparative overview is to consider, in relation to one another, the six ethical perspectives discussed in the preceding chapters. What are the defining assumptions and arguments of these perspectives as historically constituted and intellectually coherent patterns of thought? How does each handle the basic questions of war/peace ethics? Where do they differ, and which of these differences are fundamental? Can we identify areas of actual or potential agreement? Clearly, in a broad comparative inquiry of this kind, the focus must be on general themes rather than on the nuances of each perspective.

Basic Assumptions

The ethics of war and peace in the modern states system is addressed most directly by natural law and political realism, which can be understood as two sides of a continuing dialogue.

The natural law tradition is an attempt to give systematic expression to the moral point of view. Central to it is the idea of a rationally knowable system of moral precepts—natural law—imposing duties on all persons as rational beings. It is these precepts, and not the consequences of one's acts, that provide the standard of right and wrong in conduct. Moreover, the precepts of natural law must be distinguished from positive law or custom. And because they govern all conduct, they apply to public as well as private life.

Political realism is often identified with moral skepticism, the view that morality has no place in public life. But it is better understood as arguing only that there are severe *limits* to morality in public life. Moral constraints exist, but they may have to be set aside for "reasons of state." Realism is a kind of particularistic consequentialism: it seeks to guide conduct by evaluating the consequences of action (especially the actions of public officials) for the interests, security, or survival of the state. Realism thus acknowledges the authority of morality—up to a point. But it does not flinch from aggression or the deliberate killing of innocents, if such measures are required to protect the public safety. Moral constraints are to be respected where possible, but they do not have overriding authority.

Both realism and natural law offer ethical guidance for the conduct of foreign policy, and the tension between them can be seen in diplomatic practice, in international law, in "just war theory," and in the military codes of states. If the traditions of Judaism and Islam do not fit comfortably into this debate, it is not because they are unconcerned with the tension between moral law and political expediency, but because their ideas about "international relations" are different from those of realism and natural law.

Judaism has been peculiarly insulated from the realities of diplomacy and war. The rabbis who argued among themselves in the Jewish communities of the diaspora were more concerned (in their discussions of this topic) with biblical exegesis than with their own political situation. Their debate, even when it moves beyond the wars of Joshua and David, has for two millennia focused on hypothetical Jewish wars, for only since 1948 has there once again been a Jewish state, and therefore actual Jewish wars. Insofar as one can find a Jewish "international ethics" in this rabbinic legacy, it is largely one that offers guidance for isolated communities of Jews embedded in a non-Jewish, and recurrently hostile, environment.

For Islam, the primary community is the notionally expanding community of believers (*umma*). The "international ethics" of this Muslim community, which is neither a diaspora nor a state, is concerned with relations between rival religious communities, not states. The moral ideas it draws upon in discussing these relations, however, hold all human relations to the constraints of divine law. Muslim war/peace ethics, though only indirectly focused on interstate relations, is therefore always concerned with the lawfulness of war, demanding moral justification for the decision to use force and for the way it is used.

Like Judaism and Islam, Christian pacifism has not been primarily concerned with articulating principles to guide the conduct of states. It offers a critique of statecraft, but is barred from developing a practical ethic for using armed force as an instrument of policy by its blanket repudiation of what it calls "violence" and by its concern for individual commitment to Christian faith and fellowship. As Ted Koontz points out, the kind of pacifism that is driven by religious and moral commitment to nonviolence can be distinguished both from an "abolitionist" commitment to transforming the world through the creation of new institutions for settling disputes peacefully and from the view that existing communities can be defended against aggression by "nonviolent resistance." But all three members of the nonviolence family challenge the view, implicit in realist and natural law ideas of necessity and last resort, that force can be presumed to be effective.

Feminist thought on war and peace is relatively undeveloped, perhaps because women have been excluded from decisions to make wars and from actually fighting them, and because self-conscious feminism itself is relatively new. Like Christian pacifists, feminists set themselves in opposition to a political world they feel they have not made. By questioning received assumptions, feminism invites us to rethink questions of war and peace, and it problematizes the gendered identity of women as civilians and men as soldiers. But there is as yet no settled feminist ethical tradition, only a diversity of feminist idioms: Marxist, liberal, radical, maternalist, etc. Feminists remain divided concerning the ethics of war and peace.

Conceptions of War and Peace

In Judaism, Islam, and Christianity the idea of peace has two dimensions. All three religions distinguish true peace from mere truce. The Hebrew *shalom* is the cessation of fighting, a period of rest following surrender or victory, but it is also a permanent condition of perfection to be realized only with the coming of the messiah. In Islam, permanent peace, *salam*, is possible only on the basis of God's law, which requires that we acknowledge God's authority over us. And because the God to whom we must submit is the God of Islam, this peace can be enjoyed only within the Muslim community. It is the condition that prevails within the expanding realm of Islam and that will someday, with the ultimate conversion or subjugation of all non-Muslims, prevail everywhere. For natural law, true peace is not the mere absence of violence but an ordered tranquility in which war would never be an attractive option. Peace is the willing cooperation of individuals within a community, and of communities within a larger community of communities. A similar view of peace is held by those committed to Christian pacifism, though the pacifist may perceive violence where the natural lawyer does not. But the Christian pacifist also stresses how, by repaying evil with good, by forgiving the wrongdoer while resisting wrongdoing, one can be at peace with one's enemies even in the midst of war.

War, too, has a dual reference in these traditions: it is both the actual clash of armies and a metaphor for disorder. The Hebrew word for war, *milkhama*, refers to Jewish battles, actual or notional, but it also stands for the violent conditions in which Jewish communities both before and during the diaspora have struggled for existence. The Arabic words for war include *qital*, fighting or battle, and *harb*, discord or strife (as in *dar al-harb*, the domain beyond the sway of Islam, which is a domain of not-peace). More familiar to non-Muslims is *jihad*, a word with many meanings: to exert oneself; to exert oneself against resistance and thus to struggle; to struggle in behalf of Islam; and to struggle against the enemies of Islam. Given these connotations, it is not surprising that the religious imperative of jihad should be used to justify the use of armed force, and not only by those committed to Islamic revival or those who, like Saddam Hussein in the Gulf War, disingenuously exploit revivalist sentiment. But the identification of jihad with war is, in Muslim discourse, always an interpretation of its core meaning: the striving to reject evil that goes on in every soul, and that receives its collective expression in the duty of the Islamic community to realize a divinely sanctioned ethical system. Only in some contexts, then, does jihad mean actual armed conflict; often, it is closer to an expression like "the war on poverty" (with an added dimension of religious duty) than it is to "just war."

War, in realist discourse, is an instrument of policy. But it is also a permanent condition of fear and insecurity. Either the imperative of self-preservation (Hobbes) or the logic of war itself (Clausewitz) tends to drive policy beyond the limits of moral restraint: as the Romans said, "Necessity knows no law." And in feminist discourse, war is often understood to be the manifestation or consequence of male aggression, male power, and a male-dominated social order; peace, in contrast, is the expression of feminine benevolence, sociability, and nonviolence (though many feminists challenge these understandings). War is also a metaphor for the relations between men and women, which suggests that peace would involve a profound alteration of these relations—at the very least, an end to male domination.

Given its commitment to nonviolence, Christian pacifism is reluctant not only to offer judgments of the rights and wrongs of war but even to distinguish different kinds of war. It is, in fact, inclined to include all kinds of coercion, force, violence, war, and oppression in the blanket category of "violence."

Attitudes toward War and Nonviolence

None of these viewpoints is inherently militarist. All view war as at best a means and not as an end in itself. On what is this presumption against war based? What support can be found in each perspective for nonviolent or abolitionist attitudes?

Realism comes closest, in its Machiavellian moments, to finding positive value in war. But if we understand realism to be a state-centric form of consequentialism, it cannot be said to be committed to war as a way of life; rather, its attitude is a pragmatic one in which war is chosen or rejected as an instrument of policy according to circumstances. There is in realism, nevertheless, a bias against nonviolence: the use of force may sometimes be imprudent, but a refusal on principle to use it is foolhardy. Nonviolence is helpless in the face of ruthless adversaries: it can neither thwart their aims nor transform their characters. Nor can we hope to transform the character of international relations by establishing a world government, for (as Kant observes) this would only trade international for civil war. On the reasons for this pessimism, realists divide, some basing their doubts on theology or on a theory of human nature, others simply on experience and on skepticism regarding the claims of utopian politics.

Whereas some Christians accept the necessity of force, others argue that their faith commits Christians to the practice of nonviolence: using force, they argue, is incompatible with the principles of love, forbearance, forgiveness, and reconciliation. Also, there may be more effective and less costly ways to resist aggression and to settle conflicts. But the main concern of the Christian pacifist is to create and sustain a community of believers committed to living according to these principles "defenselessly," and to accepting the suffering to which this choice can lead. Catholic natural law, in contrast, teaches that though war is an evil, the use of military force may be permissible in some situations. But its justice can never be presumed. Furthermore, even where the cause is just, a war can be justly begun only if authentic efforts to avoid it through compromise have proven fruitless: war is justly chosen only when it is forced upon one, and even then one must seek only to resist aggression and not intend to kill.[1]

Judaism and Islam are even less traditions of nonviolence. Although there is disagreement within the tradition, on the whole Judaism accepts resistance, fighting, and killing as necessary for self-defense. The rabbis assume that enmity toward Jews and the need to fight is the normal condition of things in a premessianic world, but they neither glorify war nor condemn it. And there are no wars of conversion in Judaism: a Jewish holy war is a war of extermination, though the conditions justifying wars like those fought against Amalek and Canaan may never be repeated. Islam is more ambivalent. The call (*da'wa*) to serve Islam can be pursued through war if unbelievers refuse either to convert or to accept the status of a religious minority within the realm of Islam. Muslims who die in response to the da'wa are blessed by Allah, but the glorification of violence that one can find in modern fundamentalist thought has few precedents in the tradition. Armed jihad is rejected by those who, though faithful to the mission of Islam, insist that belief cannot be secured by force and that religious diversity is tolerable. For Muslims who hold views of this sort, nonviolent propagation of the faith is both expedient and proper. They find warrant for nonviolence in the Qur'an and in Muhammad's commitment to nonviolent resistance during his early years in Mecca. Even the Prophet's reluctant endorsement of limited warfare after his move to Medina can be taken to support the view that fighting is undesirable for Muslims, and that it is permissible only if there is no other effective way to resist aggression against the faith.

Christian pacifism repudiates the instrumental acceptance of war found in other perspectives. War is sin, a kind of human idolatry. In a world of war, Christians cannot be anything but nonviolent if they are faithful followers of Christ. This nonviolence does not entail complete refusal to cooperate with the world, however. Pacifists can hold government positions almost as easily as those committed to just war principles: both will face situations in which their commitments clash with policy, forcing them to take a stand. Pacifists can (some say must) participate in the world by serving their neighbors, and they must look for nonviolent ways to perform this service while seeking to transform the world so that war will cease to be an option.

Feminism is ambivalent about war, actual and metaphorical. When it is identified with rights, privileges, and opportunities from which women have been wrongly excluded, war can be seen as an activity that should be opened up to female participation. Identified as a pathology of the male-dominated social order, war ("the war system") can be seen as a way of life to be reformed by female virtues. Identified with gender relations, specifically with male domination itself, war is not the lawless anarchy (the war of all against all) anatomized by Hobbes, but an entrenched patriarchy (the war of men against women) to be resisted and, ultimately, overturned by abolishing the gender system. As Elshtain puts it, "Feminism has not quite known whether to fight men or to join them; whether to lament sex differences and deny their importance or to acknowledge and even celebrate such differences; whether to condemn all wars outright or to extol women's contributions to war efforts."[2] Hence the diversity of historical images of women in relation to war: the female patriot, the female as embodying the ideal of peace in a (male) world of war, and the female moralist committed to the practice of "maternal thinking" or an "ethic of care."

Grounds for War

What grounds for war, if any, are recognized within these perspectives? What criteria are used to distinguish justifiable from unjustifiable wars? Let's begin with political realism and natural law, for it is from the dialectic between them that we have the ancient yet still evolving idea of "just war."

For the realist, war is an instrument of state purposes to be used when it seems useful. But rules constraining the resort to arms can also be useful, and should be observed for the same reason. It follows that the rules cannot be allowed to obstruct the use of force where observing them would interfere with the protection of important national interests. States may use armed force not only to defend themselves against attack but also to avoid a dangerous loss of power. Though preempting an imminent threat might be justified morally as self-defense, a state may have to act "aggressively," and therefore "unjustly," to deal with more distant threats to national security. Realists often oppose such preventive war on prudential grounds, but realism itself has no principled objection to it.

Because natural law is concerned with articulating these "principled objections," we usually see it as more restrictive than political realism. Thus, the principle of self-defense is more constraining than the realist's expansive goal of self-preservation. And even in properly defensive wars, those against whom the defender fights must merit attack by having committed aggression. Moreover, aggressors cannot justly defend themselves against counterattack. Nevertheless, its principles sometimes make natural law seem more, not less, permissive than realism. It is more permissive, for example, when it recognizes as a ground for war the righting of a wrong done, either by restoring the damage done to the victim or by punishing the wrongdoer.[3] But the natural law tradition seems to be moving away from the view that war is a legitimate way to punish wrongdoing. A state cannot, as moralists once presumed, wage punitive war against entire communities. Increasing doubts about a practice of self-help in which states go beyond defending themselves to punish one another raise the question of whether armed reprisals can be justified by natural law.

In addition, as we have seen, the natural law tradition holds that a war cannot be justly begun if there is a reasonable prospect of avoiding it by nonviolent means. There must also be some reasonable hope of success, and the foreseeable side-effects of the war must not be excessive. But these precepts cannot be mechanically applied. They imply judgments of what is sometimes called "proportionality," but which Finnis argues is really a matter of fairness: fairness, because such judgments are to be made *not* by weighing objectively commensurable benefits and costs, but by striving to be impartial in assessing the justice and injustice of accepting the harms resulting from each of the alternatives being considered.

Many Jews seem to think that their tradition supports "just war" precepts like those of natural law. But rabbinic discourse down through the centuries has produced a rather different set of principles. Insofar as a war is seen as fighting undertaken by a Jewish sovereign or community, it is either a war commanded by God to conquer and later defend the land of Israel, or a war of expansion permitted to David as king. The rabbinic dichotomy of commanded and permitted wars is certainly quite different from the natural law distinction between just and unjust wars. As Walzer points out, the former is incomplete, for it suggests a (missing) third category of wars, those neither commanded nor permitted but forbidden. But there is disagreement whether (as Walzer suggests) the absence of a category of prohibited war indicates a willingness to tolerate wars of aggression, that is, wars fought to extend a king's domain or enhance his greatness, or whether (as Ravitzky argues) this absence should be taken as evidence that the prohibition of such wars is taken for granted. Walzer may be right that the distinction between commanded and permitted wars is an "academic" one, surviving precisely in the absence of politics. If so, then perhaps as it is tested, the distinction will give way to more familiar categories.

This does not mean that there are not explicit sources and arguments in the tradition on which a condemnation of aggressive war might be based. Some rabbis, for example, rationalized the wars of the Jewish kings by arguing that, in a world of nations permanently hostile to Israel, *any* war against other nations was in effect defensive. This argument implies the idea of what we would now call "preventive war." Yet broad though the ground it offers may be, the argument implies at least the possibility of criticism. A few commentators have explored this possibility, distinguishing between attacks on nations that are only potential enemies and attacks on those clearly preparing to invade Israel—distinguishing, that is, between broadly preventive and narrowly preemptive war. Other commentators suggest that permitted wars may be fought only against savage peoples—those who fail to observe the Noahide precepts forbidding incest, murder, robbery, idolatry, etc., and among such peoples only against the most utterly depraved. Because neither Christians nor Muslims are savages, according to this definition, war against them is not permitted. But despite these arguments, the rabbinic debate has been less concerned with the grounds for permitted war than with the conditions that must be met before such a war could be undertaken. Instead of principled objections, it offers procedural constraints—for example, that the war must be approved by the (long-defunct) Sanhedrin. In this way, the rabbis hoped to limit wars of aggression in the face of biblical passages endorsing them.

As in Jewish tradition, much of the casuistry of Islam has religious rather than practical significance. Medieval Muslim legal discussion was intended to rationalize the earliest Islamic conquests, and to reconcile the militancy of the expansionist period with the tolerance and nonviolence of many Qur'anic verses. There seems to be no developed conception in traditional Islam, however, of war as a practice among states. Nor is there much that resembles European ideas of interstate aggression and self-defense. Fighting is conceived as taking place between loosely organized parties of believers and unbelievers, and its justification is invariably religious: war is justified to advance the faith against resistance, or to defend Muslim lands against conquest by unbelievers. In the modern West, a "just war" is a finite response to a particular threat, but Islam retains a worldview within which war is an instrument (frowned on by some and celebrated by others) in the permanent struggle to establish the universal dominion of Islam.

Muslim jurists have nevertheless had to deal with the wars of Muslim rulers, and, despite the categories they bring to bear, their concerns are not entirely unlike those that have shaped European just war thinking. For example, they have had to face the problem of distinguishing authorized from unauthorized wars, in response to which they have developed the doctrine that only a lawful ruler (*imam*) of the Muslim community, or those acting by the ruler's authority, can initiate a jihad to expand the Muslim community. (This doctrine has, of course, been abused by rulers seeking to justify their wars of conquest and gain.) It would be surprising if Muslim writers had not sought to reconcile Islamic categories with the situation created by the imposition on the Muslim world of European ideas of sovereignty and international relations. In response to this situation, some Muslim writers interpret jihad as forbidding wars of aggression against other states, but as permitting defensive wars, wars of national liberation, and humanitarian intervention.[4]

Christian pacifism is more ambivalent than one might think about whether force can ever be rightly used, and not only because those we have been calling abolitionists and nonviolent resisters sometimes favor collective security, humanitarian intervention, or other ways of using force to protect peace or resist injustice. Even strict pacifists may tolerate the use of force by governments, despite the fact that it is forbidden for Christians, tacitly approving at least some wars while refusing to participate in them.[5] And the argument that Christians must seek to transform the world through nonviolent action, so that armed force is no longer needed, implies the need for (and therefore the propriety of) using force in the world as it is. But Christian pacifists are understandably reluctant to be drawn into debates about what the proper uses of force might be, and the tradition therefore has no general theory of just war, even for those who are not Christian pacifists and who may be responsible for governing.

Feminism has no consistent position on the grounds for war, nor have feminists given the issue sustained attention. Unlike Christian pacifism, which demands nonviolence as a matter of principle, feminist pacifism often reflects the essentialist view that women are inherently peaceful. Such feminists assume that a world ruled by women would be a world without war. More common than feminist pacifism, however, is the kind of feminism that draws on liberal internationalism and relies on just war ideas to condemn wars of aggression and support wars of liberation. The application to international affairs of the ethics of care yields an antiwar feminism situated uneasily between pacifist and just war convictions. For radical feminism, men in general have long waged an undeclared war on women, a war that has taken the form of institutionalized oppression and violence. Often the metaphor is one of the "colonization" of women by men, which points toward a revolution by women against the colonizer.

Resistance to Political Authority

How do the viewpoints we are considering deal with conflicts within the community, in contrast to conflicts with outsiders? Are there situations in which they might permit such uses of force against incumbent governments as tyrannicide, revolution, or a war of national liberation? Do they recognize the practice of conscientious objection?

In an ethic of law as command, there is always at least an implicit ground for resistance to the commands of a king, and this ground is the commands of God. The rabbinic tradition makes this subordination of the king's laws to those of God explicit. But, doubtless because of the subservient position of the Jews throughout most of their history, resistance to the wicked orders of even a gentile king is more likely to take the form of disobedience than of rebellion. Only in modern times are there Jewish revolutionaries as well as martyrs: it is Zionism rather than the rabbinic tradition that celebrates the Maccabean revolt as a war of national liberation. The generous biblical and talmudic exemptions from military service are probably better seen as a procedural device for constraining royal wars than as an anticipation of the modern (Protestant) idea of conscientious objection, though commentators have begun to search for a biblical warrant for the Jewish conscientious objector.

In the Muslim world, the issue of resistance to illegitimate authority is dramatically illustrated by fundamentalist hostility not only to the West but to the governments of Muslim states, which are seen as the products of colonialism and as corrupted by Western influences. The idea of a jihad to restore the Muslim world to a more complete adherence to Islam therefore makes more sense in the context of debates about the politics of Muslim governments than it does from the perspective of Western liberalism. One obstacle to calling for jihad against Muslim governments, however, is the requirement that it must be properly authorized. The debate over who can and cannot properly authorize a jihad is, therefore, an aspect of the larger debate over religious and political authority now raging throughout the Muslim world.

The idea of a rational (as opposed to a revealed) higher law as a ground for resisting political authority is most fully developed in the tradition of natural law. Efforts to overthrow one's own government are justified only when that government has usurped legitimate authority, or, if legitimate, when it governs in a way that is grossly unjust. When such a government attacks its own subjects, private citizens may rightly resist its attack with force, though this resistance must respect the same constraints that govern the conduct of war against an external aggressor. Private citizens may not punish an unjust ruler, however, any more than they may impose private vengeance on an ordinary criminal. The natural law tradition recognizes a distinction between the usurper and the legitimate but unjust ruler: whereas the latter may retain the authority to rule, the former is a kind of bandit who may be overthrown to protect the community from his depredations.

Short of revolutionary violence, a government may (in some cases must) be resisted when its laws require the performance of gravely immoral acts or where its policies are evil. Evil laws should be disobeyed and evil policies thwarted. Natural law also permits symbolic resistance (civil disobedience), provided it does not itself involve significant moral wrongs. And it may even permit refusal to participate in military service, not only to avoid involvement in an immoral war, but because such service, even in a just war, may be incompatible with the fulfillment of a person's religious (and perhaps other kinds of) commitment.[6] In no case are officials excused from the responsibility to give reasons justifying a war, or citizens from the responsibility to weigh the cogency of those reasons and to refuse to serve in or actively support a war that they deem, upon reflection, to be unjust.

Realism divides on the issue of civil resistance, depending on whether the state is seen as intrinsically valuable or merely as an instrument for pursuing what is valuable. Whereas the intrinsic view implies that suppression of dissent is the normal order of things (for citizens are servants of the state), the instrumental view limits suppression to situations of emergency (for the state, to serve its citizens, must be protected against threats to its existence). Even a liberal state, then, must sometimes suspend the rule of law.

Though realist arguments are routinely used to justify the repression of internal as well as external threats to the state, realism has no consistent position on revolution or secession. It can only evaluate resistance to authority on consequentialist grounds: if armed revolt can establish a better community, there is no reason why it should be ruled out, just as the use of force to preserve an existing community cannot be ruled out. Moreover, as a consequentialist ethic focused on the interests of a given community, realism can adopt different communities as the objects of its prudential concern. Consequentialist arguments based on the interests of communities defined by class, nationality, or gender closely resemble (in form if not in content) those based on traditional reasons of state.

Christian pacifists require no special theory of political authority; Christians must simply recognize that authority exists and deal with the implications of that recognition. For the early Christians, the injunction to obey Caesar was a reminder that though they were powerless, God was not. Such an attitude is of course not possible for post-Constantinian Christianity, which must deal with the implications of possessing power. Christian pacifists attempt to deal with these implications by arguing that the church not only must renounce violence but must use its power to overcome the violence of others as well. For some, this has meant a commitment to a nonviolent revolution to overthrow oppressive regimes and to establish liberal-democratic principles. Others argue that the church must resist being co-opted by liberals into thinking it has a stake in maintaining the existence of one state in preference to others. Feminists are also ambivalent about resisting injustice, some arguing for militant action and others counselling withdrawal. Most agree that women must eschew methods that simply replicate the crimes of men; they must resist male violence without themselves becoming violent.

Intentions and Motives

How do the various perspectives see issues regarding the intention or motive with which one acts, in contrast to the issue of the external conformity of one's acts with moral standards? Are intentions and motives different? Are acts of war rendered unjust if done for the wrong motives?

Natural law discourse clearly distinguishes intentions and motives. There is a sense in which acts are defined by the intentions that give rise to them; an act is what it is because of the intention that informs it. Further, not only is its intention part of the act, but to intend is itself to choose and therefore to act. In contrast, motives are not choices but the emotional circumstances moving ("motivating") one toward or away from particular choices. One might say that intentions are the "why" of action (what is aimed at), motives its "spirit," the state of mind of the agent (individual or collective) and the emotions influencing choice. Intentions are always morally relevant, but motives have moral significance only when they affect what is intended and done.

For natural law, then, both intentions and motives can be relevant to judgments regarding the moral rightness of a choice to fight. And this relevance can be highly constraining, for the choice must be right in every respect. If the ostensible ground of one's act is just (one is choosing military action to reverse an unjust conquest, for example), but what one intends cannot be justified (perhaps the choice is being made by a government to bolster its domestic political standing, or involves a campaign of devastation designed to punish the conqueror or prevent future aggression), then the act cannot be justified. An act may satisfy many moral criteria or have good consequences, but if it is chosen for the wrong reasons, it is wrong. One's motives in waging a war can also be an important consideration in judging it morally: to fight out of hatred or for the pleasures of battle is always wrong. Furthermore, because social as well as individual acts can have a "spirit," a nation's policies can be corrupted by the evil motives of its leaders and citizens if those motives have affected the choice of these policies.

The issue of intent is relevant to a dispute between natural law and pacifism over whether choosing to fight is necessarily to reject peace by willing the death and suffering of one's enemies. According to Finnis, even resistance to aggression cannot justify an intent to kill. War is never a license to kill, and deadly means are properly chosen not to kill those one is fighting but only to thwart their attacks. That one can foresee death as the consequence of resisting an attacker does not mean that one intends to kill, provided that one's choice in resisting is only to thwart the attack and that the foreseen deaths are the result of using the only available means of resistance. It follows, as Boyle points out, that a war fought without willing the deaths of enemy soldiers—that is, one fought in circumstances in which peace does not exist or is threatened, and where one's intent is to achieve or restore peace by resisting an enemy while causing as little harm to that enemy as possible—is a war that does not require that one turn one's heart against peace in the way that pacifists assume one must whenever one fights.[7] If this is correct, what divides the natural lawyer and the pacifist is how they apply the principle that forbids actively willing the deaths of one's enemies (itself an interpretation of the principle that evil should not be done so that good may come), not their adherence to that principle itself.

Intentions and motives are secondary in rabbinic discussions of war and peace—though hardly in rabbinic ethics generally—for the rabbis often seem to accept any motive as well as any cause as sufficient for a permitted war. With few explicit exceptions, like Maimonides' suggestion that a Jewish king should fight only to further religious and moral ends, the intentions of Jewish rulers in waging war are simply not discussed. The intentions of non-Jewish rulers, in contrast, are presumed to be evil. Their wars may have historical significance as part of God's plan, but that does not mean that they understand or intend to carry out God's commands; they are his instruments, not his agents.

Political realists also approach the ethics of statecraft with a conception of human action far less nuanced than that of natural law. A standard maxim of realist prudence is that in dealing with actual or potential adversaries, one should concern oneself with their capabilities, not their intentions. Behind this maxim is the premise that intentions are, if not unknowable, at least unreliable—or, in more cynical versions of realism, that everyone intends evil. To the degree that realism is consequentialist, the agent's own intentions are not particularly important, either: if what matters in judging an act is its consequences, then neither intentions nor motives have much ethical significance.

Realists do, however, sometimes cast aspersions on the motives of those who act (or urge others to act) on the basis of moral principles, accusing them of hypocrisy or of being more concerned with keeping their own hands clean than with avoiding disaster ("moralism"), and they sometimes argue that the prudent pursuit of self-interest is a better guide to conduct than morality is. But there is in realism another line of argument that urges an "ethic of responsibility" according to which one must "dirty one's hands," if necessary, for the good of the community one serves. This is a motive-based ethic, rather than an ethic of either principles or consequences. The ruler who invokes it says, in effect, "trust me" (to act for the good of the people). In this strand of realism, which is itself a kind of moralism, one's motives redeem the lies one must tell or the murders one must commit for reasons of state.

It is in Christian pacifism and in feminism, however, that the substitution of judgment and sentiment for abstract reasoning (moral or prudential) has gone furthest. For some feminists, ethics is neither principled nor consequentialist but a matter of developing the appropriate emotional disposition or character, a skill for managing human relationships in a caring way. Morality is a practice of sympathy and affection, not a system of principles or a calculus of consequences. Christian pacifists, too, often put the emphasis on morality as a way of life, one in which love (and worship, which is an expression of love) has a central place. Both are inclined to see the renunciation of violence as essential to the practice of care or love and to the reconciliation of those in conflict with one another. Because both understand morality as a practice involving reason and emotion, Christian pacifism and the feminist ethics of care give more significance to motives than do other perspectives. Both, however, insist that love (or care) is not only a sentiment but also an inherent quality of actions aimed at securing what is good for those who are loved. For pacifists, especially, this can mean an insistence on avoiding harm rather than on acting to rectify injustice—an insistence that may arise from suspicions regarding the motives of those with power, who so often use it to injure while pretending benevolence.

The Conduct of War

What constraints on the conduct of war do the perspectives recognize? How do they deal with problems that arise when moral and prudential considerations pull against one another?

Though every ethical viewpoint recognizes the existence of moral limits on the conduct of war, the implications of this recognition are explored most systematically within the tradition of natural law. According to this tradition, the choices made in conducting a war are governed by the same moral considerations as the decision to initiate it. Both governments and soldiers must intend to fight on just grounds, and their choices must not be motivated by hatred or other doubtful motives. They must avoid causing disproportionate ("unfair") destruction in pursuit of military ends. Above all, they must not intend, either as an end or as a means to an end, the deaths of innocents.

The moral force of this last constraint, often called the principle of discrimination or noncombatant immunity, is not undermined by uncertainties in distinguishing combatants from noncombatants. The population of any community includes many who are without question noncombatants, and methods of warfare like terror bombing or threats to employ such methods (as in the case of nuclear deterrence) are clearly barred. But one may choose to conduct military operations one knows will harm noncombatants, provided that such harm is unavoidable and that it is proportionate (in the sense that it is the result of an impartial choice in which, for example, "enemy" noncombatants are treated no more harshly than those of "friendly" or "neutral" parties).

Christian pacifism, by its blanket condemnation of war, bars itself from articulating an ethic of military conduct. But some Christian pacifists acknowledge that not all forms of violence are the same, and therefore that if force *is* used, it must be used with discrimination. Distinctions between moral and immoral conduct in war are implicit, for example, in the argument, often made by pacifists, that the destructiveness of modern weapons has made it increasingly difficult to distinguish war from terrorism. Christian pacifism sidelines *ius in bello* issues because its aim is not to develop a casuistry of fighting but to re-center the debate by drawing the line between war and peace rather than between fighting fair and fighting dirty.

Political realism accepts the principles of necessity and proportionality as constraints on the conduct of war, for (as it understands them) these principles are simply applications of the consequentialist prudence that constitutes its ethical core. But the principle of noncombatant immunity, if recognized at all, must be set aside when conformity to it interferes with the effective conduct of war. Realism also denies that in calculating whether an act is proportionate, one must consider impartially the interests of everyone affected by it: the loss of one's own soldiers or citizens is more properly counted a cost than the loss of enemy soldiers or civilians. In contrast to natural law and even to other forms of consequentialism (like utilitarianism), realist proportionality privileges the interests of one side over the interests of others.

In Islam, constraints on the conduct of war can be traced back to the pre-Islamic "rules of the game" of intertribal warfare. These rules forbade fighting during certain periods of the year and condemned excessive destruction, reflecting both a code of honor that protected the weak—women, children, the aged, and prisoners—and the view that fighting is instrumental to an end. But these rules of war are reinforced by the morality of the Qur'an and the *sunna* (the practice of the Prophet). If the purpose of war is to order the world on Islamic principles, then indiscriminate killing and destruction are forbidden because they neither respect nor further this end. Despite many differences, then, the idea of jihad resembles the Western idea of just war not only in presuming that peace is the end of war but also in insisting that the values of peace govern the conduct of war.

The issue is more complicated in rabbinic Judaism. Just as the absence of a category of forbidden wars complicates the task of rabbinic casuists, so does the biblical command to exterminate the Canaanites in conquering the land of Israel. Whatever limits on the conduct of war the tradition would recognize must be reconciled with these biblical precedents. The rabbis accomplish this reconciliation either by ignoring these passages or by interpreting them to forbid further wars of extermination: the command to "conquer" the land of Israel, for example, is often read as an injunction to settle the land peacefully. But they do not explicitly forbid such wars.

Though Jewish tradition does at times explicitly distinguish combatants and noncombatants (as when Maimonides condemns the wanton destruction of property), more often it does not. The reasons for this rabbinic failure to develop the idea of noncombatant immunity, Walzer suggests, probably lie not in the morality of the rabbis (who had clear ideas about the impropriety of killing the innocent) but in the absence of Jewish armies whose conduct would require regulation. The only context in which the issue is discussed at length is that of siege warfare, regarding which it is sometimes argued that those who wish to flee a besieged city should be allowed to leave. Modern Judaism has developed principles (the so-called "purity of arms" doctrine) that prohibit direct attacks on noncombatants, but the authority of these principles is not firmly established by the traditional sources, their wide acceptance notwithstanding. But the biblical and other passages that might be used to support these principles are there, waiting to be given authority by current interpreters.

Morality in Extremity

What is the force of moral considerations in situations of extremity? Can constraints on the initiation and conduct of war be set aside in emergencies? What constitutes an authentic emergency or situation of extremity?

What may be called the "argument from extremity" holds that, though one must in general behave morally, in situations where either individual lives or the survival of a community are threatened, moral constraints may be violated in order to meet that threat. These are sometimes called "cases of necessity," an expression that suggests that moral considerations may have to be set aside for consequential reasons.[8]

A version of this argument has long been acknowledged in Judaism, on the ground that the law was given so that Jews might live by it, not die by it. Thus, it is accepted that certain laws (like those that ban fighting on the sabbath) may if necessary be set aside. But no emergency, some hold, can justify violating the laws against murder ("bloodshed" is the term the rabbis use), idolatry, or incest. To interpret the intentional killing of noncombatants as murder and therefore as forbidden, even to preserve the community, is to offer a plausible but not necessarily authoritative interpretation of the tradition. On this interpretation, danger to a Jewish community cannot justify violating the most basic principles of Jewish morality, for to permit these principles to be abandoned would shatter the integrity of Judaism. Less grave violations of the rules of war, like ignoring rules that forbid the destruction of property, may be permissible in emergencies for the sake of "saving lives," that is, on the ground of necessity. But there are other views. Some rabbinic interpreters argue that the threat of destruction may in certain cases justify bloodshed. Others argue that if you must die rather than commit bloodshed, then you cannot fight even to defend your community against aggression. War, they suggest, is already a corrupted situation, and if you are caught in it different rules may apply.

The natural law tradition distinguishes constraints on war that are based on positive law or custom, and that have moral force for reasons of fairness and reciprocity, from those that embody the exceptionless moral precepts of natural law. Whereas customary constraints may be ignored in situations of extremity, the precepts of natural law may not, because they follow from the principle that evil may not be done so that good may come. This principle is basic because if it is denied, the obligations of morality turn on consequential considerations, and natural law as a system of choice-guiding precepts collapses. In extremity, a community may rightly choose to set aside the positive rules that exist for human convenience, but precepts like those forbidding aggression or the deliberate infliction of harm on the innocent must be respected unconditionally. It is these bedrock prohibitions that lie behind the natural law maxim "Let justice be done though the heavens fall."

The logic of Christian pacifism in dealing with the question of extremity is similar to that of natural law, but pacifists draw the line between the normal and the extreme in a different place. Instead of asking whether the rules of warfare can be overridden in extreme situations, they deny that preserving individual lives or a human community can ever be a reason for setting aside the prohibition of war. The Christian pacifist, however, defends this conclusion on religious rather than natural law grounds: our Christian duty is to obey God's laws, trusting that, if we do, God's purposes will be realized. It is not our duty to try to further these purposes by violating these laws: we are not to help God make history come out right. We are responsible for the consequences of our acts, but our first responsibility is to obey God. We must not identify extremity with threats to our own lives and communities: to put the fortunes of any person or community above obedience to God's laws is a kind of idolatry.

Extremity poses a smaller problem for political realism (and therefore also for the realist type of feminism) than it does for perspectives that believe certain moral duties to be absolutely binding. In realism, as in consequentialism generally, moral rules—which are never more than instrumental—are likely to be set aside long before a community is faced with disaster. Either consequentialist cost-benefit reasoning is substituted for the judgments of morality (eliminating the need for an escape clause in extreme situations), or morality is often pushed aside because disaster is a possible consequence of any loss of power (which means that there are many potential situations of extremity). In either case, the realist view is that where important communal interests are threatened, those acting for it must act prudently rather than morally. Since this "must" cannot itself be given a moral interpretation,[9] the claim is that, in emergencies, officials either cannot on consequential grounds afford to be morally constrained or do not have a choice: they are psychologically compelled to ignore morality. According to the latter argument, necessity excuses as well as justifies. Without it, realism is left in the awkward position of substituting one absolute (national security) for another (the moral law).

Though many realists insist on the argument from extremity, for the reasons just given, others accept as prudential wisdom the contrary argument that the rules of war have been framed for situations of grave danger. Many of these rules are expressly concerned with regulating conduct in situations of personal or communal emergency, and these at least should not be set aside when such situations arise. Something like this reasoning is reflected in standard military versions of the laws of war, which treat noncombatant immunity as an absolute standard even though they offer a cost-benefit rationale for it. It should be noticed that these positive codes join natural law in rejecting the compromise proposed by Jeff McMahan, according to which morality is understood to permit the violation of *any* moral constraint under certain conditions. From the standpoint of international as well as natural law, the "commonsense morality" that appears to converge with political realism is, like realism itself, a morality already corrupted by consequentialist rationalization.

Conclusion

In an important way, realism and natural law are united with one another and opposed to the other viewpoints: each offers a practical ethic of international relations where the others do not. Realism and natural law can be understood as two sides of a single debate: whether principles or consequences have priority in guiding the conduct of *states*. Both assume that the state is a moral agent, a collective person, and seek to guide judgments concerning the rights and wrongs of state conduct. In each, moralists have attempted to articulate principles of statecraft by drawing on an ethic of personal conduct—realists applying prudential maxims and natural lawyers applying the moral precepts of natural law.

The other viewpoints do not discuss the conduct of states in this way—but for different reasons. Islamic thought is shaped by the struggle between Islam and non-Islam. For this reason, and because the idea of the territorial state is alien to the tradition, Islamic moralists are inclined to ignore the system of states. They therefore find it hard to adapt Islamic principles to international relations and to war between states.

The attention of rabbinic Judaism, too, is focused on something other than war between states. In discussing war, the rabbis appeal not to personal morality but to biblical passages about the wars of Jewish kings. This gives Jewish tradition a nostalgic or utopian quality—if there were a Jewish state, what could it do? Where the tradition does attempt to deal with the practical issues of relations between states, it often "spiritualizes" war by interpreting the relevant biblical passages in a nonliteral manner (though, as Ravitzky points out, the post-Constantinian Christian tradition treats the pacifist teachings of the New Testament in the same way). There is much in Jewish ethics that could be applied generally to state conduct, including the so-called Jewish natural law of the Noahide commandments.[10] But the rabbinic tradition seldom applies these commandments, or the moral principles that spring from them, to the conduct of the biblical Jewish sovereigns, and it does not concern itself at all with the conduct of Gentiles. Because Jews today take it for granted that morality applies to international relations, they find it hard to believe that the tradition often challenges this view, and that the rabbinic judgments are often at odds with ordinary moral principles.

Islam and Judaism are (at least in modern times) religious communities on the defensive. They therefore tend to see the international system as an alien institution, not as an inclusive international society in which Jewish or Islamic states are related to other states on the basis of common moral rules. Realism and natural law, which developed long before the modern age, have come to terms with the international system and have thus been able to articulate an ethic of foreign policy and war. But Judaism and Islam, as traditions, have not yet embraced such an ethic. With some exceptions, each still reflects the outlook of a people preoccupied with conversion (Islam) or with resisting conversion (the Jews). For realism and natural law, diplomacy and war are the normal order of things and call for practical ethical guidance; for Judaism and Islam, they are symptoms of a condition to be endured in the interregnum before a new order is established.

The messianism of Christian pacifism may help to explain why it, too, has failed to develop an ethic of statecraft. Pacifist ethics is not primarily concerned with the state as a moral agent but with how individuals should think about their own conduct in relation to war. Listening to rabbinic and pacifist arguments, one feels that one is listening to the views of people who are not in power and who are not worried about the decisions people in power must make. The rabbis puzzle over problems of religious rather than practical significance, whereas Christian pacifists argue about what it means to be nonviolent in a violent world. This remoteness from practical politics is also evident in feminism. Insofar as they are concerned with war and peace, then, Judaism, pacifism, and feminism offer guidance about how Jews, pacifists, or women should behave in a world dominated by Gentiles, nonpacifists, or men. If Muslims stand apart, it is perhaps because Islam expects to triumph in this world and the others do not.

Notes

1. See below, under "Intentions and Motives."

2. Chapter 11 above.

3. The distinction between these various grounds for war is not always clear. Self-defense merges imperceptibly into restitutory warfare against a conqueror and into protecting other victims of aggression. And punishment is hard to distinguish from self-defense when the emphasis is on deterrence rather than on retribution.

4. As Sohail Hashmi suggests in Chapter 8 above, Muslims can be particularly open to humanitarian intervention because Islam assigns little importance to territorial sovereignty.

5. Though self-defense needs no elaborate justification for those whose outlook is shaped by natural law, the Christian pacifist may find it easier to accept the use of force to protect the innocent—which can be seen as an expression of love for one's neighbor—than to protect, and therefore prefer, one's own self.

6. See Boyle's discussion of this point in Chapter 2 above, under "Resistance to Political Authority."

7. See Boyle, Chapter 2 above, under "War and Peace."

8. Alan Donagan, *The Theory of Morality* (Chicago: University of Chicago Press, 1978), ch. 6.

9. I try to explain why in "Nuclear War and the Argument from Extremity," in Avner Cohen and Steven Lee, eds., *Nuclear Weapons and the Future of Humanity* (Totowa, NJ: Rowman and Allanheld, 1986), 289–305.

10. See Ravitzky, Chapter 6 above, and David Novak, *Jewish Social Ethics* (New York: Oxford University Press, 1992).

CHAPTER 14

Divine Justice, Evil, and Tradition: Comparative Reflections

Richard B. Miller

THIS BOOK INVITES us to examine several approaches to the ethics of war and peace, and to do so comparatively and cross-culturally. It is premised on the idea that conversation across traditions and cultures is itself a good, that mutual understanding is beneficial in a world ravaged by conflict, human suffering, and ongoing suspicion. Cross-cultural comparison is seldom only an academic task. It is often joined to the hope that dialogue can reduce the occasions of political violence and cultural animosity, that familiarity more often hinders than breeds contempt. Thus we are invited to locate areas for conversation across cultures and traditions, or at least to consider where ethical traditions share common ground.

Here I wish to call attention to general philosophical and religious concepts that illumine the extent to which Catholic natural law, political realism, Judaism, Islam, Christian nonviolence, and feminism might find resources for dialogue. As the previous essays reveal, each of these perspectives provides ethical guidelines for conduct in war and peace. But each tradition does so by drawing from a wider constellation of beliefs and symbols without which those guidelines would be incomplete, if not unintelligible. Moreover, each tradition includes abundant materials for developing its ethical norms and directives, requiring those who interpret it to make judgments about which sources are (or ought to be) most authoritative or representative.

With these concerns about beliefs, symbols, and interpretation in mind, I will cluster my comments under three rubrics: (1) the implications of theology for ethics, especially concerning the morality of extremity in war; (2) the different symbolisms of evil in moral discourse about war; and (3) hermeneutical observations about the problem of representing a tradition.

THEODICY AND MORALITY

Several of the perspectives discussed in this volume adopt the counterintuitive notion that war is not the opposite of peace. According to the Catholic natural law tradition, a just war aims to restore peace, understood as harmony and the tranquility of order; in Judaism, final peace is messianic and eschatological, a condition that may be brought about by violent means; in Islam, war is the instrument through which the abode of peace will triumph over the *dar al-harb*. Yet, however counterintuitive such notions may be, they are intelligible given some basic cosmological considerations about God's relation to history or nature. Such theological considerations, moreover, have direct bearing on what may and may not be done in the course of war itself.

In Judaism, Islam, and the Catholic natural law tradition, war is joined to peace as part of a divine ordering of the cosmos and human history, an ordering that is believed to be just. Jews and Muslims ascertain divine justice from God's actions in history, as these actions are described in sacred texts and authoritative commentary (*midrash* and *tafsir*, respectively). Here the task of practical reasoning is interpretive and analogical: it must ascertain the requirements of the divine will for situations that resemble past events in which God has acted or revealed clear directives.

Catholic natural lawyers draw inferences about the requirements of justice from the order of being, created by God. This theological dimension is not explicitly developed in John Finnis's rendition of the Catholic natural law tradition, but it has an important role to play in that tradition's understanding of peace and humanity's enjoyment of the supreme good.[1] Human intentions, when regulated by natural law, cohere with divinely ordered purposes. For Aquinas, we participate in divine reason insofar as we ascertain dictates of natural law, some of which are self-evident and others of which can be inferred from essential human ends.[2] Such ends, the basis for human fulfillment in this life, bear the imprint of the divine design. They imitate—that is, both "mirror" and "are caused by"—the eternal law, the mind of God. For this reason, Aquinas remarks that the natural law is the eternal law's participation in rational creatures (*participatio legis aeternae in rationali creatura*).[3] According to Aquinas, moreover, the eternal ideas of the created order—the blueprint of the cosmos—reside in the mind of God. These ideas serve as the exemplars for the cosmic design, the ordering of things to their respective ends.[4]

This attention to God in relation to history or nature means that Jews, Muslims, and Catholic natural lawyers typically understand war and peace within a larger cosmology, one that is constrained by the conviction of *theodicy*, or divine justice. In Judaism and Islam, God commands war as part of an overall aim of establishing peace and well-being in the future; in the Catholic natural law tradition, war is to be carried out in accordance with the designs of nature, which bear the imprint of a divine, rational Creator.

To be sure, a divine-command morality differs from the Catholic natural law: the former reveals God's will, whereas the latter connects divine purposes to reason and natural processes. But such differences should not be exaggerated, since divine-command morality and Catholic natural law morality both place great weight on divine sovereignty over human affairs. God is, respectively, either the stage manager or the set designer of political life. Understood as either Providence or Designer, God (and God's purposes) provides strong sanction for the institution of war as a vehicle for realizing peace. In none of these traditions is war intrinsically evil. Invoking the history of revelation, documented in sacred scriptures, or the notion that self-defense is a natural, rational duty, these traditions embrace the idea that war can be an instrument for providing human beings their just due.

Attention to divine ordering and justice helps account for the proper grounds for war, the proper intentions or motives for war, the relationship between war and peace, and the limits of political obligation in these three traditions. Moreover—and most importantly—this outlook helps explain a notable reticence surrounding the morality of extremity in Judaism, Catholic natural law, and Islam. War is justified when it coheres with providential or natural purposes, but decisions *in* war must be disciplined by the belief that the cosmos is finally on the side of justice. Accordingly, theodicy produces an *ethical constraint* on the conduct of war in these traditions, especially regarding the morality of means.

Stated simply, for those who embrace the idea of theodicy, it is inconceivable that divine revelation or the natural law would command some kind of evil so that good may come.[5] Theodicy, in short, mitigates crude realism or utilitarian calculations in war. The conviction that the cosmos is on the side of justice means that the right will always be joined to the good, although the realization of the good might lie in the future. If, by contrast, those who are righteous will suffer for their righteousness, the system seems unfair, and reflects badly on the morality of Providence. Similarly, if evil must be done so that good may come, then it would seem that the unjust have an advantage over the just, whose actions seem futile by comparison.

Accordingly, theodicy rules out an ethic of necessity, or sacrificing moral duties for reasons of prudence or utility. Instead, these three traditions generally hold to the idea that virtue will be its own reward, either now or later. In an ethic constrained by the belief in divine justice, we need not sacrifice morality to prudence, or ethics to necessity, because the good has been guaranteed to those who follow righteousness. The individual is freed, then, from having to make history "come out right."[6] Instead, virtuous individuals must place themselves within a larger whole—either a divinely ordered historical process, or a rationally designed set of natural ends.

A morality of extremity, then, seems to be excluded by the idea of cosmic justice. Yet in two instances, our authors mention the possibility of exceptions. Michael Walzer reports a talmudic example in which the rabbis discuss God's immoral commands to Saul. Similarly, Bassam Tibi calls attention to the Islamic precept, "Necessity overrides the forbidden," adding that the criteria for determining emergencies are vague. Yet, given what I have said about theodicy as providing an ethical constraint on the conduct of war, these examples are anomalous because they suggest that evil is condoned to achieve good. Judaism, Catholic natural law morality, and Islam adhere to a cosmology with a just God, and a just God ought not to permit such an ethic. A God who allows such an ethic would seem less perfect than a God who requires both means and ends to be moral.

Here we must observe an obvious difference with the tradition of realism, even the highly disciplined version discussed by David Mapel. As I have said, realist concessions to necessity, even if only occasional, are (or should be) inconceivable to an ethic shaped by belief in divine justice. Indeed, if we understand the epistemological implications of theodicy correctly, the main issue between a traditional Muslim, Jew, or Catholic natural lawyer, on the one hand, and a realist, on the other, would turn on whether claims of necessity are self-deceiving. For an ethic constrained by belief in theodicy, the concept of permitting morality to be sacrificed to necessity is premised on an untruthful, or at least deficient, vision of the good.

Realists can respond to these concerns in one of two ways. First, they may acknowledge the importance of divine justice for an ethic of war, but might nonetheless resist a morality of absolute rules when it comes to settling matters about war's means. Among Christian realists, for example, Reinhold Niebuhr counsels some restraint in war, arguing that since humans cannot successfully adopt a posture of holiness, their aims in war ought to be restricted to modest ends. For Niebuhr, statecraft should be directed toward eradicating evil and creating relatively just political arrangements, not toward establishing "holy" regimes. The Christian, he asserts, "worships a God whose goodness (holiness) transcends all forms of goodness known in history, all of which are tainted with sin."[7] For Niebuhr, the ends of holiness and righteousness lie beyond history, which is finally in God's control. Those who adopt an ethic of total war, or holy war, arrogate to themselves a power to direct history that exceeds the limits of human knowledge and virtue. For finite human beings, only a war of limited ends is warranted.

Niebuhr understands war's means to be set by the criterion of proportionality, not of discrimination as an indefeasible rule.[8] In his mind, absolute rules incline us to be self-righteous and legalistic in our assessments of human action. "Legalism" denotes the characteristically Protestant anxiety that rigorous moral codes lead us to become sanctimonious and pharisaical when evaluating others' actions. With an ethic of absolutes, we are liable to commit the sin of pride. Niebuhr's ethic of limited means is thus unable to generate a strict set of immunities for noncombatants.

Once again, the danger of arrogating to ourselves more virtue than is warranted in a sinful history is relevant to the ethics of war. The idea that holiness and righteousness are beyond history places limits on the kinds of judgment that we can make about the methods used in war. An outlook that is wary of pharisaism thus allows for considerable liberty (and vagueness) about what may be permitted short of total war. In this way, Niebuhr argues *both* in behalf of the relevance of theology for setting the proper ends of war *and* for a more relaxed basis for assessing the means of war, which may leave open the door for killing in the name of necessity or utility.

Second, realists might respond to concerns about divine justice by saying that ethical constraints imposed by a belief in theodicy distract us from the more modest and manageable issues that surround the morality of extremity. For many realists, the key issue is not whether concessions to necessity suggest that the unjust have an advantage over the just. Instead, the issue is whether it is worse to allow an evil or to commit one. To this, realists usually add that history provides limited options in which to exercise justice.[9] So, realists could say, we all agree that injustice occurs when nefarious forces tyrannize innocent people. If those forces are especially effective and well organized, the realist might argue that using immoral means as a way of protecting innocent people may be the lesser of two evils in a world of limited alternatives. Disagreements between realists and Jews, Muslims, and Catholic natural lawyers would turn, then, not on the issue of theodicy, but on the issue of whether permitting an injustice is worse than committing one. For the realist, the latter is not always or obviously more troubling than the former, especially when the suffering of present and future generations is at stake.[10]

Christian pacifism differs from Judaism, Islam, and the Catholic natural law tradition because its practitioners draw a sharp distinction between war and peace. In contrast to the view that God has commanded war in the past, or the natural law view that war can serve the end of peace, the Christian pacifist believes that a new dispensation has begun: the peaceable kingdom inaugurated by Jesus. This conviction allows representatives of Christian pacifism to distance themselves from other points of view by adopting a dualistic framework, sharply distinguishing between worldly and divine power, the "house of fear" and the "house of love," the conduct of war and the virtue of peace. The main idea is that non-Christian beliefs about God's actions in history, natural law morality, and political realism have inaccurate notions of power, and must be replaced by the paradoxical story of God's power-in-death.

As Ted Koontz writes, many Christian pacifists adhere to the seemingly irrational notion that the meaning of history is displayed not in worldly struggles and triumphs, but in Jesus's crucifixion. This paradox has important epistemological implications: what is foolishness to the world is in fact godly wisdom, as disclosed in the New Testament. The effect of this perspective is to call into question conventional modes of rationality. The problem of war is managed first and foremost not along ethical lines, but in terms of a theologically informed epistemology: in war we are deceived about what is really and effectively powerful.

Yet even here the belief in divine justice is indispensable. Central to Christian pacifism is the conviction that those who adhere to their moral convictions can be assured that the heavens will not fall. Indeed, as Koontz points out, Christian pacifists sharply distinguish between the heavens and political life; even if the latter fall, the overall order of life continues to reside in God's care.

This theological outlook has important ethical implications. It means, among other things, that the extremity posed by war cannot override the more comprehensive virtues of peaceableness. Indeed, if nonviolence is required by belief in a just God, then Christian pacifists need not worry about the political consequences of their views, since theodicy assures us that good will come to those who believe (and behave) rightly. Here, too, emphasis falls on belief in divine sovereignty, although with fewer connections between God's ordering of history and human politics than we witness in the dominant religious traditions in the West.[11]

Jews, Catholic natural lawyers, Muslims, and Christian pacifists who believe that the cosmos is on the side of justice need not exclude *tout court* a belief in tragedy, the idea that moral experience may sometimes include regrettable events or intractable evil. Unjust suffering, incomprehensible twists of fate, or undue distress are all recognized as ineradicable features of everyday life. But within Judaism, Christianity, and Islam the key question is, how ought one to respond to these kinds of events? Traditionally, the presence of evil in the world has not sufficed to undermine the belief in divine justice. Rather, it has sharpened ethical questions about what individuals may do to mitigate the presence of evil without succumbing to its temptations.

Symbolisms of Evil

Attention to the reality of evil, then, is scarcely foreign to religious beliefs about providential justice. And, as the essays in this volume make clear, human wrongdoing is frequently associated with the causes of war and events within war. But how the various traditions symbolize the reality of evil is by no means simple or monolithic. The essays in this collection draw upon alternative paradigms of evil, suggesting two quite different visions of war. I will call these visions the "intentional" or "virtue" paradigm, as opposed to the "contamination" or "defilement" model.[12]

According to the first model, the chief symbols of evil in war are *internal* to the agents engaged in battle. In particular, war is seen as caused by an other who is guilty of *pleonexia*, or "grasping," the Greek vice of avarice. War is occasioned by those who lack self-restraint, individuals or groups who are ruled by their passions. This attention to the moral psychology of war lies at the heart of Plato's account of the causes of conflict in the *Republic*: internal disorder wreaks disorder between individuals and communities. Similarly, psychological factors shape the rejection of war in much of the tradition of Christian nonviolence. Citing James 4:1–2a (RSV), Koontz calls attention to pacifists' anxieties about the evils of war: "What causes wars, and what causes fightings among you? Is it not your passions that are at war with your members? You desire and do not have; so you kill. And you covet and cannot obtain; so you fight and wage war." Accordingly, war is seen as occasioned by greed and collective egoism, disruptive impulses, and a weakness of moral character.

Although just war theory obviously departs from Christian nonviolence by permitting the use of lethal force to settle disputes, it nonetheless holds to the view that war is justified only if it avoids these same psychological evils: malice, a delight in destruction, a thirst for cruelty. In Western ethics, this line of symbolism finds its roots in Augustine and occupies a central place in the Catholic natural law tradition. By definition, a just war is an institution that is not intrinsically immoral. Yet war can be the occasion of sin if one's passions get caught up in bloodshed, heedless destruction, or the passion for vengeance. Indeed, on this point the Catholic natural law tradition has a great affinity with feminism, as represented by Jean Bethke Elshtain: in either case, the test of morality is to engage in political action with a chastened civic virtue, one in which the *raison de guerre* is denied its totalizing temptations. Even for realists, interiority is sometimes important. As Mapel reports, some realists argue that a statesman's motives can redeem actions that would otherwise produce dirty hands.

This attention to passions, motives, and virtue stands in contrast with a line of symbolism in Judaism and Islam that I have called the "defilement" paradigm. Here the symbolism points not so much to the interior regions of agency as to the abominations of idolatry and the sources of contamination.[13] One purpose of preventive war in Judaism, Walzer writes, is to "diminish the heathen so that they do not come up against [the Israelites]." Maimonides envisions the messianic war as intending "the elimination of idolatry from the world." Similarly, in Islam the object of *qital* is to fight against polytheists, or idolaters. In these traditions, those against whom one should fight are construed as more *other*, more alien, than the enemy in the first paradigm. As Walzer notes, the Jewish literature shows a keen sense of "prevailing hostility" (*eivah*) between those inside and those outside the religious community. Owing to their strangeness, outsiders are not to be tolerated; indeed, they are to be removed or subdued.

Moreover, in this second paradigm, war is not so much a trial of rightly ordered relations and intentions as it is an instrument of purity in an environment that is otherwise dangerous or unclean. The symbols are, or ought to be, more material and tangible than those we find in the first paradigm. War protects the people of Israel or Islam from wrongful contact, defending the faithful from the dangers of religious pollution and association with idolaters. Thus, it should come as no surprise that the grounds for war, or the practices within war, may be more militant and less tolerant than standard versions of the just war tradition. War is not simply an instrument of peace and harmony, it is literally iconoclastic, an instrument to rid the world of its graven images or polytheistic practices.

The difference between these paradigms, then, is between disordered passions on the one hand, and purity and danger on the other. In each case, moreover, our attention is called to the relation between war and identity, especially the anxiety that moral identity might be corrupted. But each model provides a different way to understand identity, evil, and the relation between the two. In the first model, evil is largely negative: it is a privation of good, a *dis*ordered intention, motive, or relation. Here evil is like a bodily organ that has become dysfunctional. In the second model, however, evil is largely positive: it has its own energy and presence, together with a certain tangibility. In this case, evil is more like a virus, with its own agency and mobility.

In addition, each paradigm suggests a certain "porousness" between the interior regions of the agent and the external world, but the way in which these regions affect each other is quite different. Consider again the virtue paradigm: when the passions are disordered, there is the danger that violence will escalate and lead to dangerous external consequences. The greater thirst for killing jeopardizes the lives of others. Hence the need to control the passions, either in an ethic of Christian nonviolence or in a just war. Otherwise those involved in war will become guilty of the vices that caused war in the first place: avarice, hatred, or lack of temperance. In the second model, the line of movement goes the other way, from the external to the internal. If the idols are not removed, there is the danger that their impurities will contaminate the religious community from without.

These different symbolisms might help us understand why, as Walzer and Tibi suggest, Judaism and Islam hold views of war that do not fit neatly into the categories of the just war tradition. Just war criteria, as Finnis's essay makes clear, operate according to the symbols of evil typical of the first paradigm. But the symbols of pollution and iconoclasm suggest different understandings of human agency, different sins that war might occasion, and different problems that war must rectify.

Hermeneutical Questions

A final set of observations surrounds the problem of interpreting and representing a tradition. Given the diversity of events, practices, and intellectual resources that shape the life of any tradition, what data are to be included in an author's account of that tradition? What is eligible and what is irrelevant in the representation of a tradition? These questions are necessarily complicated by our idea of what constitutes a "tradition," understood in formal, general terms. That is, how one constructs an account of a specific tradition will be a function, in some measure, of *prior* interpretive decisions about what a tradition looks like, conceived in the abstract.

David Kelsey has done some helpful work on a related subject, namely, the task of using the Bible to support an argument in Christian theology.[14] Kelsey likens the question, "How should theologians use scripture?" to the statement, "Let's play ball." How one conceives of "playing ball" depends largely upon what kind of game one has in mind: basketball differs from soccer, which differs from volleyball, etc. Similarly, appeals to scripture in theology are constrained by how the Bible is conceived as a whole. If it is conceived as a collection of snippets of enduring advice, then one's appeals will doubtless draw upon wisdom materials, and one's theology will in all likelihood include much aphoristic, this-worldly advice. If, however, the Bible is viewed as the revelation of law, then one's theology will doubtless assume legal and apodictic overtones. To take a third possibility, if one conceives the Bible as a series of paradigmatic events, histories with moral messages, then emphasis will fall on narrative rather than on wisdom or law. Or, to take a fourth alternative, if the Bible is viewed as a source for prophetic commentary and ideological critique, then one's use of scripture will draw more from its political literature than from its aphorisms, laws, or stories. Proverbs, Leviticus, Exodus, and Amos would assume different levels of prominence in one's use of the Bible, depending on one's conception of the text in its entirety. A theologian's use of biblical passages, in short, is the product of prior interpretive judgments about scripture as a whole, judgments that have no small effect on what is privileged as authoritative.

This volume provides quite diverse decisions about what constitutes a tradition. These decisions, in turn, bear directly upon what our authors consider to be representative or authoritative material in the traditions they seek to describe. Yet in their representations of their respective traditions, what they include and exclude is not always obvious.

Consider, first, the Catholic natural law tradition. As depicted by John Finnis, this tradition is an ethical theory at the heart of which stands an account of essential human purposes and ends. The goal of the theory is to inform individual consciences about how aims should be directed. Moreover, the tradition is depicted as having achieved consensus on many issues: the justification of war, indefeasibility of noncombatant immunity, and political obligation, to name three.

The advantage of viewing this tradition as a theory is that it enables Finnis to insert his voice into this account of natural law morality, allowing for a critical, reconstructive appropriation of its main tenets. On these grounds he shows that, by the tradition's own logic, it erroneously allowed for wars of punishment in addition to wars of self-defense. The disadvantage is that representing Catholic natural morality as a theory with a strong consensus may obscure real differences or substantive changes within the tradition itself.

The problem, stated differently, concerns streamlining the Catholic natural law tradition. Consider, for example, the issue of religion as a grounds for war. As represented here, the Catholic natural law tradition does not include differences of religion or wrong belief as grounds for war; traditionally, war was justified in terms of self-defense or punishment of wrongdoing. But in fact these grounds were general enough to allow religious sanctions to justify the use of lethal force. In the *City of God*, for example, Augustine provides a basis for wars on religious grounds that later just war theorists would have to revise. According to Augustine, false religion is an injustice against God, a disordered relation. Accordingly, force could be used to set relations in their proper proportion, to correct a wrong.[15] Viewing lethal force as an instrument to restore the order required by peace, Augustine sanctioned war to repair the relation between God and infidels, who deny God His just due. If war can help to restore proper relations between communities contending over temporal goods, such as property or the right to rule, then war can certainly repair the *ordo pacis* when the stakes are higher, as when eternal goods such as religious truth are at stake. For this reason, Augustine knew no ecumenism.

Yet things were to change in the sixteenth century. Owing to the work of Vitoria and Suarez, religious factors were removed as grounds for a just war. Writing during the Spanish conquest of the Americas, Vitoria and Suarez self-consciously secularized the criterion of just cause, arguing that religion was irrelevant either to self-defense or to the rectification of wrongdoing.[16] And they did so, it should be noted, not by arguing that the traditional view was logically inconsistent, but by revising its substantive understanding of justice. The core of their argument was that matters of faith were irrelevant to claims of title to dominion. This effort to secularize the traditional view of just cause turned on the claim that wrong belief did not deny indigenous populations rightful dominion over their land. Territorial dominion is only a temporal, natural good, the argument went, to be separated from supernatural matters of faith and religion. Accordingly, those Spaniards who sought war against Native Americans would have to find a sanction other than paganism for seizing their cities and property.

The point of this example is to illustrate internal fissures within a tradition, to remind us that the Catholic natural law tradition does not speak with one voice about the grounds for war. Instead, early modern just war theorists had to struggle to define the limits according to which harmony, the tranquility of order, and the rectification of wrongdoing could sanction the use of lethal force. That they overtly and covertly quarrelled with their authoritative sources over substantive matters leaves us with less than a streamlined view of the tradition as a whole.

Tibi provides a second view of what constitutes a tradition: a deposit of juridical decisions that presuppose a fixed, unchanging worldview. This worldview emerged prior to the development of the sovereign state system and is thus inimical to many current assumptions about international relations. Muslims (like Jews, as Walzer reports) have difficulty reckoning with the fact of sovereign statehood. Tibi's representation of the Islamic tradition as fixed and final allows for little (if any) "cultural accommodation" to changing circumstances in politics or history.

Here the idea of the development of doctrine or the historicity of doctrine might allow for more hermeneutical flexibility than we see suggested by Tibi. In modern Christianity, by way of comparison, there has been a quest to demythologize religious dogma and to understand the relativity and historicity of doctrinal formulations. This awareness of historicity has allowed for interpretive flexibility, given the philosophical conviction (found in the work of Friedrich Schleiermacher and Ernst Troeltsch) that religious teachings are historical and contextual.[17] The effect of this contextualization is to require ongoing interpretation of religious beliefs given new cultural and political developments. The authoritative sources cited by Tibi, in contrast, represent religious teachings as ahistorical and unchanging. Thus we might ask: in order to adjust to modern institutions like the sovereign state, does Islam need the revolution of historical consciousness?

Tibi's chapter suggests an affirmative answer, and on this hermeneutical point Sohail Hashmi enters the discussion. Hashmi presents Islamic ethics as dynamic and evolutionary, adapting to changes in international relations and Islamic attitudes toward Westerners. In this view, tradition is polyvalent and adaptive. The implications of its foundational sources require ongoing interpretation, given the changing cultural, political, and economic contexts in which Muslims find themselves.

Walzer's account of Judaism is similar to Hashmi's presentation of Islamic ethics, providing a third example of how we might construe a tradition. For Walzer, tradition is neither an ethical theory nor a timeless worldview, but an ongoing argument, a conversation. In Judaism, this conversation takes the form of textual commentary, carried out over generations by an educated male elite that was (unlike Muslim jurists) exiled from centers of political and military authority. Owing to this lack of power, rabbis were forced to discuss war largely in speculative terms, in the abstract. Here, too, we might ask what this notion of tradition emphasizes, and what it excludes, in its depiction of Jewish moral reflection.

Walzer acknowledges the problem that surrounds selection, interpretation, and representation when he remarks that "if the [Jewish] tradition is to serve contemporary uses, it must address itself to the full range of Jewish experience." Like Tibi, Walzer is aware that premodern assumptions within religious traditions may hinder cultural accommodation today. Yet the problem to which Walzer alludes—the limits of Jewish reflections about war and power—may well be a function of his own principle of selection. Why is the Jewish tradition reducible or equivalent to the teachings of the rabbis on war, removed as they were from power politics? Dependent upon these sources alone, Jews are left with few resources with which to assess the morality of gentile wars. Such sources obviously lack a vocabulary for secular social criticism. By this view of the tradition, how could a Jew evaluate the Gulf War? Could an American Jew draw ethical resources from Jewish sources to evaluate the morality of the Vietnam War?

One way to address these questions is to ask whether Judaism offers resources for a natural law morality, which would furnish more general, humanistic principles for evaluating policy and statecraft. Jews seeking to move beyond rabbinic materials might find norms for social criticism in the Noahide covenant, which focuses on God's relationship not with Israel but with humanity as a whole (Gen. 9:1–17). As part of this covenant, God recalls the law against murder, the validity of which is grounded in creation: humans are made in God's image (Gen. 9:6). Ethical inferences might thus be developed from the notion of *imago Dei*, the idea that human beings have inherent dignity because they bear the image and likeness of God (cf. Gen. 1:26; Ps. 8). Such biblical materials can serve as a resource for crafting more generalizable ethics of war, human rights, and political action, grounded in the natural good of human well-being. Walzer may have philosophical doubts about natural law morality or the notion of *imago Dei*, but for the purposes of representing Judaism's resources, such reservations are beside the point.[18] A fuller rendition of Judaism may include not just a divine command morality, but also some version of natural law morality, drawing from biblical materials.[19]

Like Finnis's account of the natural law tradition, Mapel's account of realism represents it as an ethical theory. In addition, Mapel sees realism as a set of views along a spectrum: both unity and difference exist within the realist camp. The common thread in realism is the rejection of deontology or "moralism" in its ethics of statecraft. But realists differ about when principles are to give way to the demands of prudence or utility. For some realists, the interests of the state are central and ought never to be compromised, regardless of the moral principles at stake. Less radical realists are willing to sacrifice moral principles only as a last resort—for example, in a situation of supreme emergency.

I have already indicated why an account of divine justice would resist even moderate views of realism, and how realists might rejoin. But here we are focusing on the hermeneutical challenge of representing a tradition, and on this score we should note the merits of Mapel's account. The advantage of his approach is that he allows for some obvious differences within a common group. Mapel thus invites us to view traditions as family resemblances, where views overlap. In order to identify a tradition, then, we need not find strict uniformity about specific problems or opinions; we may proceed with more modest expectations, seeking to find an overlapping consensus. The fact of variety within the realist tradition does not imply confusion or anarchy of meaning about what constitutes a "realist." To distinguish realists from nonrealists we need only to reason analogically, attempting to determine where similarities are sufficient to justify a common classification.

A similar view of tradition is implied by Elshtain's treatment of feminism, although it includes greater diversity than we find among realists. Here tradition is conceived as a series of discourses that derive from the common source of women's experience. Again we find an attempt to join unity and difference and reckon with the fact of intratraditional pluralism.

In Elshtain's account, the attempt to detect a family resemblance among feminists oscillates between two poles. On the one hand, feminism is depicted in terms of the literatures of women who have addressed various forms of political and social combat. On the other hand, feminism is conceived as a form of ideological criticism, resisting the hegemony of patriarchal values. The former seeks to articulate the voices of women, however much some of them remain complicit with patriarchal institutions (the Spartan Mother, for example); the latter expresses greater resistance to institutions in which women are subordinated to male power. The family resemblance lies in the fact that feminism articulates a vocabulary of social criticism, seeking to situate the voices and experiences of women in the public realm.

Perhaps the most notable feature of this tradition is that it is historically self-conscious, aware of its origins and political genealogy. As Elshtain makes plain, feminism has scarcely emerged *de novo*; it has rather sought to extend the implications of Enlightenment philosophy beyond its patriarchal articulations. Feminism both depends upon and resists liberal ideals, and thus stands in tension with one of the chief institutions of liberal philosophy, the nation-state. This genealogy has left feminist political philosophers wary about their roots. Here the knowledge of a tradition's genealogy leads to the conclusion that it must appropriate the resources of critical theory to engage in ongoing social criticism. Hence (for Elshtain) the need to adopt an ironist rhetoric, which remains connected with political institutions without compromising the quest for liberation from oppression.

Koontz's interpretation of Christian nonviolence sharpens the distinction between the importance of experience on the one hand, and intratraditional pluralism on the other. As a result, Koontz depicts the tradition of Christian nonviolence as having two dimensions. The first is that of *praxis* as foundational for identity. The Christian pacifist, for example, begins with the "first language" of experience, especially as it is shaped by symbol and worship. Here the tradition of Christian nonviolence is depicted principally as a way of life, rather than a discursive argument. Emphasis falls on pacifism as a way of seeing and of being. Discursive arguments, Koontz's "second language," may be needlessly intellectualistic. If we have to think or argue about what to do, then we are less than fully socialized; for those whose identity is intact, in contrast, moral action should be thoroughly habituated.

Koontz presents an additional dimension in his interpretation of Christian nonviolence: it is pluralistic, a family of overlapping types (pacifism, abolitionism, nonviolent resistance). These types are held together by an understanding of power that eschews military methods. Power resides in example and persuasion (pacifism), reason and education (abolitionism), or withdrawal of consent (nonviolent resistance). Moreover, practitioners of nonviolence reject a consequentialist morality, especially the morality of extremity. Drawing on their faith in God's providential direction, as I have noted, members of this family feel no need to make history come out right. The majority view the presumption against war as absolute, never to be compromised; those who are less radical are willing to participate in war only as a last resort, to end all wars. In either case war is evil, and the main question is whether it is to be avoided or removed from human affairs.

This typological account of Christian nonviolence, like Mapel's interpretation of realism, enables us to understand a tradition as composed of family resemblances, combining unity and plurality. Once again we are asked to think about similarities and differences within a tradition and to ascertain where or to what extent its various components overlap.

Conclusion

My analysis is meant to suggest that comparative reflections about war and peace operate along two levels. First, we can compare by examining how the various traditions contribute to our collective understanding of the morality of killing and political decision-making. Here reference to theological beliefs and symbols helps to clarify points of convergence and divergence concerning specific ethical issues like the causes of war, the evils in war, or the morality of extremity. But left to these matters alone, comparison would be incomplete and perhaps deceptive. We must also take into account how the traditions are conceived *as traditions*, understood in the abstract. Whether a tradition is construed as an argument, a premodern worldview, an ongoing textual commentary, a family resemblance, a series of discourses from a common source of experience, or a form of *praxis* will have no small bearing upon the extent to which it is open to comparison and dialogue from without.

For *formal* reasons, in other words, some traditions will have more (or less) reason to "converse" than will other traditions, given some basic assumptions about how to approach political philosophy and ethics. On these formal grounds it would be difficult to imagine what practitioners of Christian nonviolence, as depicted by Koontz, and the representatives of the Catholic natural law tradition, as depicted by Finnis, would have to say to each other. The former's first language is nondiscursive, whereas the latter's is discursive. Yet we might expect considerable dialogue between pacifists and feminists given that both traditions rely upon experience, especially the experience of being marginalized by centers of power. Natural lawyers and realists have strong reasons to engage in dialogue, given their similar orientations to political philosophy as a discursive, theoretical practice. Judaism and Islam must both struggle to bring their traditional beliefs into dialogue with modernity, and in this regard may find resources to engage each other as well.

Willingness to converse at this formal level, of course, does not imply agreement about more specific issues in the ethics of war and peace. The experience of marginalization may lead pacifists and feminists to adopt quite different attitudes toward the morality of violence, as the examples of the nonviolent resister and Spartan Mother make clear. The idea that tradition is a form of argument in Catholic natural law and realism by no means suggests that representatives of these traditions will agree about the morality of extremity. I call attention to these formal aspects only to show that complex factors facilitate (or hinder) conversation in a world of moral and religious diversity. Convergences among and divergences between traditions operate at more than one level, and we would be mistaken to concentrate our attention (and hopes) on specific ethical and political issues alone.[20]

Notes

1. Finnis attempts to provide an account of the natural law, especially its grounds of obligation, in nontheological terms. See John Finnis, *Natural Law and Natural Rights* (Oxford: Oxford University Press, 1980), pt. 2 and passim.

2. St. Thomas Aquinas *Summa theologiae* I-II q. 94 a. 2.

3. Aquinas *Summa theologiae* I-II q. 91 a. 2.

4. Aquinas *Summa theologiae* I q. 44 a. 3; see also I q. 2 a. 3. It is true, as Finnis argues, that the knowledge of God is not necessary as a ground for the natural law's obligation. A Thomist need not say that natural virtue is obligatory because it is commanded by God. For Aquinas, as for the Stoics and for the Greeks in general, virtue is its own reward. Yet even if Aquinas can separate grounds for moral motivation from knowledge of God's will, that does not mean that he can separate the objective structures of natural justice from the overall justice of God as designer of creation. The former is an epistemological issue, the latter an ontological one.

5. Finnis's embrace of this outlook appears in John Finnis, *Fundamentals in Ethics: Tradition, Revision, and Truth* (Washington, DC: Catholic University of America Press, 1991), 105–6.

6. For a discussion of anticonsequentialism in just war theory and pacifism, see Paul Ramsey, *Speak Up for Just War or Pacifism: A Critique of the United Methodist Bishops' Pastoral Letter "In Defense of Creation,"* with an epilogue by Stanley Hauerwas (State Park: Pennsylvania State University Press, 1988).

7. Reinhold Niebuhr, "Just or Holy?" *Christianity and Crisis* 1 (3 Nov. 1941), 1.

8. For a discussion, see James F. Childress, *Moral Responsibility in Conflicts* (Baton Rouge: Louisiana State University Press, 1982), 29–61.

9. This, too, is a theme in Niebuhr's writings. See, for example, Reinhold Niebuhr, *Christianity and Power Politics* (New York: Charles Scribner's Sons, 1940), ch. 1.

10. I take this to be the gist of Michael Walzer's notion of "supreme emergency" in *Just and Unjust Wars* (New York: Basic Books, 1977), ch. 16. Realists sometimes ask us not only to embrace the lesser of two evils, but to do so with the welfare of a community's children (and their children) in mind. Perhaps this is why the survival of the state, or the community, plays an important role in realism: the community provides the material (and other) conditions for the lives of future generations.

11. See, for example, Menno Simons, *The Complete Writings of Menno Simons, c. 1496–1561* (Scottdale, PA: Herald Press, 1956), 582–622.

12. Here I am drawing loosely on the work of Paul Ricoeur, *The Symbolism of Evil*, trans. Emerson Buchanan (Boston: Beacon Press, 1967).

13. For an illuminating discussion, see Mary Douglas, *Purity and Danger: An Analysis of the Concepts of Pollution and Taboo* (London: Ark Paperbacks, 1984).

14. David Kelsey, *Uses of Scripture in Recent Theology* (Philadelphia: Fortress Press, 1975).

15. Augustine, *City of God*, trans. Henry Bettenson, with an introduction by David Knowles (New York: Penguin Books, 1972), bk. 19, paras. 23, 24. For a discussion, see John Langan, "Elements of St. Augustine's Just War Theory," *Journal of Religious Ethics* 12 (Spring 1984), 19–39.

16. See *Francisco de Vitoria: Political Writings*, ed. Anthony Pagden and Jeremy Lawrance (Cambridge: Cambridge University Press, 1991), 233–92, 302–3; Francisco Suarez, "On War," in *War and Christian Conscience*, ed. Arthur Holmes (Grand Rapids, MI: Baker Book House, 1975), 212–14.

17. See Friedrich Schleiermacher, *The Christian Faith*, ed. H. R. Mackintosh and J. S. Stewart (Philadelphia: Fortress Press, 1976), paras. 15, 19; Ernst Troeltsch, *The Social Teaching of the Christian Churches*, trans. Olive Wyon, with an introduction by H. Richard Niebuhr (Chicago: University of Chicago Press, 1981).

18. In all likelihood, Walzer would say that a theory of natural morality is thin and overly general, as opposed to a more contextual, local morality, which is thick and particularist. See Michael Walzer, "Moral Minimalism," in *Thick and Thin: Moral Argument at Home and Abroad* (Notre Dame, IN: University of Notre Dame Press, 1994), ch. 1.

19. In recent Jewish thought, the ethical implications of viewing the human person as an image of God are discussed in L. E. Goodman, *On Justice: An Essay in Jewish Philosophy* (New Haven, CT: Yale University Press, 1991), 28–31, 53–58, and passim; see also David Novak, *Jewish Social Ethics* (New York: Oxford University Press, 1992), 68, 135, 165, 238. For a discussion focusing on classical materials, see Michael P. Levine, "The Role of Reason in the Ethics of Maimonides: Or, Why Maimonides Could Have Had a Doctrine of Natural Law Even If He Did Not," *Journal of Religious Ethics* 14 (Fall 1986), 279–95.

20. I am grateful to Scott Alexander, Judy Granbois, Barbara Klinger, Terry Nardin, and David H. Smith for comments that enabled me to improve this chapter.

Index

abolitionism: defined, 169–70; historical Christian, 170–71, 184
aggression: in Islam, 131–33, 137; in Judaism, 111–12, 119; realist justification of, 83–86; realist perception of, 59–61

Beautiful Soul: feminist realism concept of, 223; moral convictions of, 216–18, 238
benevolence (feminism), 234

casuistry: in Catholic natural law tradition, 42; double-effect doctrine, 44–45
civil disobedience (natural law tradition), 32–33
combatants, in natural law tradition, 26–27, 34
competent authority, in *ius ad bellum* doctrine, 83
conduct of war: Christian pacifist position, 188–89; constraints, 258–60; Islam, 133, 161–64; in Judaism, 106–10; natural law tradition, 25–26; realist position on, 65–68
conformism, Islamic, 134, 135, 138, 140
conquest commandment (in halakhic tradition), 117
conscientious objection: natural law tradition, 48; right of, 49

defense: as justification for war, 33, 47; in political realism, 55–56. *See also* self-defense
defensive wars (Judaism), 117–18
discrimination: in conduct of war, 27; *ius in bello* requirement for, 88; in realist perception of war, 66–67, 88–91
double-effect doctrine, 44–45, 66–67
dualism, ethical, 206

ethical thought, comparative, 9–10
ethics: Christian, 197–98; Christian pacifism, 189–93; comparative international, 4–8; of international relations (realism), 58; in Islam, 128; of war and peace in Islam, 135, 146
ethics of care (feminism), 233–38
excuse, necessity as, 73
exemptions, Jewish permitted wars, 103–4
extremity. *See* morality in extremity

fairness (natural law tradition), 20, 27–28, 34, 251
feminism: converted to pacifism, 221; grounds for war, 253; intentions and motives, 258; position on war and peace, 222, 246–47; radical, 229–33; resistance to political authority, 255–56

good life (realism), 71–72
grounds for war: Christian pacifism, 183–85, 253; feminism, 253; Islam, 131–33, 141, 155–61, 252–53; Judaism, 99–102, 251–52; natural law tradition, 20–24, 46–47, 251; realist position, 58–61

harm, intended and unintended: in principle of double effect, 66–67; in proportionality requirement of *ius ad bellum*, 86–87
human action, natural law tradition, 44–45

innocence, material, 8
innocents. *See* noncombatants
intention: defined, 63; realist use of term, 64. *See also* motive and intention
Islam: conduct of war, 259–60; as mission of peace, 132; resistance to political authority, 254; war as justification for spread of, 131–32; war/peace ethics, 246
Islamic fundamentalism, 135, 137–39, 159–61
Islamic law (*shari'a*): contemporary relevance, 147–48; in Qur'an, 148–51; war against unbelievers, 139–40
ius ad bellum doctrine: proportionality requirement, 86–87; requirements in, 83, 86
ius in bello: discrimination requirement, 88; double-effect doctrine in, 44–45, 66–67; intended or unintended harm, 66–67; judgments of proportionality, 67–68; realist position, 55; with rejection of double-

ius in bello (cont.)
effect doctrine, 66–67; traditional understanding of basis for, 66–68

jihad: conformist interpretation, 134–35, 138; in contemporary Islam, 146–47; fundamentalist interpretation, 135, 137–39, 159–61; goal of, 161, 252; grounds for war in, 156–57; Islamic debate over interpretation, 131–33, 146, 248; as just war, 146
Judaism: attention to diplomacy and war, 246; conduct of war, 260; intentions and motives, 257; morality in extremity, 260–61; resistance to political authority, 254. *See also* wars, commanded (Judaism); wars, permitted (Judaism); wars, prohibited (Judaism)
just cause: in *ius ad bellum* doctrine, 83; in ordinary morality, 84–86; realist position, 83–84
justice, radical feminism, 21
just war: Alexander of Hales, 18; of Aquinas, 18–19; Christian pacifist view, 189–93; discrimination as principle of, 67; doctrine of Christianity, 123; Islam, 131–33, 266; jihad as, 146; Judaism, 265–66; of natural law tradition, 24–25, 41–43, 251, 265; preconditions for (Alexander of Hales), 18; realist perception, 58–61; war to disseminate Islam, 131; Western concept, 131. *See also* unjust wars

last resort, in *ius ad bellum* doctrine, 83
liberalism, feminism in, 214–15
love: as motivation of Christian pacifism, 187–88; in natural law tradition, 17
loyalty: in realism, 81; in Weak Realism, 83

maternal thinking (Ruddick), 236
messianic war, Judaism, 99
military revolution, Islam, 129–30
Moderate Realism, 81–82
moral constraints: Catholic natural law tradition, 26–28; in Islamic conduct of war, 133
moralism in foreign policy (realist view), 60–61
morality: Catholic natural law conception, 44–45, 48; concept in Strong Realism, 81; of feminists, 234; in foreign policy (realist view), 60–61; in individual life, 69; at level of individual action, 81; in natural law tradition, 44–45, 245; presumption against preemptive and preventive wars, 85–86; of realism, 54–55, 57, 60–61, 74, 245; realist conception of, 233–34; realist just cause, 83–86; realist views of relationship to prudence, 69; rejection of *ius ad bellum* proportionality argument, 86
morality in extremity: Christian pacifist tradition, 189–93; in Judaism, 110–11; natural law tradition, 28–30; realist perception of, 68–73
moral necessity, 72
moral norms (Aquinas), 26
moral principles: application to individual actions, 42; formulation in terms of peace, 43; natural law tradition, 17
moral skepticism, in Strong Realism, 80
motive: defined, 63; in realist tradition, 64–65; with rejection of double-effect doctrine, 67
motive and intention: in Christian pacifist tradition, 187–88; in Judaism, 104–6; natural law tradition, 17–20, 44–46; realist perception, 63–65

natural law tradition: activities of differing moral character, 40–42; conduct of war, 258–59; ethical guidance of, 246; intention and motives, 256–57; moral constraints, 26–28; morality in extremity, 261; moral point of view in, 245
necessity of realism, 72–73
noncombatants: natural law tradition, 26–27, 34, 45; realist view of wartime fate, 55, 66, 88–91; in war, 26–27
nonviolence: attitudes of Christian pacifists, 182–83, 249; Christian, 169–73, 182–83; conception of Christian (Douglass), 204–5; grounds for war in Christian, 183–85; interpretations of Christian, 203–11; irresponsible (Niebuhr), 200; of Judaism and Islam, 249; natural law tradition, 251; realist bias against, 248–49; realist position, 57–58. *See also* pacifism
nonviolent resistance: as form of Christian nonviolence, 169–73; historical Christian, 171–72

obedience (natural law tradition), 51–52
Osgood, Robert, 69

pacifism: in Catholic teaching, 49; defined, 169–70; feminism converted to, 221; feminist antiwar, 214; nonexistence of Islamic, 131, 150–51; realist position on, 57. *See also* nonviolence
pacifism, Christian: arguments for, 199–203; conduct of war, 259; effect of different typologies, 197–99; grounds for war, 253; historical, 170, 184–85; intentions and motives, 258; morality in extremity, 261; position on war and peace, 246; resistance to political authority, 186, 255
partiality, 81
patriarchy, radical feminism, 231–32
patriotic realism, 69–70
peace: conception of Christian (Douglass), 205; idea in Judaism, Islam, and Christianity, 247; idea of temporary peace under Islam, 130; in Islam based on religious conversion or submission, 130; Islamic fundamentalist interpretation of, 138; Jewish interpretation of, 96–97; Maimonides's conditions for, 116; natural law, 41, 247; in realism, 56–57; as temporary armistices in Islam, 140
peacemaking: Douglass's conception, 205; nonviolent (Ruddick), 237
political authority: Christian pacifist resistance to, 186–87; resistance to, 253–56; resistance in Judaism, 102–4; resistance in natural law tradition, 30–33, 47–52; resistance in realist perception, 61–63, 253
practice (*sunna*) of Prophet Muhammad, 151–55
preemptive war (realism), 59–60, 85
preventive war (realism), 60, 85
proportionality: *ius ad bellum* requirement, 83, 86; natural law perception, 24–25; in principle of double effect, 66–68; realist perception, 86–88
prudence: natural law tradition, 28; realist views of relationship to morality, 57–58, 69
purity of arms doctrine (Judaism), 109–10

Qur'an: Islamic law (*shari'a*) in, 148–51; as source of ethics of war and peace, 128–31, 148–51

realism: central claim of, 68–69; conduct of war, 259; criticism of, 56, 61–62; intentions and motives of, 257; morality in extremity of, 261–62; perception of morality, 245; proportionality concept in, 67–68; resistance to political authority in, 61–63, 253; varieties of, 78–83. *See also* Moderate Realism; patriotic realism; Strong Realism; Weak Realism
reasonable hope of success, 83
reason of state: distinction between patriotic and liberal, 61–63; patriotic (realist tradition), 69–70
repression (realism), 63
resistance: in Christian pacificism to political authority, 186–87; in Judaism to political authority, 102–4; in natural law to political authority, 30–33, 47–52; to political authority, 253–56; radical feminist ethics of, 232–33; in realism to political authority, 61–63, 253
restraint (Judaism), 106
right intention, in *ius ad bellum* doctrine, 83
rules of war, 28–29

sabbath laws ignored (Judaism), 110
self-defense: in Judaism, 99; in natural law tradition, 19, 21–23, 33–34, 250–51; of realism, 61
self-preservation of state (realism), 68–73
separatism, radical feminism, 232
siege law (Judaism), 108–9
Spartan Mother tradition, 215–16, 229–30
state, the: concept in Islam, 140–41; in four variants of Moderate Realism, 81–83; Hobbes, 70; morality in conduct of, 68–73; realist perception of, 57–63, 70, 73; in Weak Realism, 83
Strong Realism: moral version of state and individual action, 79–81; nonmoral version, 80
symbolisms of evil, 270–73

theodicy, 265–70
tradition: Catholic natural law, 274; Christian pacifism, 278–79; feminism, 277–78; Islam, 275–76; Judaism, 276–77; realism, 277

unfairness. *See* fairness
universalist egoism, in Strong Realism, 80–81

unjust war: Islam, 131–33; Muslim versions of, 140; natural law tradition, 41–43; when non-Muslims attack Muslims, 131

violence (Judaism), 109

war: Bull's definition, 56; Christian pacifist views, 182–83, 185, 248–50; Christian theory of, 123–24; Clausewitz's definition, 56; concept with spread of Islam, 129; conditions to be met for war (Judaism), 99–100; defense as justification for, 33; feminist perception, 248, 250; idea in Judaism, Islam, and Christianity, 247–48; Islamic fundamentalist interpretation, 138–39; Jewish perception of, 97; justification in natural law tradition, 33; of Maimonides, 100; moral justification under Islam, 130–33; moral justification within natural law tradition, 41–42; non-Jewish, 105; postbiblical Jewish theory of, 123–24; radical feminist approach to, 230–31; realist perception, 56, 248; against unbelievers (Islam), 137–39. *See also* conduct of war; grounds for war; just war; preemptive war; preventive war; unjust war
war and peace: Catholic thinking on ethics of, 40–44, 205–6; Christian tradition, 122–24; conceptions of Christian pacifism, 180–82; conceptions in Qur'an, 128–31, 147–51; conformism of al-Azhar, 135–37; conformism of Moroccan Islam, 134–35; ethics of Islam, 129, 140, 141, 146, 148–51; ethics of (Ruddick), 235–38; ethics in *sunna* of Prophet Muhammad, 151–55; Jewish theory of, 95–96, 122–24; natural law tradition, 15–17; of political realism, 55–57; present feminist thinking, 221–22; women's history in relation to, 215–16
wars, commanded (Judaism): by God, 111; in Jewish writings, 97–98; Maimonides, 105; violation of prohibitions in, 110–11
wars, permitted (Judaism): conditions for undertaking, 111, 252; contemporary interpretation, 117–18; defensive wars, 117; grounds for, 100–101; individuals not bound to fight, 103–4; in Jewish writings, 97–98, 100; of kings of Israel, 118; three kinds, 119; traditional view, 251; two kinds, 100, 115, 119
wars, prohibited (Judaism): contemporary interpretation, 119–20; defined, 122; halakhic tradition, 116–19, 122; in Jewish religious tradition, 97–98, 115
wars of conquest (Judaism), 105–6
wartime emergencies (Judaism), 110–11
Weak Realism, 83
Women's Peace Party, 220